Lecture Notes in Computer

T0238133

Ana Bove Luís Soares Barbosa
Alberto Pardo Jorge Sousa Pinto (Eds.)

Language Engineering and Rigorous Software Development

International LerNet ALFA Summer School 2008
Piriapolis, Uruguay, February 24 - March 1, 2008
Revised Tutorial Lectures

Springer

Volume Editors

Ana Bove
Chalmers University of Technology
Department of Computer Science and Engineering
412 96 Göteborg, Sweden
E-mail: bove@chalmers.se

Luís Soares Barbosa
Universidade do Minho, Departamento de Informática
Campus de Gualtar, 4700-320 Braga, Portugal
E-mail: lsb@di.uminho.pt

Alberto Pardo
Universidad de la República
Facultad de Ingeniería, Instituto de Computación
Julio Herrera y Reissig 565 - Piso 5, 11300 Montevideo, Uruguay
E-mail: pardo@fing.edu.uy

Jorge Sousa Pinto
Universidade do Minho, Departamento de Informática
Campus de Gualtar, 4700-320 Braga, Portugal
E-mail: jsp@di.uminho.pt

Library of Congress Control Number: 2009930949

CR Subject Classification (1998): D.2, D.3, I.6, F.3, K.6.3

LNCS Sublibrary: SL 2 – Programming and Software Engineering

ISSN 0302-9743

ISBN 978-3-642-03152-6 Springer Berlin Heidelberg New York

springer.com

Typesetting: Camera-ready by author, data conversion by Scientific Publishing Services, Chennai, India
Printed on acid-free paper SPIN: 12716449 06/3180 5 4 3 2 1 0

Preface

This volume contains the lecture notes from the courses offered at the International Summer School on Language Engineering and Rigorous Software Development, held in Piriápolis, Uruguay, from February 25 to March 1, 2008.

The aim of the school was the dissemination of advanced scientific knowledge in the areas of programming languages and rigorous methods for software development. The school was oriented to computer science graduate students and researchers, with an interest in formal techniques for the design and construction of software systems as well as programming languages.

The school was organized in the context of the LERnet (Language Engineering and Rigorous Software Development) project. LERnet is a project of the ALFA programme of the European Commission for co-operation between higher education institutions of the European Union and Latin America. The institutions that participate in the LERnet project are the following:

- Chalmers Tekniska Högskola, Sweden
- Institut National de la Recherche en Informatique et Automatique (INRIA), France
- Universidad de Castilla-La Mancha, Spain
- Universidad Católica de Santiago del Estero, Argentina
- Universidad EAFIT, Colombia
- Universidade Federal de Minas Gerais, Brazil
- Universidade do Minho, Portugal
- Universidad Nacional de San Luis, Argentina
- Universidad Politécnica de Valencia, Spain
- Universidad de la República, Uruguay
- Universiteit Utrecht, The Netherlands

The project oversees the mobility of PhD students from Latin America to the European Union and vice versa for a period of up to 18 months, to pursue research activities in the scope of their PhD projects. LERnet has funded the mobility of 21 doctorate students who thus had the opportunity to develop part of their work integrated in top teams in the area of their respective projects. This summer school was organized as a complementary activity of LERnet, and as such it included a student workshop where the grantholders had the opportunity to present, discuss, and obtain feedback on the progress of their work.

The relevance of the material contained in this volume reflects the increasing importance of programming language-based methods for reasoning about properties of software. Type systems play a prominent role among such methods, being as they are fundamental ingredients of programming languages and proof assistants. Types can also be used for establishing properties of software, such as information flow security. These proceedings include the lecture notes of three courses on type theory: an introductory tutorial by Herman Geuvers, a course on type-based termination by Gilles Barthe, Benjamim Grégoire and Colin Riba, and a practical introduction to dependent types by Ana Bove and Peter Dybjer.

Type theory as used in the Coq proof assistant is also the basis for Yves Bertot's encoding in Coq of a static analyzer based on abstract interpretation, a semantics-based method. His study shows how a tool of undeniable practical interest can be formally understood and reasoned about. A different kind of encoding is used in the tutorial on combinator parsing by Doaitse Swierstra, which shows the advantages of embedding domain-specific languages into a programming language with a powerful type system and well-studied semantics.

A study by J.N. Oliveira of extended static checking using a point-free transform completes the volume. This is a novel approach to the treatment of the proof obligations generated when reasoning about properties of software. The approach advocates the use of algebraic methods to complement the more traditional use of logic.

Together these contributions will be an invaluable tool for graduate students and researchers looking forward to keeping up to date with the latest developments in rigorous approaches to software development.

We thank Adriana Carvalho and all the members of her team at the Bureau of International Relations at Minho, who were responsible for managing the project, including the participation of the project's grantholders in the event.

Finally, we would also like to express our gratitude to the school's sponsors, and thank the members of the Local Organizing Committee for the seamless organization and very enjoyable setting in which the school took place.

January 2009

Ana Bove
Luis Soares Barbosa
Alberto Pardo
Jorge Sousa Pinto

Organization

The LerNet Summer School was organised by the Universidad de la República, Uruguay.

Program Chair

Jorge Sousa Pinto	Minho University, Portugal

Scientific Committee

Ana Bove	Chalmers University, Sweden
Luis Soares Barbosa	Minho University, Portugal
Alberto Pardo	Universidad de la República, Uruguay
Jorge Sousa Pinto	Minho University, Portugal

Organizing Committee

Ana Bove	Chalmers University, Sweden
Carlos Luna	Universidad de la República, Uruguay
Alberto Pardo	Universidad de la República, Uruguay
Luis Sierra	Universidad de la República, Uruguay

Referees

A. Abel	P. Dybjer	C. McBride
R. Backhouse	M. Florido	C. Riba
Y. Bertot	H. Geuvers	
C. Camarão	P. Gorm Larsen	

Sponsoring Institutions

PEDECIBA (Programa de Desarrollo de las Ciencias Básicas, Uruguay)
CSIC (Comisión Sectorial de Investigación Científica, Universidad de la República)
TATA Consultancy Services
Microsoft Uruguay

Table of Contents

Introduction to Type Theory

Herman Geuvers

Radboud University Nijmegen, The Netherlands
Technical University Eindhoven, The Netherlands

1 Overview

These notes comprise the lecture "Introduction to Type Theory" that I gave at the Alpha Lernet Summer School in Piriapolis, Uruguay in February 2008. The lecture was meant as an *introduction* to typed λ-calculus for PhD. students that have some (but possibly not much) familiarity with logic or functional programming. The lecture consisted of 5 hours of lecturing, using a beamer presentation, the slides of which can be found at my homepage[1]. I also handed out exercises, which are now integrated into these lecture notes.

In the lecture, I attempted to give an introductory overview of type theory. The problem is: there are so many type systems and so many ways of defining them. Type systems are used in programming (languages) for various purposes: to be able to find simple mistakes (e.g. caused by typing mismatches) at compile time; to generate information about data to be used at runtime, ... But type systems are also used in theorem proving, in studying the the foundations of mathematics, in proof theory and in language theory.

In the lecture I have focussed on the use of type theory for compile-time checking of functional programs and on the use of types in proof assistants (theorem provers). The latter combines the use of types in the foundations of mathematics and proof theory. These topics may seem remote, but as a matter of fact they are not, because they join in the central theme of these lectures:

Curry-Howard isomorphism of formulas-as-types
(and proofs-as-terms)

This isomorphism amounts to two readings of typing judgments

$$M : A$$

- M is a term (program, expression) of the data type A
- M is a proof (derivation) of the formula A

The first reading is very much a "programmers" view and the second a "proof theory" view. They join in the implementation of proof assistants using type systems, where a term (proof) of a type (formula) is sought for interactively between the user and the system, and where terms (programs) of a type can also be used to define and compute with functions (as algorithms).

[1] `url: http://www.cs.ru.nl/H.Geuvers/Uruguay2008SummerSchool.html/`

A. Bove et al. (Eds.): LerNet ALFA Summer School 2008, LNCS 5520, pp. 1–56, 2009.

For an extensive introduction into the Curry-Howard isomorphism, we refer to [39].

The contents of these notes is as follows.

1. Introduction: what are types and why are they not sets?
2. Simply typed λ-calculus (Simple Type Theory) and the Curry Howard isomorphism
3. Simple Type Theory: "Curry" type assignment, principle type algorithm and normalization
4. Polymorphic type theory: full polymorphism and ML style polymorphism
5. Dependent type theory: logical framework and type checking algorithm

In the course, I have also (briefly) treated higher order logic, the λ-cube, Pure Type Systems and inductive types, but I will not do that here. This is partly because of space restrictions, but mainly because these notes should be of a very introductory nature, so I have chosen to treat lesser things in more detail.

2 Introduction

2.1 Types and Sets

Types are not sets. Types are a bit like sets, but types give syntactic information, e.g.

$$3 + (7 * 8)^5 : \mathsf{nat}$$

whereas sets give semantic information, e.g.

$$3 \in \{n \in \mathbb{N} \mid \forall x, y, z \in \mathbb{N}^+(x^n + y^n \neq z^n)\}$$

Of course, the distinction between syntactical and semantical information can't always be drawn that clearly, but the example should be clear: $3+(7*8)^5$ is of type nat simply because 3, 7 and 8 are natural numbers and $*$ and $+$ are operations on natural numbers. On the other hand, $3 \in \{n \in \mathbb{N} \mid \forall x, y, z \in \mathbb{N}^+(x^n+y^n \neq z^n)\}$, because there are no positive x, y, z such that $x^n + y^n = z^n$. This is an instance of 'Fermat's last Theorem', proved by Wiles. To establish that 3 is an element of that set, we need a *proof*, we can't just read it off from the components of the statement. To establish that $3 + (7 * 8)^5 : \mathsf{nat}$ we don't need a proof but a *computation*: our "reading the type of the term" is done by a simple computation.

One can argue about what can be "just read off", and what not; a simple criterion may be whether there is an algorithm that establishes the fact. So then we draw the line between "is of type" (:) and "is an element of" ($\in$) as to whether the relation is decidable or not. A further refinement may be given by arguing that a type checking algorithm should be of low complexity (or compositional or syntax directed).

There are very many different type theories and also mathematicians who base their work on set theory use types as a *high level ordering mechanism*, usually in an informal way. As an example consider the notion of *monoid*, which is defined as a tuple $\langle A, \cdot, e \rangle$, where A is a set, $\cdot$ a binary operation on A and e an element of A, satisfying the monoidic laws. In set theory, such an ordered pair $\langle a, b \rangle$ is typically defined as $\{\{a\}, \{a, b\}\}$, and with that we can define ordered triples, but one usually doesn't get into those details, as they are irrelevant *representation issues*: the only thing that is relevant for an ordered pair is that one has *pairing* and *projection* operators, to create a pair and to take it apart. This is exactly how an ordered pair would be defined in type theory: if A and B are types, then $A \times B$ is a type; if $a : A$ and $b : B$, then $\langle a, b \rangle : A \times B$; if $p : A \times B$, then $\pi_1\, p : A$, $\pi_2\, t : B$ and moreover $\pi_1 \langle a, b \rangle = a$ and $\pi_2 \langle a, b \rangle = b$. So mathematicians use a kind of high level typed language, to avoid irrelevant representation issues, even if they may use set theory as their foundation. However, this high level language plays a more important role than just a language, as can be seen from the problems that mathematicians study: whether $\sqrt{2}$ is an element of the set π is not considered a relevant question. A mathematician would probably not even considered this as a meaningful question, because *the types don't match*: π isn't a set but a number. (But in set theory, everything is a set.) Whether $\sqrt{2} \in \pi$ depends on the actual representation of the real numbers as sets, which is quite arbitrary, so the question is considered irrelevant.

We now list a number of issues and set side by side how set theory and type theory deal with them.

Collections. Sets are "collections of things", where the things themselves are again sets. There are all kinds of ways for putting things together in a set: basically (ignoring some obvious consistency conditions here) one can just put all the elements that satisfy a property together in a set. Types are collections of objects of the same intrinsic nature or the same structure. There are specific ways of forming new types out of existing ones.

Existence. Set theory talks about what things *exist*. The infinity axiom states that an infinite set exists and the power set axiom states that the set of subsets of a set exists. This gives set theory a clear *foundational* aspect, apart from its informal use. It also raises issues whether a "choice set" exists (as stated by the axiom of choice) and whether *inaccessible cardinals* exist. (A set X such that for all sets Y with $|Y| < |X|$, $|2^Y| < |X|$.) Type theory talks about how things can be *constructed* (syntax, expressions). Type theory defines a formal *language*. This puts type theory somewhere in between the research fields of software technology and proof theory, but there is more: being a system describing what things can be *constructed*, type theory also has something to say about the *foundations of mathematics*, as it also – just like set theory – describes what exists (can be constructed) and what not.

Extensionality versus intensionality. Sets are extensional: Two sets are equal if they contain the same elements. For example $\{n \in \mathbb{N} \mid \exists x, y, z \in \mathbb{N}^+(x^n + y^n = z^n)\} = \{0, 1, 2\}$. So set equality is undecidable. In general it requires a proof to establish the equality of two sets. Types are intensional[2]. Two types are equal

[2] But the first version of Martin-Löf's type theory is extensional – and hence has undecidable type checking. This type theory is the basis of the proof assistant Nuprl[10].

if they have the same *representation*, something that can be verified by simple syntactic considerations. So, $\{n \mid \exists x, y, z : \mathsf{nat}^+(x^n + y^n \neq z^n)\} \neq \{n \mid n = 0 \vee n = 1 \vee n = 2\}$ because these two types don't have the same representation. Of course, one may wonder what types these are exactly, or put differently, what an object of such a type is. We'll come to that below.

Decidability of $:$, *undecidability of* $\in$. Membership is undecidable in set theory, as it requires a proof to establish $a \in A$. Typing (and type checking) is decidable[3]. Verifying whether M is of type A requires purely syntactic methods, which can be cast into a *typing algorithm.* As indicated before, types are about syntax: $3 + (7 * 8)^5 : \mathsf{nat}$, because 3, 7, 8 are of type nat and the operations take objects of type nat to nat. Similarly, $\frac{1}{2}\Sigma_{n=0}^{\infty} 2^{-n} : \mathbb{N}$ is not a typing judgment, because one needs additional information to know that the sum is divisible by 2.

The distinction between syntax and semantics is not always as sharp as it seems. The more we know about semantics (a model), the more we can formalize it and "turn it into syntax". For example, we can turn

$$\{n \in \mathbb{N} \mid \exists x, y, z \in \mathbb{N}^+(x^n + y^n = z^n)\}$$

into a (syntactic) type , with decidable type checking , if we take as its terms pairs

$$\langle n, p\rangle : \{n : \mathsf{nat} \mid \exists x, y, z : \mathsf{nat}^+(x^n + y^n = z^n)\}$$

where p is a proof of $\exists x, y, z \in \mathsf{nat}^+(x^n + y^n = z^n)$. If we have decidable proof checking, then it is decidable whether a given pair $\langle n, p\rangle$ is typable with the above type or not.

In these notes, we will study the formulas-as-types and proof-as-terms embedding, which gives syntactic representation of proofs that can be *type checked* to see whether they are correct and what formula (their type) they prove. So with such a representation, proof checking is certainly decidable. We can therefore summarize the difference between set theory and type theory as the difference between *proof checking* (required to check a typing judgment), which is decidable and *proof finding* (which is required to check an element-of judgment) which is not decidable.

2.2 A Hierarchy of Type Theories

In this paper we describe a numbers of type theories. These could be described in one framework of the λ-cube or Pure Type Systems, but we will not do that here. For the general framework we refer to [5,4]. This paper should be seen (and used) as a very introductory paper, that can be used as study material for researchers interested in type theory, but relatively new to the field.

Historically, untyped λ-calculus was studied in much more depth and detail (see [3]) before the whole proliferation of types and related research took

[3] But there are type systems with undecidable type checking, for example the Curry variant of system F (see Section 5.2). And there are more exceptions to this rule.

off. Therefore, in overview papers, one still tends to first introduce untyped λ-calculus and then the typed variant. However, if one knows nothing about either subjects, typed λ-calculus is more natural then the untyped system, which – at first sight – may seem like a pointless token game with unclear semantics. So, we start off from the simply typed λ- calculus.

The following diagrams give an overview of the lectures I have given at the Alfa Lernet Summer School. The first diagram describes simple type theory and polymorphic type theory, which comes in two flavors: à la Church and à la Curry. Apart from that, I have treated a weakened version of λ2, corresponding to polymorphism in functional languages like ML. This will also be discussed in this paper. A main line of thought is the formulas-as-types embedding, so the corresponding logics are indicated in the left column.

The second diagram deals with the extension with dependent types. In the lectures I have treated all systems in the diagram, but in these notes, only the first row will be discussed: first order dependent type theory λP and two ways of interpreting logic into it: a *direct encoding* of minimal predicate logic and a *logical framework* encoding of many different logics. The first follows the Curry-Howard version of the formulas-as-types embedding, which we also follow for λ→ and λ2. The second follows De Bruijn's version of the formulas-as-types embedding, where we encode a logic in a context using dependent types. The rest of the diagram is not treated here, but it is treated on the slides[4].

Logic		TT a la Church	Also known as	TT a la Curry
PROP	$\overset{\text{f-as-t}}{\longrightarrow}$	λ→	STT	λ→
PROP2	$\overset{\text{f-as-t}}{\longrightarrow}$	λ2	system F	λ2

						Remarks
PRED	$\overset{\text{f-as-t}}{\longrightarrow}$	λP		LF	$\overset{\text{f-as-t}}{\longleftarrow}$	Many logics
HOL	$\overset{\text{f-as-t}}{\longrightarrow}$	λHOL				language of HOL is STT
HOL	$\overset{\text{f-as-t}}{\longrightarrow}$	CC	Calc. of Constr.			
		PTS				different PTSs for HOL

3 Simple Type Theory λ→

In our presentation of the simple type theory, we have just arrow types. This is the same as the original system of [9], except for the fact that we allow type variables, whereas Church starts form two base types ι and o. A very natural extension is the one with product types and possibly other type constructions (like sum types, a unit type, ...). A good reference for the simple type theory extended with product types is [27].

[4] url: `http://www.cs.ru.nl/H.Geuvers/Uruguay2008SummerSchool.html/`

Definition 1. *The types of* $\lambda\rightarrow$ *are*

$$\mathsf{Typ} := \mathsf{TVar} \mid (\mathsf{Typ}{\rightarrow}\mathsf{Typ})$$

where TVar *denotes the countable set of type variables.*

Convention 2.
- *Type variables will be denoted by* $\alpha, \beta, \gamma, \ldots$. *Types will be denoted by* $\sigma, \tau, \ldots$.
- *In types we let* brackets associate to the right *and we* omit outside brackets*:* $(\alpha{\rightarrow}\beta){\rightarrow}(\beta{\rightarrow}\gamma){\rightarrow}\alpha{\rightarrow}\gamma$ *denotes* $(\alpha{\rightarrow}\beta){\rightarrow}((\beta{\rightarrow}\gamma){\rightarrow}(\alpha{\rightarrow}\gamma))$

Example 1. The following are types: $(\alpha{\rightarrow}\beta){\rightarrow}\alpha$, $(\alpha{\rightarrow}\beta){\rightarrow}((\beta{\rightarrow}\gamma){\rightarrow}(\alpha{\rightarrow}\gamma))$. Note the higher order structure of types: we read $(\alpha{\rightarrow}\beta){\rightarrow}\alpha$ as the *type of functions that take functions from* α *to* β *to values of type* α.

Definition 3. *The* terms *of* $\lambda\rightarrow$ *are defined as follows*

- *There are countably many typed variables* $x_1^\sigma, x_2^\sigma, \ldots$, *for every* σ.
- *Application: if* $M : \sigma{\rightarrow}\tau$ *and* $N : \sigma$, *then* $(M\,N) : \tau$
- *Abstraction: if* $P : \tau$, *then* $(\lambda x^\sigma.P) : \sigma{\rightarrow}\tau$

So the binary application operation is not written. One could write $M \cdot N$, but that is not done in λ-calculus. The λ is meant to *bind* the variable in the *body*: in $\lambda x^\sigma.M$, x^σ is bound in M. We come to that later.

The idea is that $\lambda x^\sigma.M$ is the function $x \mapsto M$ that takes an input argument P and produces the output $M[x := P]$, M *with* P *substituted for* x. This will be made precise by the β*-reduction rule*, which is the computation rule to deal with λ-terms. We come to this in Definition 6.

Convention 4.
- *Term variables will be denoted by* $x, y, z, \ldots$. *Terms will be denoted by* $M, N, P, \ldots$.
- *Type annotations on variables will only be written at the* λ*-abstraction: we write* $\lambda x^\sigma.x$ *instead of* $\lambda x^\sigma.x^\sigma$.
- *In term applications we let* brackets associate to the left *and we* omit outside brackets *and brackets around iterations of abstractions:* $M\,N\,P$ *denotes* $((M\,N)\,P)$ *and* $\lambda x^{\alpha\rightarrow\beta}.\lambda y^{\beta\rightarrow\gamma}.\lambda z^\alpha.xz(yz)$ *denotes* $(\lambda x^{\alpha\rightarrow\beta}.(\lambda y^{\beta\rightarrow\gamma}.(\lambda z^\alpha.((xz)(yz)))))$

Examples 2. For every type σ we have the term $\mathbf{I}_\sigma := \lambda x^\sigma.x$ which is of type $\sigma{\rightarrow}\sigma$. This is the *identity combinator* on σ.

For types σ and τ we have the term $\mathbf{K}_{\sigma\tau} := \lambda x^\sigma.\lambda y^\tau.x$ of type $\sigma{\rightarrow}\tau{\rightarrow}\sigma$. This term, called the K *combinator* takes two inputs and returns the first.

Here are some more interesting examples of typable terms:
$\lambda x^{\alpha\rightarrow\beta}.\lambda y^{\beta\rightarrow\gamma}.\lambda z^\alpha.y(xz) : (\alpha{\rightarrow}\beta){\rightarrow}(\beta{\rightarrow}\gamma){\rightarrow}\alpha{\rightarrow}\gamma$,
$\lambda x^\alpha.\lambda y^{(\beta\rightarrow\alpha)\rightarrow\alpha}.y(\lambda z^\beta.x) : \alpha{\rightarrow}((\beta{\rightarrow}\alpha){\rightarrow}\alpha){\rightarrow}\alpha$.

To show that a term is of a certain type, we have to "build it up" using the inductive definition of terms (Definition 3). For $\lambda x^{\alpha\rightarrow\beta}.\lambda y^{\beta\rightarrow\gamma}.\lambda z^\alpha.y(xz)$, we find the type as follows:

- If $x : \alpha{\to}\beta$, $y : \beta{\to}\gamma$ and $z : \alpha$, then $xz : \beta$,
- so $y(xz) : \gamma$,
- so $\lambda z^{\alpha}.y(xz) : \alpha{\to}\gamma$,
- so $\lambda y^{\beta\to\gamma}.\lambda z^{\alpha}.y(xz) : (\beta{\to}\gamma){\to}\alpha{\to}\gamma$,
- so $\lambda x^{\alpha\to\beta}.\lambda y^{\beta\to\gamma}.\lambda z^{\alpha}.y(xz) : (\alpha{\to}\beta){\to}(\beta{\to}\gamma){\to}\alpha{\to}\gamma$

In λ-calculus (and type theory) we often take a number of λ-abstractions together, writing $\lambda x^{\sigma} y^{\tau}.x$ for $\lambda x^{\sigma}.\lambda y^{\tau}.x$. The conventions about types and applications fit together nicely. If $F : \sigma{\to}\tau{\to}\rho$, $M : \sigma$ and $P : \tau$, then

$$F\,M : \tau{\to}\rho \quad \text{and} \quad F\,M\,P : \rho$$

Given the bracket convention for types, every type of $\lambda{\to}$ can be written as

$$\sigma_1{\to}\sigma_2{\to}\ldots{\to}\alpha$$

with α a type variable.

The lack of product types is largely circumvented by dealing with functions of multiple arguments by *Currying*: We don't have $F : \sigma \times \tau \to \rho$ but instead we can use $F : \sigma{\to}\tau{\to}\rho$, because the latter F is a function that takes two arguments, of types σ and τ, and produces a term of type ρ.

3.1 Computation, Free and Bound Variables, Substitution

A λ-term of the form $(\lambda x^{\sigma}.M)P$ is a β- redex (*red*ucible *ex*pression). A redex can be *contracted*:

$$(\lambda x^{\sigma}.M)P \longrightarrow_{\beta} M[x := P]$$

where $M[x := P]$ denotes M with P substituted for x.

As an example, we have $(\lambda x^{\sigma}.\lambda y^{\tau}.x)P \longrightarrow_{\beta} \lambda y^{\tau}.P$. But what if $P = y$? then $(\lambda x^{\sigma}.\lambda y^{\tau}.x)y \longrightarrow_{\beta} \lambda y^{\tau}.y$, which is clearly not what we want, because the *free* y has become *bound* after reduction. The λ is a binder and we have to make sure that free variables don't get bound by a substitution. The solution is to *rename* bound variables before substitution.

Definition 5. *We define the notions of free and bound variables of a term, FV and BV.*

$$\begin{aligned} FV(x) &= \{x\} & BV(x) &= \emptyset \\ FV(MN) &= FV(M) \cup FV(N) & BV(MN) &= BV(M) \cup BV(N) \\ FV(\lambda x^{\sigma}.M) &= FV(M) \setminus \{x\} & BV(\lambda x^{\sigma}.M) &= BV(M) \cup \{x\} \end{aligned}$$

$M \equiv N$ or $M =_{\alpha} N$ if M is equal to N modulo renaming of bound variables. *A* closed *term is a term without free variables; closed terms are sometimes also called* combinators.

The renaming of bound variable x is done by taking a "fresh" variable (i.e. one that does not yet occur in the term, either free or bound), say y and replace all bound occurrences of x by y and λx by λy.

Examples 3. – $\lambda x^\sigma.\lambda y^\tau.x \equiv \lambda x^\sigma.\lambda z^\tau.x$
– $\lambda x^\sigma.\lambda y^\tau.x \equiv \lambda y^\sigma.\lambda x^\tau.y$. This equality can be obtained by first renaming y to z, then x to y and then z to y.
– NB we also have $\lambda x^\sigma.\lambda y^\tau.y \equiv \lambda x^\sigma.\lambda x^\tau.x$. This equality is obtained by renaming the second x to y in the second term.

In the last example, we observe that our description of renaming above is slightly too informal. It is not symmetric, as we cannot rename y in the first term to x, and we may at some point not wish to rename with a completely fresh variable, but just with one that is not "in scope". We leave it at this and will not give a completely formal definition, as we think that the reader will be capable of performing α-conversion in the proper way. Fully spelled out definitions can be found in [11,24,3].

The general idea of (typed) λ-calculus is that we don't distinguish between terms that are α convertible: we consider terms *modulo α-equality* and we don't distinguish between $\lambda x^\sigma.\lambda y^\tau.x$ and $\lambda x^\sigma.\lambda z^\tau.x$. This implies that all our operations and predicates should be defined on α-equivalence classes, a property that we don't verify for every operation we define, but that we should be aware of.

When reasoning about λ-terms we use concrete terms (and not α-equivalence classes). We will avoid terms like $\lambda x^\sigma.\lambda x^\tau.x$, because they can be confusing. In examples we always rename bound variables such that no clashes can arise. This is known as the *Barendregt convention*: when talking about a set of λ-terms, we may always assume that all free variables are different from the bound ones and that all bound variables are distinct.

Before reduction or substitution, we rename (if necessary):

$$(\lambda x^\sigma.\lambda y^\tau.x)y \equiv (\lambda x^\sigma.\lambda z^\tau.x)y \longrightarrow_\beta \lambda z^\tau.y$$

Definition 6. *The notions of one-step β-reduction, $\longrightarrow_\beta$, multiple-step β-reduction, $\twoheadrightarrow_\beta$, and β-equality, $=_\beta$ are defined as follows.*

$$\begin{aligned}(\lambda x^\sigma.M)N &\longrightarrow_\beta M[x := N]\\ M \longrightarrow_\beta N \Rightarrow M\,P &\longrightarrow_\beta N\,P\\ M \longrightarrow_\beta N \Rightarrow P\,M &\longrightarrow_\beta P\,N\\ M \longrightarrow_\beta N \Rightarrow \lambda x^\sigma.M &\longrightarrow_\beta \lambda x^\sigma.N\end{aligned}$$

$\twoheadrightarrow_\beta$ is the transitive reflexive closure of $\longrightarrow_\beta$. $=_\beta$ is the transitive reflexive symmetric closure of $\longrightarrow_\beta$.

The type $(\sigma\to\sigma)\to\sigma\to\sigma$ is called the type of *numerals over* σ, nat_σ. The way to encode natural numbers as closed terms of type nat_σ is as follows.

$$c_n := \lambda f^{\sigma\to\sigma}.\lambda x^\sigma.f^n(x)$$

where

$$f^n(x) \text{ denotes } \underbrace{f(\ldots f(f}_{n \text{ times } f}\ x))$$

So $c_2 := \lambda f^{\sigma\to\sigma}.\lambda x^\sigma.f(f\,x)$. These are also known as the *Church numerals*. (For readability we don't denote the dependency of c_n on the type σ, but leave it implicit.) A Church numeral c_n denotes the n-times iteration: it is a higher order function that takes a function $f : \sigma\to\sigma$ and returns the n-times iteration of f.

Example 4. We show a computation with the Church numeral c_2: we apply it to the identity $\mathbf{I}_\sigma$.

$$\begin{aligned}
\lambda z^\sigma.c_2\,\mathbf{I}_\sigma\,z &\equiv \lambda z^\sigma.(\lambda f^{\sigma\to\sigma}.\lambda x^\sigma.f(f\,x))\mathbf{I}_\sigma\,z\\
&\longrightarrow_\beta \lambda z^\sigma.(\lambda x^\sigma.\mathbf{I}_\sigma(\mathbf{I}_\sigma\,x))z\\
&\longrightarrow_\beta \lambda z^\sigma.\mathbf{I}_\sigma(\mathbf{I}_\sigma\,z)\\
&\longrightarrow_\beta \lambda z^\sigma.\mathbf{I}_\sigma\,z\\
&\longrightarrow_\beta \lambda z^\sigma.z \equiv \mathbf{I}_\sigma
\end{aligned}$$

In the above example, we see that at a certain point there are several ways to reduce: we can contract the inner or the outer redex with $\mathbf{I}_\sigma$. In this case the result is exactly the same. In general there are many redexes within a term that can be reduced, and they may all yield a different result. Often we want to fix a certain method for reducing terms, or we only want to contract redexes of a certain shape. This can be observed in the following example.

Examples 5. Define the $\mathbf{S}$ combinator as follows.

$$\mathbf{S} := \lambda x^{\sigma\to\sigma\to\sigma}.\lambda y^{\sigma\to\sigma}.\lambda z^\sigma.x\,z(y\,z) \;:\; (\sigma\to\sigma\to\sigma)\to(\sigma\to\sigma)\to\sigma\to\sigma$$

Then $\mathbf{S}\,\mathbf{K}_{\sigma\sigma}\,\mathbf{I}_\sigma : \sigma\to\sigma$ and

$$\mathbf{S}\,\mathbf{K}_{\sigma\sigma}\,\mathbf{I}_\sigma \longrightarrow_\beta (\lambda y^{\sigma\to\sigma}.\lambda z^\sigma.\mathbf{K}_{\sigma\sigma}\,z(y\,z))\mathbf{I}_\sigma$$

There are several ways of reducing this term further:

$$\begin{aligned}
(\lambda y^{\sigma\to\sigma}.\lambda z^\sigma.\mathbf{K}_{\sigma\sigma}\,z(y\,z))\mathbf{I}_\sigma &\quad \text{is a redex}\\
\mathbf{K}_{\sigma\sigma}\,z &\quad \text{is a redex}
\end{aligned}$$

$$\begin{aligned}
(\lambda y^{\sigma\to\sigma}.\lambda z^\sigma.\mathbf{K}_{\sigma\sigma}\,z(y\,z))\mathbf{I}_\sigma &\longrightarrow_\beta \lambda z^\sigma.\mathbf{K}_{\sigma\sigma}\,z(\mathbf{I}_\sigma\,z)\\
&\equiv \lambda z^\sigma.(\lambda p^\sigma\,q^\sigma.p)\,z(\mathbf{I}_\sigma\,z)\\
&\longrightarrow_\beta \lambda z^\sigma.(\lambda q^\sigma.z)\,(\mathbf{I}_\sigma\,z)\\
\textit{Call by Value} \qquad &\longrightarrow_\beta \lambda z^\sigma.(\lambda q^\sigma.z)z\\
&\longrightarrow_\beta \lambda z^\sigma.z
\end{aligned}$$

But also

$$\begin{aligned}
(\lambda y^{\sigma\to\sigma}.\lambda z^\sigma.\mathbf{K}_{\sigma\sigma}\,z(y\,z))\mathbf{I}_\sigma &\equiv (\lambda y^{\sigma\to\sigma}.\lambda z^\sigma.(\lambda p^\sigma\,q^\sigma.p)\,z(y\,z))\mathbf{I}_\sigma\\
&\longrightarrow_\beta (\lambda y^{\sigma\to\sigma}.\lambda z^\sigma.(\lambda q^\sigma.z)(y\,z))\mathbf{I}_\sigma\\
&\longrightarrow_\beta \lambda z^\sigma.(\lambda q^\sigma.z)\,(\mathbf{I}_\sigma\,z)\\
\textit{Call by Name} \qquad &\longrightarrow_\beta \lambda z^\sigma.z
\end{aligned}$$

In the previous example we have seen that the term $\lambda z^\sigma.(\lambda q^\sigma.z)\,(\mathbf{I}_\sigma\, z)$ can be reduced in several ways. *Call-by-name* is the ordinary β-reduction, where one can contract any β-redex. In *call-by-value*, one is only allowed to reduce $(\lambda x.M)N$ if N is a *value*, where a value is an abstraction term or a variable ([34]). So to reduce a term of the form $(\lambda x.M)((\lambda y.N)P)$ "call-by-value", we first have to contract $(\lambda y.N)P$. Call-by-value restricts the number of redexes that is allowed to be contracted, but it does not prescribe which is the next redex to contract. More restrictive variations of β-reduction are obtained by defining a *reduction strategy* which is a recipe that describes for every term which redex to contract. Well-known reduction strategies are *left-most outermost* or *right-most innermost*. To understand these notions it should be observed that redexes can be *contained in another*, e.g. in $(\lambda x.M)((\lambda y.N)P)$ or in $(\lambda x.(\lambda y.N)P)Q$, but they can also be *disjoint*, in which case there's always one to the left of the other. Other reduction strategies select a set of redexes and contract these simultaneously (a notion that should be defined first of course). For example, it is possible to define the simultaneous contraction of all redexes in a term, which is usually called a *complete development*. We don't go into the theory of reduction strategies or developments here, but refer to the literature [3]. Reduction in simple type theory enjoys some important properties that we list here. We don't give any proofs, as they can be found in the standard literature [5].

Theorem 1. *The simple type theory enjoys the following important properties.*

- *Subject Reduction*
  If $M : \sigma$ and $M \longrightarrow_\beta P$, then $P : \sigma$.
- *Church-Rosser*
  If M is a well-typed term in $\lambda\!\!\rightarrow$ and $M \twoheadrightarrow_\beta P$ and $M \twoheadrightarrow_\beta N$, then there is a (well-typed) term Q such that $P \twoheadrightarrow_\beta Q$ and $N \twoheadrightarrow_\beta Q$.
- *Strong Normalization*
  If M is well-typed in $\lambda\!\!\rightarrow$, then there is no infinite β-reduction path starting from M.

Subject reduction states – looking at it from a programmers point of view – that well-typed programs don't go wrong: evaluating a program $M : \sigma$ to a value indeed returns a value of type σ. Church-Rosser states that it doesn't make any difference for the final value *how* we reduce: we always get the same value. Strong Normalization states that no matter how one evaluates, one always obtains a value: there are no infinite computations possible.

3.2 Simple Type Theory Presented with Derivation Rules

Our definition of $\lambda\!\!\rightarrow$ terms (Definition 3) is given via a standard inductive definition of the terms. This is very close to Church' [9] original definition. A different presentation can be given by presenting the inductive definition of the terms in rule form:

$$\frac{}{x^\sigma : \sigma} \qquad \frac{M : \sigma\to\tau \quad N : \sigma}{MN : \tau} \qquad \frac{P : \tau}{\lambda x^\sigma.P : \sigma\to\tau}$$

The advantage is that now we also have a *derivation tree*, a proof of the fact that the term has that type. We can reason over these derivations.

In the above presentations, the set of free variables of a term is a global notion, that can be computed by the function FV. This is sometimes felt as being a bit imprecise and then a presentation is given with *contexts* to explicitly declare the free variables of a term.

$$x_1 : \sigma_1, x_2 : \sigma_2, \ldots, x_n : \sigma_n$$

is a context, if all the x_i are distinct and the σ_i are all $\lambda\!\!\rightarrow$-types. Contexts are usually denoted by Γ and we write $x \in \Gamma$ if x is one of the variables declared in Γ.

Definition 7. *The* derivation rules *of* $\lambda\!\!\rightarrow$ *à la Church are as follows.*

$$\frac{x{:}\sigma \in \Gamma}{\Gamma \vdash x : \sigma} \quad \frac{\Gamma \vdash M : \sigma{\rightarrow}\tau \quad \Gamma \vdash N : \sigma}{\Gamma \vdash MN : \tau} \quad \frac{\Gamma, x{:}\sigma \vdash P : \tau}{\Gamma \vdash \lambda x{:}\sigma.P : \sigma{\rightarrow}\tau}$$

We write $\Gamma \vdash_{\lambda\rightarrow} M : \sigma$ *if there is a derivation using these rules with conclusion* $\Gamma \vdash M : \sigma$.

So note that – apart from the context – we now also write the type as a declaration in the λ-abstraction (and not as a superscript): $\lambda x : \sigma.x$ instead of $\lambda x^\sigma.x$. This presents us with a slightly different view on the base syntax: we don't see the variables as being typed (x^σ), but we take the view of a countably infinite collection of untyped variables that we assign a type to in the context (the free variables) or in the λ-abstraction (the bound variables).

To relate this Definition with the one of 3, we state – without proof – the following fact, where we ignore the obvious isomorphism that "lifts" the types in the λ-abstraction to a superscript.

Fact 1. *If* $\Gamma \vdash M : \sigma$*, then* $M : \sigma$ *(Definition 3) and* $FV(M) \subseteq \Gamma$.
If $M : \sigma$ *(Definition 3), then* $\Gamma \vdash M : \sigma$*, where* Γ *consists exactly of declarations of all the* $x \in FV(M)$ *to their corresponding types.*

As an example, we give a complete derivation of $\vdash \mathbf{K}_{\sigma\tau} : \sigma \rightarrow \tau \rightarrow \sigma$.

$$\cfrac{\cfrac{x : \sigma, y : \tau \vdash x : \sigma}{x : \sigma \vdash \lambda y{:}\tau.x : \tau \rightarrow \sigma}}{\vdash \lambda x{:}\sigma.\lambda y{:}\tau.x : \sigma \rightarrow \tau \rightarrow \sigma}$$

Derivations of typing judgments tend to get quite broad, because we are constructing a derivation tree. Moreover, this tree may contain quite a lot of duplications. So, when we are looking for a term of a certain type, the tree format may not be the most efficient and easy-to-use. We therefore introduce a *Fitch style representation* of typing derivations, named after the logician Fitch, who has developed a natural deduction system for logic in this format, also called *flag deduction* style [16]. We don't show that these two derivation styles derive the same set of typable terms, because it should be fairly obvious. (And a precise proof involves quite some additional notions and notation.)

Definition 8. *The Fitch style presentation of the rules of $\lambda\!\to$ is as follows.*

$$
\begin{array}{l|l|l}
1 & x:\sigma & \\
\cline{2-2}
2 & \quad\ldots & \\
3 & \quad\ldots & \\
4 & \quad M:\tau & \\
5 & \lambda x{:}\sigma.M:\sigma\to\tau & \textit{abs},\ 1,\ 4
\end{array}
\qquad
\begin{array}{l|ll}
1 & \ldots & \\
2 & \ldots & \\
3 & M:\sigma\to\tau & \\
4 & \ldots & \\
5 & \ldots & \\
6 & N:\sigma & \\
7 & \ldots & \\
8 & M\,N:\tau & \textit{app},\ 3,\ 6
\end{array}
$$

abs-rule *app-rule*

In a Fitch deduction, a hypothesis is introduced by "raising a flag", e.g. the $x:\sigma$ in the left rule. A hypothesis is discharged when we "withdraw the flag", which happens at line 5. In a Fitch deduction one usually numbers the lines and refers to them in the *motivation* of the lines: the "abs,1, 4" and the "app, 3, 6" at the end of lines 5 and 7.

Some remarks apply.

- It should be understood that one can raise a flag under an already open flag (one can nest flags), but the variable x in the newly raised flag should be *fresh*: it should not be declared in any of the open flags.
- In the app-rule, the order of the M and N can of course be different. Also the terms can be in a "smaller scope", that is: $M:\sigma$ may be higher in the deduction under less flags. Basically the M and N should just be "in scope", where a flag-ending ends the scope of all terms that are under that flag.

We say that a Fitch deduction derives the judgement $\Gamma\vdash M:\sigma$ if $M:\sigma$ is on the last line of the deduction the raised flags together form the context Γ.

Example 6. We show an example of a derivation of a term of type

$$(\alpha\to\beta\to\gamma)\to(\alpha\to\beta)\to\alpha\to\gamma$$

We show the derivation in two stages, to indicate how one can use the Fitch deduction rules to incrementally construct a term of a given type.

$$
\begin{array}{l|l}
1 & x:\alpha\to\beta\to\gamma \\
\cline{2-2}
2 & \quad y:\alpha\to\beta \\
3 & \qquad z:\alpha \\
4 & \qquad ?? \\
5 & \qquad ?? \\
6 & \qquad ?:\gamma \\
7 & \quad \lambda z{:}\alpha.?:\alpha\to\gamma \\
8 & \lambda y{:}\alpha\to\beta.\lambda z{:}\alpha.?:(\alpha\to\beta)\to\alpha\to\gamma \\
9 & \lambda x{:}\alpha\to\beta\to\gamma.\lambda y{:}\alpha\to\beta.\lambda z{:}\alpha.?:(\alpha\to\beta\to\gamma)\to(\alpha\to\beta)\to\alpha\to\gamma
\end{array}
$$

$$
\begin{array}{r|l}
1 & x : \alpha\to\beta\to\gamma \\
2 & \quad y : \alpha\to\beta \\
3 & \quad\quad z : \alpha \\
4 & \quad\quad x\, z : \beta\to\gamma \\
5 & \quad\quad y\, z : \beta \\
6 & \quad\quad x\, z(y\, z) : \gamma \\
7 & \quad \lambda z{:}\alpha.x\, z(y\, z) : \alpha\to\gamma \\
8 & \lambda y{:}\alpha\to\beta.\lambda z{:}\alpha.x\, z(y\, z) : (\alpha\to\beta)\to\alpha\to\gamma \\
9 & \lambda x{:}\alpha\to\beta\to\gamma.\lambda y{:}\alpha\to\beta.\lambda z{:}\alpha.x\, z(y\, z) : (\alpha\to\beta\to\gamma)\to(\alpha\to\beta)\to\alpha\to\gamma
\end{array}
$$

Exercises 1. 1. Construct a term of type$(\delta\to\delta\to\alpha)\to(\alpha\to\beta\to\gamma)\to(\delta\to\beta)\to\delta\to\gamma$
2. Construct two terms of type $(\delta\to\delta\to\alpha)\to(\gamma\to\alpha)\to(\alpha\to\beta)\to\delta\to\gamma\to\beta$
3. Construct a term of type $((\alpha\to\beta)\to\alpha)\to(\alpha\to\alpha\to\beta)\to\alpha$
4. Construct a term of type $((\alpha\to\beta)\to\alpha)\to(\alpha\to\alpha\to\beta)\to\beta$ (Hint: use the previous exercise.)

3.3 The Curry-Howard Formulas-as-Types Correspondence

Using the presentation of $\lambda\!\to$ with derivation rules, it is easier to make the *Curry-Howard formulas-as-types* correspondence precise. The idea is that there are two readings of a judgement $M : \sigma$:

1. term as algorithm/program, type as specification :
   M is a function of type σ
2. type as a proposition, term as its proof :
   M is a proof of the proposition σ

More precisely, the Curry-Howard formulas-as-types correspondence states that there is a natural one-to-one correspondence between typable terms in $\lambda\!\to$ and derivations in *minimal proposition logic.* Looking at it from the logical point of view: the judgement $x_1 : \tau_1, x_2 : \tau_2, \ldots, x_n : \tau_n \vdash M : \sigma$ can be read as *M is a proof of σ from the assumptions $\tau_1, \tau_2, \ldots, \tau_n$.*

Definition 9. *The system of minimal proposition logic* PROP *consists of*

- *implicational propositions, generated by the following abstract syntax:*

$$\mathsf{prop} ::= \mathsf{PropVar} | (\mathsf{prop}\to\mathsf{prop})$$

- *derivation rules (Δ is a set of propositions, σ and τ are propositions)*

$$
\frac{\sigma\to\tau \quad \sigma}{\tau}\ \to\text{-}E
\qquad\qquad
\begin{array}{c}
[\sigma]^j \\
\vdots \\
\dfrac{\tau}{\sigma\to\tau}\ [j]\to\text{-}I
\end{array}
$$

We write $\Delta \vdash_{\mathrm{PROP}} \sigma$ if there is a derivation using these rules with conclusion σ and non-discharged assumptions *in Δ.*

Note the difference between a context, which is basically a *list*, and a *set* of assumptions. Logic (certainly in natural deduction) is usually presented using a *set* of assumptions, but there is no special reason for not letting the assumptions be a list, or a multi-set.

We now give a precise definition of the formulas-as-types correspondence. For this we take the presentation of PROP with lists (so Δ is a list in the following definition). As a matter of fact the *formulas-as-types* part of the definition is trivial: a proposition in PROP is just a type in $\lambda\!\to$, but the most interesting part of the correspondence is the *proofs-as-terms* embedding, maybe best called the *deductions-as-term* embedding. For PROP, this part is also quite straightforward, but we describe it in detail nevertheless.)

Definition 10. *The* deductions-as-terms *embedding from derivation of* PROP *to term of* $\lambda\!\to$ *is defined inductively as follows. We associate to a list of propositions Δ a context Γ in the obvious way by replacing σ_i in Δ with $x_i : \sigma_i \in \Gamma$. On the left we give the inductive clause for the derivation and on the right we describe on top of the line the terms we have (by induction) and below the line the term that the derivation gets mapped to.*

$$\frac{}{\Delta \vdash \sigma}\,\sigma \in \Delta \quad \rightsquigarrow \quad \frac{}{\Gamma \vdash x : \sigma}\,x : \sigma \in \Gamma$$

$$\frac{\sigma\!\to\!\tau \quad \sigma}{\tau}\,{\to}\text{-}E \quad \rightsquigarrow \quad \frac{\Gamma_1 \vdash M : \sigma\!\to\!\tau \quad \Gamma_2 \vdash N : \sigma}{\Gamma_1 \cup \Gamma_2 \vdash M\,N : \tau}$$

$$\frac{\begin{array}{c}[\sigma]^j \\ \vdots \\ \tau\end{array}}{\sigma\!\to\!\tau}\,[j]\,{\to}\text{-}I \quad \rightsquigarrow \quad \frac{\Gamma, x : \sigma \vdash M : \tau}{\Gamma \vdash \lambda x{:}\sigma.M : \sigma\!\to\!\tau}$$

We denote this embedding by $\overline{-}$, *so if $\mathcal{D}$ is a derivation from* PROP, $\overline{\mathcal{D}}$ *is a* $\lambda\!\to$*-term.*

For a good understanding we give a detailed example.

Example 7. Consider the following natural deduction derivation PROP and the term in $\lambda\!\to$ it gets mapped to.

$$\cfrac{\cfrac{\cfrac{\cfrac{\cfrac{[\alpha\!\to\!\beta\!\to\!\gamma]^3 \quad [\alpha]^1}{\beta\!\to\!\gamma} \qquad \cfrac{[\alpha\!\to\!\beta]^2 \quad [\alpha]^1}{\beta}}{\gamma}}{\alpha\!\to\!\gamma}\,1}{(\alpha\!\to\!\beta)\!\to\!\alpha\!\to\!\gamma}\,2}{(\alpha\!\to\!\beta\!\to\!\gamma)\!\to\!(\alpha\!\to\!\beta)\!\to\!\alpha\!\to\!\gamma}\,3 \quad \mapsto \quad \begin{array}{l}\lambda x{:}\alpha\!\to\!\beta\!\to\!\gamma.\lambda y{:}\alpha\!\to\!\beta.\lambda z{:}\alpha.xz(yz) \\ \quad : (\alpha\!\to\!\beta\!\to\!\gamma)\!\to\!(\alpha\!\to\!\beta)\!\to\!\alpha\!\to\!\gamma\end{array}$$

To create the term on the right, it is best to decorate the deduction tree with terms, starting from the leaves (decorated by variables) and working downwards, finally creating a term for the root node that is the λ-term that corresponds to the whole deduction.

$$\dfrac{\dfrac{\dfrac{\dfrac{[x:\alpha{\to}\beta{\to}\gamma]^3 \quad [z:\alpha]^1}{xz:\beta{\to}\gamma} \qquad \dfrac{[y:\alpha{\to}\beta]^2 \quad [z:\alpha]^1}{yz:\beta}}{\dfrac{xz(yz):\gamma}{\lambda z{:}\alpha.xz(yz):\alpha{\to}\gamma}1}}{\lambda y{:}\alpha{\to}\beta.\lambda z{:}\alpha.xz(yz):(\alpha{\to}\beta){\to}\alpha{\to}\gamma}2}{\lambda x{:}\alpha{\to}\beta{\to}\gamma.\lambda y{:}\alpha{\to}\beta.\lambda z{:}\alpha.xz(yz):(\alpha{\to}\beta{\to}\gamma){\to}(\alpha{\to}\beta){\to}\alpha{\to}\gamma}3$$

Theorem 2 (Soundness, Completeness of formulas-as-types)

1. *If $\mathcal{D}$ is a natural deduction in* PROP *with conclusion σ and non-discharged assumption in Δ, then*

$$\boldsymbol{x}:\boldsymbol{\Delta}\vdash\overline{\mathcal{D}}:\sigma \text{ in } \lambda{\to}.$$

2. *If $\Gamma \vdash M:\sigma$ in $\lambda{\to}$, then there is a derivation of σ from the Δ in* PROP, *where Δ is Γ without the variable-assignments.*

We don't give the proofs, as they are basically by a straightforward induction. The second part of the Theorem can be strengthened a bit: we can construct a derivation $\mathcal{D}$ out of the term M, as an inverse to the mapping $\overline{-}$. So, the formulas-as-types correspondence constitutes an *isomorphism* between derivations in PROP and well-typed terms in $\lambda{\to}$.

Exercise 2. Add types to the λ-abstractions and give the derivation that corresponds to the term $\lambda x.\lambda y.y(\lambda z.y\,x):(\gamma{\to}\varepsilon){\to}((\gamma{\to}\varepsilon){\to}\varepsilon){\to}\varepsilon$.

In the λ-calculus we have a notion of computation, given by β-reduction: $(\lambda x{:}\sigma.M)P \longrightarrow_\beta M[x:=P]$. Apart from that, there is also a notion of η-reduction: $\lambda x{:}\sigma.M\,x \longrightarrow_\eta M$ if $x \notin \mathrm{FV}(M)$. The idea of considering these terms as equal is quite natural, because they behave exactly the same as functions: $(\lambda x{:}\sigma.M\,x)P \longrightarrow_\beta M\,P$. In a typed setting, it is very natural to consider the rule in the opposite direction, because then one can make sure that every term of a function type has a normal form that is a λ-abstraction. Of course this requires a proviso to prevent an infinite η-reduction of the form $x \longrightarrow_\eta \lambda y{:}\sigma.x\,y \longrightarrow_\eta \lambda y{:}\sigma.(\lambda z{:}\sigma.x\,z)y\ldots$

In natural deduction we also have a notion of computation: *cut-elimination* or *detour-elimination.* If one introduces a connective and then immediately eliminates it again, this is called a cut or a detour. A *cut* is actually a *rule* in the sequent calculus representation of logic and the *cut-elimination* theorem in sequent calculus states that the cut-rule is derivable and thus superfluous. In natural deduction, we can eliminate detours, which are often also called cuts, a terminology that we will also use here.

Definition 11. *A* cut *in a deduction in minimal propositional logic is a place where an* $\to$*-I is immediately followed by an elimination of that same* $\to$*. Graphically (*$\mathcal{D}_1$ *and* $\mathcal{D}_2$ *denote deductions):*

$$\dfrac{\dfrac{\begin{matrix}[\sigma]^1\\ \mathcal{D}_1\\ \tau\end{matrix}}{\sigma\to\tau}\,1 \qquad \dfrac{\mathcal{D}_2}{\sigma}}{\tau}$$

Cut-elimination *is defined by replacing the cut in a deduction in the way given below.*

$$\dfrac{\dfrac{\begin{matrix}[\sigma]^1\\ \mathcal{D}_1\\ \tau\end{matrix}}{\sigma\to\tau}\,1 \qquad \dfrac{\mathcal{D}_2}{\sigma}}{\tau} \quad\longrightarrow\quad \begin{matrix}\mathcal{D}_2\\ \sigma\\ \mathcal{D}_1\\ \tau\end{matrix}$$

So every occurrence of the discharged assumption $[\sigma]^1$ *in* $\mathcal{D}_1$ *is replaced by the deduction* $\mathcal{D}_2$*.*

It is not hard to prove that eliminating a cut yields a well-formed natural deduction again, with the same conclusion. The set of non-discharged assumptions remains the same or shrinks. (In case there is no occurrence of $[\sigma]^1$ at all; then $\mathcal{D}_2$ is removed and also its assumptions.) That this process terminates is not obvious: if $[\sigma]^1$ occurs several times, $\mathcal{D}_2$ gets copied, resulting in a larger deduction.

Lemma 2. *Cut-elimination in* PROP *corresponds to* β*-reduction in* $\lambda\!\to$*: if* $\mathcal{D}_1 \longrightarrow_{cut} \mathcal{D}_2$*, then* $\overline{\mathcal{D}_1} \longrightarrow_\beta \overline{\mathcal{D}_2}$

The proof of this Lemma is indicated in the following diagram.

$$\dfrac{\dfrac{\begin{matrix}[x:\sigma]^1\\ \mathcal{D}_1\\ M:\tau\end{matrix}}{\lambda x{:}\sigma.M:\sigma\to\tau}\,1 \qquad \dfrac{\mathcal{D}_2}{P:\sigma}}{(\lambda x{:}\sigma.M)P:\tau} \quad\longrightarrow_\beta\quad \begin{matrix}\mathcal{D}_2\\ P:\sigma\\ \mathcal{D}_1\\ M[x:=P]:\tau\end{matrix}$$

To get a better understanding of the relation between cut-elimination and β-reduction, we now study an example.

Example 8. Consider the following proof of $A{\to}A{\to}B, (A{\to}B){\to}A \vdash B$.

$$\dfrac{\dfrac{\dfrac{\dfrac{A{\to}A{\to}B \quad [A]^1}{A{\to}B} \quad [A]^1}{B}}{A{\to}B} \qquad \dfrac{(A{\to}B){\to}A \qquad \dfrac{\dfrac{\dfrac{A{\to}A{\to}B \quad [A]^1}{A{\to}B} \quad [A]^1}{B}}{A{\to}B}}{A}}{B}$$

It contains a cut: a $\to$-I directly followed by an $\to$-E. We now present the same proof after reduction

$$\dfrac{\dfrac{A{\to}A{\to}B \qquad \dfrac{(A{\to}B){\to}A \qquad \dfrac{\dfrac{\dfrac{A{\to}A{\to}B \quad [A]^1}{A{\to}B} \quad [A]^1}{B}}{A{\to}B}}{A}}{A{\to}B} \qquad \dfrac{(A{\to}B){\to}A \qquad \dfrac{\dfrac{\dfrac{A{\to}A{\to}B \quad [A]^1}{A{\to}B} \quad [A]^1}{B}}{A{\to}B}}{A}}{B}$$

We now present the same derivations of $A{\to}A{\to}B, (A{\to}B){\to}A \vdash B$, now with term information

$$\dfrac{\dfrac{\dfrac{\dfrac{p : A{\to}A{\to}B \quad [x : A]^1}{p\,x : A{\to}B} \quad [x : A]^1}{p\,x\,x : B}}{\lambda x{:}A.p\,x\,x : A{\to}B} \qquad \dfrac{q : (A{\to}B){\to}A \qquad \dfrac{\dfrac{\dfrac{p : A{\to}A{\to}B \quad [x : A]^1}{p\,x : A{\to}B} \quad [x : A]^1}{p\,x\,x : B}}{\lambda x{:}A.p\,x\,x : A{\to}B}}{q(\lambda x{:}A.p\,x\,x) : A}}{(\lambda x{:}A.p\,x\,x)(q(\lambda x{:}A.p\,x\,x)) : B}$$

The term contains a β-redex: $(\lambda x{:}A.p\,x\,x)\,(q(\lambda x{:}A.p\,x\,x))$ We now present the reduced proof of $A{\to}A{\to}B, (A{\to}B){\to}A \vdash B$ with term info. For reasons of page size we summarize the derivation of $q(\lambda x{:}A.p\,x\,x) : A$ as $\mathcal{D}$. So

$$\dfrac{\boxed{\;\mathcal{D}\;}}{q(\lambda x{:}A.p\,x\,x) : A} \quad := \quad \dfrac{q : (A{\to}B){\to}A \qquad \dfrac{\dfrac{\dfrac{p : A{\to}A{\to}B \quad [x{:}A]^1}{p\,x : A{\to}B} \quad [x{:}A]^1}{p\,x\,x : B}}{\lambda x{:}A.p\,x\,x : A{\to}B}}{q(\lambda x{:}A.p\,x\,x) : A}$$

This is the sub-derivation that gets copied under cut-elimination (β-reduction).

$$\dfrac{\dfrac{p : A{\to}A{\to}B \quad \dfrac{\boxed{\mathcal{D}}}{q(\lambda x{:}A.p\,x\,x) : A}}{p(q(\lambda x{:}A.p\,x\,x)) : A{\to}B} \qquad \dfrac{\boxed{\mathcal{D}}}{q(\lambda x{:}A.p\,x\,x) : A}}{p(q(\lambda x{:}A.p\,x\,x))(q(\lambda x{:}A.p\,x\,x)) : B}$$

4 Type Assignment versus Typed Terms

4.1 Untyped λ-Calculus

Simple Type Theory is not very expressive: one can only represent a limited number of functions over the nat_σ (see the paragraph after Definition 6) data types in $\lambda{\to}$. We can allow more functions to be definable by relaxing the type constraints. The most flexible system is to have no types at all.

Definition 12. *The terms of the untyped λ-calculus, Λ, are defined as follows.*

$$\Lambda ::= \mathit{Var} \mid (\Lambda\,\Lambda) \mid (\lambda\,\mathit{Var}.\Lambda)$$

Examples are the well-known combinators that we have already seen in a typed fashion: $\mathbf{K} := \lambda x\,y.x$, $\mathbf{S} := \lambda x\,y\,z.x\,z(y\,z)$. But we can now do more: here are some well-known untyped λ-terms $\omega := \lambda x.x\,x$, $\Omega := \omega\,\omega$. The notions of β-reduction and β-equality generalize from the simple typed case, so we don't repeat it here. An interesting aspect is that we can now have *infinite reductions*. (Which is impossible in $\lambda{\to}$, as that system is Strongly Normalizing.) The simplest infinite reduction is the following *loop*:

$$\Omega \longrightarrow_\beta \Omega$$

A term that doesn't loop but whose reduction path contains infinitely many different terms is obtained by putting $\omega_3 := \lambda x.x\,x\,x$, $\Omega_3 := \omega_3\omega_3$. Then:

$$\Omega_3 \longrightarrow_\beta \omega_3\,\omega_3\,\omega_3 \longrightarrow_\beta \omega_3\,\omega_3\,\omega_3\,\omega_3 \longrightarrow_\beta \ldots$$

The untyped λ-calculus was defined by Church [9] and proposed as a system to capture the notion of *mechanic computation*, for which Turing proposed the notion of Turing machine. An important property of the untyped λ-calculus is that it is *Turing complete*, which was proved by Turing in 1936, see [13]. The power of Λ lies in the fact that you can *solve recursive equations*.

A recursive equation is a question of the following kind:

- Is there a term M such that

$$M\,x =_\beta x\,M\,x?$$

– Is there a term M such that

$$M\,x =_\beta \mathsf{if}\,(\mathsf{Zero}\,x)\,\mathsf{then}\,1\,\mathsf{else}\,\mathsf{Mult}\,x\,(M\,(\mathsf{Pred}\,x))?$$

So, we have two expressions on either side of the $=_\beta$ sign, both containing an unknown M and we want to know whether a solution for M exists.

The answer is: **yes**, if we can rewrite the equation to one of the form

$$M =_\beta \boxed{\ldots M \ldots} \tag{1}$$

Note that this is possible for the equations written above. For example the first equation is solved by a term M that satisfies $M =_\beta \lambda x.x\,M\,x$.

That we can solve equation of the form (1) is because every term in the λ-calculus has a *fixed point*. Even more: we have a *fixed point combinator*.

Definition 13. – *The term M is a* fixed point *of the term P if $P\,M =_\beta M$.*
– *The term Y is a* fixed point combinator *if for every term P, $Y\,P$ is a fixed point of P, that is if*

$$P\,(Y\,P) =_\beta Y\,P.$$

In the λ-calculus we have various fixed point combinators, of which the Y-combinator is the most well-known one: $Y := \lambda f.(\lambda x.f(x\,x))(\lambda x.f(x\,x))$.

Exercise 3. Verify that the Y as defined above is a fixed point combinator: $P\,(Y\,P) =_\beta Y\,P$ for every λ-term P.

Verify that $\Theta := (\lambda x\,y.y(x\,x\,y))(\lambda x\,y.y(x\,x\,y))$ is also a fixed point combinator that is even *reducing*: $\Theta\,P \twoheadrightarrow_\beta P\,(\Theta\,P)$ for every λ-term P.

The existence of fixed-points is the key to the power of the λ-calculus. But we also need natural numbers and booleans to be able to write programs. In Section 3 we have already seen the *Church numerals*:

$$c_n := \lambda f.\lambda x.f^n(x)$$

where

$$f^n(x) \text{ denotes } \underbrace{f(\ldots f(f}_{n \text{ times } f}\ x))$$

The successor is easy to define for these numerals: $\mathsf{Suc} := \lambda n.\lambda f\,x.f(n\,f\,x)$. Addition can also be defined quite easily, but if we are lazy we can also use the fixed-point combinator. We want to solve

$$\mathsf{Add}\,n\,m := \mathsf{if}\,(\mathsf{Zero}\,n)\,\mathsf{then}\,m\,\mathsf{else}\,\mathsf{Add}\,(\mathsf{Pred}\,n)\,m)$$

where Pred is the predecessor function, Zero is a test for zero and $\mathsf{if}\ldots\mathsf{then}\ldots\mathsf{else}$ is a case distinction on booleans. The booleans can be defined by

$$\mathsf{true} := \lambda x\,y.x$$
$$\mathsf{false} := \lambda x\,y.y$$
$$\mathsf{if}\,b\,\mathsf{then}\,P\,\mathsf{else}\,Q := b\,P\,Q.$$

Exercise 4. 1. Verify that the booleans behave as expected:
if true then P else $Q =_\beta P$ and if false then P else $Q =_\beta Q$.
2. Define a test-for-zero Zero on the Church numerals :$\mathsf{Zero}\, c_0 =_\beta \mathsf{true}$ and $\mathsf{Zero}\, c_{n+1} =_\beta \mathsf{false}$. (Defining the predecessor is remarkably tricky!)

Apart from the natural numbers and booleans, it is not difficult to find encodings of other data, like lists and trees. Given the expressive power of the untyped λ-calculus and the limited expressive power of $\lambda\!\!\rightarrow$, one may wonder why we want types. There are various good reasons for that, most of which apply to the the "typed versus untyped programming languages" issue in general.

Types give a (partial) specification. Types tell the programmer – and a person reading the program — what a program (λ-term) does, to a certain extent. Types only give a very partial specification, like $f : \mathbb{N} \rightarrow \mathbb{N}$, but depending on the type system, this information can be enriched, for example: $f : \Pi n : \mathbb{N}.\exists m : \mathbb{N}.m > n$, stating that f is a program that takes a number n and returns an m that is larger than n. In the Chapter by Bove and Dybjer, one can find examples of that type and we will also come back to this theme in this Chapter in Section 6.

"Well-typed programs never go wrong" (Milner). The *Subject Reduction property* guarantees that a term of type σ remains to be of type σ under evaluation. So, if M : `nat` evaluates to a value v, we can be sure that v is a natural number.

The type checking algorithm detects (simple) mistakes. Types can be checked at compile time (*statically*) and this is a simple but very useful method to detect simple mistakes like typos and applying functions to the wrong arguments. Of course, in a more refined type system, type checking can also detect more subtle mistakes.

Typed terms always terminate(?). In typed λ-calculi used for representing proofs (following the Curry-Howard isomorphism), the terms are always terminating, and this is seen as an advantage as it helps in proving consistency of logical theories expressed in these calculi. In general, termination very much depends on the typing system. In this paper, all type systems only type terminating (strongly normalizing) λ-terms, which also implies that these systems are not Turing complete. Type systems for programming languages will obviously allow also non-terminating calculations. A simple way to turn $\lambda\!\!\rightarrow$ into a Turing complete language is by adding fixed point combinators (for every type σ) $Y_\sigma : (\sigma\!\rightarrow\!\sigma)\!\rightarrow\!\sigma$ with the reduction rule $Y f \rightarrow f(Y f)$. This is basically the system PCF, first defined and studied by Plotkin [35].

Given that we want types, the situation with a system like $\lambda\!\!\rightarrow$ as presented in Section 3, is still unsatisfactory from a programmers point of view. Why would the programmer have to write all those types? The compiler should compute the type information for us!

For M an *untyped* term, we want the type system to *assign* a type σ to M (or say that M is not typable). Such a type system is called a *type assignment system*, or also *typing à la Curry* (as opposed to the *typing à la Church* that we have seen up to now).

4.2 Simple Type Theory à la Church and à la Curry

We now set the two systems side-by-side: $\lambda\!\!\to$ à la Church and à la Curry.

Definition 14. *In $\lambda\!\!\to$ à la Curry, the terms are*

$$\Lambda ::= Var \mid (\Lambda\,\Lambda) \mid (\lambda\, Var.\Lambda)$$

In $\lambda\!\!\to$ à la Church, the terms are

$$\Lambda_{Ch} ::= Var \mid (\Lambda_{Ch}\,\Lambda_{Ch}) \mid (\lambda\, Var{:}\sigma.\Lambda_{Ch})$$

where σ ranges over the simple types, as defined in Definition 1.

These sets of terms are just the *preterms*. The typing rules will select the *well-typed* terms from each of these sets.

Definition 15. *The typing rules of $\lambda\!\!\to$ à la Church and $\lambda\!\!\to$ à la Curry are as follows. (The ones for the Church system are the same as the ones in Definition 7.)*
$\lambda\!\!\to$ (à la Church):

$$\frac{x{:}\sigma \in \Gamma}{\Gamma \vdash x : \sigma} \quad \frac{\Gamma \vdash M : \sigma{\to}\tau \quad \Gamma \vdash N : \sigma}{\Gamma \vdash MN : \tau} \quad \frac{\Gamma, x{:}\sigma \vdash P : \tau}{\Gamma \vdash \lambda x{:}\sigma.P : \sigma{\to}\tau}$$

$\lambda\!\!\to$ (à la Curry):

$$\frac{x{:}\sigma \in \Gamma}{\Gamma \vdash x : \sigma} \quad \frac{\Gamma \vdash M : \sigma{\to}\tau \quad \Gamma \vdash N : \sigma}{\Gamma \vdash MN : \tau} \quad \frac{\Gamma, x{:}\sigma \vdash P : \tau}{\Gamma \vdash \lambda x.P : \sigma{\to}\tau}$$

The rules à la Curry can of course also be given in the Fitch style, which is the style we use when giving derivations of typings.

Exercise 5. Give a full derivation of

$$\vdash \lambda x.\lambda y.y(\lambda z.y\,x) : (\gamma{\to}\varepsilon){\to}((\gamma{\to}\varepsilon){\to}\varepsilon){\to}\varepsilon$$

in Curry style $\lambda\!\!\to$

We can summarize the differences between *Typed Terms* and *Type Assignment* as follows:

- With typed terms (typing à la Church), we have terms with type information in the λ-abstraction: $\lambda x{:}\alpha.x : \alpha{\to}\alpha$. As a consequence:
  - Terms have unique types,
  - The type is directly computed from the type info in the variables.
- With type assignment (typing à la Curry), we assign types to untyped λ-terms: $\lambda x.x : \alpha{\to}\alpha$. As a consequence:
  - Terms do not have unique types,
  - A *principal type* can be computed (using unification).

Examples 9. – Typed Terms:

$$\lambda x{:}\alpha.\lambda y{:}(\beta{\to}\alpha){\to}\alpha.y(\lambda z{:}\beta.x)$$

has only the type $\alpha{\to}((\beta{\to}\alpha){\to}\alpha){\to}\alpha$

– Type Assignment: $\lambda x.\lambda y.y(\lambda z.x)$ can be assigned the types
  - $\alpha{\to}((\beta{\to}\alpha){\to}\alpha){\to}\alpha$
  - $(\alpha{\to}\alpha){\to}((\beta{\to}\alpha{\to}\alpha){\to}\gamma){\to}\gamma$
  - ...

  with $\alpha{\to}((\beta{\to}\alpha){\to}\gamma){\to}\gamma$ being the *principal type*, a notion to be defined and discussed later.

There is an obvious connection between Church and Curry typed $\lambda{\to}$, given by the *erasure map*.

Definition 16. *The* erasure *map* $|-|$ *from* $\lambda{\to}$ *à la Church to* $\lambda{\to}$ *à la Curry is defined by erasing all type information:*

$$\begin{aligned} |x| &:= x \\ |M\,N| &:= |M|\,|N| \\ |\lambda x:\sigma.M| &:= \lambda x.|M| \end{aligned}$$

So, e.g. $|\lambda x{:}\alpha.\lambda y{:}(\beta{\to}\alpha){\to}\alpha.y(\lambda z{:}\beta.x))| = \lambda x.\lambda y.y(\lambda z.x))$.

Theorem 3. *If* $M:\sigma$ *in* $\lambda{\to}$ *à la Church, then* $|M|:\sigma$ *in* $\lambda{\to}$ *à la Curry.*
If $P:\sigma$ *in* $\lambda{\to}$ *à la Curry, then there is an* M *such that* $|M|\equiv P$ *and* $M:\sigma$ *in* $\lambda{\to}$ *à la Church.*

The proof is by an easy induction on the derivation.

4.3 Principal Types

We now discuss the notion of a principal type in $\lambda{\to}$ à la Curry. We will describe an algorithm, the *principal type algorithm*, that, given a closed untyped term M, computes a type σ if M is typable with type σ in $\lambda{\to}$, and "reject" if M is not typable. Moreover, the computed type σ is "minimal" in the sense that all possible types for M are substitution instances of σ.

Computing a principal type for M in $\lambda{\to}$ à la Curry proceeds as follows:

1. Assign a type variable to every variable x in M.
2. Assign a type variable to every *applicative sub-term* of M.
3. Generate a (finite) set of equations E between types that need to hold in order to ensure that M is typable.
4. Compute a "minimal substitution" S, substituting types for type variables, that makes all equations in E hold. (This is a *most general unifier* for E.)
5. With S compute the type of M.

The algorithm described above can fail only if their is no unifying substitution for E. In that case we return "reject" and conclude that M is not typable. An *applicative sub-term* is a term that is not a variable and does not start with a λ. (So it is a sub-term of the form $P\,Q$). One could label all sub-terms with a type variable, but that just adds superfluous overhead. We show how the algorithm works by elaborating an example.

Example 10. We want to compute the principal type of $\lambda x.\lambda y.y(\lambda z.yx)$.

1. Assign type variables to all term variables: $x : \alpha, y : \beta, z : \gamma$.
2. Assign type variables to all applicative sub-terms: $y\,x : \delta$, $y(\lambda z.y\,x) : \varepsilon$. These two steps yield the following situation, where we indicate the types of the variables and applicative sub-terms by super- and subscripts.

$$\lambda x^{\alpha}.\lambda y^{\beta}.\underbrace{y^{\beta}(\lambda z^{\gamma}.\overbrace{y^{\beta}x^{\alpha}}^{\delta})}_{\varepsilon}$$

3. Generate equations between types, necessary for the term to be typable:

$$E = \{\beta = \alpha{\to}\delta, \beta = (\gamma{\to}\delta){\to}\varepsilon\}$$

   The equation $\beta = \alpha{\to}\delta$ arises from the sub-term $\overbrace{y^{\beta}x^{\alpha}}^{\delta}$, which is of type δ if β is a function type with domain α and range δ. The equation $\beta = (\gamma{\to}\delta){\to}\varepsilon$ arises from the sub-term $\underbrace{y^{\beta}(\lambda z^{\gamma}.\overbrace{y\,x}^{\delta})}_{\varepsilon}$, which is of type ε if β is a function type with domain $\gamma{\to}\delta$ and range ε.
4. Find a most general substitution (a *most general unifier*) for the type variables that solves the equations:

$$S := \{\alpha := \gamma{\to}\delta,\ \ \beta := (\gamma{\to}\delta){\to}\varepsilon,\ \ \delta := \varepsilon\}$$

5. The *principal type* of $\lambda x.\lambda y.y(\lambda z.yx)$ is now

$$(\gamma{\to}\varepsilon){\to}((\gamma{\to}\varepsilon){\to}\varepsilon){\to}\varepsilon$$

Exercise 6. 1. Compute the principal type for $\mathbf{S} := \lambda x.\lambda y.\lambda z.x\,z(y\,z)$
2. Which of the following terms is typable? If it is, determine the *principal type*; if it isn't, show that the typing algorithm rejects the term.
   (a) $\lambda z\,x.z(x(\lambda y.y\,x))$
   (b) $\lambda z\,x.z(x(\lambda y.y\,z))$
3. Compute the principal type for $M := \lambda x.\lambda y.x(y(\lambda z.x\,z\,z))(y(\lambda z.x\,z\,z))$.

We now introduce the notions required for the principal types algorithm.

Definition 17. – *A* type substitution *(or just substitution) is a map S from type variables to types. As a function, we write it* after the type, *so σS denotes the result of carrying out substitution S on σ.*

- *Most substitutions we encounter are the identity on all but a finite number of type variables, so we often denote a substitution as* $[\alpha_1 := \sigma_1, \ldots, \alpha_n := \sigma_n]$. *We view a type substitution as a function that is carried out* in parallel *so* $[\alpha := \beta{\rightarrow}\beta, \beta := \alpha{\rightarrow}\gamma]$ *applied to* $\alpha{\rightarrow}\beta$ *results in* $(\beta{\rightarrow}\beta){\rightarrow}\alpha{\rightarrow}\gamma$.
- *We can compose substitutions in the obvious way:* $S;T$ *is obtained by first performing* S *and then* T.
- *A* unifier *of the types* σ *and* τ *is a substitution that "makes* σ *and* τ *equal", i.e. an* S *such that* $\sigma S = \tau S$.
- *A* most general unifier *(or mgu) of the types* σ *and* τ *is the "simplest substitution" that makes* σ *and* τ *equal, i.e. an* S *such that*
  - $\sigma S = \tau S$
  - *for all substitutions* T *such that* $\sigma T = \tau T$ *there is a substitution* R *such that* $T = S; R$.

All these notions generalize to lists instead of pairs σ, τ. We say that S *unifies* the list of equations $\sigma_1 = \tau_1, \ldots, \sigma_n = \tau_n$ if $\sigma_1 S = \tau_1 S, \ldots, \sigma_n S = \tau_n S$, that is: S makes all equations true.

The crucial aspect in the principal type algorithm is the computability of a *most general unifier* for a set of type equations. The rest of the algorithm should be clear from the example and we don't describe it in detail here.

Definition 18. *We define the algorithm* U *that, when given a list of type equations* $E = \langle\sigma_1 = \tau_1, \ldots, \sigma_n = \tau_n\rangle$ *outputs a substitution* S *or "reject" as follows.* U *looks at the first type equation* $\sigma_1 = \tau_1$ *and depending on its form it outputs:*

- $U(\langle\alpha = \alpha, \ldots, \sigma_n = \tau_n\rangle) := U(\langle\sigma_2 = \tau_2, \ldots, \sigma_n = \tau_n\rangle)$.
- $U(\langle\alpha = \tau_1, \ldots, \sigma_n = \tau_n\rangle) :=$ *"reject" if* $\alpha \in FV(\tau_1)$, $\tau_1 \neq \alpha$.
- $U(\langle\alpha = \tau_1, \ldots, \sigma_n = \tau_n\rangle) :=$ $[\alpha := \tau_1, U(\langle\sigma_2[\alpha := \tau_1] = \tau_2[\alpha := \tau_1], \ldots, \sigma_n[\alpha := \tau_1] = \tau_n[\alpha := \tau_1]\rangle)]$, *if* $\alpha \notin FV(\tau_1)$.
- $U(\langle\sigma_1 = \alpha, \ldots, \sigma_n = \tau_n\rangle) := U(\langle\alpha = \sigma_1, \ldots, \sigma_n = \tau_n\rangle)$
- $U(\langle\mu{\rightarrow}\nu = \rho{\rightarrow}\xi, \ldots, \sigma_n = \tau_n\rangle) := U(\langle\mu = \rho, \nu = \xi, \ldots, \sigma_n = \tau_n\rangle)$

Theorem 4. *The function* U *computes the* most general unifier *of a set of equations* E. *That is,*

- *If* $U(E) =$ *"reject", then there is no substitution* S *that unifies* E.
- *If* $U(E) = S$, *then* S *unifies* E *and for all substitutions* T *that unify* E, *there is a substitution* R *such that* $T = S; R$ *(*S *is most general).*

Definition 19. *The type* σ *is a* principal type *for the closed untyped* λ*-term* M *if*

- $M : \sigma$ *in* $\lambda{\rightarrow}$ *à la Curry*
- *for all types* τ, *if* $M : \tau$, *then* $\tau = \sigma S$ *for some substitution* S.

Theorem 5 (Principal Types). *There is an algorithm* PT *that, when given a closed (untyped)* λ*-term* M, *outputs*

- *A principal type* σ *such that* $M : \sigma$ *in* $\lambda\!\!\rightarrow$ *à la Curry.*
- *"reject" if* M *is not typable in* $\lambda\!\!\rightarrow$ *à la Curry.*

The algorithm is the one we have described before. We don't give it in formal detail, nor the proof of its correctness, but refer to [5] and [40]. This algorithm goes back to the type inference algorithm for simply typed lambda calculus of Hindley [23], which was independently developed by Milner [29] and extended to the weakly polymorphic case (see Section 5.1). Damas [12] has proved it correct and therefore this algorithm is often referred to as the Hindley-Milner or Damas-Milner algorithm.

If one wants to type an *open term* M, i.e. one that contains free variables, one is actually looking for what is known as a *principal pair*, consisting of a context Γ and a type σ such that $\Gamma \vdash M : \sigma$ and if $\Gamma' \vdash M : \tau$, then there is a substitution S such that $\tau = \sigma S$ and $\Gamma' = \Gamma S$. (A substitution extends straightforwardly to contexts.) However, there is a simpler way of attacking this problem: just apply the PT algorithm for closed terms to $\lambda x_1 \ldots \lambda x_n.M$ where $x_1, \ldots, x_n$ is the list of free variables in M.

The following describes a list of typical decidability problems one would like to have an algorithm for in a type theory.

Definition 20

$\vdash M : \sigma?$	Type Checking Problem	*TCP*
$\vdash M : ?$	Type Synthesis *or* Type Assginment Problem	*TSP, TAP*
$\vdash ? : \sigma$	Type Inhabitation Problem	*TIP*

Theorem 6. *For* $\lambda\!\!\rightarrow$*, all problems defined in Definition 20 are decidable, both for the Curry style and for the Church style versions of the system.*

For Church style, TCP and TSP are trivial, because we can just "read off" the type from the term that has the variables in the λ-abstractions decorated with types. For Curry style, TSP is solved by the PT algorithm. This also gives a way to solve TCP: to verify if $M : \sigma$, we just compute the principal type of M, say τ, and verify if σ is a substitution instance of τ (which is decidable).

In general, one may think that TCP is easier than TSP, but they are (usually) equivalent: Suppose we need to solve the TCP $M\,N : \sigma$. The only thing we can do is to solve the TSP $N :?$ and if this gives answer τ, solve the TCP $M : \tau\!\rightarrow\!\sigma$. So we see that these problems are tightly linked.

For Curry systems, TCP and TSP soon become undecidable if we go beyond $\lambda\!\!\rightarrow$. In the next section we will present the polymorphic λ-calculus, whose Curry style variant has an undecidable TCP.

TIP is decidable for $\lambda\!\!\rightarrow$, as it corresponds to *provability* in PROP, which is known to be decidable. This applies to both the Church and Curry variants, because they have the same inhabited types (as a consequence of Theorem 3). TIP is undecidable for most extensions of $\lambda\!\!\rightarrow$, because TIP corresponds to provability in some logic and provability gets easily undecidable (e.g. already in very weak systems of predicate logic).

As a final remark: if we add a context to the problems in Definition 20, the decidability issues remain the same. For TIP, the problem is totally equivalent since

$$x_1 : \sigma_1, \ldots, x_n : \sigma_n \vdash ? : \sigma \iff \vdash ? : \sigma_1 \to \ldots \to \sigma_n \to \sigma$$

For the Church system, TSP is also totally equivalent:

$$x_1 : \sigma_1, \ldots, x_n : \sigma_n \vdash M :? \iff \vdash \lambda x_1{:}\sigma_1 . \ldots \lambda x_n{:}\sigma_n . M :?$$

and similarly for TCP.

For the Curry system, the situation is slightly different, because in the TSP $\Gamma \vdash M :?$ the free variables are "forced" to be of specific types, which they are not in $\vdash \lambda \boldsymbol{x}.M :?$. Nevertheless, also if we add a context, TSP and TCP remain decidable and the principal type technique that we have described still works.

4.4 Properties of $\lambda\!\to$; Normalization

We now list the most important meta-theoretic properties of $\lambda\!\to$.

Theorem 7. – *For $\lambda\!\to$ à la Church:* Uniqueness of types
If $\Gamma \vdash M : \sigma$ and $\Gamma \vdash M : \tau$, then $\sigma = \tau$.
- Subject Reduction
If $\Gamma \vdash M : \sigma$ and $M \longrightarrow_\beta N$, then $\Gamma \vdash N : \sigma$.
- Strong Normalization
If $\Gamma \vdash M : \sigma$, then all β-reductions from M terminate.

These are proved using the following more basic properties of $\lambda\!\to$.

Proposition 1. – Substitution property
If $\Gamma, x : \tau, \Delta \vdash M : \sigma$, $\Gamma \vdash P : \tau$, then $\Gamma, \Delta \vdash M[x := P] : \sigma$.
- Thinning
If $\Gamma \vdash M : \sigma$ and $\Gamma \subseteq \Delta$, then $\Delta \vdash M : \sigma$.

The proof of these properties proceeds by induction on the typing derivation – where we sometimes first have to prove some auxiliary Lemmas that we haven't listed here – except for the proof of Strong Normalization, which was first proved by Tait [38]. As Strong Normalization is such an interesting property and it has an interesting proof, we devote the rest of this section to it. We first study the problem of *Weak Normalization*, stating that every term has (a reduction path to) a normal form.

Definition 21. – *A λ-term M is* weakly normalizing *or WN if there is a reduction sequence starting from M that terminates.*
- *A λ-term M is* strongly normalizing *or SN if all reduction sequences starting from M terminate.*

A type system is WN if all well-typed terms are WN, and it is SN if all well-typed terms are SN.

What is the problem with normalization?

- Terms may get larger under reduction
  $(\lambda f.\lambda x.f(fx))P \longrightarrow_\beta \lambda x.P(Px)$, which blows up if P is large.
- Redexes may get multiplied under reduction.
  $(\lambda f.\lambda x.f(fx))((\lambda y.M)Q) \longrightarrow_\beta \lambda x.((\lambda y.M)Q)(((\lambda y.M)Q)x)$
- New redexes may be created under reduction.
  $(\lambda f.\lambda x.f(fx))(\lambda y.N) \longrightarrow_\beta \lambda x.(\lambda y.N)((\lambda y.N)x)$

To prove WN, we would like to have a reduction strategy that does not create new redexes, or that makes the term shorter in every step. However, this idea is too naive and impossible to achieve. We can define a more intricate notion of "size" of a term and a special reduction strategy that decreases the size of a term at every step, but to do that we have to analyze more carefully what can happen during a reduction. We give the following Lemma about "redex creation", the proof of which is just a syntactic case analysis.

Lemma 3. *There are four ways in which "new" β-redexes can be created in a β-reduction step.*

- Creation
$$(\lambda x.\ldots(x\,P)\ldots)(\lambda y.Q) \longrightarrow_\beta \ldots(\lambda y.Q)P\ldots$$
  Here we really create a new redex, by substituting a λ-abstraction for a variable that is in function position.
- Multiplication
$$(\lambda x.\ldots x\ldots x\ldots)((\lambda y.Q)R) \longrightarrow_\beta \ldots(\lambda y.Q)R\ldots(\lambda y.Q)R\ldots$$
  Here we copy (possibly many times) an existing redex, thereby creating new ones.
- Hidden redex
$$(\lambda x.\lambda y.Q)R\,P \longrightarrow_\beta (\lambda y.Q[x := R])P$$
  Here the redex $(\lambda y.Q)P$ was already present in a hidden form, being "shaded" by the λx; it is revealed by contracting the outer redex.
- Identity
$$(\lambda x.x)(\lambda y.Q)R \longrightarrow_\beta (\lambda y.Q)R$$
  This is a different very special case of a "hidden redex": by contracting the identity, the redex $(\lambda y.Q)R$ is revealed.

We now define an appropriate size and an appropriate reduction strategy that proves weak normalization. The proof is originally due to Turing and was first written up by Gandy [17].

Definition 22. *The* height *(or order) of a type $h(\sigma)$ is defined by*

- $h(\alpha) := 0$
- $h(\sigma_1 \to \ldots \to \sigma_n \to \alpha) := max(h(\sigma_1), \ldots, h(\sigma_n)) + 1.$

The idea is that the height of a type σ is at least 1 higher than of any of the domains types occurring in σ. In the definition, we use the fact that we can write types in a "standard form" $\sigma_1 \to \ldots \to \sigma_n \to \alpha$. But it is equivalent to define h directly by induction over the definition of types, as is stated in the following exercise.

Exercise 7. Prove that the definition of h above is equivalent to defining

- $h(\alpha) := 0$
- $h(\sigma \to \tau) := \max(h(\sigma) + 1, h(\tau))$.

Definition 23. *The* height *of a redex* $(\lambda x{:}\sigma.P)Q$ *is the height of the type of* $\lambda x{:}\sigma.P$.

As an example, we look at the "identity" redex creation case of lemma 3. Note that the height of the redex in $(\lambda x{:}\sigma.x)(\lambda y{:}\tau.Q)R$ is $h(\sigma)+1$ and that the height of the redex in its reduct, $(\lambda y{:}\tau.Q)R$, is $h(\sigma)$. (Note that the type of $\lambda y{:}\tau.Q)$ is just σ.) So the created redex has lesser height.

This will be the key idea to our reduction strategy: we will select a redex whose reduction only creates redexes of lesser height.

Definition 24. *We assign a* measure m *to the terms by defining*

$$m(N) := (h_r(N), \#N)$$

where

- $h_r(N) =$ *the maximum height of a redex in* N,
- $\#N =$ *the number of redexes of maximum height* $h_r(N)$ *in* N.

The measures of terms are ordered in the obvious *lexicographical* way:

$$(h_1, x) <_l (h_2, y) \text{ iff } h_1 < h_2 \text{ or } (h_1 = h_2 \text{ and } x < y).$$

Theorem 8 (Weak Normalization). *If* P *is a typable term in* $\lambda\!\to$, *then there is a terminating reduction starting from* P.

Proof. Pick a redex of maximum height $h_r(P)$ inside P that does not contain any other redex of height $hr(P)$. Note that this is always possible: If R_1 and R_2 are redexes, R_1 is contained in R_2 or the other way around. Say we have picked $(\lambda x{:}\sigma.M)N$.

Reduce this redex, to obtain $M[x := N]$. We claim that *this does not create a new redex of height* $h_r(P)$ $(\star)$. This is the important step and the proof is by analyzing the four possibilities of redex creation as they are given in Lemma 3. We leave this as an exercise.

If we write Q for the reduct of P, then, as a consequence of $(\star)$, we find that $m(Q) <_l m(P)$. As there are no infinitely decreasing $<_l$ sequences, this process must terminate and then we have arrived at a normal form.

Exercise 8. Check claim $(\star)$ in the proof of Theorem 8. (Hint: Use Lemma 3.)

Strong Normalization for $\lambda\!\to$ is proved by constructing a *model* of $\lambda\!\to$. We give the proof for $\lambda\!\to$ à la Curry. The proof is originally due to Tait [38], who proposed the interpretation of the $\to$ types as given below. Recently, combinatorial proofs have been found, that give a "measure" to a typed λ-term and then prove that this measure decreases *for all* reduction steps that are possible. See [26].

Definition 25. *The interpretation of $\lambda\!\to$-types is defined as follows.*

- $[\![\alpha]\!] := \mathsf{SN}$ *(the set of strongly normalizing λ-terms).*
- $[\![\sigma\!\to\!\tau]\!] := \{M \mid \forall N \in [\![\sigma]\!](MN \in [\![\tau]\!])\}$.

Note that the interpretation of a function type is countable: it is not (isomorphic to) the full function space, but it contains only the functions from $[\![\sigma]\!]$ to $[\![\tau]\!]$ that can be λ-*defined*, i.e. are representable by a λ-term. This set is obviously countable. We have the following closure properties for $[\![\sigma]\!]$.

Lemma 4. *1.* $[\![\sigma]\!] \subseteq \mathsf{SN}$
2. $xN_1 \dots N_k \in [\![\sigma]\!]$ *for all* x, σ *and* $N_1, \dots, N_k \in \mathsf{SN}$.
3. If $M[x := N]\boldsymbol{P} \in [\![\sigma]\!]$, $N \in \mathsf{SN}$, *then* $(\lambda x.M)N\boldsymbol{P} \in [\![\sigma]\!]$.

Proof. All three parts are by induction on the structure of σ. The first two are proved simultaneously. (NB. In the case of $\sigma = \rho\!\to\!\tau$ for the proof of (1), we need that $[\![\rho]\!]$ is non-empty, which is guaranteed by the induction hypothesis for (2).) For (1) also use the fact that, if $M\,N \in \mathsf{SN}$, then also $M \in \mathsf{SN}$.

Exercise 9. Do the details of the proof of Lemma 4.

Proposition 2

$$\left.\begin{array}{r} x_1{:}\tau_1, \dots, x_n{:}\tau_n \vdash M : \sigma \\ N_1 \in [\![\tau_1]\!], \dots, N_n \in [\![\tau_n]\!] \end{array}\right\} \Rightarrow M[x_1 := N_1, \dots, x_n := N_n] \in [\![\sigma]\!]$$

Proof. By induction on the derivation of $\Gamma \vdash M : \sigma$, using (3) of the Lemma 4.

Corollary 1 (Strong Normalization for $\lambda\!\to$). *$\lambda\!\to$ is SN*

Proof. By taking $N_i := x_i$ in Proposition 2. (Note that $x_i \in [\![\tau_i]\!]$ by Lemma 4.) Then $M \in [\![\sigma]\!] \subseteq \mathsf{SN}$.

Exercise 10. Verify the details of the Strong Normalization proof. That is, prove Proposition 2 in detail by checking the inductive cases.

In the Strong Normalization proof, we have constructed a model that has the special nature that the interpretation of the function space is countable. If one thinks about semantics in general, one of course can also take the full set-theoretic function space as interpretation of $\sigma\!\to\!\tau$. We elaborate a little bit on this point, mainly as a reference for a short discussion in the Section on polymorphic λ-calculus.

We say that $\lambda\rightarrow$ *has a simple set-theoretic model.* Given sets $[\![\alpha]\!]$ for type variables α, define

$$[\![\sigma\rightarrow\tau]\!] := [\![\tau]\!]^{[\![\sigma]\!]} \text{ (set theoretic function space } [\![\sigma]\!] \rightarrow [\![\tau]\!])$$

Now, if any of the base sets $[\![\alpha]\!]$ is infinite, then there are higher and higher infinite cardinalities among the $[\![\sigma]\!]$, because the cardinality of $[\![\sigma\rightarrow\tau]\!]$ is always strictly larger than that of $[\![\sigma]\!]$.

There are smaller models, e.g.

$$[\![\sigma\rightarrow\tau]\!] := \{f \in [\![\sigma]\!] \rightarrow [\![\tau]\!] \,|\, f \text{ is definable}\}$$

where *definability* means that it can be constructed in some formal system. This restricts the collection to a *countable* set. As an example we have seen in the SN proof the following interpretation

$$[\![\sigma\rightarrow\tau]\!] := \{f \in [\![\sigma]\!] \rightarrow [\![\tau]\!] \,|\, f \text{ is } \lambda\text{-definable}\}$$

The most important thing we want to note for now is that in $\lambda\rightarrow$ we have a lot of freedom in choosing the interpretation of the $\rightarrow$-types. In the polymorphic λ-calculus, this is no longer the case.

5 Polymorphic Type Theory

Simple type theory $\lambda\rightarrow$ is not very expressive: we can only define generalized polynomials as functions [37] and we don't have a clear notion of data types. Also, in simple type theory, we cannot 'reuse' a function. For example, $\lambda x{:}\alpha.x : \alpha\rightarrow\alpha$ and $\lambda x{:}\beta.x : \beta\rightarrow\beta$, which is twice the identity in slightly different syntactic form. Of course, in the Curry version we have $\lambda x.x : \alpha\rightarrow\alpha$ and $\lambda x.x : \beta\rightarrow\beta$, but then still we can't have *the same term* $\lambda x.x$ being of type $\alpha\rightarrow\alpha$ and of type $\beta\rightarrow\beta$ *at the same time.* To see what we mean with that, consider the following term that we can type

$$(\lambda y.y)(\lambda x.x)$$

In the Church version, this would read, e.g.

$$(\lambda y{:}\sigma\rightarrow\sigma.y)(\lambda x{:}\sigma.x)$$

which shows that we can type this term with type $\sigma\rightarrow\sigma$. To type the two identities with the same type at the same time, we would want to type the following (of which the term above is a one-step reduct):

$$(\lambda f.f\,f)(\lambda x.x).$$

But this term is not typable: f should be of type $\sigma\rightarrow\sigma$ and of type $(\sigma\rightarrow\sigma)\rightarrow\sigma\rightarrow\sigma$ at the same time, which we can't achieve in $\lambda\rightarrow$.

We want to define functions that can treat types *polymorphically.* We add types of the form $\forall\alpha.\sigma$.

Examples 11. – $\forall\alpha.\alpha\to\alpha$
If $M : \forall\alpha.\alpha\to\alpha$, then M can map any type to itself.
– $\forall\alpha.\forall\beta.\alpha\to\beta\to\alpha$
If $M : \forall\alpha.\forall\beta.\alpha\to\beta\to\alpha$, then M can take two inputs (of arbitrary types) and return a value of the first input type.

There is a weak and a strong version of polymorphism. The first is present in most functional programming languages, therefore also called *ML style polymorphism*. The second allows more types and is more immediate if one takes a logical view on types. We first treat the weak version.

5.1 Typed λ-Calculus with Weakly Polymorphic Types

Definition 26. *In* weak λ2 *(the system with* weak polymorphism*) we have the following additional types*

$$\mathsf{Typ}_w := \forall\alpha.\mathsf{Typ}_w | \mathsf{Typ}$$

where Typ *is the collection of λ→-types as defined in Definition 1.*

So, the weak polymorphic types are obtained by adding $\forall\alpha_1.\dots.\forall\alpha_n.\sigma$ for σ a λ→-type.

We can formulate polymorphic λ-calculus in Church and in Curry style. As for λ→, the two systems are different in the type information that occurs in the terms, but now the difference is larger: in polymorphic λ-calculus we also have abstractions over types.

Definition 27. *The terms of* weak λ2 *à la Church are defined by*

$$\Lambda_2^{ch} ::= Var \mid (\Lambda_2^{ch}\,\Lambda_2^{ch}) \mid (\lambda Var{:}\mathsf{Typ}.\Lambda_2^{ch}) \mid (\lambda \mathsf{TVar}.\Lambda_2^{ch}) \mid \Lambda_2^{ch}\,\mathsf{Typ}$$

The terms of the Curry version of the calculus are of course just Λ. This means that in the Curry version we will not record the abstractions over type variables. This is made precise in the following rules.

Definition 28. *The* Derivation rules *for* weak λ2 *(ML-style polymorphism) in Church style are as follows*

$$\frac{x:\sigma\in\Gamma}{\Gamma\vdash x:\sigma} \quad \frac{\Gamma,x:\sigma\vdash M:\tau}{\Gamma\vdash\lambda x{:}\sigma.M:\sigma\to\tau}\ \textit{if}\ \sigma,\tau\in\mathsf{Typ} \quad \frac{\Gamma\vdash M:\sigma\to\tau \quad \Gamma\vdash N:\sigma}{\Gamma\vdash MN:\tau}$$

$$\frac{\Gamma\vdash M:\sigma}{\Gamma\vdash\lambda\alpha.M:\forall\alpha.\sigma}\ \alpha\notin FV(\Gamma) \quad \frac{\Gamma\vdash M:\forall\alpha.\sigma}{\Gamma\vdash M\tau:\sigma[\alpha:=\tau]}\ \textit{if}\ \tau\in\mathsf{Typ}$$

Definition 29. *The* derivation rules *for* weak λ2 *(ML-style polymorphism) in Curry style are as follows.*

$$\frac{x:\sigma\in\Gamma}{\Gamma\vdash x:\sigma} \quad \frac{\Gamma,x:\sigma\vdash M:\tau}{\Gamma\vdash\lambda x.M:\sigma\to\tau}\ \textit{if}\ \sigma,\tau\in\mathsf{Typ} \quad \frac{\Gamma\vdash M:\sigma\to\tau \quad \Gamma\vdash N:\sigma}{\Gamma\vdash MN:\tau}$$

$$\frac{\Gamma \vdash M : \sigma}{\Gamma \vdash M : \forall \alpha.\sigma}\ \alpha \notin FV(\Gamma) \qquad \frac{\Gamma \vdash M : \forall \alpha.\sigma}{\Gamma \vdash M : \sigma[\alpha := \tau]}\ \textit{if } \tau \in \mathsf{Typ}$$

Examples 12. 1. In $\lambda 2$ à la Curry: $\lambda x.\lambda y.x : \forall \alpha.\forall \beta.\alpha {\to} \beta {\to} \alpha$.

2. In $\lambda 2$ à la Church we have the following, which is the same term as in the previous case, but now with type information added: $\lambda \alpha.\lambda \beta.\lambda x{:}\alpha.\lambda y{:}\beta.x : \forall \alpha.\forall \beta.\alpha {\to} \beta {\to} \alpha$.
3. In $\lambda 2$ à la Curry: $z : \forall \alpha.\alpha {\to} \alpha \vdash z\, z : \forall \alpha.\alpha {\to} \alpha$.
4. In $\lambda 2$ à la Church, we can annotate this term with type information to obtain: $z : \forall \alpha.\alpha {\to} \alpha \vdash \lambda \alpha.z\,(\alpha {\to} \alpha)\,(z\,\alpha) : \forall \alpha.\alpha {\to} \alpha$.
5. We do *not* have $\vdash \lambda z.z\, z : \ldots$

We can make flag deduction rules for this system as follows.

$$\begin{array}{r|l}
1 & \quad x : \sigma \\ \hline
2 & \quad \ldots \\
3 & \quad \ldots \\
4 & \quad M : \tau \\
5 & \lambda x{:}\sigma.M : \sigma \to \tau
\end{array}
\qquad
\begin{array}{r|l}
1 & \ldots \\
2 & \ldots \\
3 & M : \sigma \to \tau \\
4 & \ldots \\
5 & \ldots \\
6 & N : \sigma \\
7 & \ldots \\
8 & M\,N : \tau
\end{array}$$

if $\sigma, \tau \in \mathsf{Typ}$

$$\begin{array}{r|l}
1 & \quad \alpha \\ \hline
2 & \quad \ldots \\
3 & \quad \ldots \\
4 & \quad M : \sigma \\
5 & \lambda \alpha.M : \forall \alpha.\sigma
\end{array}
\qquad
\begin{array}{r|l}
1 & \ldots \\
2 & \ldots \\
3 & M : \forall \alpha.\sigma \\
4 & \ldots \\
5 & \ldots \\
6 & M\,\tau : \sigma[\alpha := \tau]
\end{array}$$

if α fresh

The "freshness" condition in the rule means that α should *not occur free above the flag.* In terms of contexts, this means precisely that the type variable that we intend to abstract over does not occur in the context Γ. The freshness condition excludes the following wrong flag deduction.

$$\text{WRONG}\quad
\begin{array}{r|l}
1 & f : \alpha {\to} \beta \\ \hline
2 & \quad \alpha \\ \hline
3 & \qquad x : \alpha \\ \hline
4 & \qquad f\,x : \beta \\
5 & \quad \lambda x.f\,x : \alpha {\to} \beta \\
6 & \lambda x.f\,x : \forall \alpha.\alpha {\to} \beta
\end{array}$$

Of course, we should not be able to derive

$$f : \alpha \to \beta \vdash \lambda x.f\,x : \forall \alpha.\alpha \to \beta$$

Examples 13. Here are the first four examples of 12, now with flag deductions. In the first row we find the derivations in the Church systems, in the second row the ones in the Curry system.

$$\begin{array}{ll}
1 & \mid \alpha \\
2 & \mid \mid \beta \\
3 & \mid \mid \mid x : \alpha \\
4 & \mid \mid \mid \mid y : \beta \\
5 & \mid \mid \mid \lambda y{:}\beta.x : \beta \to \alpha \\
6 & \mid \mid \lambda x{:}\alpha.\lambda y{:}\beta.x : \alpha \to \beta \to \alpha \\
7 & \mid \lambda \beta.\lambda x{:}\alpha.\lambda y{:}\beta.x : \forall \beta.\alpha \to \beta \to \alpha \\
8 & \lambda \alpha.\lambda \beta.\lambda x{:}\alpha.\lambda y{:}\beta.x : \forall \alpha.\forall \beta.\alpha \to \beta \to \alpha
\end{array}$$

$$\begin{array}{ll}
1 & \mid z : \forall \alpha.\alpha \to \alpha \\
2 & \mid \mid \alpha \\
3 & \mid \mid z\,\alpha : \alpha \to \alpha \\
4 & \mid \mid z\,(\alpha \to \alpha) : (\alpha \to \alpha) \to \alpha \to \alpha \\
5 & \mid \mid z\,(\alpha \to \alpha)(z\,\alpha) : \alpha \to \alpha \\
6 & \mid \lambda \alpha.z\,(\alpha \to \alpha)(z\,\alpha) : \forall \alpha.\alpha \to \alpha
\end{array}$$

$$\begin{array}{ll}
1 & \mid \alpha \\
2 & \mid \mid \beta \\
3 & \mid \mid \mid x : \alpha \\
4 & \mid \mid \mid \mid y : \beta \\
5 & \mid \mid \mid \lambda y.x : \beta \to \alpha \\
6 & \mid \mid \lambda x.\lambda y.x : \alpha \to \beta \to \alpha \\
7 & \mid \lambda x.\lambda y.x : \forall \beta.\alpha \to \beta \to \alpha \\
8 & \lambda x.\lambda y.x : \forall \alpha.\forall \beta.\alpha \to \beta \to \alpha
\end{array}$$

$$\begin{array}{ll}
1 & \mid z : \forall \alpha.\alpha \to \alpha \\
2 & \mid \mid \alpha \\
3 & \mid \mid z : \alpha \to \alpha \\
4 & \mid \mid z : (\alpha \to \alpha) \to \alpha \to \alpha \\
5 & \mid \mid z\,z : \alpha \to \alpha \\
6 & \mid z\,z : \forall \alpha.\alpha \to \alpha
\end{array}$$

In the types, $\forall$ only occurs on the outside. Therefore, in programming languages (that usually follow a Curry style typing discipline) it is usually left out and all type variables are *implicitly universally quantified over*. This means that one doesn't write the $\forall$, so the types are restricted to Typ and hence we don't have the last two rules. That any type variable can be instantiated with a type, is then made formal by changing the variable rule into

$$\frac{}{\Gamma, x{:}\forall \boldsymbol{\alpha}.\sigma \vdash x : \sigma[\boldsymbol{\alpha} := \boldsymbol{\tau}]} \text{ if } \boldsymbol{\tau} \subseteq \mathsf{Typ}$$

This should be read as that σ doesn't contain any $\forall$ anymore. So we have universal types only in the context (as types of declared variables) and only at this place we can instantiate the $\forall\alpha$ with types, which must be simple types. It can be proven that this system is equivalent to $\lambda 2$ à la Curry in the following sense. Denote by $\vdash_v$ the variant of the weak $\lambda 2$ rules à la Curry where we don't have rules for $\forall$ and the adapted rule for variables just described. Then

$$\Gamma \vdash_v M : \sigma \Rightarrow \Gamma \vdash M : \sigma$$
$$\Gamma \vdash M : \forall \boldsymbol{\alpha}.\sigma \Rightarrow \Gamma \vdash_v M : \sigma[\boldsymbol{\alpha} := \boldsymbol{\tau}]$$

This is proved by induction on the derivation, using a Substitution Lemma that holds for all type systems that we have seen so far and that we therefore state here in general.

Lemma 5 (Substitution for types). *If $\Gamma \vdash M : \sigma$, then $\Gamma[\alpha := \tau] \vdash M : \sigma[\alpha := \tau]$, for all systems à la Curry defined so far.*
For the Church systems we have types in the terms. Then the Substitution Lemma states: If $\Gamma \vdash M : \sigma$, then $\Gamma[\alpha := \tau] \vdash M[\alpha := \tau] : \sigma[\alpha := \tau]$.

For all systems, this Lemma is proved by a straightforward induction over the derivation.

With weak polymorphism, type checking is still decidable: the principal types algorithm can be extended to incorporate *type schemes*: types of the form $\forall\alpha.\sigma$. We have observed that weak polymorphism allows terms to have many (polymorphic) types, but we cannot abstract over variables of these types. This is allowed with *full polymorphism*, also called *system F style polymorphism.*

5.2 Typed λ-Calculus with Full Polymorphism

Definition 30. *The types of* λ2 *with* full (system F-style) polymorphism *are*

$$\mathsf{Typ}_2 := \mathsf{TVar} \mid (\mathsf{Typ}_2 {\rightarrow} \mathsf{Typ}_2) \mid \forall\alpha.\mathsf{Typ}_2$$

1. *The derivation rules for* λ2 *with* full (system F-style) polymorphism *in Curry style are as follows. (Note that* σ *and* τ *range over* Typ_2*.)*

$$\frac{x:\sigma \in \Gamma}{\Gamma \vdash x:\sigma} \quad \frac{\Gamma, x:\sigma \vdash M:\tau}{\Gamma \vdash \lambda x.M : \sigma{\rightarrow}\tau} \quad \frac{\Gamma \vdash M : \sigma{\rightarrow}\tau \quad \Gamma \vdash N:\sigma}{\Gamma \vdash MN:\tau}$$

$$\frac{\Gamma \vdash M:\sigma}{\Gamma \vdash M : \forall\alpha.\sigma}\ \alpha \notin FV(\Gamma) \qquad \frac{\Gamma \vdash M : \forall\alpha.\sigma}{\Gamma \vdash M : \sigma[\alpha := \tau]}$$

2. *The derivation rules for* λ2 *with* full (system F-style) polymorphism *in Church style are as follows. (Again, note that* σ *and* τ *range over* Typ_2*.)*

$$\frac{x:\sigma \in \Gamma}{\Gamma \vdash x:\sigma} \quad \frac{\Gamma, x:\sigma \vdash M:\tau}{\Gamma \vdash \lambda x{:}\sigma.M : \sigma{\rightarrow}\tau} \quad \frac{\Gamma \vdash M : \sigma{\rightarrow}\tau \quad \Gamma \vdash N:\sigma}{\Gamma \vdash MN:\tau}$$

$$\frac{\Gamma \vdash M:\sigma}{\Gamma \vdash \lambda\alpha.M : \forall\alpha.\sigma}\ \alpha \notin FV(\Gamma) \qquad \frac{\Gamma \vdash M : \forall\alpha.\sigma}{\Gamma \vdash M\tau : \sigma[\alpha := \tau]}$$

So now, $\forall$ can also occur deeper in a type. We can write flag deduction rules for the full λ2 in the obvious way, for both the Curry and the Church variant of the system. We now give some examples that are only valid with full polymorphism.

Examples 14. – $\lambda 2$ à la Curry: $\lambda x.\lambda y.x : (\forall\alpha.\alpha)\to\sigma\to\tau$.
– $\lambda 2$ à la Church: $\lambda x{:}(\forall\alpha.\alpha).\lambda y{:}\sigma.x\tau : (\forall\alpha.\alpha)\to\sigma\to\tau$.

Here are the flag deductions that prove the two typings in the Examples.

1	$x : \forall\alpha.\alpha$	(flag)
2	$\quad y : \sigma$	(flag)
3	$\quad x\,\tau : \tau$	
4	$\lambda y{:}\sigma.x\,\tau : \sigma\to\tau$	
5	$\lambda x{:}\forall\alpha.\alpha.\lambda y{:}\sigma.x\,\tau : (\forall\alpha.\alpha)\to\sigma\to\tau$	

1	$x : \forall\alpha.\alpha$	(flag)
2	$\quad y : \sigma$	(flag)
3	$\quad x : \tau$	
4	$\lambda y.x : \sigma\to\tau$	
5	$\lambda x.\lambda y.x : (\forall\alpha.\alpha)\to\sigma\to\tau$	

In $\lambda 2$ we use the following abbreviations for types: $\bot := \forall\alpha.\alpha$, $\top := \forall\alpha.\alpha\to\alpha$. The names are derived from the behavior of the types. From a term of type $\bot$, we can create a term of any type: $\lambda x{:}\bot.x\sigma : \bot\to\sigma$ for any type σ. So $\bot$ is in some sense the "smallest type". Also, $\bot$ is empty: there is no closed term of type $\bot$. On the other hand, $\top$ is the type with one canonical closed element: $\lambda\alpha.\lambda x{:}\alpha.x : \top$. We can now also type a term like $\lambda x.x\,x$.

Examples 15. – In Curry $\lambda 2$: $\lambda x.xx : \bot\to\bot$, $\lambda x.xx : \top\to\top$
– In Church $\lambda 2$: $\lambda x{:}\bot.x(\bot\to\bot)x : \bot\to\bot$, $\lambda x{:}\top.x\,\top\,x : \top\to\top$.
– In Church $\lambda 2$: $\lambda x{:}\bot.\lambda\alpha.x(\alpha\to\alpha)(x\alpha) : \bot\to\bot$, $\lambda x{:}\top.\lambda\alpha.x(\alpha\to\alpha)(x\alpha) : \top\to\top$.

We show two typings in the previous example by a flag deduction.

1	$x : \bot$	(flag)
2	$\quad \alpha$	(flag)
3	$\quad x : \alpha\to\alpha$	
4	$\quad x : \alpha$	
5	$\quad x\,x : \alpha$	
6	$x\,x : \forall\alpha.\alpha$	
7	$\lambda x{:}\bot.x\,x : \bot\to\bot$	

1	$x : \top$	(flag)
2	$x\,\top : \top\to\top$	
3	$x\,\top\,x : \top$	
4	$\lambda x{:}\top.x\,\top\,x : \top\to\top$	

Exercises 11. 1. Verify using a flag deduction that in Church $\lambda 2$: $\lambda x{:}\top.\lambda\alpha.x(\alpha\to\alpha)(x\alpha) : \top\to\top$.
2. Verify using a flag deduction that in Curry $\lambda 2$: $\lambda x.xx : \top\to\top$
3. Find a type in Curry $\lambda 2$ for $\lambda x.x\,x\,x$
4. Find a type in Curry $\lambda 2$ for $\lambda x.x\,x\,(x\,x)$

With full polymorphism, type checking becomes undecidable [41] for the Curry version of the system. For the Church version it is clearly still decidable, as we have all necessary type information in the term.

Definition 31. *We define the* erasure map *from $\lambda 2$ à la Church to $\lambda 2$ à la Curry as follows.*

$$\begin{array}{llll}|x| & := x & & \\ |\lambda x{:}\sigma.M| & := |\lambda x.M| & |\lambda\alpha.M| & := |M| \\ |MN| & := |M|\,|N| & |M\sigma| & := |M|\end{array}$$

We have the following proposition about this erasure map, that relates the Curry and Church systems to each other.

Proposition 3. *If $\Gamma \vdash M : \sigma$ in $\lambda 2$ à la Church, then $\Gamma \vdash |M| : \sigma$ in $\lambda 2$ à la Curry.*
If $\Gamma \vdash P : \sigma$ in $\lambda 2$ à la Curry, then there is an M such that $|M| \equiv P$ and $\Gamma \vdash M : \sigma$ in $\lambda 2$ à la Church.

The proof is by straightforward induction on the derivations. We don't give the details. In the Examples of 12, 14 and 15, we can see the Proposition at work: an erasure of the Church style derivation gives a Curry style derivation. The other way around: any Curry style derivation can be "dressed up" with type information to obtain a Church style derivation. The undecidability of type checking in $\lambda 2$ à la Curry can thus be rephrased as: we cannot algorithmically reconstruct the missing type information in an untyped term. In Example 15 we have seen two completely different ways to "dress up" the term $\lambda x.x\,x$ to make it typable in $\lambda 2$-Church. This is a general pattern: there are many possible ways to add typing information to an non-typable term to make it typable in $\lambda 2$-Church.

We have opposed "weak polymorphism" to "full polymorphism" and we referred to the first also as ML-style polymorphism. It is the case that polymorphism in most functional programming languages is weaker than full polymorphism, and if we restrict ourselves to the pure λ-calculus, it is just the weak polymorphic system that we have described. However, to regain some of the "full polymorphism", ML has additional constructs, like *let polymorphism.*

$$\frac{\Gamma \vdash M : \sigma \quad \Gamma, x : \sigma \vdash N : \tau}{\Gamma \vdash \mathsf{let}\, x = M \,\mathsf{in}\, N : \tau} \text{ for } \tau \text{ a } \lambda{\rightarrow}\text{-type}, \sigma \text{ a } \lambda 2\text{-type}$$

We can see a term $\mathsf{let}\, x = M \,\mathsf{in}\, N$ as a β-redex $(\lambda x{:}\sigma.N)M$. So the let-rule allows the formation of a β-redex $(\lambda x{:}\sigma.N)M$, for σ a polymorphic type, while we cannot form the abstraction term $\lambda x{:}\sigma.N : \sigma{\rightarrow}\tau$. So it is still impossible to have a universal quantifier deeper inside a type, though we can have a polymorphic term as a subterm of a well-typed term. For the extension of the principal type algorithm to include weak polymorphism with lets we refer to [30].

Exercise 12. 1. Type the term $(\lambda f.f\,f)(\lambda x.x)$ in (full) $\lambda 2$-Curry.
2. Type the term $\mathsf{let}\, f = \lambda x.x \,\mathsf{in}\, f\,f$ in weak $\lambda 2$-Curry with the let-rule as given above.

5.3 Meta-theoretic Properties

We now recall the decidability issues of Definition 20 and look into them for $\lambda 2$.

Theorem 9. *Decidability properties of the (weak and full) polymorphic λ-calculus*

- *TIP is decidable for the weak polymorphic λ-calculus, undecidable for the full polymorphic λ-calculus.*

– *TCP and TSP are equivalent.*

TCP	*à la Church*	*à la Curry*
ML-style	*decidable*	*decidable*
System F-style	*decidable*	*undecidable*

With full polymorphism (system F), untyped terms contain too little information to compute the type [41]. TIP is equivalent to provability in logic. For full $\lambda 2$, this is *second order intuitionistic proposition logic* (to be discussed in the next Section), which is known to be undecidable. For weak $\lambda 2$, the logic is just a very weak extension of PROP which is decidable.

5.4 Formulas-as-Types for Full λ2

There is a formulas-as-types isomorphism between full system-F style $\lambda 2$ and second order proposition logic, PROP2.

Definition 32. *Derivation rules of* PROP2*:*

$$\frac{\begin{array}{c}\tau_1 \ldots \tau_n \\ \vdots \\ \sigma\end{array}}{\forall\alpha.\sigma}\ \forall\text{-}I,\ \text{if } \alpha \notin FV(\tau_1, \ldots, \tau_n) \qquad \frac{\forall\alpha.\sigma}{\sigma[\alpha := \tau]}$$

NB This is constructive second order proposition logic: *Peirce's law*

$$\forall\alpha.\forall\beta.((\alpha{\to}\beta){\to}\alpha){\to}\alpha$$

is not derivable (so there is no closed term of this type). The logic only has implication and universal quantification, but the other connectives are now definable.

Definition 33. *Definability of the other intuitionistic connectives.*

$$\begin{aligned}\bot &:= \forall\alpha.\alpha \\ \sigma\wedge\tau &:= \forall\alpha.(\sigma{\to}\tau{\to}\alpha){\to}\alpha \\ \sigma\vee\tau &:= \forall\alpha.(\sigma{\to}\alpha){\to}(\tau{\to}\alpha){\to}\alpha \\ \exists\alpha.\sigma &:= \forall\beta.(\forall\alpha.\sigma{\to}\beta){\to}\beta\end{aligned}$$

Proposition 4. *All the standard constructive deduction rules (elimination and introduction rules) are derivable using the definitions in 33.*

Example 16. We show the derivability of the $\wedge$-elimination rule by showing how to derive σ from $\sigma \wedge \tau$:

$$\frac{\dfrac{\forall\alpha.(\sigma{\to}\tau{\to}\alpha){\to}\alpha}{(\sigma{\to}\tau{\to}\sigma){\to}\sigma} \qquad \dfrac{\dfrac{[\sigma]^1}{\tau{\to}\sigma}}{\sigma{\to}\tau{\to}\sigma}\,1}{\sigma}$$

There is a formulas-as-types embedding of PROP2 into $\lambda 2$ that maps deductions to terms. It can be defined inductively, as we have done for PROP and $\lambda\!\rightarrow$ in Definition 10. We don't give the definitions, but illustrate it by an example.

Example 17. The definable $\wedge$-elimination rule in PROP2 under the deductions-as-terms embedding yields a λ-terms that "witnesses" the construction of an object of type σ out of an object of type $\sigma \wedge \tau$.

$$\dfrac{\dfrac{M : \forall\alpha.(\sigma{\to}\tau{\to}\alpha){\to}\alpha}{M\sigma : (\sigma{\to}\tau{\to}\sigma){\to}\sigma} \qquad \dfrac{\dfrac{[x:\sigma]^1}{\lambda y{:}\tau.x : \tau{\to}\sigma}}{\lambda x{:}\sigma.\lambda y{:}\tau.x : \sigma{\to}\tau{\to}\sigma}\,1}{M\sigma(\lambda x{:}\sigma.\lambda y{:}\tau.x) : \sigma}$$

So the following term is a "witness" for the $\wedge$-elimination.

$$\lambda z{:}\sigma{\wedge}\tau.z\,\sigma\,(\lambda x{:}\sigma.\lambda y{:}\tau.x) : (\sigma \wedge \tau){\to}\sigma$$

Exercise 13. Prove the derivability of some of the other logical rules:

1. Define $\mathsf{inl} : \sigma \to \sigma \vee \tau$
2. Define pairing : $\langle -, - \rangle : \sigma \to \tau \to \sigma \times \tau$
3. Given $f : \sigma{\to}\rho$ and $g : \tau{\to}\rho$, construct a term $\mathsf{case}\ f\,g : \sigma \vee \tau{\to}\rho$

5.5 Data Types in λ2

In $\lambda\!\rightarrow$ we can define a type of "natural numbers over a type σ": $(\sigma{\to}\sigma){\to}\sigma{\to}\sigma$. In $\lambda 2$, we can define this type polymorphically.

$$\mathsf{Nat} := \forall\alpha.(\alpha{\to}\alpha){\to}\alpha{\to}\alpha$$

This type uses the encoding of natural numbers as Church numerals

$$n \mapsto c_n := \lambda f.\lambda x.f(\ldots(f x)) \;\; n\text{-times } f$$

- $0 := \lambda\alpha.\lambda f{:}\alpha{\to}\alpha.\lambda x{:}\alpha.x$
- $S := \lambda n{:}\mathsf{Nat}.\lambda\alpha.\lambda f{:}\alpha{\to}\alpha.\lambda x{:}\alpha.f(n\,\alpha\,x\,f)$

Proposition 5. *Over the type* Nat*, functions can be defined by* iteration*: if $c : \sigma$ and $g : \sigma{\to}\sigma$, then there is a function*

$$\mathsf{It}\,c\,g : \mathsf{Nat}{\to}\sigma$$

satisfying

$$\mathsf{It}\,c\,g\,0 = c$$
$$\mathsf{It}\,c\,g\,(S\,x) = g(\mathsf{It}\,c\,g\,x)$$

Proof. $\mathsf{It}\,c\,g : \mathsf{Nat}{\to}\sigma$ is defined as $\lambda n{:}\mathsf{Nat}.n\,\sigma\,g\,c$. It is left as a (quite ease) exercise to see that this satisfies the equations.

The function It acts as an iterator: it takes a "begin value" c and a map g and n times iterates g on c, where n is the natural number input. So $\mathsf{It}\,c\,g\,n = g(\ldots(g\,c))$, with n times g.

Examples 18. 1. Addition

$$\mathsf{Plus} := \lambda n{:}\mathsf{Nat}.\lambda m{:}\mathsf{Nat}.\mathsf{It}\,m\,S\,n$$

or if we unfold the definition of It: $\mathsf{Plus} := \lambda n{:}\mathsf{Nat}.\lambda m{:}\mathsf{Nat}.n\,\mathsf{Nat}\,S\,m$, which says: iterate the $+1$ function n times on begin value m.

2. Multiplication

$$\mathsf{Mult} := \lambda n{:}\mathsf{Nat}.\lambda m{:}\mathsf{Nat}.\mathsf{It}\,0\,(\lambda x{:}\mathsf{Nat}.\mathsf{Plus}\,m\,x)\,n$$

The predecessor is notably difficult to define! The easiest way to define it is by first defining *primitive recursion* on the natural numbers. This means that if we have $c : \sigma$ and $f : \mathsf{Nat}{\to}\sigma{\to}\sigma$, we want to define a term $\mathsf{Rec}\,c\,f : \mathsf{Nat}{\to}\sigma$ satisfying

$$\begin{aligned} \mathsf{Rec}\,c\,f\,0 &= c \\ \mathsf{Rec}\,c\,f\,(S\,x) &= f\,x\,(\mathsf{Rec}\,c\,f\,x) \end{aligned}$$

(Note that if we can define functions by primitive recursion, the predecessor is just $P := \mathsf{Rec}\,0\,(\lambda x\,y : \mathsf{Nat}.x)$.)

It is known that primitive recursion can be encoded in terms of iteration, so therefore we can define the predecessor in $\lambda 2$. However, the complexity (in terms of the number of reduction steps) of this encoding is very bad. As a consequence:

$$\mathsf{Pred}(n+1) \twoheadrightarrow_\beta n$$

in a number of steps of $O(n)$.

Exercise 14. 1. Complete the details in the proof of Proposition 5

2. Verify in detail that addition and multiplication as defined in Example 18 behave as expected.
3. Define the data type $\mathsf{Three} := \forall\alpha{:}*.\alpha{\to}\alpha{\to}\alpha{\to}\alpha$.
   (a) Give three different closed inhabitants of the type Three in $\lambda 2$ à la Church: $\mathsf{one}, \mathsf{two}, \mathsf{three} : \mathsf{Three}$.
   (b) Define a function $\mathsf{Shift} : \mathsf{Three} \to \mathsf{Three}$ that does the following

$$\begin{aligned} \mathsf{Shift}\,\mathsf{one} &=_\beta \mathsf{two} \\ \mathsf{Shift}\,\mathsf{two} &=_\beta \mathsf{three} \\ \mathsf{Shift}\,\mathsf{three} &=_\beta \mathsf{one} \end{aligned}$$

Apart from the natural numbers, many other algebraic data types are definable in $\lambda 2$. Here is the example of lists over a base type A.

$$\mathsf{List}_A := \forall \alpha.\alpha \to (A \to \alpha \to \alpha) \to \alpha$$

The representation of lists over A as terms of this type uses the following encoding

$$[a_1, a_2, \ldots, a_n] \mapsto \lambda x.\lambda f.f a_1(f a_2(\ldots(f a_n x))) \quad n\text{-times } f$$

We can now define the constructors Nil (empty list) and Cons (to "cons" an element to a list) as follows.

- $\mathsf{Nil} := \lambda\alpha.\lambda x{:}\alpha.\lambda f{:}A \to \alpha \to \alpha.x$
- $\mathsf{Cons} := \lambda a{:}A.\lambda l{:}\mathsf{List}_A.\lambda\alpha.\lambda x{:}\alpha.\lambda f{:}A \to \alpha \to \alpha.f\, a(l\, \alpha\, x\, f)$

Note that the definition of Cons conforms with the representation of lists given above.

Proposition 6. *Over the type* List_A *we can define functions by* iteration*: if* $c : \sigma$ *and* $g : A \to \sigma \to \sigma$*, then there is a function*

$$\mathsf{It}\, c\, g : \mathsf{List}_A \to \sigma$$

satisfying

$$\begin{aligned} \mathsf{It}\, c\, g\, \mathsf{Nil} &= c \\ \mathsf{It}\, c\, g\, (\mathsf{Cons}\, a\, l) &= g\, a\, (\mathsf{It}\, c\, g\, l) \end{aligned}$$

Proof. $\mathsf{It}\, c\, g : \mathsf{List}_A \to \sigma$ is defined as $\lambda l{:}\mathsf{List}_A.l\, \sigma\, c\, g$. This satisfies the equations in the proposition. Basically, we have, for $l = [a_1, \ldots, a_n]$, $\mathsf{It}\, c\, g\, l = g\, a_1(\ldots(g\, a_n\, c))$ (n times g).

Example 19. A standard function one wants to define over lists is the "map" function, which given a function on the carrier type, extends it to a function on the lists over this carrier type. Given $f : \sigma \to \tau$, $\mathsf{Map}\, f : \mathsf{List}_\sigma \to \mathsf{List}_\tau$ should apply f to all elements in a list. It is defined by

$$\mathsf{Map} := \lambda f{:}\sigma \to \tau.\mathsf{It}\, \mathsf{Nil}(\lambda x{:}\sigma.\lambda l{:}\mathsf{List}_\tau.\mathsf{Cons}(f\, x)l).$$

Then

$$\begin{aligned} \mathsf{Map}\, f\, \mathsf{Nil} &= \mathsf{Nil} \\ \mathsf{Map}\, f\, (\mathsf{Cons}\, a\, k) &= \mathsf{It}\, \mathsf{Nil}(\lambda x{:}\sigma.\lambda l{:}\mathsf{List}_\tau.\mathsf{Cons}(f\, x)l)\, (\mathsf{Cons}\, a\, k) \\ &= (\lambda x{:}\sigma.\lambda l{:}\mathsf{List}_\tau.\mathsf{Cons}(f\, x)l)a(\mathsf{Map}\, f\, k) \\ &= \mathsf{Cons}(f\, a)(\mathsf{Map}\, f\, k) \end{aligned}$$

This is exactly the recursion equation for Map that we would expect.

Many more data-types can be defined in $\lambda 2$. The product of two data-types is defined in the same way as the (logical) conjunction: $\sigma \times \tau := \forall \alpha.(\sigma \to \tau \to \alpha) \to \alpha$. we have already seen how to define projections and pairing (the $\wedge$-elimination and $\wedge$-introduction rules). The disjoint union (or sum) of two data-types is defined in the same way as the logical disjunction: $\sigma + \tau := \forall \alpha.(\sigma \to \alpha) \to (\tau \to \alpha) \to \alpha$. We can define inl, inr and case. The type of binary trees with nodes in A and leaves in B can be defined as follows.

$$\mathsf{Tree}_{A,B} := \forall \alpha.(B \to \alpha) \to (A \to \alpha \to \alpha \to \alpha) \to \alpha$$

and we define $\mathsf{leaf} : B \to \mathsf{Tree}_{A,B}$ by $\mathsf{leaf} := \lambda b{:}B.\lambda \alpha.\lambda l{:}B \to \alpha.\lambda j{:}A \to \alpha \to \alpha \to \alpha.l\, b$.

Exercises 15. – Define a function of type $\mathsf{List}_A \to \mathsf{Nat}$ that computes the length of a list.
- Define $\mathsf{join} : \mathsf{Tree}_{A,B} \to \mathsf{Tree}_{A,B} \to A \to \mathsf{Tree}_{A,B}$ that takes two trees and a node label and builds a tree.
- Define a function $\mathsf{TreeSum} : \mathsf{Tree}_{\mathsf{Nat},\mathsf{Nat}} \to \mathsf{Nat}$ that computes the sum of all leaves and nodes in a binary tree.
- Give the *iteration scheme* over binary trees and show that it is definable in $\lambda 2$.

5.6 Meta-theory of λ2; Strong Normalization

Theorem 10. – *For $\lambda 2$ à la Church: Uniqueness of types*
If $\Gamma \vdash M : \sigma$ and $\Gamma \vdash M : \tau$, then $\sigma = \tau$.
- *Subject Reduction*
If $\Gamma \vdash M : \sigma$ and $M \longrightarrow_{\beta\eta} N$, then $\Gamma \vdash N : \sigma$.
- *Strong Normalization*
If $\Gamma \vdash M : \sigma$, then all β-reductions from M terminate.

The third property is remarkably complicated and we address it in detail below. The first two are proved by induction on the derivation, using some other meta-theoretic properties, that one also proves by induction over the derivation (the Substitution Property we have already seen for types; this is the same property for terms):

Proposition 7. – Substitution property
If $\Gamma, x : \tau, \Delta \vdash M : \sigma$, $\Gamma \vdash P : \tau$, then $\Gamma, \Delta \vdash M[x := P] : \sigma$.
- Thinning
If $\Gamma \vdash M : \sigma$ and $\Gamma \subseteq \Delta$, then $\Delta \vdash M : \sigma$.

We now elaborate on the proof of Strong Normalization of β-reduction for $\lambda 2$. The proof is an extension of the Tait proof of SN for $\lambda\!\to$, but it needs some crucial extra ingredients that have been developed by Girard [21]. We motivate these additional notions below.

In $\lambda 2$ à la Church there are two kinds of β-reductions:

- Kind 1, term-applied-to-term: $(\lambda x{:}\sigma.M)P \longrightarrow_\beta M[x := P]$
- Kind 2, term-applied-to-type: $(\lambda \alpha.M)\tau \longrightarrow_\beta M[\alpha := \tau]$

The second kind of reductions does no harm: (i) there are no infinite β-reduction paths with solely reductions of kind 2; (ii) if $M \longrightarrow_\beta N$ with a reduction of kind 2, then $|M| \equiv |N|$. So, if there is an infinite β-reduction in λ2-Church, then there is one in λ2-Curry and we are done if we prove SN for λ2 à la Curry.

Recall the model construction in the proof for λ→:

- $[\![\alpha]\!] := \mathsf{SN}$.
- $[\![\sigma \to \tau]\!] := \{M \mid \forall N \in [\![\sigma]\!](MN \in [\![\tau]\!])\}$.

So, now the question is: How to define $[\![\forall\alpha.\sigma]\!]$? A natural guess would be to define $[\![\forall\alpha.\sigma]\!] := \Pi_{X \in U}[\![\sigma]\!]_{\alpha:=X}$, where U is some set capturing all possible interpretations of types. This Π-set is a set of functions that take an element X of U (an interpretation of a type) and yield an element of the interpretation of σ where we assign X to α.

But now the problem is that $\Pi_{X \in U}[\![\sigma]\!]_{\alpha:=X}$ gets too big: if there is any type with more than one element (something we would require for a model), then $\mathrm{card}(\Pi_{X \in U}[\![\sigma]\!]_{\alpha:=X}) > \mathrm{card}(U)$. The cardinality of the interpretation of $\forall\alpha.\sigma$ would be larger than the set it is a member of and that's impossible. So we cannot interpret the $\forall$ as a Π-set (or a union for the same reason).

Girard has given the solution to this problem: $[\![\forall\alpha.\sigma]\!]$ should be very small:

$$[\![\forall\alpha.\sigma]\!] := \bigcap_{X \in U} [\![\sigma]\!]_{\alpha:=X}$$

This conforms with the idea that $\forall\alpha.\sigma$ is the type of terms that act *parametrically* on a type. A lot of literature has been devoted to the nature of polymorphism, for which the terminology *parametricity* has been introduced, intuitively saying that a function operates on types *without looking into them.* So a parametric function cannot act differently on Nat and Bool. This implies, e.g. that there is only one parametric function from α to α: the identity. See [1] for more on parametricity.

The second important novelty of Girard is the actual definition of U, the collection of all *possible interpretations* of types. U will be defined as SAT, the collection of *saturated sets* of (untyped) λ-terms.

Definition 34. $X \subset \Lambda$ *is* saturated *if*

- $xP_1 \dots P_n \in X$ *(for all* $x \in \mathsf{Var}$, $P_1, \dots, P_n \in \mathsf{SN}$*)*
- $X \subseteq \mathsf{SN}$
- *If* $M[x := N]\boldsymbol{P} \in X$ *and* $N \in \mathsf{SN}$, *then* $(\lambda x.M)N\boldsymbol{P} \in X$.

The definition of saturated sets basically arises by taking the closure properties that we *proved* for the interpretation of λ→-types as a *definition* of the collection of possible interpretation of λ2-types.

Definition 35. *Let* $\rho : \mathsf{TVar} \to SAT$ *be a* valuation *of type variables. Define* $[\![\sigma]\!]_\rho$ *by:*

- $[\![\alpha]\!]_\rho := \rho(\alpha)$

- $[\![\sigma\to\tau]\!]_\rho := \{M | \forall N \in [\![\sigma]\!]_\rho (MN \in [\![\tau]\!]_\rho)\}$
- $[\![\forall\alpha.\sigma]\!]_\rho := \cap_{X \in SAT}[\![\sigma]\!]_{\rho,\alpha:=X}$

Proposition 8

$$x_1 : \tau_1, \ldots, x_n : \tau_n \vdash M : \sigma \Rightarrow M[x_1 := P_1, \ldots, x_n : P_n] \in [\![\sigma]\!]_\rho$$

for all valuations ρ *and* $P_1 \in [\![\tau_1]\!]_\rho, \ldots, P_n \in [\![\tau_n]\!]_\rho$

The proof is by induction on the derivation of $\Gamma \vdash M : \sigma$.

Corollary 2. $\lambda 2$ *is SN*

Proof. Take P_1 to be x_1, ..., P_n to be x_n.

Exercise 16. Verify the details of the proof of the Proposition.

We end this section with some remarks on semantics. In the section on $\lambda\!\!\to$ we have seen that the SN proof consists of the construction of a model, where the interpretation of the function type is "small" (not the full function space). But for $\lambda\!\!\to$, there are also models where the function type is the full set-theoretic function space. These are often referred to as *set-theoretical models* of type theory.

Theorem 11 (Reynolds[36]). $\lambda 2$ *does not have a non-trivial set-theoretic model.*

This is a remarkable theorem, also because there are no requirements for the interpretation of the other constructs, only that the model is sound. The proof proceeds by showing that if $[\![\sigma\to\tau]\!] := [\![\tau]\!]^{[\![\sigma]\!]}$ (the set theoretic function space), then $[\![\sigma]\!]$ is a singleton set for every σ. We call such a model *trivial*, as all types are interpreted as the empty set or the singleton set. This is a sound interpretation, corresponding with the interpretation of the formulas of PROP2 in a classical way (suing a truth table semantics). It is also called the *proof irrelevance semantics* as all proofs of propositions are identified. As said, it is a sound model, but not a very interesting one, certainly from a programmers point of view, because all natural numbers are identified.

So we can rephrase Reynolds result as: in an interesting $\lambda 2$-model, $[\![\sigma\to\tau]\!]$ must be small.

6 Dependent Type Theory

In the paper by Bove and Dybjer, we can see "Dependent Types at Work" and that paper also gives some of the history and intuitions behind it. In this Section I will present the rules. The problem with dependent types is that "everything depends on everything", so we can't first define the types and then the terms. We will have two "universes": **type** and **kind**. Dybjer and Bove used "Set" for what I call **type**: the universe of types. (We can't have **type** : **type**, so to type **type** we need to have another universe: **type** : **kind**.)

We define first order dependent type theory, $\lambda\mathsf{P}$. This system is also known as LF (Logical Framework, [22]) The judgements of the system are of the form

$$\Gamma \vdash M : B$$

where

- Γ is a context
- M and B are terms taken from the set of *pseudo-terms.*

Definition 36. *The set of pseudo-terms is defined by*

$$\mathsf{T} ::= \mathsf{Var} \mid \mathbf{type} \mid \mathbf{kind} \mid (\mathsf{T}\mathsf{T}) \mid (\lambda x{:}\mathsf{T}.\mathsf{T}) \mid \Pi x{:}\mathsf{T}.\mathsf{T},$$

Furthermore, there is an *auxiliary* judgement

$$\Gamma \vdash$$

to denote that Γ is a *correct context.*

Definition 37. *The* derivation rules *of* $\lambda\mathsf{P}$ *are (*$\mathbf{s}$ *ranges over* $\{\mathbf{type}, \mathbf{kind}\}$*):*

$$(\mathit{base})\ \emptyset \vdash \quad (\mathit{ctxt})\ \frac{\Gamma \vdash A : \mathbf{s}}{\Gamma, x{:}A \vdash}\ \mathit{if}\ x\ \mathit{not\ in}\ \Gamma \quad (\mathit{ax})\ \frac{\Gamma \vdash}{\Gamma \vdash \mathbf{type} : \mathbf{kind}}$$

$$(\mathit{proj})\ \frac{\Gamma \vdash}{\Gamma \vdash x : A}\ \mathit{if}\ x{:}A \in \Gamma \quad (\Pi)\ \frac{\Gamma, x{:}A \vdash B : \mathbf{s} \quad \Gamma \vdash A : \mathbf{type}}{\Gamma \vdash \Pi x{:}A.B : \mathbf{s}}$$

$$(\lambda)\ \frac{\Gamma, x{:}A \vdash M : B \quad \Gamma \vdash \Pi x{:}A.B : \mathbf{s}}{\Gamma \vdash \lambda x{:}A.M : \Pi x{:}A.B} \quad (\mathit{app})\ \frac{\Gamma \vdash M : \Pi x{:}A.B \quad \Gamma \vdash N : A}{\Gamma \vdash MN : B[x := N]}$$

$$(\mathit{conv})\ \frac{\Gamma \vdash M : B \quad \Gamma \vdash A : \mathbf{s}}{\Gamma \vdash M : A}\ A =_{\beta\eta} B$$

In this type theory, we have a new phenomenon, which is the *Π-type*:

$$\Pi x{:}A.B(x) \simeq \text{the type of functions } f \text{ such that } f\,a : B(a) \text{ for all } a{:}A$$

The Π-type is a generalization of the well-known function type: if $x \notin \mathrm{FV}(B)$, then $\Pi x{:}A.B$ is just $A{\to}B$. So, we will use the arrow notation $A{\to}B$ as an abbreviation for $\Pi x{:}A.B$ in case $x \notin \mathrm{FV}(B)$. The Π rule allows to form two forms of function types in $\lambda\mathsf{P}$

$$(\Pi)\ \frac{\Gamma \vdash A : \mathbf{type} \quad \Gamma, x{:}A \vdash B : \mathbf{s}}{\Gamma \vdash \Pi x{:}A.B : \mathbf{s}}$$

- With $\mathbf{s} = \mathbf{kind}$, we can form $A{\to}A{\to}\mathbf{type}$ and $A{\to}\mathbf{type}$.
- With $\mathbf{s} = \mathbf{type}$ and $P : A{\to}\mathbf{type}$, we can form $A{\to}A$ and $\Pi x{:}A.P\,x{\to}P\,x$.

6.1 Formulas-as-Types: Minimal Predicate Logic into λP

Following the methods for $\lambda{\rightarrow}$ and $\lambda 2$, we can embed logic into first order dependent type theory following the Curry-Howard formulas-as-types embedding. For λP, we can embed *minimal first order predicate logic*, the predicate logic with just implication and universal quantification and the intuitionistic rules for these connectives. The idea is to represent *both the domains and the formulas* of the logic as types. In predicate logic we need to interpret a *signature* for the logic, that tells us which constants, functions and relations there are (and, in case of many-sortedness, which are the domains). This is not difficult but it involves some overhead when giving a precise formal definition. So, we don't give a completely formal definition but just an example.

Example 20. Minimal first order predicate logic over one domain with one constant, one unary function and two unary and one binary relation is embedded into λP by considering the context

$$\Gamma := A : \mathbf{type}, a : A, f : A{\rightarrow}A, P : A{\rightarrow}\mathbf{type}, Q : A{\rightarrow}\mathbf{type}, R : A{\rightarrow}A{\rightarrow}\mathbf{type}.$$

Implication is represented as $\rightarrow$ and $\forall$ is represented as Π:

$$\forall x{:}A.P\,x \mapsto \Pi x{:}A.P\,x$$
$$\forall x{:}A.R\,x\,x{\rightarrow}P\,x \mapsto \Pi x{:}A.R\,x\,x{\rightarrow}P\,x$$

the intro and elim rules are just λ-abstraction and application, both for implication and universal quantification.

The terms of type A act as the first order terms of the language: a, $f\,a$, $f(f\,a)$ etc. The formulas are encoded as terms of type **type**: $P\,a$, $R\,a\,a$ are the closed atomic formulas and with $\rightarrow$, Π and variables we build the first order formulas from that.

In λP, we can give a precise derivation that the context Γ is correct: $\Gamma \vdash$. These derivations are quite lengthy, because in a derivation tree the same judgment is derived several times in different branches of the tree. Therefore such derivations are best given in *flag style*. It should be clear by now how we turn a set of derivations rules into a flag format. We will usually omit derivations of the correctness of a context, but for completeness we here give one example, in flag format. We give a precise derivation of the judgment

$$A : \mathbf{type}, P : A{\rightarrow}\mathbf{type}, a : A \vdash P\,a{\rightarrow}\mathbf{type} : \mathbf{kind}$$

NB. we use the $\rightarrow$-formation rule as a degenerate case of the Π-formation rule (if $x \notin \mathrm{FV}(B)$).

$$\frac{\Gamma \vdash A : \mathbf{type} \quad \Gamma \vdash B : \mathbf{s}}{\Gamma \vdash A \rightarrow B : \mathbf{s}} \ \rightarrow\text{-form}$$

1	$\mathbf{type} : \mathbf{kind}$	
2	$A : \mathbf{type}$	ctxt-proj, 1
3	$A \to \mathbf{type} : \mathbf{kind}$	$\to$-form, 2, 1
4	$P : A \to \mathbf{type}$	ctxt-proj, 3
5	$a : A$	ctxt-proj, 2
6	$P\,a : \mathbf{type}$	app, 4, 5
7	$P\,a \to \mathbf{type} : \mathbf{kind}$	$\to$-form, 6, 1

Example 21. We illustrate the use of application and abstraction to encode elimination and introduction rules of the logic. take Γ to be the context of Example 20.

$$\Gamma \vdash \lambda z{:}A.\lambda h{:}(\Pi x, y{:}A.R\,x\,y).h\,z\,z : \Pi z{:}A.(\Pi x, y{:}A.R\,x\,y) \to R\,z\,z$$

This term is a proof of $\forall z{:}A.(\forall x, y{:}A.R(x, y)) \to R(z, z)$. The first λ encodes a $\forall$-introduction, the second λ an implication-introduction.

Example 22. We now show how to construct a term of type $(\Pi x{:}A.P\,x \to Q\,x) \to (\Pi x{:}A.P\,x) \to \Pi x{:}A.Q\,x$ in the context Γ. We do this by giving a derivation in "flag style", where we omit derivations of the well-formedness of types and contexts. We write σ for $(\Pi x{:}A.P\,x \to Q\,x) \to (\Pi x{:}A.P\,x) \to \Pi x{:}A.Q\,x$.

1	$A : \mathbf{type}$	
2	$P : A \to \mathbf{type}$	
3	$Q : A \to \mathbf{type}$	
4	$h : \Pi x{:}A.P\,x \to Q\,x$	
5	$g : \Pi x{:}A.P\,x$	
6	$x : A$	
7	$h\,x : P\,x \to Q\,x$	app, 4, 6
8	$g\,x : P\,x$	app, 5, 6
9	$h\,x(g\,x) : Q\,x$	app, 7, 8
10	$\lambda x{:}A.h\,x(g\,x) : \Pi x{:}A.Q\,x$	λ-rule, 6, 9
11	$\lambda g{:}\Pi x{:}A.P\,x.\lambda x{:}A.h\,x(g\,x) : (\Pi x{:}A.P\,x) \to \Pi x{:}A.Q\,x$	λ-rule, 5, 10
12	$\lambda h{:}\Pi x{:}A.P\,x \to Q\,x.\lambda g{:}\Pi x{:}A.P\,x.\lambda x{:}A.h\,x(g\,x) : \sigma$	λ-rule, 4, 11

So:

$$\Gamma \vdash \lambda h{:}\Pi x{:}A.P\,x \to Q\,x.\lambda g{:}\Pi x{:}A.P\,x.\lambda x{:}A.h\,x(g\,x) : \sigma$$

Exercise 17. 1. Find terms of the following types (NB $\to$ binds strongest)

$$(\Pi x{:}A.P\,x \to Q\,x) \to (\Pi x{:}A.P\,x) \to \Pi x{:}A.Q\,x$$

and

$$(\Pi x{:}A.P\,x \to \Pi z.R\,z\,z) \to (\Pi x{:}A.P\,x) \to \Pi z{:}A.R\,z\,z).$$

2. Find a term of the following type and write down the context in which this term is typed.

$$(\Pi x{:}A.P\,x{\to}Q){\to}(\Pi x{:}A.P\,x){\to}Q$$

What is special about your context? (It should somehow explicitly state that the type A is not empty.)

The representation that we have just described is called the *direct encoding* of logic in type theory. This is the formulas-as-types embedding originally due to Curry and Howard and described first in formal detail in [25]. Apart from this, there is the *LF encoding* of logic in type theory. This is the formulas-as-types embedding as it was invented by De Bruijn in his Automath project [31]. We describe it now.

6.2 LF Embedding of Logic in Type Theory

For $\lambda\!\to$, $\lambda 2$ and $\lambda\mathsf{P}$ we have seen *direct* representations of logic in type theory. Characteristics of such an encoding are:

- Connectives each have a counterpart in the type theory:

implication	$\sim$ $\to$-type
universal quantification	$\sim$ $\forall$-type

- Logical rules have their direct counterpart in type theory:

$\to$-introduction	$\sim$ λ-abstraction
$\to$- elimination	$\sim$ application
$\forall$-introduction	$\sim$ λ-abstraction
$\forall$-elimination	$\sim$ application

- the context declares a *signature*, *local variables* and *assumptions*.

There is another way of interpreting logic in type theory, due to De Bruijn, which we call the *logical framework* representation of logic in type theory. The idea is to use type theory as a framework in which various logics can be encoded by choosing an appropriate context. Characteristics of the LF encoding are:

- Type theory is used as a *meta system* for encoding ones own logic.
- The context is used as a *signature for the logic*: one chooses an appropriate context Γ_L in which the logic L (including its proof rules) is declared.
- The type system is a meta-calculus for dealing with *substitution* and *binding*.

We can put these two embeddings side by side by looking at the trivial proof of A implies A.

	proof	formula
direct embedding	$\lambda x{:}A.x$	$A{\to}A$
LF embedding	$\mathsf{imp\_intr}\,A\,A\,\lambda x{:}T\,A.x$	$T(A \Rightarrow A)$

For the LF embedding of minimal proposition logic into λP, we need the following context.

$$\begin{aligned}\Rightarrow &: \mathsf{prop}{\to}\mathsf{prop}{\to}\mathsf{prop}\\ \mathsf{T} &: \mathsf{prop}{\to}\mathbf{type}\\ \mathsf{imp\_intr} &: (A, B : \mathsf{prop})(\mathsf{T}\,A \to \mathsf{T}\,B) \to \mathsf{T}(A \Rightarrow B)\\ \mathsf{imp\_el} &: (A, B : \mathsf{prop})\mathsf{T}(A \Rightarrow B) \to \mathsf{T}\,A \to \mathsf{T}\,B.\end{aligned}$$

The idea is that prop is the type of names of propositions and that T "lifts" a name φ to the type of its proofs $T\,\varphi$. The terms imp_intr and imp_el encode the introduction and elimination for implication.

Exercise 18. Verify that $\mathsf{imp\_intr}\,A\,A\,\lambda x{:}T\,A.x : T(A \Rightarrow A)$ in the context just described.

In the following table we summarize the difference between the two encodings

Direct embedding	LF embedding
One type system : One logic	One type system : Many logics
Logical rules $\sim$ type theoretic rules	Logical rules $\sim$ context declarations

Apart from this, a direct embedding aims at describing a formulas–as-types *isomorphism* between the logic and the type theory, whereas the LF idea is to provide a system for enabling a formulas–as–types embedding for many different logics. For $\lambda{\to}$ and $\lambda 2$ there is indeed a one-one correspondence between deductions in logic and typable terms in the type theory. For the case of λP and minimal predicate logic, this is not so obvious, as we have identified the domains and the formulas completely: they are all of type **type**. This gives rise to types of the form $\Pi x{:}A.P\,x{\to}A$ and allows to form predicates over formulas, like $B : (\Pi x{:}A.R\,x\,x){\to}\mathbf{type}$, that don't have a correspondence in the logic. It can nevertheless be shown that the direct embedding of PRED into λP is complete, but that requires some effort. See [18] for details.

Now, we show some examples of logics in the logical framework LF – which is just λP. Then we exhibit the properties of LF that make this work.

Minimal propositional logic in λP Fix the signature (context) of minimal propositional logic.

$$\begin{aligned}\mathsf{prop} &: \mathbf{type}\\ \mathsf{imp} &: \mathsf{prop}{\to}\mathsf{prop}{\to}\mathsf{prop}\end{aligned}$$

As a notation we introduce

$$A \Rightarrow B \text{ for } \mathsf{imp}\,A\,B$$

The type prop is the type of 'names' of propositions. A term of type prop can not be inhabited (proved), as it is not a type. We 'lift' a name p : prop to the type of its proofs by introducing the following map:

$$\mathsf{T} : \mathsf{prop}{\to}\mathbf{type}.$$

The intended meaning of $\mathsf{T}p$ is 'the type of proofs of p'. We interpret 'p is valid' by '$\mathsf{T}p$ is inhabited'. To derive $\mathsf{T}p$ we also encode the logical derivation rules by adding to the context

$$\begin{aligned}\mathsf{imp\_intr} &: \Pi p, q : \mathsf{prop}.(\mathsf{T}p \to \mathsf{T}q) \to \mathsf{T}(p \Rightarrow q),\\ \mathsf{imp\_el} &: \Pi p, q : \mathsf{prop}.\mathsf{T}(p \Rightarrow q) \to \mathsf{T}p \to \mathsf{T}q.\end{aligned}$$

imp_intr takes two (names of) propositions p and q and a term $f : \mathsf{T}\,p \to \mathsf{T}\,q$ and returns a term of type $\mathsf{T}(p \Rightarrow q)$ Indeed $A \Rightarrow A$ is now valid: $\mathsf{imp\_intr} A\, A(\lambda x{:}\mathsf{T}\,A.x) : \mathsf{T}(A \Rightarrow A)$.

Exercise 19. Construct a term of type $\mathsf{T}(A \Rightarrow (B \Rightarrow A))$ in the context with $A, B : \mathsf{prop}$.

Definition 38. *Define Σ_{PROP} to be the signature for minimal proposition logic, PROP, as just constructed.*

Now, why would this be a "good" encoding? Are all derivations represented as terms in $\lambda\mathsf{P}$? And if a type is inhabited, is the associated formula then provable? We have the following desired properties of the encoding.

Definition 39. – Soundness *of the encoding states that*

$$\vdash_{PROP} A \Rightarrow \Sigma_{PROP}, a_1{:}\mathsf{prop}, \ldots, a_n{:}\mathsf{prop} \vdash p : \mathsf{T}\,A \text{ for some } p.$$

where $\{a_, \ldots, a_n\}$ is the set of proposition variables in A.
– Adequacy *(or completeness) states the converse:*

$$\Sigma_{PROP}, a_1{:}\mathsf{prop}, \ldots, a_n{:}\mathsf{prop} \vdash p : \mathsf{T}\,A \Rightarrow \vdash_{PROP} A$$

Proposition 9. *The LF encoding of* PROP *in* $\lambda\mathsf{P}$ *is sound and adequate.*

The proof of soundness is by induction on the derivation of $\vdash_{\mathrm{PROP}} A$. Adequacy also holds, but it is more involved to prove. One needs to define a canonical form of terms of type $\mathsf{T}\,A$ (the so called *long $\beta\eta$-normal-form*) and show that these are in one-one correspondence with proofs. See [22] for details.

Minimal predicate logic over one domain A in $\lambda\mathsf{P}$ Signature:

$$\begin{aligned}\mathsf{prop} &: \mathbf{type},\\ A &: \mathbf{type},\\ \mathsf{T} &: \mathsf{prop} \to \mathbf{type}\\ \mathsf{f} &: A \to A,\\ \mathsf{R} &: A \to A \to \mathsf{prop},\\ \Rightarrow &: \mathsf{prop} \to \mathsf{prop} \to \mathsf{prop},\\ \mathsf{imp\_intr} &: \Pi p, q : \mathsf{prop}.(\mathsf{T}p \to \mathsf{T}q) \to \mathsf{T}(p \Rightarrow q),\\ \mathsf{imp\_el} &: \Pi p, q : \mathsf{prop}.\mathsf{T}(p \Rightarrow q) \to \mathsf{T}p \to \mathsf{T}q.\end{aligned}$$

Now we encode $\forall$ by observing that $\forall$ takes a $P : A{\rightarrow}\mathsf{prop}$ and returns a proposition, so:

$$\forall : (A{\rightarrow}\mathsf{prop}){\rightarrow}\mathsf{prop}$$

Universal quantification $\forall x{:}A.(Px)$ is then translated by $\forall(\lambda x{:}A.(Px))$

Definition 40. *The signature:* Σ_{PRED} *is defined by adding to the above the following intro and elim rules for* $\forall$.

$$\begin{aligned}\forall &: (A{\rightarrow}\mathsf{prop}){\rightarrow}\mathsf{prop},\\ \forall\_\mathsf{intr} &: \Pi P{:}A{\rightarrow}\mathsf{prop}.(\Pi x{:}A.\mathsf{T}(Px)){\rightarrow}\mathsf{T}(\forall P),\\ \forall\_\mathsf{elim} &: \Pi P{:}A{\rightarrow}\mathsf{prop}.\mathsf{T}(\forall P){\rightarrow}\Pi x{:}A.\mathsf{T}(Px).\end{aligned}$$

The proof of

$$\forall z{:}A(\forall x, y{:}A.Rxy) \Rightarrow Rzz$$

is now mirrored by the proof-term

$$\begin{aligned}&\forall\_\mathsf{intr}[\_](\ \lambda z{:}A.\mathsf{imp\_intr}[\_][\_](\lambda h{:}\mathsf{T}(\forall x, y{:}A.Rxy).\\ &\qquad \forall\_\mathsf{elim}[\_](\forall\_\mathsf{elim}[\_]hz)z)\ )\end{aligned}$$

For readability, we have replaced the instantiations of the Π-type by $[\_]$.
This term is of type

$$\mathsf{T}(\forall(\lambda z{:}A.\mathsf{imp}(\forall(\lambda x{:}A.(\forall(\lambda y{:}A.\mathsf{R}xy))))(\mathsf{R}zz)))$$

Exercise 20. Construct a proof-term that mirrors the (obvious) proof of $\forall x(P\,x \Rightarrow Q\,x) \Rightarrow \forall x.P\,x \Rightarrow \forall x.Q\,x$

Proposition 10. *We have soundness and adequacy for minimal predicate logic:*

$$\vdash_{\mathrm{PRED}} \varphi \Rightarrow \Sigma_{\mathrm{PRED}}, x_1{:}A, \ldots, x_n{:}A \vdash p : \mathsf{T}\varphi,\ \textit{for some } p,$$

where $\{x_1, \ldots, x_n\}$ *is the set of free variables in* φ.

$$\Sigma_{\mathrm{PRED}}, x_1{:}A, \ldots, x_n{:}A \vdash p : \mathsf{T}\varphi \Rightarrow \vdash_{\mathrm{PRED}} \varphi$$

6.3 Meta-theory of λP

Proposition 11.
- *Uniqueness of types*
  If $\Gamma \vdash M : \sigma$ *and* $\Gamma \vdash M : \tau$, *then* $\sigma{=}_{\beta}\tau$.
- *Subject Reduction*
  If $\Gamma \vdash M : \sigma$ *and* $M \longrightarrow_{\beta} N$, *then* $\Gamma \vdash N : \sigma$.
- *Strong Normalization*
  If $\Gamma \vdash M : \sigma$, *then all* β*-reductions from* M *terminate.*

The proofs are by induction on the derivation, by first proving auxiliary lemmas like Substitution and Thinning. SN can be proved by defining a reduction preserving map from λP to λ→. Then, an infinite reduction path in λP would give rise to an infinite reduction path in λ→, so SN for λP follows from SN for λ→. See [22] for details. We now come back to the decidability questions of Definition 20.

Proposition 12. *For* λP*:*

- *TIP is undecidable*
- *TCP/TSP is decidable*

The undecidability of TIP follows from the fact that provability in minimal predicate logic is undecidable. A more straightforward proof is given in [7], by interpreting the halting problem for register machines as a typing problem (in a specific context) in λP.

We will expand on the decidability of TCP below. It is shown by defining two algorithms simultaneously: one that does type synthesis $\Gamma \vdash M :?$ and one that does *context checking*: $\Gamma \vdash ?$. This is to mirror the two forms of judgment in λP.

Remark 1. One can also introduce a *Curry variant* of λP. This is done in [2]. A related issue is whether one can type an *untyped* λ-term in λP. So, given an M, is there a context Γ, a type A and a term P such that $\Gamma \vdash P : A$ and $|P| \equiv M$. Here, $|-|$ is the erasure map defined by

$$\begin{aligned} |x| &:= x \\ |\lambda x{:}\sigma.M| &:= |\lambda x.M| \quad |MN| := |M|\,|N| \end{aligned}$$

The answer to this question is yes, because an untyped term is λP-typable iff it is typable in $\lambda{\rightarrow}$. But there is a little snag: if we *fix* the context Γ, the problem becomes undecidable, as was shown in [14], where Dowek gives a context Γ and a term M such that $\exists P, A(\Gamma \vdash P : A \wedge |P| = M)$ is equivalent to the Post correspondence problem.

6.4 Type Checking for λP

We define algorithms Ok($-$) and Type$_{_}(-)$ simultaneously:

- Ok($-$) takes a context and returns 'accept' or 'reject'
- Type$_{_}(-)$ takes a context and a term and returns a term or 'reject'.

Definition 41. *The type synthesis algorithm* Type$_{_}(-)$ *is* sound *if*

$$\text{Type}_\Gamma(M) = A \;\Rightarrow\; \Gamma \vdash M : A \textit{ (for all } \Gamma \textit{ and } M)$$

The type synthesis algorithm Type$_{_}(-)$ *is* complete *if*

$$\Gamma \vdash M : A \;\Rightarrow\; \text{Type}_\Gamma(M) =_\beta A \textit{ (for all } \Gamma \textit{ and } M)$$

Completeness only makes sense if we have uniqueness of types: only then it makes sense to check if the type that is given to us is convertible to the type computed by Type. In case we don't have uniqueness of types, one would let Type$_{_}(-)$ compute a set of possible types, one for each β-equivalence class.

Definition 42

$$
\begin{aligned}
\mathrm{Ok}(<>) &= \textit{`accept'} \\
\mathrm{Ok}(\Gamma, x{:}A) &= \mathsf{if}\ \mathrm{Type}_\Gamma(A) \in \{\mathbf{type}, \mathbf{kind}\}\ \mathsf{then}\ \mathrm{Type}_\Gamma(A)\ \mathsf{else}\ \textit{`reject'}, \\
\mathrm{Type}_\Gamma(x) &= \mathsf{if}\ \mathrm{Ok}(\Gamma)\ \mathsf{and}\ x{:}A \in \Gamma\ \mathsf{then}\ A\ \mathsf{else}\ \textit{`reject'}, \\
\mathrm{Type}_\Gamma(\mathbf{type}) &= \mathsf{if}\ \mathrm{Ok}(\Gamma)\ \mathsf{then}\ \mathbf{kind}\ \mathsf{else}\ \textit{`reject'}, \\
\mathrm{Type}_\Gamma(MN) &= \mathsf{if}\ \mathrm{Type}_\Gamma(M) = C\ \mathsf{and}\ \mathrm{Type}_\Gamma(N) = D \\
&\quad\ \mathsf{then}\ \ \mathsf{if}\ C \twoheadrightarrow_\beta \Pi x{:}A.B\ \mathsf{and}\ A =_\beta D \\
&\quad\ \qquad\ \mathsf{then}\ B[x := N]\ \mathsf{else}\ \textit{`reject'} \\
&\quad\ \mathsf{else}\ \ \textit{`reject'}, \\
\mathrm{Type}_\Gamma(\lambda x{:}A.M) &= \mathsf{if}\ \mathrm{Type}_{\Gamma,x:A}(M) = B \\
&\quad\ \mathsf{then}\ \qquad \mathsf{if}\ \mathrm{Type}_\Gamma(\Pi x{:}A.B) \in \{\mathbf{type}, \mathbf{kind}\} \\
&\quad\ \qquad\qquad\ \mathsf{then}\ \Pi x{:}A.B\ \mathsf{else}\ \textit{`reject'} \\
&\quad\ \mathsf{else}\ \textit{`reject'}, \\
\mathrm{Type}_\Gamma(\Pi x{:}A.B) &= \mathsf{if}\ \mathrm{Type}_\Gamma(A) = \mathbf{type}\ \mathsf{and}\ \mathrm{Type}_{\Gamma,x:A}(B) = s \\
&\quad\ \mathsf{then}\ s\ \mathsf{else}\ \textit{`reject'}
\end{aligned}
$$

Proposition 13. *The type checking algorithm is sound:*

$$
\begin{aligned}
\mathrm{Type}_\Gamma(M) = A &\Rightarrow \Gamma \vdash M : A \\
\mathrm{Ok}(\Gamma) = \textit{`accept'} &\Rightarrow \Gamma \vdash
\end{aligned}
$$

The proof is by simultaneous induction on the computation of Type and Ok.

For completeness, we need to prove the following simultaneously, which we would prove by induction on the derivation.

$$
\begin{aligned}
\Gamma \vdash A : \mathbf{s} &\Rightarrow \mathrm{Type}_\Gamma(A) = \mathbf{s} \\
\Gamma \vdash M : A &\Rightarrow \mathrm{Type}_\Gamma(M) =_\beta A \\
\Gamma \vdash &\Rightarrow \mathrm{Ok}(\Gamma) = \text{`accept'}
\end{aligned}
$$

The first slight strengthening of completeness is not a problem: in case the type of A is **type** or **kind**, $\mathrm{Type}_\Gamma(A)$ returns exactly **type** or **kind** (and not a term $=_\beta$-equal to it). The problem is the λ-rule, where $\mathrm{Type}_{\Gamma,x:A}(M) = C$ and $C =_\beta B$ and we know that $\mathrm{Type}_\Gamma(\Pi x{:}A.B) = \mathbf{s}$, but we need to know that $\mathrm{Type}_\Gamma(\Pi x{:}A.C) = \mathbf{s}$, because that is the side condition in the Type algorithm for the $\lambda x{:}A.M$ case.

The solution is to change the definition of Type a little bit. This is motivated by the following Lemma, which is specific to the type theory $\lambda\mathsf{P}$.

Lemma 6. *The derivable judgements of* $\lambda\mathsf{P}$ *remain exactly the same if we replace the* λ*-rule by*

$$
(\lambda')\ \frac{\Gamma, x{:}A \vdash M : B \quad \Gamma \vdash A : \mathbf{type}}{\Gamma \vdash \lambda x{:}A.M : \Pi x{:}A.B}
$$

The proof is by induction on the derivation. Now we can in the λ-case of the definition of Type replace the side condition

$$\text{if } \mathrm{Type}_\Gamma(\Pi x{:}A.B) \in \{\mathbf{type}, \mathbf{kind}\}$$

by

$$\text{if } \mathrm{Type}_\Gamma(A) \in \{\mathbf{type}\}$$

Definition 43. *We adapt the definition of* Type *in Definition 42 by replacing the λ-abstraction case by*

$$\begin{array}{rll} \mathrm{Type}_\Gamma(\lambda x{:}A.M) = & \text{if } \mathrm{Type}_{\Gamma,x:A}(M) = B & \\ & \text{then} & \text{if } \mathrm{Type}_\Gamma(A) = \mathbf{type} \\ & & \text{then } \Pi x{:}A.B \text{ else } \textit{`reject'} \\ & \text{else } \textit{`reject'}, & \end{array}$$

Then soundness still holds and we have the following.

Proposition 14

$$\begin{aligned} \Gamma \vdash A : \mathbf{s} &\Rightarrow \mathrm{Type}_\Gamma(A) = \mathbf{s} \\ \Gamma \vdash M : A &\Rightarrow \mathrm{Type}_\Gamma(M) =_\beta A \\ \Gamma \vdash &\Rightarrow \mathrm{Ok}(\Gamma) = \textit{`accept'} \end{aligned}$$

As a consequence of soundness and completeness we find that

$$\mathrm{Type}_\Gamma(M) = \text{`reject'} \quad \Rightarrow \quad M \text{ is not typable in } \Gamma$$

Completeness implies that Type terminates correctly on *all well-typed terms*. But we want that Type terminates on *all pseudo terms*: we want to assure that on a non-typable term, Type returns 'reject', which is not guaranteed by Soundness and Completeness.

To prove that $\mathrm{Type}_{\_}(-)$ terminates on all inputs, we need to make sure that $\mathrm{Type}_\Gamma(M)$ and $\mathrm{Ok}(\Gamma)$ are called on arguments of lesser size. As "size" we take the sum of the lengths of the context Γ and the term M, and then all cases are decreasing, apart from λ-abstraction and application. In the λ-abstraction case, Type is called on a pseudo-term $\Pi x{:}A.B$ that is not necessarily smaller. But our replacement of the side condition in Type for the λ-abstraction case in Definition 43 solves this problem.

In the case of application, the function Type is called on smaller inputs, but the algorithms requires β-equality and β-reduction checking:

$$\begin{array}{rll} \mathrm{Type}_\Gamma(MN) = & \text{if } \mathrm{Type}_\Gamma(M) = C \text{ and } \mathrm{Type}_\Gamma(N) = D & \\ & \text{then } \ \text{if } C \twoheadrightarrow_\beta \Pi x{:}A.B \text{ and } A =_\beta D & \\ & \qquad \text{then } B[x := N] \text{ else `reject'} & \\ & \text{else } \ \text{`reject'}, & \end{array}$$

So, we need to decide β-reduction and β-equality, which, for pseudo-terms is undecidable. The solution is that Type will only check β-equality (and reduction) for *well-typed* terms, and we know that λP is SN and CR, so this is decidable.

Proposition 15. *Termination of* Type *and* Ok*: For all pseudo-terms M and pseudo-contexts Γ,* $\mathrm{Type}_\Gamma(M)$ *terminates (in either a pseudo-term A or 'reject') and* $\mathrm{Ok}(\Gamma)$ *terminates (in either 'accept' or 'reject').*

The proof is by induction on the size of the inputs, using the Soundness (Proposition 13) and decidability of β-equality for well-typed terms in the application case.

7 Conclusion and Further Reading

In this paper we have introduced various type theories by focussing on the Curry-Howard formulas-as-types embedding and by highlighting some of the programming aspects related to type theory. As stated in the Introduction, we could have presented the type systems à la Church in a unified framework of the "λ-cube" or "Pure Type Systems", but for expository reasons we have refrained from doing so. In the PTS framework, one can study the systems $F\omega$, a higher order extension of system F, $\lambda\mathsf{HOL}$, a type systems for higher order (predicate) logic, and the Calculus of Constructions, a higher order extension of $\lambda\mathsf{P}$. Also one can generalize these systems to the logically inconsistent systems λU and $\lambda\star$ where **type** is itself a type. (These systems are computationally not inconsistent so still interesting to study.) We refer to [4,5] and the references in those papers for further reading.

In another direction, there are various typing constructs that can be added to make the theories more powerful. The most prominent one is the addition of a scheme for inductive types, which also adds an induction and a well-founded recursion principle for every inductive type. Examples are the Calculus of Inductive Constructions (CIC) and Martin-Löf type theory. The latter is introduced in the paper by Bove and Dybjer and a good reference is [32]. CIC is the type theory implemented in the proof assistant Coq and a good reference for both the theory and the tool is [6].

In the direction of programming, there is a world of literature and a good starting point is [33]. We have already mentioned PCF [35], which is the simplest way to turn $\lambda\!\!\to$ into a Turing complete language. The next thing to add are algebraic data types, which are the programmer's analogue to inductive types. Using these one can define and compute with data types of lists, trees etc. as a primitive in the language (as opposed to coding them in $\lambda 2$ as we have done in Section 5.5). Other important concepts to add, especially to the type systems à la Curry, are overloading and subtyping. A good reference for further reading is [33].

References

1. Bainbridge, E.S., Freyd, P.J., Scedrov, A., Scott, P.J.: Functorial polymorphism. Theoretical Computer Science 70, 35–64 (1990)
2. van Bakel, S., Liquori, L., Ronchi Della Rocca, S., Urzyczyn, P.: Comparing Cubes of Typed and Type Assignment Systems. Ann. Pure Appl. Logic 86(3), 267–303 (1997)

3. Barendregt, H.: The Lambda Calculus: Its Syntax and Semantics. Studies in Logic and the Foundations of Mathematics, vol. 103. North Holland, Amsterdam (1981)
4. Barendregt, H., Geuvers, H.: Proof Assistants using Dependent Type Systems. In: Robinson, A., Voronkov, A. (eds.) Handbook of Automated Reasoning, ch.18, vol. 2, pp. 1149–1238. Elsevier, Amsterdam (2001)
5. Barendregt, H.: Lambda Calculi with Types. In: Abramsky, Gabbay, Maibaum (eds.) Handbook of Logic in Computer Science, vol. 1. Clarendon (1992)
6. Bertot, Y., Castéran, P.: Interactive Theorem Proving and Program Development: Coq'Art: the Calculus of Inductive Constructions. EATCS Series: Texts in Theoretical Computer Science, 469 p. Springer, Heidelberg (2004)
7. Bezem, M., Springintveld, J.: A Simple Proof of the Undecidability of Inhabitation in λP. J. Funct. Program. 6(5), 757–761 (1996)
8. Böhm, C., Berarducci, A.: Automatic synthesis of typed λ-programs on term algebras. Theoretical Computer Science 39, 135–154 (1985)
9. Church, A.: A formulation of the simple theory of types. Journal of Symbolic Logic 5, 56–68 (1940)
10. Constable, R.L., Allen, S.F., Bromley, H.M., Cleaveland, W.R., Cremer, J.F., Harper, R.W., Howe, D.J., Knoblock, T.B., Mendler, N.P., Panangaden, P., Sasaki, J.T., Smith, S.F.: Implementing Mathematics with the Nuprl Development System. Prentice-Hall, NJ (1986)
11. Curry, H.B., Feys, R., Craig, W.: Combinatory Logic, vol. 1. North–Holland, Amsterdam (1958)
12. Damas, L., Milner, R.: Principal type-schemes for functional programs. In: POPL 1982: Proceedings of the 9th ACM SIGPLAN-SIGACT symposium on Principles of programming languages, pp. 207–212. ACM, New York (1982)
13. Davis, M. (ed.): The Undecidable, Basic Papers on Undecidable Propositions, Unsolvable Problems And Computable Functions. Raven Press, New York (1965)
14. Dowek, G.: The Undecidability of Typability in the Lambda-Pi-Calculus. In: Bezem, M., Groote, J.F. (eds.) TLCA 1993. LNCS, vol. 664, pp. 139–145. Springer, Heidelberg (1993)
15. Dowek, G.: Collections, sets and types. Mathematical Structures in Computer Science 9, 1–15 (1999)
16. Fitch, F.: Symbolic Logic, An Introduction. The Ronald Press Company (1952)
17. Gandy, R.O.: An early proof of normalization by A.M. Turing. In: Seldin, J.P., Hindley, J.R. (eds.) H.B. Curry: Essays on Combinatory Logic, Lambda Calculus and Formalism, pp. 453–455. Academic Press, London (1980)
18. Geuvers, H., Barendsen, E.: Some logical and syntactical observations concerning the first order dependent type system λP. Math. Struc. in Comp. Sci. 9(4), 335–360 (1999)
19. Girard, J.-Y., Taylor, P., Lafont, Y.: Proofs and types. Cambridge tracts in theoretical computer science, vol. 7. Cambridge University Press, Cambridge
20. Girard, J.-Y.: The system F of variable types, fifteen years later. Theoretical Computer Science 45, 159–192 (1986)
21. Girard, J.-Y.: Une extension de l'interprétation de Gödel à l'analyse et son application à l'élimination des coupures dans l'analyse et la théorie des types. In: Proceedings of the Second Scandinavian Logic Symposium. Studies in Logic and the Foundations of Mathematics, vol. 63, pp. 63–92. North-Holland, Amsterdam (1971)
22. Harper, R., Honsell, F., Plotkin, G.: A Framework for Defining Logics. In: Proceedings 2nd Annual IEEE Symp. on Logic in Computer Science, LICS 1987, Ithaca, NY, USA, June 22-25 (1987)

23. Hindley, J.R.: The principal type-scheme of an object in combinatory logic. Transactions of the American Mathematical Society 146, 29–60 (1969)
24. Hindley, J.R., Seldin, J.P.: Introduction to combinators and lambda-calculus. London Mathematical Society Student Texts. Cambridge University Press, Cambridge (1986)
25. Howard, W.: The formulas-as-types notion of construction. In: Seldin, J.P., Hindley, J.R. (eds.) H.B. Curry: Essays on Combinatory Logic, Lambda-Calculus and Formalism, pp. 479–490. Academic Press, New York (1980)
26. Joachimski, F., Matthes, R.: Short proofs of normalization for the simply- typed lambda-calculus, permutative conversions and Gödel's T. Arch. Math. Log. 42(1), 59–87 (2003)
27. Lambek, J., Scott, P.: Introduction to Higher Order Categorical Logic. Cambridge University Press, Cambridge (1986)
28. Martin-Löf, P.: Intuitionistic type theory, Bibliopolis (1984)
29. Milner, R., Robin: A Theory of Type Polymorphism in Programming. JCSS 17, 348–375 (1978)
30. Mycroft, A.: Polymorphic type schemes and recursive definitions. In: Paul, M., Robinet, B. (eds.) Programming 1984. LNCS, vol. 167, pp. 217–228. Springer, Heidelberg (1984)
31. Nederpelt, R., Geuvers, H., de Vrijer, R. (eds.): Selected Papers on Automath. Studies in Logic, vol. 133. North-Holland, Amsterdam (1994)
32. Nordström, B., Petersson, K., Smith, J.: Programming in Martin-Löf's Type Theory, An Introduction. Oxford University Press, Oxford (1990)
33. Pierce, B.C.: Types and Programming Languages. MIT Press, Cambridge (2002)
34. Plotkin, G.: Call-by-Name, Call-by-Value and the lambda-Calculus. Theor. Comp. Sci. 1(2), 125–159 (1975)
35. Plotkin, G.: LCF considered as a programming language. Theor. Comp. Sci. 5, 223–255 (1977)
36. Reynolds, J.C.: Polymorphism is not Set-Theoretic. In: Kahn, G., MacQueen, D.B., Plotkin, G. (eds.) Semantics of Data Types 1984. LNCS, vol. 173, pp. 145–156. Springer, Heidelberg (1984)
37. Schwichtenberg, H.: Definierbare Funktionen im λ-Kalkül mit Typen. Archiv für Mathematische Logik und Grundlagenforschung 17, 113–114 (1976)
38. Tait, W.W.: Intensional interpretation of functionals of finite type. J. Symbol. Logic 32(2), 187–199 (1967)
39. Urzyczyn, P., Sørensen, M.: Lectures on the Curry-Howard Isomorphism. Studies in Logic and the Foundations of Mathematics, vol. 149. Elsevier, Amsterdam (2006)
40. Wand, M.: A simple algorithm and proof for type inference. Fundamenta Informaticae X, 115–122 (1987)
41. Wells, J.B.: Typability and type-checking in the second-order λ-calculus are equivalent and undecidable. In: Proceedings of the 9th Annual Symposium on Logic in Computer Science, Paris, France, pp. 176–185. IEEE Computer Society Press, Los Alamitos (1994)

Dependent Types at Work

Ana Bove and Peter Dybjer

Chalmers University of Technology, Göteborg, Sweden
{bove,peterd}@chalmers.se

Abstract. In these lecture notes we give an introduction to functional programming with dependent types. We use the dependently typed programming language Agda which is an extension of Martin-Löf type theory. First we show how to do simply typed functional programming in the style of Haskell and ML. Some differences between Agda's type system and the Hindley-Milner type system of Haskell and ML are also discussed. Then we show how to use dependent types for programming and we explain the basic ideas behind type-checking dependent types. We go on to explain the Curry-Howard identification of propositions and types. This is what makes Agda a programming logic and not only a programming language. According to Curry-Howard, we identify programs and proofs, something which is possible only by requiring that all program terminate. However, at the end of these notes we present a method for encoding partial and general recursive functions as total functions using dependent types.

1 What Are Dependent Types?

Dependent types are types that depend on elements of other types. An example is the type A^n of vectors of length n with components of type A. Another example is the type $A^{m \times n}$ of $m \times n$-matrices. We say that the type A^n *depends* on the number n, or that A^n is a *family* of types *indexed* by the number n. Yet another example is the type of trees of a certain height. With dependent types we can also define the type of height-balanced trees of a certain height, that is, trees where the height of subtrees differ by at most one. As we will see, more complicated invariants can also be expressed with dependent type. We can have a type of sorted lists and a type of sorted binary trees (binary search trees). In fact, we shall use the strong system of dependent types of the Agda language [3,25] which is an extension of Martin-Löf type theory [19,20,21,24]. In this language we can express more or less any conceivable property. We have to say "more or less" because Gödel's incompleteness theorem sets a limit for the expressiveness of logical languages.

Parametrised types, such as the type $[A]$ of lists of elements of type A, are usually not called dependent types. These are families of types indexed by other *types*, not families of types indexed by *elements* of another type. However, in dependent type theories there is a type of *small types* (a *universe*), so that we have a type $[A]$ of lists of elements of a given small type A.

A. Bove et al. (Eds.): LerNet ALFA Summer School 2008, LNCS 5520, pp. 57–99, 2009.

Already FORTRAN allowed you to define arrays of a given dimension, and in this sense, dependent types are as old as high-level programming languages. However, the simply typed lambda calculus and the Hindley-Milner type system, on which typed functional programming languages such as ML [23] and Haskell [26] are based, do not include dependent types, only parametrised types. Similarly, the polymorphic lambda calculus System F [14] has types like $\forall X.A$ where X ranges over all types, but no quantification over elements of other types.

The type systems of typed functional programming languages have gradually been extended with new features. One example is the module system of SML; others are the arrays and the newly introduced generalised algebraic data types of Haskell [27]. Moreover, a number of experimental functional languages with limited forms of dependent types have been introduced recently. Examples include meta-ML (for meta-programming) [31], PolyP [17] and Generic Haskell [16] (for generic programming), and dependent ML [28] (for programming with "indexed" types). It turns out that many of these features can be modelled by the dependent types in the strong type system we consider in these notes.

The modern development of dependently typed programming languages has its origins in the *Curry-Howard isomorphism* between propositions and types. Already in the 1930's Curry noticed the similarity between the axioms of implicational logic

$$P \supset Q \supset P \qquad\qquad (P \supset Q \supset R) \supset (P \supset Q) \supset P \supset R$$

and types of the combinators K and S

$$A \to B \to A \qquad\qquad (A \to B \to C) \to (A \to B) \to A \to C.$$

In fact, K can be viewed as a *witness* (also *proof object*) of the truth of $P \supset Q \supset P$ and S of the truth of $(P \supset Q \supset R) \supset (P \supset Q) \supset P \supset R$. The typing rule for *application*, if f has type $A \to B$ and a has type A, then $f\ a$ has type B, corresponds to the inference rule *modus ponens*: from $P \supset Q$ and P conclude Q. Thus, there is a one-to-one correspondence between combinatory terms and proofs in implicational logic.

In a similar way product types correspond to conjunctions, and sum types (disjoint unions) to disjunctions. To extend this correspondence to predicate logic, Howard and de Bruijn introduced dependent types $A(x)$ corresponding to predicates $P(x)$. They formed indexed products $\prod x\colon D.A(x)$ and indexed sums $\sum x\colon D.A(x)$ corresponding, respectively, to universal quantifications $\forall x\colon D.P(x)$ and existential quantifications $\exists x\colon D.P(x)$. What we obtain here is a *Curry-Howard* interpretation of *intuitionistic* predicate logic. There is a one-to-one correspondence between propositions and types in a type system with dependent types. There is also a one-to-one correspondence between proofs of a certain proposition in constructive predicate logic and terms of the corresponding type. Furthermore, to accommodate equality in predicate logic, we introduce the type $a == b$ of proofs that a and b are equal. In this way, we get a Curry-Howard interpretation of predicate logic with equality. We can go even further and add the type of natural numbers with addition and multiplication, and get a Curry-Howard version of Heyting (intuitionistic) arithmetic. More about the correspondence between propositions and types can be found in Section 4.

The Curry-Howard interpretation was the basis for Martin-Löf's intuitionistic type theory [19,20,21]. In this theory propositions and types are actually identified. Although Martin-Löf's theory was primarily intended to be a foundational system for constructive mathematics, it can also be used as a programming language [20]. From the early 1980's and onwards, a number of computer systems implementing variants of Martin-Löf type theory were built. The most well-known are the NuPRL [6] system from Cornell implementing an extensional version of the theory, and the Coq [32] system from INRIA in France implementing an intensional impredicative version. The Agda system implements an intensional predicative extension of Martin-Löf type theory. It is the latest in a sequence of systems developed in Göteborg.

Systems implementing dependent type theories are often referred to as either *proof assistants* or *dependently typed programming languages*, depending on whether the emphasis is on proving or on programming. Agda is primarily designed to be a programming language, although it can be used as a proof assistant as well. It extends Martin.Löf type theory with a number of features, such as flexible mechanisms for defining new inductive data types and for defining functions by pattern matching, to make programming convenient.

About These Notes

The aim of these notes is to give a gentle introduction to dependently typed programming for a reader who is familiar with ordinary functional programming, and who has basic knowledge of logic and type systems. Although we use the Agda language, similar techniques can be used in related dependently typed programming languages such as Epigram [22] and Coq [32]. The presentation is by example: the reader is guided through a number of successively more advanced examples of what can be done with dependent types. It is useful to have a working version of Agda running while reading these notes. Instructions for how to download Agda can be found on the Agda wiki [3].

We would also like to say a few words about what we will not do.

We will not give a full definition of the Agda language with syntax and inference rules.

In order to program effectively in Agda, some understanding of the type-checking algorithm is needed, and we will discuss this briefly in Section 5. However, the full story is a complex matter beyond the scope of these notes. The basic ideas behind the present type-checking algorithm was first presented by Coquand [7]. More information about type-checking and normalisation can be found in in Norell's thesis [25], in Abel, Coquand, and Dybjer [1,2] and in Coquand, Kinoshita, Nordström, and Takeyama [8].

Programming with dependent types would be difficult without an interface where terms can be interactively refined with the aid of the type-checker. For this purpose Agda has an Emacs interface which however, will not be described here. A few words on the help provided when interactively defining a program can be found in section A.5.

The reader who wants a more complete understanding of dependent type theory should read one of the books about Martin-Löf type theory and related systems. Martin-Löf's "Intuitionistic Type Theory" [21] is a classic, although the reader should be aware that it describes an extensional version of the theory. The book by Nordström, Petersson, and Smith [24] contains a description of the later intensional theory on which Agda is based. Other books on variants of dependent type theory are by Thompson [33], by Constable et al [6] on the NuPRL-system, and by Bertot and Casteran [4] on the Coq-system. The recent lecture notes (available from the Agda wiki [3]) by Norell are a complement to the present notes. They provide a collection of somewhat more advanced examples of how to use Agda for dependently typed programming.

The present volume also contains other material which is useful for further reading. Geuvers' lecture notes provide an introduction to type theory including Barendregt's *pure type systems* and their most important meta-theoretic properties. Bertot's notes describe how dependent types (in Coq) can be used for implementing a number of concepts occurring in a course in programming language theory with the focus on abstract interpretation. Barthe, Grégoire, and Riba's notes present a method for making more powerful termination-checkers.

The rest of the notes are organised as follows. In Section 2, we show how to do ordinary functional programming in Agda. Section 3 introduces some basic dependent types and shows how to use them. In Section 4, we explain the Curry-Howard isomorphism. In Section 5 we briefly discuss some aspects of type-checking and pattern matching with dependent types. In Section 6 we show how to use Agda as a programming logic. Section 7 describes how to represent general recursion and partial functions as total functions in Agda. To avoid entering into too many details, we will postpone, as far as possible, an account of Agda's concrete syntax until Appendix A.

2 Simply Typed Functional Programming in Agda

We begin by showing how to do ordinary functional programming in Agda. We will discuss the correspondence with programming in Haskell [26], the standard lazy simply typed functional programming language. Haskell is the implementation language of the Agda system and, as one can see below, Agda has borrowed a number of features from Haskell.

Here we show how to introduce the basic data structures of truth values (a.k.a. boolean values) and natural numbers, and how to write some basic functions over them. Then, we show a first use of dependent types: how to write polymorphic programs in Agda using quantification over a type of small types.

2.1 Truth Values

We first introduce the type of truth values in Agda:

```
data Bool : Set where
  true : Bool
  false : Bool
```

This states that `Bool` is a data type with the two constructors `true` and `false`. In this particular case both constructors are also elements of the data type since they do not have any arguments. Note that the types of the constructors are explicitly given and that ":" denotes type membership in Agda. Observe also that the above definition states that `Bool` is a member of the type `Set`. This is the type of *sets* (using a terminology introduced by Martin-Löf [21]) or *small types* (mentioned in the introduction). `Bool` is a small type, but `Set` itself is not, it is a *large* type. If we added that `Set` : `Set`, the system would actually become inconsistent and hence, we would be able to prove any property.

Let us now define a simple function, negation, on truth values:

```
not : Bool -> Bool
not true = false
not false = true
```

Note that we begin by declaring the type of `not`: it is a function from truth values to truth values. Then we define the function by case analysis using pattern matching on the argument.

To give the same definition in Haskell, it will be sufficient to write the two defining equations. The Haskell type system will then infer that `not` has the type `Bool -> Bool` by using the Hindley-Milner type inference algorithm. In Agda we cannot infer types in general, but we can always *check* whether a certain term has a certain type provided it is *normal*. The reason for this is that the type-checking algorithm in Agda uses *normalisation (simplification)*, and without the normality restriction it may not terminate. We will discuss some aspects of type-checking dependent types in Section 3, but the full story is a complex matter which is beyond the scope of these notes.

Agda checks that patterns cover all cases and does not accept functions with missing patterns. The following definition will not be accepted:

```
not : Bool -> Bool
not true = false
```

Agda will complain that it misses the case for `not false`. In Section 4 we explain why all programs in Agda must be total.

We can define binary functions in a similar way, and we can even use pattern matching on both arguments:

```
equiv : Bool -> Bool -> Bool
equiv true true = true
equiv true false = false
```

```
equiv false true = false
equiv false false = true
```

In Agda, we can define *infix* and *mix-fix operators*. Agda is more permissive (than Haskell) about which characters can be part of the operator's name, and about the number and the position of its arguments. One indicates the places of the arguments of the operators with underscore ("_"). For example, disjunction on truth values is usually an infix operator and it can be declared in Agda as follows:

```
_||_ : Bool -> Bool -> Bool
```

As in Haskell, variables and the wild card character "_" can be used in patterns to denote an arbitrary argument of the appropriate type. Wild cards are often used when the variable does not appear on the right hand side of an equation:

```
true || _ = true
_ || true = true
_ || _ = false
```

We can define the precedence and association of infix operators much in the same way as in Haskell, the higher number the stronger the binding:

```
infixl 60 _||_
```

From now on, we assume operators are defined with the right precedence and association, and therefore do not write unnecessary parentheses in our examples.

We should also mention that one can use Unicode in Agda – a much appreciated feature which makes it possible to write code which looks like "mathematics". We will only use ASCII in these notes however.

Exercise: Define some more truth functions, such as conjunction and implication.

2.2 Natural Numbers

The type of natural numbers is defined as the following data type:

```
data Nat : Set where
  zero : Nat
  succ : Nat -> Nat
```

In languages such as Haskell, such data types are usually known as *recursive*: a natural number is either `zero` or the successor of another natural number. In constructive type theory, one usually refers to them as *inductive types* or *inductively defined types*.

We can now define the predecessor function:

```
pred : Nat -> Nat
pred zero = zero
pred (succ n) = n
```

We can define addition and multiplication as recursive functions (note that application of the prefix `succ` operator has higher precedence than the infix operators `+` and `*`, and that `*` has higher precedence than `+`):

```
_+_ : Nat -> Nat -> Nat
zero + m = m
succ n + m = succ (n + m)
```

```
_*_ : Nat -> Nat -> Nat
zero * n = zero
succ n * m = n * m + m
```

They are examples of functions defined by *primitive* recursion in the first argument. We have two cases: a base case for `zero`, and a step case where the value of the function for `succ n` is defined in terms of the value of the function for `n`.

Given a first order data type, we distinguish between *canonical* and *non-canonical* forms. Elements on canonical form are built up by constructors only, whereas non-canonical elements might contain defined functions. For example, `true` and `false` are canonical forms, but `(not true)` is a non-canonical form. Moreover, `zero`, `succ zero`, `succ (succ zero)`, ..., are canonical forms, whereas `zero + zero` and `zero * zero` are not. Neither is the term `succ (zero + zero)`.

Remark. The above notion of canonical form is sufficient for the purpose of these notes, but Martin-Löf used another notion for the semantics of his theory [20]. He instead considers *lazy canonical forms*, that is, it suffices that a term begins with a constructor to be considered a canonical form. For example, `succ (zero + zero)` is a lazy canonical form, but not a "full" canonical form. Lazy canonical forms are appropriate for lazy functional programming languages, such as Haskell, where a constructor should not evaluate its arguments.

We can actually use decimal representation for natural numbers by using some built-in definitions. Agda also provides built-in definitions for addition and multiplication of natural numbers that are faster than our recursive definitions; see Appendix A.2 for information on how to use the built-in representation and operations. In what follows, we will sometimes use decimal representation and write 3 instead of `succ (succ (succ zero))` for example.

Although the natural numbers with addition and multiplication can be defined in the same way in Haskell, one normally uses the primitive type `Int` of integers instead. The Haskell system interprets the elements of `Int` as binary machine integers, and addition and multiplication are performed by the hardware adder and multiplier.

Exercise: Write the cut-off subtraction function - the function on natural numbers, which returns 0 if the second argument is greater than or equal to the first. Also write some more numerical functions like $<$ or $\leqslant$.

2.3 Lambda Notation and Polymorphism

Agda is based on the typed lambda calculus. We have already seen that application is written by juxtaposition. Lambda abstraction is either written *Curry-style*

```
\x -> e
```

without a type label on the argument x, or *Church-style*

```
\(x : A) -> e
```

with a type label. The Curry- and Church-style identity functions are

```
\x -> x : A -> A                    \(x : A) -> x : A -> A
```

respectively. See Appendix A.3 for more ways to write abstractions in Agda.

The above typings are valid for any type A, so \x -> x is polymorphic, that is, it has many types. Haskell would infer the type

```
\x -> x :: a -> a
```

for a *type variable* a. (Note that Haskell uses "::" for type membership.) In Agda, however, we have no type variables. Instead we can express the fact that we have a family of identity functions, one for each small type, as follows:

```
id : (A : Set) -> A -> A
id = \(A : Set) -> \(x : A) -> x
```

or as we have written before

```
id A x = x
```

We can also mix these two possibilities:

```
id A = \ x -> x
```

From this follows that id A : A -> A is the identity function on the small type A, that is, we can apply this "generic" identity function id to a type argument A to obtain the identity function from A to A (it is like when we write $\mathtt{id}_A$ in mathematics for the identity function on a set A).

Here we see a first use of dependent types: the type A -> A *depends* on the variable A : Set ranging over the small types. We see also Agda's notation for *dependent function types*; the rule says that if A is a type and B[x] is a type which depends on (is indexed by) (x : A), then (x : A) -> B[x] is the type of functions f mapping arguments (x : A) to values f x : B[x].

If the type-checker can figure out the value of an argument, we can use a wild card character:

```
id _ x : A
```

Here, the system deduces that the wild card character should be filled in by A.

We now show how to define the K and S combinators in Agda:

```
K : (A B : Set) -> A -> B -> A
K _ _ x _ = x

S : (A B C : Set) -> (A -> B -> C) -> (A -> B) -> A -> C
S _ _ _ f g x = f x (g x)
```

(Note the *telescopic* notation (A B : Set) above; see Appendix A.3.)

2.4 Implicit Arguments

Agda also has a more sophisticated abbreviation mechanism, *implicit arguments*, that is, arguments which are omitted. Implicit arguments are declared by enclosing their typings within curly brackets (braces) rather than ordinary parentheses. As a consequence, if we declare the argument `A : Set` of the identity function as implicit, we do not need to lambda-abstract over it in the definition:

```
id : {A : Set} -> A -> A
id = \x -> x
```

We can also omit it on the left hand side of a definition:

```
id x = x
```

Similarly, implicit arguments are omitted in applications:

```
id zero : Nat
```

We can always explicitly write an implicit argument by using curly brackets

`id {Nat} zero : Nat` or even `id {_} zero : Nat`.

2.5 Gödel System T

We shall now show that Gödel System T is a subsystem of Agda. This is a system of primitive recursive functionals [15] which is important in logic and a precursor to Martin-Löf type theory. In both these systems, recursion is restricted to primitive recursion in order to make sure that all programs terminate.

Gödel System T is based on the simply typed lambda calculus with two base types, truth values and natural numbers. (Some formulations code truth values as 0 and 1.) It includes constants for the constructors `true`, `false`, `zero`, and `succ` (successor), and for the conditional and primitive recursion combinators.

First we define the conditional:

```
if_then_else_ : {C : Set} -> Bool -> C -> C -> C
if true then x else y = x
if false then x else y = y
```

(Note the mix-fix syntax and the implicit argument which gives a readable version.)

The primitive recursion combinator for natural numbers is defined as follows:

```
natrec : {C : Set} -> C -> (Nat -> C -> C) -> Nat -> C
natrec p h zero = p
natrec p h (succ n) = h n (natrec p h n)
```

It is a functional (higher-order function) defined by primitive recursion. It receives four arguments: the first (which is implicit) is the return type, the second (called `p` in the equations) is the element returned in the base case, the third (called `h` in the equations) is the step function, and the last is the natural number on which we perform the recursion.

We can now use `natrec` to define addition and multiplication as follows:

```
plus : Nat -> Nat -> Nat
plus n m = natrec m (\x y -> succ y) n

mult : Nat -> Nat -> Nat
mult n m = natrec zero (\x y -> plus y m) n
```

Compare this definition of addition and multiplication in terms of `natrec`, and the one given in Section 2.2 where the primitive recursion schema is expressed by two pattern matching equations.

If we work in Agda and want to make sure that we stay entirely within Gödel system T, we must only use terms built up by variables, application, lambda abstraction, and the constants

```
true, false, zero, succ, if_then_else_, natrec
```

As already mentioned, Gödel system T has the unusual property (for a programming language) that all its typable programs terminate: not only do terms in the base types `Bool` and `Nat` terminate whatever reduction is chosen, but also terms of function type terminate; the reduction rules are β-reduction, and the defining equations for `if_then_else_` and `natrec`.

Reductions can be performed anywhere in a term, so in fact there may be several ways to reduce a term. We say then that Gödel system T is *strongly normalising*, that is, any typable term reaches a normal form whatever reduction strategy is chosen.

In spite of this restriction, we can define many numerical functions in Gödel system T. It is easy to see that we can define all primitive recursive functions (in the usual sense without higher-order functions), but we can also define functions which are not primitive recursive, such as the Ackermann function.

Gödel system T is very important in the history of ideas that led to the Curry-Howard isomorphism and Martin-Löf type theory. Roughly speaking, Gödel system T is the simply typed kernel of Martin-Löf's constructive type theory, and Martin-Löf type theory is the foundational system out of which the Agda language grew. The relationship between Agda and Martin-Löf type theory is much like the relationship between Haskell and the simply typed lambda calculus. Or perhaps it is better to compare it with the relationship between Haskell and Plotkin's PCF [29]. Like Gödel system T, PCF is based on the simply typed lambda calculus with truth values and natural numbers. However, an important difference is that PCF has a fixed point combinator which can be used for encoding arbitrary *general recursive definitions*. As a consequence we can define non-terminating functions in PCF.

Exercise: Define all functions previously given in the text in Gödel System T.

2.6 Parametrised Types

As already mentioned, in Haskell we have parametrised types such as the type `[a]` of lists with elements of type `a`. In Agda the analogous definition is as follows:

```
data List (A : Set) : Set where
  [] : List A
  _::_ : A -> List A -> List A
```

First, this expresses that the type of the list former is

```
List : Set -> Set
```

Note also that we placed the argument type `(A : Set)` to the left of the colon. In this way, we tell Agda that `A` is a *parameter* and it becomes an implicit argument to the constructors:

```
[]   : {A : Set} -> List A
_::_ : {A : Set} -> A -> List A -> List A
```

The list constructor `_::_` ("cons") is an infix operator, and we can declare its precedence as usual.

Note that this list former only allows us to define lists with elements in arbitrary *small* types, not with elements in arbitrary types. For example, we cannot define lists of sets using this definition, since sets form a *large* type.

Now, we define the map function, one of the principal polymorphic list combinators, by pattern matching on the list argument:

```
map : {A B : Set} -> (A -> B) -> List A -> List B
map f [] = []
map f (x :: xs) = f x :: map f xs
```

Exercise: Define some more list combinators like for example `foldl` or `filter`. Define also the list recursion combinator `listrec` which plays a similar rôle as `natrec` does for natural numbers.

Another useful parametrised types is the binary Cartesian product, that is, the type of pairs:

```
data _X_ (A B : Set) : Set where
  <_,_> : A -> B -> A X B
```

We define the two projection functions as:

```
fst : {A B : Set} -> A X B -> A
fst < a , b > = a

snd : {A B : Set} -> A X B -> B
snd < a , b > = b
```

A useful list combinator that converts a pair of lists into a list of pairs is `zip`:

```
zip : {A B : Set} -> List A -> List B -> List (A X B)
zip [] [] = []
zip (x :: xs) (y :: ys) = < x , y > :: zip xs ys
zip _ _ = []
```

Usually we are only interested in zipping lists of equal length. The third equation states that the elements that remain from a list when the other list has been emptied will not be considered in the result. We will return to this later, when we write a dependently typed versions `zip` function in Section 3.

Exercise: Define the sum `A + B` of two small types `A` and `B` as a parametrised data type. It has two constructors: `inl`, which injects an element of `A` into `A + B`, and `inr`, which injects an element of `B` into `A + B`. Define a combinator `case` which makes it possible to define a function from `A + B` to a small type `C` by cases. (Beware that Agda does not support overloading of names except constructor names of different data types, so you cannot define the type `_+_` in a file where the definition of the addition of natural numbers is defined with the name `+` and is in scope.)

2.7 Termination-Checking

In mainstream functional languages one can use general recursion freely; as a consequence we can define partial functions. For example, in Haskell we can define our own division function as (beware of the possible name clash)

```
div m n = if (m < n) then 0 else 1 + div (m - n) n
```

This definition should not be accepted by Agda, since `div` is a partial function: it does not terminate if `n` is zero, whereas Agda requires that all functions terminate.

How can we ensure that all functions terminate? One solution is to restrict all recursion to primitive recursion, like in Gödel system T. We should then only be allowed to define functions by primitive recursion (including primitive list recursion, etc), but not by general recursion as is the case of the function `div`. This is indeed the approach taken in Martin-Löf type theory: all recursion is *primitive* recursion, where primitive recursion should be understood as a kind of *structural* recursion on the *well-founded* data types. We will not go into these details, but the reader is referred to Martin-Löf's book [21] and Dybjer's schema for inductive definitions [10].

Working only with this kind of structural recursion (in one argument at a time) is often inconvenient in practice. Therefore, the Göteborg group has chosen to use a more general form of termination-checking in Agda (and its predecessor ALF). A correct Agda program is one which passes both type-checking and termination-checking, and where the patterns in the definitions cover the whole domain. We will not explain the details of Agda's termination-checker, but limit ourselves to noting that it allows us to do pattern matching on several arguments simultaneously and to have recursive calls to *structurally smaller* arguments. In this way, we have a generalisation of primitive recursion which is practically useful, and still lets us remain within the world of total functions where logic is available via the Curry-Howard correspondence. Agda's termination-checker has not yet been documented and studied rigorously. If Agda will be used as a system for formalising mathematics rigorously, it is advisable to stay within a well-specified subset such as Martin-Löf type theory [24] or Martin-Löf type theory with inductive [10] and inductive-recursive definitions [11,13].

Most programs we have written above only use simple case analysis or primitive (structural) recursion in one argument. An exception is the `zip` function, which has been defined by structural recursion on both arguments simultaneously. This function is obviously terminating and it is accepted by the termination-checker. The `div` function is partial and is of course, not accepted by the termination-checker. However, even a variant which rules out division by zero, but uses repeated subtraction is rejected by the termination-checker although it is actually terminating. The reason is that the termination-checker does not recognise the recursive call to `(m - n)` as structurally smaller. The reason is that subtraction is not a constructor for natural numbers, so further reasoning is required to deduce that the recursive call is actually on a smaller argument (with respect to some well-founded ordering).

When Agda cannot be sure that a recursive function will terminate, it marks the name of the defined function in orange. However, the function is "accepted" nevertheless: Agda leaves it to you to decide whether you want to continue working without its blessing.

In Section 7 we will describe how partial and general recursive functions can be represented in Agda. The idea is to replace a partial function by a total function with an extra argument: a proof that the function terminates on its arguments.

The search for more powerful termination-checkers for dependently typed languages is a subject of current research. Here it should be noted again that it is not sufficient to ensure that all programs of base types terminate, but that programs of all types reduce to normal forms. This involves reducing open terms, which leads to further difficulties. See for example the recent Ph.D. thesis by Wahlstedt [34].

3 Dependent Types

3.1 Vectors of a Given Length

Now it is time to introduce some real dependent types. Consider again the `zip` function that we have presented at the end of Section 2.6, converting a pair of lists into a list of pairs. One could argue that we cannot turn a pair of lists into a list of pairs, unless the lists are equally long. The third equation in the definition of `zip` in page 67 tells us what to do if this is not the case: `zip` will simply cut off the longer list and ignore the remaining elements.

With dependent types we can ensure that the "bad" case never happens. We can use the dependent type of lists of a certain length, often referred to as the dependent type of vectors.

How can we define the dependent type of vectors of length n? There are actually two alternatives.

Recursive family: We define it by induction on n, or put differently, by primitive recursion on n.

Inductive family: We define it as a family of data types by declaring its constructors together with their types. This is just like the definition of the data type of ordinary lists, except that the length information is now included in the types of the constructors.

Below, we will show how to define vectors in Agda in both ways. In the remainder of the notes we will, however, mostly use inductive families. This should not be taken as a statement that inductive families are always more convenient than recursive ones. When both methods are applicable, one needs to carefully consider how they will be used before choosing the one or the other. For each inductive family we define below, the reader should ask him/herself whether there is an alternative recursive definition and if so, write it in Agda.

Vectors as a Recursive Family. In mathematics we might define vectors of length n by induction on n:

$$A^0 = 1$$
$$A^{n+1} = A \times A^n$$

In Agda (and Martin-Löf type theory) this definition is written as follows.

```
Vec : Set -> Nat -> Set
Vec A zero = Unit
Vec A (succ n) = A X Vec A n
```

where `Unit` is the unit type, that is, the type with only one element

```
data Unit : Set where
  <> : Unit
```

Before, we have only used primitive recursion for defining functions where the range is in a given set (in a given small type). Here, we have an example where we use primitive recursion for defining a family of sets, that is, a family of elements in a given large type.

We can now define the `zip` function by induction on the length:

```
zip : {A B : Set} -> (n : Nat) ->
      Vec A n -> Vec B n -> Vec (A X B) n
zip zero v w = <>
zip (succ n) < a , v > < b , w > = < < a , b > , zip n v w >
```

In the base case we return the empty vector, which is defined as the unique element of the unit type. Note that this is type-correct since the right hand side has type `Vec (A X B) zero` which is defined as the type `Unit`. The equation for the step case is type-correct since the right hand side has type

```
Vec (A X B) (succ n) = (A X B) X (Vec (A X B) n),
```

and similarly for the type of the arguments on the left hand side. Agda uses these definitions (which are given by equations) during type-checking to reduce type expressions to their normal form. We will discuss type-checking dependent types in more detail in Section 5.

Exercise: Write the functions `head`, `tail`, and `map` for the recursive vectors.

Vectors as an Inductive Family. We can also define vectors inductively as the following *indexed family* of data types:

```
data Vec (A : Set) : Nat -> Set where
  [] : Vec A zero
  _::_ : {n : Nat} -> A -> Vec A n -> Vec A (succ n)
```

As before, we define the set of vectors for each length `n`, but this time we do not do induction on the length but instead give constructors which generate vectors of different lengths. The constructor `[]` generates a vector of length 0, and `_::_` generates a vector of length ($\mathtt{n} + 1$) from a vector of length `n` by adding an element at the beginning.

Such a data type definition is also called an *inductive family*, or an *inductively defined family of sets*. This terminology comes from constructive type theory, where data types such as `Nat` and `(List A)` are called *inductive types*.

Remark. Beware of terminological confusion. As we have mentioned before, in programming languages one instead talks about *recursive types* for such data types defined by declaring the constructors with their types. This may be a bit confusing since we used the word *recursive family* for a different notion. There is a reason for the terminological distinction between data types in ordinary functional languages, and data types in languages where all programs terminate. In the latter, we will not have any non-terminating numbers or non-terminating lists. The set-theoretic meaning of such types is therefore simple: just build the set inductively generated by the constructors, see [9] for details. In a language with non-terminating programs, however, the semantic domains are more complex. One typically considers various kinds of *Scott domains* which are complete partially orders.

Note that `(Vec A n)` has two arguments: the small type `A` of the elements in the vector, and the length `n` of type `Nat`. Here `A` is a parameter in the sense that it remains the same throughout the definition: for a given `A` we define the family `Vec A : Nat -> Set`. In contrast, `n` is not a parameter since it varies in the types of the constructors. Non-parameters are often called *indices* and we can say that `Vec A` is an inductive family *indexed* by the natural numbers. In the definition of a data type in Agda, parameters are placed to the left of the colon and become implicit arguments to the constructors, whilst indices are placed to the right (observe where the parameter `(A : Set)` and the index type `Nat` appear in the definition of the data type of vectors).

We can now define a version of `zip` where the type ensures that the arguments are equally long vectors and moreover, that the result maintains this length:

```
zip : {A B : Set} -> (n : Nat) ->
      Vec A n -> Vec B n -> Vec (A X B) n
zip zero [] [] = []
zip (succ n) (x :: xs) (y :: ys) = < x , y > :: zip n xs ys
```

Let us analyse this definition. We pattern match on the first vector (of type `Vec A n`) and get two cases. When the vector is empty then it must be the case that `n` is zero. If we now pattern match on the second vector we get only one case, the empty vector, since the type of the second vector must be `Vec B zero`. The type of the result is `Vec (A X B) zero` and hence, we return the empty vector. When the first vector is not empty, that is, it is of the form `(x :: xs)` (for `x` and `xs` of the corresponding type), then the length of the vector should be `(succ n)` for some number `n`. Now again, the second vector should also have length `(succ n)` and hence be of the form `(y :: ys)` (for `y` and `ys` of the corresponding type). The type of `zip` tells us that the result should be a vector of length `(succ n)` of elements of type `A X B`. Note that the third equation we had before (in page 67) is ruled out by type-checking, since it covered a case where the two input vectors have unequal length. In Section 5 we will look into type-checking dependent types in more detail.

Another much discussed problem in computer science is what to do when we try to take the head or the tail of an empty list. Using vectors we can easily forbid these cases:

```
head : {A : Set} {n : Nat} -> Vec A (succ n) -> A
head (x :: _) = x

tail : {A : Set} {n : Nat} -> Vec A (succ n) -> Vec A n
tail (_ :: xs) = xs
```

The cases for the empty vector will not type-check.

Standard combinators for lists often have corresponding variants for dependent types; for example,

```
map : {A B : Set} {n : Nat} -> (A -> B) -> Vec A n -> Vec B n
map f [] = []
map f (x :: xs) = f x :: map f xs
```

3.2 Finite Sets

Another interesting example is the dependent type of finite sets, here defined as an inductive family.

```
data Fin : Nat -> Set where
  fzero : {n : Nat} -> Fin (succ n)
  fsucc : {n : Nat} -> Fin n -> Fin (succ n)
```

For each `n`, the set `(Fin n)` contains exactly `n` elements; for example, `(Fin 3)` contains the elements `fzero`, `fsucc fzero` and `fsucc (fsucc fzero)`.

This data type is useful when we want to access the element at a certain position in a vector: if the vector has `n` elements and the position of the element is given by `(Fin n)`, we are sure that we access an element inside the vector. Let us look at the type of such a function:

```
_!_ : {A : Set} {n : Nat} -> Vec A n -> Fin n -> A
```

If we pattern match on the vector (we work with the inductive definition of vectors), we have two cases, the empty vector and the non-empty one. If the vector is non-empty, then we know that `n` should be of the form `(succ m)` for some `(m : Nat)`. Now, the elements of `Fin (succ m)` are either `fzero` and then we should return the first element of the vector, or `(fsucc i)` for some `(i : Fin m)` and then we recursively call the function to look for the `i`th element in the tail of the vector.

What happens when the vector is empty? Here `n` must be zero. According to the type of the function, the fourth argument of the function is of type `(Fin 0)` which has no elements. This means that there is no such case. In Agda this function can be expressed as follows:

```
_!_ : {A : Set} {n : Nat} -> Vec A n -> Fin n -> A
[] ! ()
(x :: xs) ! fzero = x
(x :: xs) ! fsucc i = xs ! i
```

The `()` in the second line above states that there are no elements in `(Fin 0)` and hence, that there is no equation for the empty vector. So `[] ! ()` is not an equation like the others, it is rather an annotation which tells Agda that there is no equation. The type-checker will of course check that this is actually the case.

We will discuss empty sets more in Section 4.

Exercise: Rewrite the function `_!!_` so that it has the following type:

```
_!!_ : {A : Set}{n : Nat} -> Vec A (succ n) -> Fin (succ n) -> A
```

This will eliminate the empty vector case, but which other cases are needed?

Exercise: Give an alternative definition of `Fin` as a recursive family.

3.3 More Inductive Families

Just as we can use dependent types for defining lists of a certain length, we can use them for defining binary trees of a certain height:

```
data DBTree (A : Set) : Nat -> Set where
  dlf : A -> DBTree A zero
  dnd : {n : Nat} -> DBTree A n -> DBTree A n ->
        DBTree A (succ n)
```

With this definition, any given `(t : DBTree A n)` is a perfectly balanced tree with 2^n elements and information in the leaves.

Exercise: Modify the above definition in order to define the height balanced binary trees, that is, binary trees where the difference between the heights of the left and right subtree is at most one.

Exercise: Define lambda terms as an inductive family indexed by the maximal number of free variables allowed in the term. Try also to define typed lambda terms as an inductive family indexed by the type of the term.

4 Propositions as Types

As we already mentioned in the introduction, Curry observed in the 1930's that there is a one-to-one correspondence between propositions in *propositional logic* and types. In the 1960's, de Bruijn and Howard introduced dependent types because they wanted to extend Curry's correspondence to *predicate logic*. Through the work of Scott [30] and Martin-Löf [19], this correspondence became the basic building block of a new foundational system for constructive mathematics: Martin-Löf's *intuitionistic type theory*.

We shall now show how intuitionistic predicate logic with equality is a subsystem of Martin-Löf type theory by realising it as a theory in Agda.

4.1 Propositional Logic

The idea behind the Curry-Howard isomorphism is that each *proposition* is interpreted as the *set* of its proofs. To emphasise that "proofs" here are "first-class" mathematical object one often talks about *proof objects*. In constructive mathematics they are often referred to as *constructions*. A proposition is *true* iff its set of proofs is inhabited; it is *false* iff its set of proofs is empty.

We begin by defining *conjunction*, the connective "and", as follows:

```
data _&_ (A B : Set) : Set where
  <_,_> : A -> B -> A & B
```

Let `A` and `B` be two propositions represented by their sets of proofs. Then, the first line states that `A & B` is also a set (a set of proofs), representing the conjunction of `A` and `B`. The second line states that all elements of `A & B`, that is, the proofs of `A & B`, have the form `< a , b >`, where `(a : A)` and `(b : B)`, that is, `a` is a proof of `A` and `b` is a proof of `B`. We note that the definition of conjunction is nothing but the definition of the *Cartesian product* of two sets: an element of the Cartesian product is a pair of elements of the component sets. We could equally well have defined

```
_&_ : Set -> Set -> Set
A & B = A X B
```

This is the Curry-Howard *identification* of conjunction and Cartesian product.

It may surprise the reader familiar with propositional logic, that all proofs of `A & B` are pairs (of proofs of `A` and proofs of `B`). In other words, that all such proofs are obtained by applying the constructor of the data type for `&` (sometimes one refers to this as the rule of `&`-*introduction*). Surely, there must be other ways to prove a conjunction, since there are many other axioms and inference rules. The explanation of this mystery is that we distinguish between *canonical proofs* and *non-canonical* proofs. When we say that all proofs of `A & B` are pairs of proofs of `A` and proofs of `B`, we actually mean that all *canonical* proofs of `A & B` are pairs of *canonical* proofs of `A` and *canonical* proofs of `B`. This is the so called *Brouwer-Heyting-Kolmogorov (BHK)*-interpretation of logic, as refined and formalised by Martin-Löf.

The distinction between canonical proofs and non-canonical proofs is analogous to the distinction between canonical and non-canonical elements of a set; see Section 2.2. As we have already mentioned, by using the rules of computation we can always reduce a non-canonical natural number to a canonical one. The situation is analogous for sets of proofs: we can always reduce a non-canonical proof of a proposition to a canonical one using simplification rules for proofs. We shall now see examples of such simplification rules.

We define the two rules of &-elimination as follows

```
fst : {A B : Set} -> A & B -> A
fst < a , b > = a

snd : {A B : Set} -> A & B -> B
snd < a , b > = b
```

Logically, these rules state that if `A & B` is true then `A` and `B` are also true. The justification for these rules uses the definition of the set of canonical proofs of `A & B` as the set of pairs `< a , b >` of canonical proofs `(a : A)` and of canonical proofs `(b : B)`. It immediately follows that if `A & B` is true then `A` and `B` are also true.

The proofs

```
fst < a , b > : A                  snd < a , b > : B
```

are *non-canonical*, but the *simplification rules* (also called equality rules, computation rules, reduction rules) explain how they are converted into canonical ones:

```
fst < a , b > = a                  snd < a , b > = b
```

The definition of *disjunction* (connective "or") follows similar lines. According to the BHK-interpretation a (canonical) proof of `A \/ B` is *either* a (canonical) proof of `A` *or* a (canonical) proof of `B`:

```
data _\/_ (A B : Set) : Set where
  inl : A -> A \/ B
  inr : B -> A \/ B
```

Note that this is nothing but the definition of the *disjoint union* of two sets: disjunction corresponds to disjoint union according to Curry-Howard. (Note that we use the *disjoint* union rather than the ordinary union.)

At the end of Section 2.6 you were asked to define the disjoint union of two sets `A` and `B`. Once we have defined `A + B`, we can define `\/` in terms of `+` in the same way as we defined `&` in terms of `X` above:

```
_\/_ : Set -> Set -> Set
A \/ B = A + B
```

Furthermore, the rule of \/-elimination is nothing but the rule of case analysis for a disjoint union:

```
case : {A B C : Set} -> A \/ B -> (A -> C) -> (B -> C) -> C
case (inl a) d e = d a
case (inr b) d e = e b
```

We can also introduce the proposition which is always true, that we call `True`, which corresponds to the unit set (see page 70) according to Curry-Howard:

```
data True : Set where
  <> : True
```

The proposition `False` is the proposition that is false by definition, and it is nothing but the empty set according to Curry-Howard. This is the set which is defined by stating that it has no canonical elements.

```
data False : Set where
```

This set is sometimes referred as the "absurdity" set and denoted by $\bot$.

The rule of $\bot$-elimination states that if one has managed to prove `False`, then one can prove any proposition `A`. This can of course only happen if one started out with contradictory assumptions. It is defined as follows:

```
nocase : {A : Set} -> False -> A
nocase ()
```

The justification of this rule is the same as the justification of the existence of an empty function from the empty set into an arbitrary set. Since the empty set has no elements there is nothing to define; it is definition by *no cases*. Recall the explanation on page 72 when we used the notation `()`.

Note that to write "no case" in Agda, that is, cases on an empty set, one writes a "dummy case" `nocase ()` rather than actually no cases. The dummy case is just a marker that tells the Agda-system that there are no cases to consider. It should not be understood as a case analogous with the lines defining `fst`, `snd`, and `case` above.

As usual in constructive logic, to prove the negation of a proposition is the same as proving that the proposition in question leads to absurdity:

```
Not : Set -> Set
Not A = A -> False
```

According to the BHK-interpretation, to prove an implication is to provide a *method* for transforming a proof of `A` into a proof of `B`. When Brouwer pioneered this idea about 100 years ago, there were no computers and no models of computation. But in modern constructive mathematics in general, and in Martin-Löf type theory in particular, a "method" is usually understood as a *computable function* (or computer program) which transforms proofs. Thus we define *implication* as function space. To be clear, we introduce some new notation for implications:

```
_==>_ : (A B : Set) -> Set
A ==> B = A -> B
```

The above definition is not accepted in Martin-Löf's own version of propositions-as-sets. The reason is that each proposition should be defined by stating what its canonical proofs are. A canonical proof should always begin with a *constructor*, but a function in `A -> B` does not, unless one considers the lambda-sign (the symbol \ in Agda for variable abstraction in a function) as a constructor.

Instead, Martin-Löf defines implication as a set with one constructor:

```
data _==>_ (A B : Set) : Set where
  fun : (A -> B) -> A ==> B
```

If `==>` is defined in this way, a canonical proof of `A ==> B` always begins with the constructor `fun`. The rule of `==>`-elimination (modus ponens) is now defined by pattern matching:

```
apply : {A B : Set} -> A ==> B -> A -> B
apply (fun f) a = f a
```

This finishes the definition of propositional logic inside Agda, except that we are of course free to introduce other connectives, such as *equivalence* of propositions:

```
_<==>_ : Set -> Set -> Set
A <==> B  =   (A ==> B) & (B ==> A)
```

Exercise: Prove your favourite tautology from propositional logic. Beware that you will not be able to prove the *law of the excluded middle* `A \/ Not A`. This is a consequence of the definition of disjunction, can you explain why?. The law of the excluded middle is not available in intuitonistic logic, only in classical logic.

4.2 Predicate Logic

We now move to predicate logic and introduce the *universal* and *existential quantifiers.*

The BHK-interpretation of universal quantification (for all) ∀ `x : A. B` is similar to the BHK-interpretation of implication: to prove ∀ `x : A. B` we need to provide a method which transforms an arbitrary element `a` of the domain `A` into a proof of the proposition `B[x:=a]`, that is, the proposition `B` where the free variable `x` has been instantiated (substituted) by the term `a`. (As usual we must avoid capturing free variables.) In this way we see that universal quantification is interpreted as the *dependent function space*. An alternative name is *Cartesian product of a family of sets*: a universal quantifier can be viewed as the conjunction of a family of propositions. Another common name is the "Π-set", since Cartesian products of families of sets are often written Π`x : A. B`.

```
Forall : (A : Set) -> (B : A -> Set) -> Set
Forall A B = (x : A) -> B x
```

Remark. Note that implication can be defined as a special case of universal quantification: it is the case where `B` does not depend on `(x : A)`.

For similar reasons as for implication, Martin-Löf does not accept the above definition in his version of the BHK-interpretation. Instead he defines the universal quantifier as a data type with one constructor:

```
data Forall (A : Set) (B : A -> Set) : Set where
  dfun : ((a : A) -> B a) -> Forall A B
```

Exercise: Write the rule for ∀-elimination.

According to the BHK-interpretation, a proof of ∃x : A. B consists of an element (a : A) and a proof of B[x:=a].

```
data Exists (A : Set) (B : A -> Set) : Set where
  [_,_] : (a : A) -> B a -> Exists A B
```

Note the similarity with the definition of conjunction: a proof of an existential proposition is a pair [a , b], where (a : A) is a *witness*, an element for which the proposition (B a) is true, and (b : B a) is a *proof* object of this latter fact.

Thinking in terms of Curry-Howard, this is also a definition of the *dependent product.* An alternative name is then the *disjoint union of a family of sets*, since an existential quantifier can be viewed as the disjunction of a family of propositions. Another common name is the "Σ-set", since disjoint union of families of sets are often written Σx : A. B.

Given a proof of an existential proposition, we can extract the witness:

```
dfst : {A : Set} {B : A -> Set} -> Exists A B -> A
dfst [ a , b ] = a
```

and the proof that the proposition is indeed true for that witness:

```
dsnd : {A : Set}{B : A -> Set} -> (p : Exists A B) -> B (dfst p)
dsnd [ a , b ] = b
```

As before, these two rules can be justified in terms of canonical proofs.

We have now introduced all rules needed for a Curry-Howard representation of *untyped* constructive predicate logic. We only need a special (unspecified) set D for the domain of the quantifiers.

However, Curry-Howard immediately gives us a *typed* predicate logic with a very rich type-system. In this typed predicate logic we have further laws. For example, there is a dependent version of the \/-elimination:

```
dcase : {A B : Set} -> {C : A \/ B -> Set} -> (z : A \/ B) ->
        ((x : A) -> C (inl x)) -> ((y : B) -> C (inr y)) -> C z
dcase (inl a) d e = d a
dcase (inr b) d e = e b
```

Similarly, we have the dependent version of the other elimination rules, for example the dependent version of the ⊥-elimination is as follows:

```
dnocase : {A : False -> Set} -> (z : False) -> A z
dnocase ()
```

Exercise: Write the dependent version of the remaining elimination rules.

Exercise: Prove now a few tautologies from predicate logic. Be aware that while classical logic always assumes that there exists an element we can use in the proofs, this is not the case in constructive logic. When we need an element of the domain set, we must explicitly state that such an element exists.

4.3 Equality

Martin-Löf defines equality in predicate logic [18] as the set inductively generated by the reflexive rule. This definition was then adapted to intuitionistic type theory [19], where the *equality* relation is given a propositions-as-sets interpretation as the following inductive family:

```
data _==_ {A : Set} : A -> A -> Set where
  refl : (a : A) -> a == a
```

This states that `(refl a)` is a canonical proof of `a == a`, provided `a` is a canonical element of `A`. More generally, `(refl a)` is a canonical proof of `a' == a''` provided both `a'` and `a''` have `a` as their canonical form (obtained by simplification).

The rule of ==-elimination is the rule which allows us to substitute equals for equals:

```
subst : {A : Set} -> {C : A -> Set} -> {a' a'' : A} ->
        a' == a'' -> C a' -> C a''
subst (refl a) c = c
```

This is proved by pattern matching: the only possibility to prove `a' == a''` is if they have the same canonical form `a`. In this case, (the canonical forms of) `C a'` and `C a''` are also the same; hence they contain the same elements.

4.4 Induction Principles

In Section 2.5 we have defined the combinator `natrec` for primitive recursion over the natural numbers and used it for defining addition and multiplication. Now we can give it a more general dependent type than before: the parameter `C` can be a family of sets over the natural numbers instead of simply a set:

```
natrec : {C : Nat -> Set} -> (C zero) ->
         ((m : Nat) -> C m -> C (succ m)) -> (n : Nat) -> C n
natrec p h zero = p
natrec p h (succ n) = h n (natrec p h n)
```

Because of the Curry-Howard isomorphism, we know that `natrec` does not necessarily need to return an ordinary element (like a number, or a list, or a function) but also a proof of some proposition. The type of the result of `natrec` is determined by `C`. When defining `plus` or `mult`, `C` will be instantiated to the constant family `(\n -> Nat)` (in the dependently typed version of `natrec`). However, `C` can be a property (propositional function) of the natural numbers, for example, "to be even" or "to be a prime number". As a consequence, `natrec` can not only be used to define functions over natural numbers but also to prove propositions over the natural numbers. In this case, the type of `natrec` expresses the principle of *mathematical induction*: if we prove a property for 0, and prove the property for $m + 1$ assuming that it holds for m, then the property holds for arbitrary natural numbers.

Suppose we want to prove that the two functions defining the addition in Section 2 (`+` and `plus`) give the same result. We can prove this by induction, using `natrec` as follows (let `_==_` be the propositional equality defined in Section 4.3):

```
eq-plus-rec : (n m : Nat) -> n + m == plus n m
eq-plus-rec n m = natrec (refl m) (\k' ih -> eq-succ ih) n
```

Here, the proof `eq-succ : {n m : Nat} -> n == m -> succ n == succ m` can also be defined (proved) using `natrec`. (Actually, the Agda system cannot infer what `C` –in the definition of `natrec`– would be in this case so, in the proof of this property, we would actually need to explicitly write the implicit argument as `{(\k -> k + m == plus k m)}`.)

Exercise: Prove `eq-succ` and `eq-mult-rec`, the equivalent to `eq-plus-rec` but for `*` and `mult`.

As we mentioned before, we could define structural recursion combinators analogous to the primitive recursion combinator `natrec` for any inductive type (set). Recall that inductive types are introduced by a `data` declaration containing its constructors and their types. These combinators would allow us both to define functions by structural recursion, and to prove properties by structural induction over those data types. However, we have also seen that for defining functions, we actually did not need the recursion combinators. If we want to, we can express structural recursion and structural induction directly using pattern matching (this is the alternative we have used in most examples in these notes). In practice, this is usually more convenient when proving and programming in Agda, since the use of pattern matching makes it easier to both write the functions (proofs) and understand what they do.

Let us see how to prove a property by induction without using the combinator `natrec`. We use pattern matching and structural recursion instead:

```
eq-plus : (n m : Nat) -> n + m == plus n m
eq-plus zero m = refl m
eq-plus (succ n) m = eq-succ (eq-plus n m)
```

This function can be understood as usual. First, the function takes two natural numbers and produces an element of type `n + m == plus n m`. Because of the Curry-Howard isomorphism, this element happens to be a proof that the addition of both numbers is the same irrespectively of whether we add them by using `+` or by using `plus`. We proceed by cases on the first argument. If `n` is 0 we need to give a proof of (an element of type) `0 + m == plus 0 m`. If we reduce the expressions on both sides of `_==_`, we see that we need a proof of `m == m`. This proof is simply `(refl m)`. The case where the first argument is `(succ n)` is more interesting: here we need to return an element (a proof) of `succ (n + m) == succ (plus n m)` (after making the corresponding reductions for the successor case). If we have a proof of `n + m == plus n m`, then applying the function `eq-succ` to that proof will do it. Observe that the recursive call to `eq-plus` on the number `n` gives us exactly a proof of the desired type.

Exercise: Prove `eq-succ` and `eq-mult` using pattern matching and structural recursion.

Remark. According to the Curry-Howard interpretation, a proof by structural induction corresponds to a definition of a function by structural recursion: recursive calls correspond to the use of induction hypotheses.

5 Type-Checking Dependent Types

Type-checking dependent types is considerably more complex than type-checking (non-dependent) Hindley-Milner types. Let us now look more closely at what happens when type-checking the `zip` function on vectors.

```
zip : {A B : Set} -> (n : Nat) ->
      Vec A n -> Vec B n -> Vec (A X B) n
zip zero [] [] = []
zip (succ n) (x :: xs) (y :: ys) = < x , y > :: zip n xs ys
```

There are several things to check in this definition.

First, we need to check that the type of `zip` is well-formed. This is relatively straightforward: we check that `Set` is well-formed, that `Nat` is well-formed, that `(Vec A n)` is well-formed under the assumptions that `(A : Set)` and `(n : Nat)`, and that `(Vec B n)` is well-formed under the assumptions that `(B : Set)` and `(n : Nat)`. Finally, we check that `(Vec (A X B) n)` is well-formed under the assumptions `(A : Set)`, `(B : Set)` and `(n : Nat)`.

Then, we need to check that the left hand sides and the right hand sides of the equations have the same well-formed types. For example, in the first equation `(zip zero [] [])` and `[]` must have the type `(Vec (A X B) zero)`; etc.

5.1 Pattern Matching with Dependent Types

Agda requires patterns to be *linear*, that is, the same variable must not occur more than once. However, situations arise when one is tempted to repeat a variable. To exemplify this, let us consider a version of the `zip` function where we explicitly write the index of the second constructor of vectors:

```
zip : {A B : Set} -> (n : Nat) ->
      Vec A n -> Vec B n -> Vec (A X B) n
```

```
zip zero [] [] = []
zip (succ n) (_::_ {n} x xs) (_::_ {n} y ys) =
                                  < x , y > :: zip n xs ys
```

The type-checker will complain since the variable n occurs three times. Trying to avoid this non-linearity by writing different names

```
zip (succ n) (_::_ {m} x xs) (_::_ {h} y ys) = ....
```

or even the wild card character instead of a variable name

```
zip (succ n) (_::_ {_} x xs) (_::_ {_} y ys) = ....
```

will not help. The type-checker must check that, for example, the vector (_::_ {m} x xs) has size (succ n) but it does not have enough information for deducing this. What to do? The solution is to distinguish between what is called *accessible patterns*, which arise from explicit pattern matching, and *inaccessible patterns*, which arise from index instantiation. Inaccessible patterns must then be prefixed with a "." as in

```
zip (succ n) (_::_ .{n} x xs) (_::_ .{n} y ys) =
                                  < x , y > :: zip n xs ys
```

The accessible parts of a pattern must form a well-formed linear pattern built from constructors and variables. Inaccessible patterns must refer only to variables bound in the accessible parts. When computing the pattern matching at run time only the accessible patterns need to be considered, the inaccessible ones are guaranteed to match simply because the program is well-typed. For further reading about pattern matching in Agda we refer to Norell's Ph.D. thesis [25].

It is worth noting that patterns in indices (that is, inaccessible ones) are not required to be constructor combinations. Arbitrary terms may occur as indices in inductive families, as the following definition of the image of a function (taken from [25]) shows:

```
data Image {A B : Set} (f : A -> B) : B -> Set where
  im : (x : A) -> Image f (f x)
```

If we want to define the right inverse of f for a given (y : B), we can pattern match on a proof that y is in the image of f:

```
inv : {A B : Set} (f : A -> B) -> (y : B) -> Image f y -> A
inv f .(f x) (im x) = x
```

Observe that the term y should be instantiated to (f x), which is not a constructor combination.

5.2 Normalisation during Type-Checking

Let us now continue to explain type-checking with dependent types. Consider the following definition of the append function over vectors, where _+_ is the function defined in Section 2.2:

```
_++_ : {A : Set} {n m : Nat} -> Vec A n -> Vec A m ->
        Vec A (n + m)
[] ++ ys = ys
(x :: xs) ++ ys = x :: (xs ++ ys)
```

Let us analyse what happens "behind the curtains" while type-checking the equations of this definition. Here we pattern match on the first vector. If it is empty, then we return the second vector unchanged. In this case `n` must be `zero`, and we know by the first equation in the definition of `_+_` that `zero + m = m`. Hence, we need to return a vector of size `m`, which is exactly the type of the argument `ys`. If the first vector is not empty, then we know that `n` must be of the form `(succ n')` for some `(n' : Nat)`, and we also know that `(xs : Vec A n')`. Now, by definition of `_+_`, append must return a vector of size `succ (n' + m)`. By definition of append, we have that `(xs ++ ys : Vec A (n' + m))`, and by the definition of (the second constructor of) the data type of vectors we know that adding an element to a vector of size `(n' + m)` returns a vector of size `succ (n' + m)`. So here again, the resulting term is of the expected type.

This example shows how we simplify (normalise) expressions during type checking. To show that the two sides of the first equation for append have the same type, the type-checker needs to recognise that `zero + m = m`, and to this end it uses the first equation in the definition of `_+_`. Observe that it simplifies an *open* expression: `zero + m` contains the free variable `m`. This is different from the usual situation: when evaluating a term in a functional programming language, equations are only used to simplify *closed* expressions, that is, expressions where there are no free variables.

Let us now consider what would happen if we define addition of natural numbers by recursion on the second argument instead of on the first. That is, if we would have the following definition of addition, which performs the task equally well:

```
_+'_ : Nat -> Nat -> Nat
n +' zero = n
n +' succ m = succ (n +' m)
```

Will the type-checker recognise that `zero +' m = m`? No, it is not sufficiently clever. To check whether two expressions are equal, it will only use the defining equations in a left-to-right manner and this is not sufficient. It will not try to do induction on `m`, which is what is needed here.

Let us see how this problem typically arises when programming in Agda. One of the key features of Agda is that it helps us to construct a program step-by-step. In the course of this construction, Agda will type-check half-written programs, where the unknown parts are represented by terms containing ?-signs. The part of the code denoted by "?" is called a *goal*, something that the programmer has left to do. Agda type-checks such half-written programs, tells us whether it is type-correct so far, and also tells the types of the goals; see Appendix A.5 for more details.

Here is a half-written program for append defined by pattern matching on its first argument; observe that the right hand sides are not yet written:

```
_++'_ : {A : Set} {n m : Nat} -> Vec A n -> Vec A m ->
        Vec A (n +' m)
[] ++' ys = ?
(x :: xs) ++' ys = ?
```

In the first equation we know that `n` is `zero`, and we know that the resulting vector should have size `(zero +' m)`. However, the type-checker does not know at this stage what the result of `(zero +' m)` is. The attempt to refine the first goal with the term `ys` will simply not succeed. If one looks at the definition of `_+'_`, one sees that the type-checker only knows the result of an addition when the *second* number is either `zero` or of the form `succ` applied to another natural number. But so far, we know nothing about the size `m` of the vector `ys`. While we know from school that addition on natural numbers is commutative and hence, `zero +' m == m +' zero` (for some notion of equality over natural numbers, as for example the one defined in Section 4.3), the type-checker has no knowledge about this property unless we prove it. What the type-checker does know is that `m +' zero = m` by definition of the new addition. So, if we are able to prove that `zero +' m == m +' zero`, we will know that `zero +' m == m`, since terms that are defined to be equal are replaceable.

Can we finish the definition of the append function, in spite of this problem? The answer is yes. We can prove the following substitutivity rule:

```
substEq : {A : Set} -> (m : Nat) -> (zero +' m) == m ->
          Vec A m -> Vec A (zero +' m)
```

which is just a special case of the more general substitutivity rule defined in 4.3 (prove `substEq` using `subst` as an exercise). We can then instantiate the "?" in the first equation with the term

```
substEq m (eq-z m) ys : Vec A (zero +' m)
```

where `eq-z m` is a proof that `zero +' m == m`. This proof is an explicit *coercion* which changes the type of `ys` to the appropriate one. It is of course undesirable to work with terms which are decorated with logical information in this way, and it is often possible (but not always) to avoid this situation by judicious choice of definitions.

Ideally, we would like to have the following *substitutivity* rule:

$$\frac{\texttt{ys} : \texttt{Vec A m} \qquad \texttt{zero} +' \texttt{m} == \texttt{m}}{\texttt{ys} : \texttt{Vec A} (\texttt{zero} +' \texttt{m})}$$

This rule is actually available in *extensional intuitionistic type theory* [20,21], which is the basis of the NuPRL system [6]. However, the drawback of extensional type theory is that we loose normalisation and decidability of type-checking. As a consequence, the user has to work on a lower level since the system cannot check equalities automatically by using normalisation. NuPRL compensates for this by using so called *tactics* for proof search. Finding a suitable compromise between the advantages of extensional and intensional type theory is a topic of current research.

Remark. Notice the difference between the equality we wrote above as _==_ and the one we wrote as _=_. Here, the symbol _=_, which we have used when introducing the definition of functions, stands for *definitional equality*. When two terms `t` and `t'` are defined to be equal, that is, they are such that `t = t'`, then the type-checker can tell that they are the same by reducing them to normal form. Hence, substitutivity is automatic and the type-checker will accept a term `h` of type `(C t)` whenever it expects a term of type `(C t')` and vice versa, without needing extra logical information.

The symbol _==_ stands, in these notes, for a *propositional equality*, see Section 4.3. It is an equivalence relation, it is substitutive, and `t = t'` implies `t == t'`.

6 Agda as a Programming Logic

In Sections 2 and 3 we have seen how to write functional programs in type theory. Those programs include many of the programs one would write in a standard functional programming language such as Haskell. There are several important differences however. Agda requires all programs to terminate whereas Haskell does not. In Agda we need to cover all cases when doing pattern matching, but not in Haskell. And in Agda we can write programs with more complex types, since we have dependent types. For example, in Section 4 we have seen how to use the Curry-Howard isomorphism to represent propositions as types in predicate logic.

In this section, we will combine the aspects discussed in the previous sections and show how to use Agda as a programming logic. In other words, we will use the system to prove properties of our programs. Observe that when we use Agda as a programming logic, we limit ourselves to programs that pass Agda's termination-checker. So we need to practise writing programs which use structural recursion, maybe simultaneously in several arguments.

To show the power of dependent types in programming we consider the program which inserts an element into a binary search tree. Binary search trees are binary trees whose elements are sorted. We approach this problem in two different ways.

In our first solution we work with binary trees as they would be defined in Haskell, for example. Here, we define a predicate that checks when a binary tree is sorted and an insertion function that, when applied to a sorted tree, returns a sorted tree. We finally show that the insertion function behaves as expected, that is, that the resulting tree is indeed sorted. This approach is sometimes called *external programming logic*: we write a program in an ordinary type system and afterwards we prove a property of it. The property is a logical "comment".

In our second solution, we define a type which only contains sorted binary trees. So these binary trees are sorted by construction. The data type of sorted binary trees is defined simultaneously with two functions which check that the elements in the subtrees are greater (smaller) than or equal to the root (respectively). This is an example of an *inductive-recursive* definition [11,12]. This is a kind of definition available in Agda which we have not yet encountered. We then define an insertion function over those trees, which is also correct by construction: its type ensures that sorted trees are mapped into sorted trees. This approach is sometimes called *integrated* or *internal programming logic*: the logic is integrated with the program.

We end this section by sketching alternative solutions to the problem. The interested reader can test his/her understanding of dependent types by filling all the gaps in the ideas we mention here.

Due to space limitations, we will not be able to show *all* proofs and codes in here. In some cases, we will only show the types of the functions and explain what they do (sometimes this is obvious from the type). We hope that by now the reader has enough knowledge to fill in the details on his or her own.

In what follows let us assume we have a set `A` with an inequality relation `<=` that is total, anti-symmetric, reflexive and transitive:

```
A : Set
_<=_ : A -> A -> Set
tot : (a b : A) -> (a <= b) \/ (b <= a)
antisym : {a b : A} -> a <= b -> b <= a -> a == b
refl : (a : A) -> a <= a
trans : {a b c : A} -> a <= b -> b <= c -> a <= c
```

Such assumptions can be declared as *postulates* in Agda. They can also be module parameters (see Appendix A.1).

We shall use a version of binary search trees which allows multiple occurrences of an element. This is a suitable choice for representing multi-sets. If binary search trees are used to represent sets, it is preferable to keep just one copy of each element only. The reader can modify the code accordingly as an exercise.

6.1 The Data Type of Binary Trees and the Sorted Predicate

Let us define the data type of binary trees with information on the nodes:

```
data BTree : Set where
  lf : BTree
  nd : A -> BTree -> BTree -> BTree
```

We want to define the property of being a sorted tree. We first define when all elements in a tree are smaller than or equal to a certain given element (below, the element `a`):

```
all-leq : BTree -> A -> Set
all-leq lf a = True
all-leq (nd x l r) a = (x <= a) & all-leq l a & all-leq r a
```

What does this definition tell us? The first equation says that all elements in the empty tree (just a leaf with no information) are smaller than or equal to `a`.

The second equation considers the case where the tree is a node with root `x` and subtrees `l` and `r`. (From now on we take the convention of using the variables `l` and `r` to stand for the left and the right subtree, respectively). The equation says that all elements in the tree `(nd x l r)` will be smaller than or equal to `a` if `x <= a`, that is, `x` is smaller than or equal to `a`, and also all elements in both `l` and `r` are smaller than or equal to `a`. Notice the two structurally recursive calls in this definition.

Remark. Note that this is a recursive definition of a set. In fact, we could equally well have chosen to return a truth value in `Bool` since the property `all-leq` is *decidable*. In general, a property of type `A -> Bool` is decidable, that is, there is an algorithm which for an arbitrary element of `A` decides whether the property holds for that element or not. A property of type `A -> Set` may not be decidable, however. As we learn in computability theory, there is no general method for looking at a proposition (e.g. in predicate logic) and decide whether it is true or not. Similarly, there is no general method for deciding whether a `Set` in Agda is inhabited or not.

Exercise: Write the similar property which is true when all elements in a tree are greater than or equal to a certain element:

```
all-geq : BTree -> A -> Set
```

Finally, a tree is sorted when its leaves increase from right to left:

```
Sorted : BTree -> Set
Sorted lf = True
Sorted (nd a l r) = (all-geq l a & Sorted l) &
                    (all-leq r a & Sorted r)
```

The empty tree is sorted. A non-empty tree will be sorted if all the elements in the left subtree are greater than or equal to the root, if all the elements in the right subtree are smaller than or equal to the root, and if both subtrees are also sorted. (The formal definition actually requires the proofs in a different order, but we can prove that `&` is commutative, hence the explanation is valid.)

Let us now define a function which inserts an element in a sorted tree in the right place so that the resulting tree is also sorted.

```
insert : A -> BTree -> BTree
insert a lf = nd a lf lf
insert a (nd b l r) with tot a b
... | inl _ = nd b l (insert a r)
... | inr _ = nd b (insert a l) r
```

The empty case is easy. To insert an element into a non-empty tree we need to compare it to the root of the tree to decide whether we should insert it into the right or into the left subtree. This comparison is done by `(tot a b)`.

Here we use a new feature of Agda: the `with` construct which lets us analyse `(tot a b)` before giving the result of `insert`. Recall that `(tot a b)` is a proof that either a <= b or b <= a. The insertion function performs case analysis on this proof. If the proof has the form (inl _) then a <= b (the actual proof of this is irrelevant, which is denoted by a wild card character) and we (recursively) insert a into the right subtree. If b <= a (this is given by the fact that the result of (tot a b) is of the form inr _) we insert a into the left subtree.

The with construct is very useful in the presence of inductive families; see Appendix A.4 for more information.

Observe that the type of the function neither tells us that the input tree nor that the output tree are sorted. Actually, one can use this function to insert an element into a unsorted tree and obtain another unsorted tree.

So how can we be sure that our function behaves correctly when it is applied to a sorted tree, that is, how can we be sure it will return a sorted tree? We have to prove it.

Let us assume we have the following two proofs:

```
all-leq-ins : (t : BTree) -> (a b : A) -> all-leq t b ->
              a <= b -> all-leq (insert a t) b

all-geq-ins  : (t : BTree) -> (a b : A) -> all-geq t b ->
              b <= a -> all-geq (insert a t) b
```

The first proof states that if all elements in the tree t are smaller than or equal to b, then the tree that results from inserting an element a such that a <= b, is also a tree where all the elements are smaller than or equal to b. The second proof can be understood similarly.

We can now prove that the tree that results from inserting an element into a sorted tree is also sorted. Note that a proof that a non-empty tree is sorted consist of four subproofs, structured as a pair of pairs of proofs; recall that the constructor of a pair of proofs is the mix-fix operator <_,_> (see Section 4.1).

```
sorted : (a : A) -> (t : BTree) -> Sorted t ->
         Sorted (insert a t)
sorted a lf _ = < < <> , <> > , < <> , <> > >
sorted a (nd b l r) < < pl1 , pl2 > , < pr1 , pr2 > >
   with tot a b
... | inl h = < < pl1 , pl2 > ,
                < all-leq-ins r a b pr1 h , sorted a r pr2 > >
... | inr h = < < all-geq-ins l a b pl1 h , sorted a l pl2 > ,
                < pr1 , pr2 > >
```

Again, the empty case is easy. Let t be the tree (nd b l r). The proof that t is sorted is given here by the term < < pl1 , pl2 > , < pr1 , pr2 > > where pl1 : all-geq l b, pl2 : Sorted l, pr1 : all-leq r b, and pr2 : Sorted r. Now, the actual resulting tree, (insert a t), will depend on how the element a compares to the root b. If a <= b, with h being a proof of that statement, we leave the left subtree unchanged and we insert the new element in the right subtree. Since both the left subtree and the root remain the same, the proofs that all the elements in the left subtree are greater than or equal to the root, and the proof that the left subtree is sorted, are the same as before. We construct the corresponding proofs for the new right subtree `(insert a r)`. We know by `pr1` that all the elements in `r` are smaller than or equal to `b`, and by `h` that `a <= b`. Hence, by applying `all-leq-ins` to the corresponding arguments we obtain one of the proofs we need, that is, a proof that all the elements in `(insert a r)` are smaller than or equal to `b`. The last proof needed in this case is a proof that the tree `(insert a r)` is sorted, which is obtained by the inductive hypothesis. The case where `b <= a` is similar.

This proof tells us that if we start from the empty tree, which is sorted, and we only add elements to the tree by repeated use of the function `insert` defined above, we obtain yet another sorted tree.

Alternatively, we could give the insertion function the following type:

```
insert : A -> (t : BTree) -> Sorted t ->
         Exists BTree (\(t' : BTree) -> Sorted t')
```

This type expresses that both the input and the output trees are sorted: the output is a pair consisting of a tree and a proof that it is sorted. The type of this function is a more refined *specification* of what the insertion function does. An insert function with this type needs to manipulate both the output trees and the proof objects which are involved in verifying the sorting property. Here, computational information is mixed with logical information. Note that the information that the initial tree is sorted will be needed to produce a proof that the resulting tree will also be sorted.

Exercise: Write this version of the insertion function.

6.2 An Inductive-Recursive Definition of Binary Search Trees

The idea here is to define a data type of sorted binary trees, that is, a data type where binary trees are sorted already by construction.

What would such a data type look like? The data type must certainly contain a constructor for the empty tree, since this is clearly sorted. What should the constructor for the node case be? Let `BSTree` be the type we want to define, that is, the type of sorted binary trees. If we only want to construct sorted trees, it is not enough to provide a root `a` and two sorted subtrees `l` and `r`, we also need to know that all elements in the left subtree are greater than or equal to the root (let us denote this by `l >=T a`), and that all elements in the right subtree are smaller than or equal to the root (let us denote this by `r <=T a`). The fact that both subtrees are sorted can be obtained simply by requiring that both subtrees have type `BSTree`, which is the type of sorted binary trees.

The relations `(_>=T_)` and `(_<=T_)` are defined by recursion on `BSTree`. Moreover, they appear in the types of the constructors of `BSTree`. This is a phenomenon that does not arise when defining data types in ordinary functional programming. Is it really a consistent definition method? The answer is yes, such mutual *inductive-recursive* definitions [11,12] are constructively valid. Inductive-recursive definitions increase the *proof-theoretic strength* of the theory since they can be used for defining large universes analogous to large cardinals in set theory.

The definitions of both relations for the empty tree are trivial. If we want to define when all the elements in a non-empty tree with root `x` and subtrees `l` and `r` are greater than or equal to an element `a`, that is, `(snd x l r _ _) >=T a`, we need to check that `a <= x` and that `r >=T a`. Notice that since this tree is sorted, it should be the case that `l >=T x` and hence, that `l >=T a` (prove this "transitivity" property), so we do not need to explicitly ask for this relation to hold. The condition `a <= x` might also seem redundant, but it is actually needed unless we consider the singleton tree as a special case. If we simple remove that condition from the definition we present below, it is easy to see that we could prove `t >=T a` for any tree `t` and element `a`. The definition of the relation `_<=T_` for non-empty trees is analogous.

The formal definition of the data type together with these two relations is as follows:

```
mutual
  data BSTree  : Set where
    slf : BSTree
    snd : (a : A) -> (l r : BSTree) -> (l >=T a) ->
          (r <=T a) -> BSTree

  _>=T_ : BSTree -> A -> Set
  slf >=T a = True
  (snd x l r _ _) >=T a = (a <= x) & (r >=T a)

  _<=T_ : BSTree -> A -> Set
  slf <=T a = True
  (snd x l r _ _) <=T a = (x <= a) & (l <=T a)
```

Remark. We tell Agda that we have a mutual definition by prefixing it with the keyword `mutual` (see Appendix A.1). This keyword is used for all kinds of mutual definitions: mutual inductive definitions, mutual recursive definitions, and mutual inductive-recursive definitions.

Exercise: Define a function

```
bst2bt : BSTree -> BTree
```

that converts sorted binary trees into regular binary tree by simply keeping the structure and forgetting all logical information.

Prove that the tree resulting from this conversion is sorted:

```
bst-sorted : (t : BSTree) -> Sorted (bst2bt t)
```

Define also the other conversion function, that is, the functions that takes a regular binary tree that is sorted and returns a sorted binary tree:

```
sorted-bt2bst : (t : BTree) -> Sorted t -> BSTree
```

Let us return to the definition of the insertion function for this data type. Let us simply consider the non-empty tree case from now on. Similarly to how we defined the function `insert` above, we need to analyse how the new element to insert (called `a` below) compares with the root of the tree (called `x` below) in order to decide in which subtree the element should be actually inserted. However, since we also need to provide extra information in order to make sure we are constructing a sorted tree, the work does not end here. We must show that all the elements in the new right subtree are smaller than or equal to `x` when `a <= x` (this proof is called `sins-leqT` below), or that all the elements in the new left subtree are greater than or equal to `x` when `x <= a` (this proof is called `sins-geqT` below).

```
mutual
  sinsert : (a : A) -> BSTree -> BSTree
  sinsert a slf = snd a slf slf <> <>
  sinsert a (snd x l r pl pr) with (tot a x)
  ... | inl p = snd x l (sinsert a r) pl (sins-leqT a x r pr p)
  ... | inr p = snd x (sinsert a l) r (sins-geqT a x l pl p) pr

  sins-geqT : (a x : A) -> (t : BSTree) -> t >=T x -> x <= a ->
              (sinsert a t) >=T x
  sins-geqT _ _ slf _ q = < q , <> >
  sins-geqT a x (snd b l r _ _) < h1 , h2 > q with tot a b
  ... | inl _ = < h1 , sins-geqT a x r h2 q >
  ... | inr _ = < h1 , h2 >

  sins-leqT : (a x : A) -> (t : BSTree) -> t <=T x -> a <= x ->
              (sinsert a t) <=T x
  sins-leqT _ _ slf _ q = < q , <> >
  sins-leqT a x (snd b l r _ _) < h1 , h2 > q with tot a b
  ... | inl _ = < h1 , h2 >
  ... | inr _ = < h1 , sins-leqT a x l h2 q >
```

Let us study in detail the second equation in the definition of `sins-geqT`. The reader should do a similar analysis to make sure he/she understands the rest of the code as well. Given `a`, `x` and `t` such that `t >=T x` and `x <= a`, we want to show that if we insert `a` in `t`, all elements in the resulting tree are also greater than or equal to `x`. Let `t` be a node with root `b` and subtrees `l` and `r`. Let `q` be the proof that `x <= a`. In this case, the proof of `t >=T x` is a pair consisting of a proof `h1 : x <= b` and a proof `h2 : r >=T x`. In order to know what the resulting tree will look like, we analyse the result of the expression `(tot a b)` with the `with` construct. If `a <= b`, we leave the left subtree unchanged and we add `a` in the right subtree. The root of the resulting tree is still `b`. To prove the desired result in this case we need to provide a proof that `x <= b`, in this case `h1`, and a proof that `(sinsert a r >=T x)`, which is given by the induction hypothesis since `r` is a subterm of `t` and `r >=T x` (given by `h2`). In the case where `b <= a` we insert `a` into the left subtree and hence, the desired result is simply given by the pair `< h1 , h2 >`.

6.3 Bounded Binary Search Trees

There are more ways to define binary search trees. When programming with dependent types, it is crucial to use effective definitions, and trying different alternatives is often worth-while. When proving, one pays an even higher price for poor design choices than when programming in the ordinary way.

For the binary search trees example, another possibility is to define bounded binary search trees, that is binary search trees where all the elements are between a lower and upper bound. This gives a smooth way to define an inductive family indexed by these bounds. In this way we do not need an inductive-recursive definition but only an inductive definition. The type of the insertion function will now specify the bounds of the resulting tree.

Exercise: Define bounded binary search trees with an insertion function in Agda. How can we define a type of unbounded binary search trees from the type of bounded ones?

Write functions converting between the different kinds of binary trees discussed above.

7 General Recursion and Partial Functions

In Section 2.7 we mentioned that Agda's type-checker will not itself force us to use primitive recursion; we can use general recursion which then will be checked -and rejected- by the termination-checker. In this way, the type-checker will allow us to define partial functions such as division, but they will not pass the termination-checker. Even total functions like the quicksort algorithm will not be accepted by the termination-checker because the recursive calls are not to *structurally* smaller arguments.

We have also mentioned that in order to use Agda as a programming logic, we should restrict ourselves to functions that pass both the type-checker and the termination-checker. In addition, the Agda system checks that definitions by pattern matching cover all cases. This prevents us from writing partial functions (recursive or not) such as a head function on lists, which does not have a case for empty lists. (Note that Agda always performs termination-checking and coverage-checking in connection with type-checking. The user does not need to call them explicitly.)

Ideally, we would like to define in Agda more or less any function that can be defined in Haskell, and also we would like to use the expressive power provided by dependent types to prove properties about those functions.

One way to do this has been described by Bove and Capretta [5]. Given the definition of a general recursive function, the idea is to define a domain predicate that characterises the inputs on which the function will terminate.

A general recursive function of n arguments will be represented by an Agda-function of $n + 1$ arguments, where the extra (and last) argument is a proof that the n first arguments satisfy the domain predicate. The domain predicate will be defined inductively, and the $n + 1$-ary function will be defined by structural recursion on its last argument. The domain predicate can easily and automatically be determined from the recursive equations defining the function. If the function is defined by nested recursion, the domain predicate and the $n + 1$-ary function need to be defined simultaneously: they form a simultaneous inductive-recursive definition, just like in the binary search trees in the previous section.

We illustrate Bove and Capretta's method by showing how to define division on natural numbers in Agda; for further reading on the method we refer to [5].

Let us first give a slightly different Haskell version of the division function:

```
div m n | m < n = 0
div m n | m >= n = 1 + div (m - n) n
```

This function cannot be directly translated into Agda for two reasons. First, and less important, Agda does not provide Haskell conditional equations. Second, and more fundamental, this function would not be accepted by Agda's termination-checker since it is defined by general recursion, which might lead to non-termination. For this particular example, when the second argument is zero the function is partial since it will go on for ever computing the second equation.

But, as we explained in Section 2.7, even ruling out the case when `n` is zero would not help. Although the recursive argument to the function actually decreases when `0 < n` (for the usual notions of –cut-off– `_-_` and of the less-than relation on the natural numbers), the recursive call is not on a *structurally* smaller argument. Hence, the system does not realise that the function will actually terminate because `(m - n)` is not structurally smaller than `m` (there is obvious room for improvement here and, as already mentioned, making more powerful termination-checkers is a topic of current research).

What does the definition of `div` tell us? If `(m < n)`, then the function terminates (with the value 0). Otherwise, if `(m >= n)`, then the function terminates on the inputs `m` and `n` provided it terminates on the inputs `(m - n)` and `n`. This actually amounts to an inductive definition of a domain predicate expressing on which pairs of natural numbers the division algorithm terminates. If we call this predicate `DivDom`, we can express the text above by the following two rules:

$$\frac{\mathtt{m} < \mathtt{n}}{\mathtt{DivDom\ m\ n}} \qquad \frac{\mathtt{m} >= \mathtt{n} \qquad \mathtt{DivDom}\ (\mathtt{m} - \mathtt{n})\ \mathtt{n}}{\mathtt{DivDom\ m\ n}}$$

Given the Agda definition of the two relations

```
_<_ : Nat -> Nat -> Set
_>=_ : Nat -> Nat -> Set
```

we can easily define an inductive predicate for the domain of the division function as follows:

```
data DivDom : Nat -> Nat -> Set where
  div-dom-lt : (m n : Nat) -> m < n -> DivDom m n
  div-dom-geq : (m n : Nat) -> m >= n -> DivDom (m - n) n ->
                DivDom m n
```

Observe that there is no proof of `(DivDom m 0)`. This corresponds to the fact that `(div m 0)` does not terminate for any `m`. The constructor `div-dom-lt` cannot be used to obtain such a proof since we will not be able to prove that `(m < 0)` (assuming the relation was defined correctly). On the other hand, if we want to use the constructor `div-dom-geq` to build a proof of `(DivDom m 0)`, we first need to build a proof of `(DivDom (m - 0) 0)`, which means, we first need a proof of `(DivDom m 0)`! Moreover, if `n` is not zero, then there is precisely one way to prove `(DivDom m n)` since either `(m < n)` or `(m >= n)`, but not both.

Exercise: Define in Agda the two relations

```
_<_ : Nat -> Nat -> Set
_>=_ : Nat -> Nat -> Set
```

We can now represent division as an Agda function with a third argument: a proof that the first two arguments belong to the domain of the function. Formally, the function is defined by pattern matching on this last argument, that is, on the proof that the two arguments satisfy the domain predicate `DivDom`.

```
div : (m n : Nat) -> DivDom m n -> Nat
div .m .n (div-dom-lt m n p) = zero
div .m .n (div-dom-geq m n p q) = 1 + div (m - n) n q
```

(Observe also the "." notation in the definition of `div`, which was explained in Section 5.)

Pattern matching on `(DivDom m n)` gives us two cases. In the first case, given by `div-dom-lt`, we have that `(p : m < n)`. Looking at the Haskell version of the algorithm, we know that we should simply return zero here. In the second case, given by `div-dom-geq`, we have that `(p : m >= n)` and that `(m - n)` and `n` satisfy the relation `DivDom` (with `q` a proof of this). If we look at the Haskell version of the algorithm, we learn that we should now recursively call the division function on the arguments `(m - n)` and `n`. Now, in the Agda version of this function, unlike in the Haskell one, we also need to provide a proof that `DivDom (m - n) n`, but this is exactly the type of `q`.

The definition of the division function is now accepted both by the type-checker and by the termination-checker and hence, we can use Agda as a programming logic and prove properties about the division function, as we showed in Section 6.

However, it is worth noting that in order to use the function `div` (either to run it or to prove something about it) we need to provide a proof that its arguments satisfy the domain predicate for the function. When the actual domain of the function is easy to identify, it might be convenient to prove a lemma, once and for all, establishing the set of elements for which the domain predicate is satisfied. For our example, this lemma could have the following type:

```
divdom : (m n : Nat) -> Not (n == zero) -> DivDom m n
```

Then, given the numbers `m` and `n` and a proof `p` that `n` is not zero, we can call the division function simply as `(div m n (divdom m n p))`.

References

1. Abel, A., Coquand, T., Dybjer, P.: On the algebraic foundation of proof assistants for intuitionistic type theory. In: Garrigue, J., Hermenegildo, M.V. (eds.) FLOPS 2008. LNCS, vol. 4989, pp. 3–13. Springer, Heidelberg (2008)
2. Abel, A., Coquand, T., Dybjer, P.: Verifying a semantic beta-eta-conversion test for Martin-Löf type theory. In: Audebaud, P., Paulin-Mohring, C. (eds.) MPC 2008. LNCS, vol. 5133, pp. 29–56. Springer, Heidelberg (2008)
3. Agda wiki (2008), `appserv.cs.chalmers.se/users/ulfn/wiki/agda.php`
4. Bertot, Y., Castéran, P.: Interactive Theorem Proving and Program Develpment. Coq'Art: The Calculus of Inductive Constructions. Springer, Heidelberg (2004)
5. Bove, A., Capretta, V.: Modelling general recursion in type theory. Mathematical Structures in Computer Science 15, 671–708 (2005)
6. Constable, R.L., et al.: Implementing Mathematics with the NuPRL Proof Development System. Prentice-Hall, Englewood Cliffs (1986)
7. Coquand, T.: An algorithm for testing conversion in type theory. In: Logical Frameworks, pp. 255–279. Cambridge University Press, Cambridge (1991)
8. Coquand, T., Kinoshita, Y., Nordström, B., Takeyama, M.: A simple type-theoretic language: Mini-tt. In: Levy, J.-J., Bertot, Y., Huet, G., Plotkin, G. (eds.) From Semantics to Computer Science: Essays in Honor of Gilles Kahn, pp. 139–164. Cambridge University Press, Cambridge (2008)
9. Dybjer, P.: Inductive sets and families in Martin-Löf's type theory and their set-theoretic semantics. In: Logical Frameworks, pp. 280–306. Cambridge University Press, Cambridge (1991)
10. Dybjer, P.: Inductive families. Formal Aspects of Computing 6, 440–465 (1994)
11. Dybjer, P.: A general formulation of simultaneous inductive-recursive definitions in type theory. Journal of Symbolic Logic 65(2) (June 2000)
12. Dybjer, P., Setzer, A.: A finite axiomatization of inductive-recursive definitions. In: Girard, J.-Y. (ed.) TLCA 1999. LNCS, vol. 1581, pp. 129–146. Springer, Heidelberg (1999)
13. Dybjer, P., Setzer, A.: Indexed induction-recursion. Journal of Logic and Algebraic Programming 66(1), 1–49 (2006)
14. Girard, J.Y.: Une extension de l'interprétation de Gödel à l'analyse, et son application à l'elimination des coupures dans l'analyse et la théorie des types. In: Fenstad, J.E. (ed.) Proceedings of the Second Scandinavian Logic Symposium, pp. 63–92. North-Holland Publishing Company, Amsterdam (1971)
15. Gödel, K.: Über eine bisher noch nicht benutze erweitrung des finiten standpunktes. Dialectica 12 (1958)
16. Hinze, R.: A new approach to generic functional programming. In: Proceedings of the 27th Annual ACM SIGPLAN-SIGACT Symposium on Principles of Programming Languages, Boston, Massachusetts (January 2000)
17. Jansson, P., Jeuring, J.: PolyP — a polytypic programming language extension. In: POPL 1997, pp. 470–482. ACM Press, New York (1997)

18. Martin-Löf, P.: Hauptsatz for the Intuitionistic Theory of Iterated Inductive Definitions. In: Fenstad, J.E. (ed.) Proceedings of the Second Scandinavian Logic Symposium, pp. 179–216. North-Holland Publishing Company, Amsterdam (1971)
19. Martin-Löf, P.: An Intuitionistic Theory of Types: Predicative Part. In: Rose, H.E., Shepherdson, J.C. (eds.) Logic Colloquium 1973, pp. 73–118. North-Holland Publishing Company, Amsterdam (1975)
20. Martin-Löf, P.: Constructive mathematics and computer programming. In: Logic, Methodology and Philosophy of Science, VI, 1979, pp. 153–175. North-Holland, Amsterdam (1982)
21. Martin-Löf, P.: Intuitionistic Type Theory. Bibliopolis (1984)
22. McBride, C.: Epigram: Practical programming with dependent types. In: Vene, V., Uustalu, T. (eds.) AFP 2004. LNCS, vol. 3622, pp. 130–170. Springer, Heidelberg (2005)
23. Milner, R., Tofte, M., Harper, R., MacQueen, D.: The Definition of Standard ML. MIT Press, Cambridge (1997)
24. Nordström, B., Petersson, K., Smith, J.M.: Programming in Martin-Löf's Type Theory. An Introduction. Oxford University Press, Oxford (1990)
25. Norell, U.: Towards a practical programming language based on dependent type theory. PhD thesis, Department of Computer Science and Engineering, Chalmers University of Technology, SE-412 96 Göteborg, Sweden (September 2007)
26. Peyton Jones, S. (ed.): Haskell 98 Language and Libraries The Revised Report. Cambridge University Press, Cambridge (2003)
27. Peyton Jones, S., Vytiniotis, D., Weirich, S., Washburn, G.: Simple unification-based type inference for GADTs. In: ICFP 2006: Proceedings of the Eleventh ACM SIGPLAN International Conference on Functional Programming, pp. 50–61. ACM Press, New York (2006)
28. Pfenning, F., Xi, H.: Dependent Types in practical programming. In: Proc. 26th ACM Symp. on Principles of Prog. Lang., pp. 214–227 (1999)
29. Plotkin, G.D.: LCF considered as a programming language. Theor. Comput. Sci. 5(3), 225–255 (1977)
30. Scott, D.: Constructive validity. In: Symposium on Automatic Demonstration. Lecture Notes in Mathematics, vol. 125, pp. 237–275. Springer, Berlin (1970)
31. Taha, W., Sheard, T.: Metaml and multi-stage programming with explicit annotations. Theor. Comput. Sci. 248(1-2), 211–242 (2000)
32. The Coq development team. The Coq proof assistant (2008), `coq.inria.fr/`
33. Thompson, S.: Type Theory and Functional Programming. Addison-Wesley, Reading (1991)
34. Wahlstedt, D.: Dependent Type Theory with Parameterized First-Order Data Types and Well-Founded Recursion. PhD thesis, Chalmers University of Technology (2007) ISBN 978-91-7291-979-2

A More about the Agda System

Documentation about Agda with examples (both programs and proofs) and instructions on how to download the system can be found on the Agda Wiki page `http://appserv.cs.chalmers.se/users/ulfn/wiki/agda.php`. Norell's Ph.D thesis [25] is a good source of information about the system and its features.

A.1 Short Remarks on Agda Syntax

Indentation. When working with Agda, beware that, as in Haskell, indentation plays a major role.

White Space. Agda likes white spaces; the following typing judgement is not correct:

```
not:Bool->Bool
```

The reason is that the set of characters is not partitioned into those which can be used in operators and those which can be used in identifiers (or other categories), since doing that for the full set of Unicode characters is neither tractable nor desirable. Hence, strings like `xs++ys` and `a->b` are treated as one token.

Comments. Comments in Agda are as in Haskell. Short comments begin with "`--`" followed by whitespace, which turns the rest of the line into a comment. Long comments are enclosed between `{-` and `-}`; whitespace separates these delimiters from the rest of the text.

Postulates. Agda has a mechanism for assuming that certain constructions exist, without actually defining them. In this way we can write down postulates (axioms), and reason on the assumption that these postulates are true. We can also introduce new constants of given types, without constructing them. Beware that this allows us to introduce an element in the empty set.

Postulates are introduced by the keyword `postulate`. Some examples are

```
postulate S : Set
postulate one : Nat
postulate _<=_ : Nat -> Nat -> Set
postulate zero-lower-bound : (n : Nat) -> zero <= n
```

Here we introduce a set `S` about which we know nothing; an arbitrary natural number `one`; and a binary relation `<=` on natural numbers about which we know nothing but the fact that `zero` is a least element with respect to it.

Modules. All definitions in Agda should be inside a module. Modules can be parametrised and can contain submodules. There should only be one main module per file and it should have the same name as the file. We refer to the Agda Wiki for details.

Mutual Definitions. Agda accepts mutual definitions: mutually inductive definitions of sets and families, mutually recursive definitions of functions, and mutually inductive-recursive definitions [11,13].

A block of mutually recursive definitions is introduced by the keyword `mutual`.

A.2 Built-In Representation of Natural Numbers

In order to use decimal representation for natural numbers and the built-in definitions for addition and multiplication of natural numbers, one should give the following code to Agda (for the names of the data type, constructors and operation given in these notes):

```
{-# BUILTIN NATURAL Nat #-}
{-# BUILTIN ZERO zero #-}
{-# BUILTIN SUC succ #-}
{-# BUILTIN NATPLUS _+_ #-}
{-# BUILTIN NATTIMES _*_ #-}
```

Internally, closed natural numbers will be represented by Haskell integers and addition of closed natural numbers will be computed by Haskell integer addition.

A.3 More on the Syntax of Abstractions and Function Definitions

Repeated lambda abstractions are common. Agda allows us to abbreviate the Church-style abstractions

`\(A : Set) -> \(x : A) -> x` as `\(A : Set) (x : A) -> x`

If we use Curry-style and omit type labels, we can abbreviate

`\A -> \x -> x` as `\A x -> x`

Telescopes. When several arguments have the same types, as `A` and `B` in

```
K : (A : Set) -> (B : Set) -> A -> B -> A
```

we do not need to repeat the type:

```
K : (A B : Set) -> A -> B -> A
```

This is called *telescopic* notation.

A.4 The `with` Construct

The `with` construct is useful when we are defining a function and we need to analyse an intermediate result on the left hand side of the definition rather than on the right hand side. When using `with` to pattern match on intermediate results, the terms matched on are abstracted from the goal type and possibly also from the types of previous arguments.

The `with` construct is not a basic type-theoretic construct. It is rather a convenient shorthand. A full explanation and reduction of this construct is beyond the scope of these notes.

The (informal) syntax is as follows: if when defining a function `f` on the pattern `p` we want to use the `with` construct on the expression `d` we write:

```
f p with d
f p1 | q1 = e1
     :
f pn | qn = en
```

where `p1`,...,`pn` are instances of `p`, and `q1`,...,`qn` are the different possibilities for `d`. An alternative syntax for the above is:

```
f p with d
... | q1 = e1
     :
... | qn = en
```

where we drop the information about the pattern `pi` which corresponds to the equation.

There might be more than one expression `d` we would like to analyse, in which case we write:

```
f p with d1 | ... | dm
f p1 |   q11 | ... | q1m = e1
      :
f pn |   qn1 | ... | qnm = en
```

The `with` construct can also be nested. Beware that mixing nested `with` and ... notation to the left will not always behave as one would expect; it is recommended to not use the ... notation in these cases.

A.5 Goals

Agda is a system which helps us to interactively write a correct program. It is often hard to write the whole program before type-checking it, especially if the type expresses a complex correctness property. Agda helps us to build up the program interactively; we write a partially defined term, where the undefined parts are marked with "?". Agda checks that the partially instantiated program is type-correct so far, and shows us both the type of the undefined parts and the possible constrains they should satisfy. Those "unknown" terms are called *goals* and will be filled-in later, either at once or by successive refinement of a previous goal. Goals cannot be written anywhere. They may have to satisfy certain constraints and there is a *context* which contains the types of the variables that may be used when instantiating the goal. There are special commands which can be used for instantiating goals or for inspecting the context associated to a certain goal.

A Tutorial on Type-Based Termination

Gilles Barthe[1], Benjamin Grégoire[2], and Colin Riba[2]

[1] IMDEA Software, Madrid, Spain
[2] INRIA Sophia-Antipolis, France

Abstract. Type-based termination is a method to enforce termination of recursive definitions through a non-standard type system that introduces a notion of size for inhabitants of inductively defined types. The purpose of this tutorial is to provide a gentle introduction to a polymorphically typed λ-calculus with type-based termination, and to the size inference algorithm which is used to guarantee automatically termination of recursive definitions.

1 Introduction

Functional programming languages advocate the use of mathematically intuitive constructions to develop programs. In particular, functional programming languages feature mechanisms to introduce and manipulate finite datatypes such as lists and trees, and infinite datatypes such as streams and infinite trees. There are two basic ingredients to manipulate elements of a datatype: case analysis, that enables to reason by analysis on the top constructor, and fixpoints, that enable to define functions by recursion and co-recursion. Traditionally, functional programming languages allow for unrestricted fixpoints, which are subsumed by the construction

$$\frac{\Gamma, f : \tau \vdash e \ : \ \tau}{\Gamma \vdash (\mathsf{letrec}_\tau \ f = e) \ : \ \tau}$$

whose computational behavior is given by the reduction rule

$$(\mathsf{letrec}_\tau \ f = e) \quad \to \quad e[f := (\mathsf{letrec}_\tau \ f = e)]$$

Unrestricted use of fixpoints leads to typable expressions that diverge, i.e. that have an infinite reduction sequence. While non-termination is acceptable in functional programming languages, logical systems based on type theory must be terminating in order to guarantee coherence and decidability of equivalence between terms. Thus, logical systems based on type theory seek to restrict the usage of recursive definitions to enforce termination.

A standard means to enforce termination is to abandon the syntax of functional programming languages and to rely instead on combinators, known as recursors. Such recursors allow to define functions of type $d \to \sigma$, where d is an inductive datatype such as natural numbers of lists; more generally, the notion of inductive datatype captures in a type-theoretical setting the notion of least fixpoint of a monotone operator. To guarantee termination, recursors combine case

A. Bove et al. (Eds.): LerNet ALFA Summer School 2008, LNCS 5520, pp. 100–152, 2009.

analysis and structural recursion, and their reduction rules ensure that recursive calls are applied to smaller arguments. Unfortunately, recursors are not intuitive to use. Therefore, proof assistants based on type theory, such as Coq and Agda, tend to rely on an alternative approach, that maintains the syntax of functional programming languages, but imposes instead syntactic conditions that ensure termination. Restrictions concern both the typing rule and the reduction rule. Restrictions for the typing rule impose conditions, both on the type τ and on the expression e, under which recursive definitions are well-formed. Essentially, the type τ must be of the form $d \to \sigma$, where d is an inductive datatype, as for recursors. Then, the expression e must be of the form $\lambda x : d.\ b$ where b can only make recursive calls to f on arguments that are structurally smaller than x. Finally, reductions must be restricted to the case where e is applied to an expression of the form $c\ \boldsymbol{t}$ for some constructor c. While the first and third restrictions are easily enforced, it is difficult to find appropriate criteria that enforce the second restriction. A common means to ensure that recursive calls are performed on smaller arguments is to define a syntactic check on the body b of recursive calls. However, such a syntactic approach is problematic, as shall be explained in the course of this chapter.

Type-based termination is an alternative approach to guarantee strong normalization of typable expressions through the use of a non-standard typing system in which inhabitants of inductive datatypes are given a size, which in turn is used to guarantee termination of recursive definitions. Type-based termination draws its inspiration from the set-theoretic and domain-theoretic semantics of inductive definitions, in which inductive sets are viewed as the upper limit of their approximation. In effect, type-based termination embeds these semantical intuitions into the syntax of the type theory, by letting inductive datatypes carry size annotations, and by restricting the rule for fixpoints

$$\frac{\Gamma, f : d^{\imath} \to \sigma \vdash e \ :\ d^{\widehat{\imath}} \to \sigma}{\Gamma \vdash (\mathsf{letrec}_{d^{\infty} \to \sigma}\ f = e)\ :\ d^{\infty} \to \sigma}$$

where d is an inductive datatype, $\imath$ is an arbitrary (i.e. implicitly quantified universally) size, $d^{\imath}$ denotes the $\imath$-approximation of d, and $d^{\widehat{\imath}}$ denotes the next approximation of d, and d^{∞} denotes the inductive datatype itself. As should appear from the typing rule, termination is enforced naturally by requiring that recursive calls, that correspond to occurrences of f in e, can only be made to smaller elements, as f only takes as arguments elements of type $d^{\imath}$.

Type-based termination benefits from essential characteristics that make it an attractive means to ensure termination of recursive definitions in a typed λ-calculus, both from the point of view of the users and of the designers of the type system. First and foremost, it is intuitive and easy to grasp, since the type system simply captures the idea that a recursive definition terminates whenever the size of arguments decreases in recursive calls. As a consequence, the type system is also predictable (i.e. it is possible to have *a priori* an intuition as to whether a definition is correct) and transparent (i.e. it is possible *a posteriori* to understand why a definition is incorrect) for users, which we view as essential properties of a formal system. Second, type-based termination is expressive: even for the simplest instance of type-based termination, in which the arithmetic of stages only builds on zero, successor and infinity, type-based termination is sufficiently powerful to encode many typed λ-calculi using syntactic termination criteria, and to provide precise typings for some functions that do not increase the size of their arguments (i.e. for unary functions the size of the result is smaller or equal than the size of the argument). Third, type-based termination is based on a solid theoretical foundation, namely that of approximation, which substantially simplifies in the development of realizability models. As shall be illustrated in Section 3.4, there is a good match between the syntax of the type system and its semantics, which facilitates the interpretation of recursive definitions in the realizability model. Fourth, type-based termination isolates in the design of the type system itself the components that are relevant for termination, i.e. constructors, case analysis, and fixpoint definitions, from the remaining components, whose syntax and typing rules are unaffected. Such a separation makes type-based termination robust to language extensions, and compatible with modular verification and separate compilation.

In summary, type-based termination appears as a suitable approach to guarantee strong normalization of typable terms, which in the near future may well supplant syntactic methods that are currently in use in logical systems based on type theory. On this account, the main objective of this tutorial is to provide a gentle introduction to type-based termination. For pedagogical purposes, we start with a review of mechanisms to introduce recursive definitions in typed λ-calculi, and proceed to define a type system that uses type-based termination. Then, we provide high-level proofs of the essential properties of the type system, in particular of strong normalization and of decidability of type inference; we explain the latter in great length, because of the complexity of the algorithm. We conclude with a brief examination of some possible extensions to our system, and a brief account of related work. For simplicity, we focus on a polymorphically typed λ-calculus, although all of the results that we present in this chapter scale up to dependent types.

2 Computations in Polymorphic Type Systems

This section presents the basic framework of this tutorial and the main problem we want to address: having a convenient way for computing in type systems issued from the Curry-Howard isomorphism, while preserving crucial logical properties such as subject reduction, strong normalization and coherence.

We start in Sect. 2.1 from Girard's System F, with terms *à la* Church, as presented in [12]. This system enjoys strong normalization and coherence, and can encode every inductive datatype and every function provably total in second order Peano arithmetic [12]. However, the algorithmic behavior of System F is unsatisfactory, since basic functions such as the predecessor function on Church's numerals is not implementable in constant time [15], and it is more generally the case of primitive recursion over all inductive datatypes, at least when the computing relation is β-reduction [16].

Hence, from a computational point of view, it is convenient to add datatypes and recursion to System F, leading to System F^{rec} presented in Sect. 2.2. However, F^{rec} lacks both strong normalization and coherence, because of general recursion and of the ability to define non well-founded datatypes.

As a first step towards a well-behaved system, we introduce in Sect. 2.3 the notion of *inductive datatype*. Then, we recall in Sect. 2.5 a syntactic termination criteria, which allows to retrieve strong normalization and coherence. The limitations of such criteria motivate the use of type-based termination, to be presented in Sect. 3.

2.1 System *F*

Types. We assume given a set $\mathcal{V}_{\mathcal{T}}$ of type variables. The set $\mathcal{T}$ of types is given by the abstract syntax:

$$\mathcal{T} ::= \mathcal{V}_{\mathcal{T}} \mid \mathcal{T} \to \mathcal{T} \mid \Pi \mathcal{V}_{\mathcal{T}}.\, \mathcal{T}$$

Types are denoted by lower-case Greek letters $\sigma, \tau, \theta, \ldots$. Free and bound variables are defined as usual. The capture-avoiding substitution of $\boldsymbol{\tau}$ for $\boldsymbol{X}$ in σ is written $\sigma[\boldsymbol{X} := \boldsymbol{\tau}]$. We let $\mathsf{FV}_{\mathcal{T}}(e)$ be the set of type variable occurring free in τ. A type τ is *closed* if $\mathsf{FV}_{\mathcal{T}}(\tau) = \emptyset$.

Example 2.1.
(i) The type of the polymorphic identity is

$$\Pi X.\, X \to X$$

(ii) It is well-known that inductive datatypes can be coded into System F, see e.g. [12]. For instance, Peano natural numbers can be encoded as *Church's numerals*, whose type is

$$\mathsf{N_{Ch}} \quad := \quad \Pi X.\, X \to (X \to X) \to X$$

From this type, we can read that Church numerals represent the free structure built from one nullary constructor (which stands for 0), and one unary constructor (which stands for the successor).
(iii) The "false" proposition is

$$\bot \quad := \quad \Pi X.\, X$$ □

Terms and reductions. We assume given a set $\mathcal{V}_{\mathcal{E}} = \{x, y, z, \ldots\}$ of *(object) variables*. The set $\mathcal{E}$ of *terms* is given by the abstract syntax:

$$\mathcal{E} ::= \mathcal{V}_{\mathcal{E}} \mid \lambda \mathcal{V}_{\mathcal{E}} : \mathcal{T}.\, \mathcal{E} \mid \Lambda \mathcal{V}_{\mathcal{T}}.\, \mathcal{E} \mid \mathcal{E}\, \mathcal{E} \mid \mathcal{E}\, \mathcal{T}$$

Free and bound variables, substitution, etc. are defined as usual. The capture-avoiding substitution of e' for x in e is written $e[x := e']$. We let $\mathsf{FV}_{\mathcal{E}}(e)$ be the set of free term variables occurring in e. We say that e is *closed* when $\mathsf{FV}_{\mathcal{E}}(e) = \emptyset$.

The reduction calculus is given by β-reduction $\rightarrow_\beta$, which is defined as the compatible closure of

$$(\lambda x : \tau.\ e)\ e' \quad \succ_\beta \quad e[x := e'] \qquad \text{and} \qquad (\Lambda X.\ e)\ \tau \quad \succ_\beta \quad e[X := \tau]$$

The relation $\rightarrow_\beta$ is confluent.

Notation 2.2. *We write $e \rightarrow^n_\beta e'$ if there is $k \leq n$ such that*

$$e \quad \underbrace{\rightarrow_\beta \quad \dots \quad \rightarrow_\beta}_{k\ times} \quad e'$$

Example 2.3.

(i) The polymorphic identity is $\Lambda X.\ \lambda x : X.\ x$.

(ii) The Church's numerals are terms of the form

$$c_n \quad := \quad \Lambda X.\ \lambda x : X.\ \lambda f : X \rightarrow X.\ f^n\ x$$

The numeral c_n encodes the natural number n by computing iterations. Indeed, the expression $c_n\,p\,f$ performs n iterations of f on p:

$$c_n\ p\ f \quad \rightarrow^*_\beta \quad \underbrace{f \cdots (f}_{n\ \text{times}}\ p) \quad = \quad f^n\ p$$

The constructors of Church's numerals are the terms Z and S defined as:

$$\begin{array}{lcl} \mathsf{Z} & := & \Lambda X.\ \lambda x : X.\ \lambda f : X \rightarrow X.\ x \\ \mathsf{S} & := & \lambda n : \mathsf{N_{Ch}}.\ \Lambda X.\ \lambda x : X.\ \lambda f : X \rightarrow X.\ f\,(n\,X\,x\,f) \end{array}$$

where $\mathsf{N_{Ch}}$ is the type of Church's numerals defined in Ex. 2.1.(ii). Given $\tau \in \mathcal{T}$, we can code *iteration at type* τ with the term $\mathsf{Iter}_\tau\ u\ v\ n\ := \ n\ \tau\ u\ v$. For all $n, u, v \in \mathcal{E}$ we have

$$\begin{array}{llll} \mathsf{Iter}_\tau\ u\ v\ \mathsf{Z} & \rightarrow^2_\beta & (\lambda x : \tau.\ \lambda f : \tau \rightarrow \tau.\ x)\ u\ v & \rightarrow^2_\beta\ u \\ \mathsf{Iter}_\tau\ u\ v\ (\mathsf{S}\ n) & \rightarrow^2_\beta & (\lambda x : \tau.\ \lambda f : \tau \rightarrow \tau.\ f\ (n\ \tau\ x\ f))\ u\ v & \rightarrow^2_\beta\ v\ (n\ \tau\ u\ v) \end{array}$$

Hence, $\mathsf{Iter}_\tau\,u\,v\,(\mathsf{S}\,n)$ β-reduces in four steps to $v\,(\mathsf{Iter}_\tau\,u\,v\,n)$. Using this iteration scheme, every function provably total in second order Peano arithmetic can be coded in System F [12]. □

Typing. A context is a map $\Gamma : \mathcal{V}_\mathcal{E} \rightarrow \mathcal{T}$ of finite domain. Given $x \notin \mathsf{dom}(\Gamma)$ we let $\Gamma, x : \tau$ be the context

$$(\Gamma, x : \tau)(y) \quad =_{\text{def}} \quad \begin{cases} \tau & \text{if } y = x \\ \Gamma(y) & \text{otherwise} \end{cases}$$

The notation $\Gamma, x : \tau$ always implicitly assumes that $x \notin \mathsf{dom}(\Gamma)$. The typing relation of System F is defined by the rules of Fig. 1.

$$\text{(var)}\ \frac{}{\Gamma, x : \sigma \vdash x : \sigma}$$

$$\text{(abs)}\ \frac{\Gamma, x : \tau \vdash e : \sigma}{\Gamma \vdash \lambda x : \tau.\ e : \tau \to \sigma} \qquad \text{(app)}\ \frac{\Gamma \vdash e : \tau \to \sigma \quad \Gamma \vdash e' : \tau}{\Gamma \vdash e\, e' : \sigma}$$

$$\text{(T-abs)}\ \frac{\Gamma \vdash e : \sigma}{\Gamma \vdash \Lambda X.\ e : \Pi X.\ \sigma}\ \text{if } X \notin \Gamma \qquad \text{(T-app)}\ \frac{\Gamma \vdash e : \Pi X.\ \sigma}{\Gamma \vdash e\, \tau : \sigma[X := \tau]}$$

Fig. 1. Typing rules of System F

Example 2.4.
(i) The polymorphic identity of Ex. 2.3.(i) can be given the type of Ex. 2.1.(i):

$$\vdash \Lambda X.\ \lambda x : X.\ x : \Pi X.\ X \to X$$

(ii) Church numerals can be given the type N_{Ch}:

$$\vdash \Lambda X.\ \lambda x : X.\ \lambda f : X \to X.\ f^n\, x : \Pi X.\ X \to (X \to X) \to X$$

Moreover, $\mathsf{Z} : \mathsf{N}_{\mathsf{Ch}}$ and $\mathsf{S} : \mathsf{N}_{\mathsf{Ch}} \to \mathsf{N}_{\mathsf{Ch}}$. Iteration can be typed as follows:

$$n : \mathsf{N}_{\mathsf{Ch}}, u : \tau, v : \tau \to \tau \vdash \mathsf{Iter}_\tau\, n\, u\, v : \tau$$ □

Some important properties. The most important properties of System F are subject reduction, strong normalization, and coherence.

Subject reduction states that types are closed under β-reduction.

Theorem 2.5 (Subject reduction). *If $\Gamma \vdash e : \tau$ and $e \to_\beta e'$, then also $\Gamma \vdash e' : \tau$.*

Terms typable in System F enjoy a very strong computational property: they are *strongly normalizing*. A term is strongly normalizing if every reduction sequence starting from it is finite. We can thus define the set SN_β of strongly β-normalizing terms as being the smallest set such that

$$\forall e.\quad (\forall e'.\quad e \to_\beta e' \implies e' \in \mathsf{SN}_\beta) \implies e \in \mathsf{SN}_\beta$$

Strong normalization is also useful for the implementation of the language, because it ensures that every reduction strategy (i.e. every way of reducing a term) is terminating. Strong normalization can be proved using the reducibility technique [12], which is sketched in Sect. 3.4.

Theorem 2.6 (Strong normalization). *If $\Gamma \vdash e : \tau$ then $e \in \mathsf{SN}_\beta$.*

We now discuss some logical properties of System F. It is easy to see that $\Gamma \vdash e : \bot$ implies $\Gamma \vdash e\,\tau : \tau$ for all type τ. According to the Curry-Howard propositions-as-types isomorphism, this means that the type $\bot$ is the false proposition: every proposition τ can be deduced from it. Therefore, having $\Gamma \vdash e : \bot$ means that everything can be deduced from Γ. From a logical perspective, it is crucial to ensure that there is no term of type $\bot$ in the empty context. This property is fortunately satisfied by System F. It can be proved by syntactical reasoning, using subject reduction and strong normalization, but a direct reducibility argument is also possible, see Sect. 3.4.

Theorem 2.7 (Coherence). *There is no term e such that* $\vdash e : \bot$.

2.2 A Polymorphic Calculus with Datatypes and General Recursion

It is well-known that System F has limited computational power, e.g. it is not possible to encode in System F a predecessor function that computes in constant time [15]. Therefore, programming languages and proof assistants rely on languages that extend the λ-calculus with new constants and rewrite rules. In this section, we discuss one such extension of System F *à la* Church, as presented in Sect. 2.1. This system, called F^{rec}, consists in adding *datatypes* and general recursion to System F. Before giving the formal definitions, we informally present the system with some examples of datatypes. We then recall some well-known examples showing that System F^{rec} lacks two of the most important properties of System F, namely termination and coherence.

Basic features. In System F^{rec}, we represent the type natural numbers using a special type constant Nat. Furthermore, the language of λ-terms is extended by two constants $\mathsf{o} : \mathsf{Nat}$ and $\mathsf{s} : \mathsf{Nat} \to \mathsf{Nat}$ representing the two constructors of Nat. All this information is gathered in the datatype definition:

$$\textbf{Datatype}\ \mathsf{Nat} := \mathsf{o} : \mathsf{Nat} \mid \mathsf{s} : \mathsf{Nat} \to \mathsf{Nat}$$

This defines Nat as the least type build from the nullary constructor o and the unary constructor s.

Example 2.8. We can now represent the number n by the term $\mathsf{s}^n\,\mathsf{o}$. □

System F^{rec} provides two ways of computing on datatypes. The first one performs the destruction of constructor-headed terms, and allows to reason by case-analysis, similarly as in functional programming languages. For instance, we can define the predecessor function as follows:

$$\mathsf{pred} := \lambda x : \mathsf{Nat}.\ \mathsf{case}_{\mathsf{Nat}}\ x\ \mathsf{of}\ \{\ \mathsf{o} \Rightarrow \mathsf{o} \mid \mathsf{s} \Rightarrow \lambda y : \mathsf{Nat}.\ y\ \}$$

This function is evaluated as follows:

$$\begin{array}{rcl} \mathsf{pred}\,\mathsf{o} & \to & \mathsf{case}_{\mathsf{Nat}}\ \mathsf{o}\ \mathsf{of}\ \{\mathsf{o} \Rightarrow \mathsf{o} \mid \mathsf{s} \Rightarrow \lambda y : \mathsf{Nat}.\ y\} \quad \to \mathsf{o} \\ \mathsf{pred}\,(\mathsf{s}\,n) & \to & \mathsf{case}_{\mathsf{Nat}}\ (\mathsf{s}\,n)\ \mathsf{of}\ \{\mathsf{o} \Rightarrow \mathsf{o} \mid \mathsf{s} \Rightarrow \lambda y : \mathsf{Nat}.\ y\} \to (\lambda y : \mathsf{Nat}.\ y)\,n \ \to\ n \end{array}$$

and is typed using the rule

$$\frac{x : \mathsf{Nat} \vdash x \ : \ \mathsf{Nat} \qquad x : \mathsf{Nat} \vdash \mathsf{o} \ : \ \mathsf{Nat} \qquad x : \mathsf{Nat} \vdash \lambda y : \mathsf{Nat}.\ y \ : \ \mathsf{Nat} \to \mathsf{Nat}}{x : \mathsf{Nat} \vdash \mathsf{case}_{\mathsf{Nat}}\ x \ \mathsf{of}\ \{\mathsf{o} \Rightarrow \mathsf{o} \mid \mathsf{s} \Rightarrow \lambda y : \mathsf{Nat}.\ y\} \ : \ \mathsf{Nat}}$$

Performing a case analysis over an expression e of type Nat means building an object of a given type, say σ, by reasoning by cases on the constructors of Nat. We therefore must provide a branch e_{o} for the case of o and a branch e_{s} for the case of s. If e evaluates to o, then the case-analysis evaluates to e_{o}, and if e evaluates to $\mathsf{s}\,n$, then the we get $e_{\mathsf{s}}\,n$:

$$\begin{array}{rcl} \mathsf{case}_\sigma\ \mathsf{o}\ \mathsf{of}\ \{\mathsf{o} \Rightarrow e_{\mathsf{o}} \mid \mathsf{s} \Rightarrow e_{\mathsf{s}}\} & \to & e_{\mathsf{o}} \\ \mathsf{case}_\sigma\ (\mathsf{s}\ n)\ \mathsf{of}\ \{\mathsf{o} \Rightarrow e_{\mathsf{o}} \mid \mathsf{s} \Rightarrow e_{\mathsf{s}}\} & \to & e_{\mathsf{s}}\ n \end{array}$$

Since this case-analysis must evaluate to a term of type σ, we must have $e_{\mathsf{o}} : \sigma$ and $e_{\mathsf{s}} : \mathsf{Nat} \to \sigma$. We therefore arrive at the general rule for case-analysis over natural numbers:

$$(\text{case})\ \frac{\Gamma \vdash e \ : \ \mathsf{Nat} \qquad \Gamma \vdash e_{\mathsf{o}} \ : \ \sigma \qquad \Gamma \vdash e_{\mathsf{s}} \ : \ \mathsf{Nat} \to \sigma}{\Gamma \vdash \mathsf{case}_\sigma\ e\ \mathsf{of}\ \{\mathsf{o} \Rightarrow e_{\mathsf{o}} \mid \mathsf{s} \Rightarrow e_{\mathsf{s}}\} \ : \ \sigma}$$

The second computing mechanism of System F^{rec} is *general recursion*. The system is equipped by a general fixpoint operator $(\mathsf{letrec}_\tau\ f = e)$, which is typed by the rule

$$(\text{rec})\ \frac{\Gamma, f \ : \ \tau \vdash e \ : \ \tau}{\Gamma \vdash (\mathsf{letrec}_\tau\ f = e) \ : \ \tau}$$

and which reduces as follows:

$$(\mathsf{letrec}_\tau\ f = e) \quad \to \quad e[f := (\mathsf{letrec}_\tau\ f = e)]$$

This allows to encode efficiently primitive recursion over natural numbers.

Example 2.9 (Gödel's System T). In F^{rec}, we can encode primitive recursion on natural numbers as follows:

$$\begin{array}{l} \mathsf{rec} := \Lambda X.\ (\mathsf{letrec}_{\mathsf{Nat} \to X}\ rec = \lambda x : \mathsf{Nat}.\ \lambda u : X.\ \lambda v : \mathsf{Nat} \to X \to X. \\ \qquad \mathsf{case}_X\ x\ \mathsf{of}\ \{\ \mathsf{o} \Rightarrow u \\ \qquad\qquad\qquad \mid \mathsf{s} \Rightarrow \lambda y : \mathsf{Nat}.\ v\ y\ (rec\ y\ u\ v)\ \} \\ \quad) : \quad \Pi X.\ \mathsf{Nat} \to (\mathsf{Nat} \to X \to X) \to X \to X \end{array}$$

Therefore, writing rec_τ for the head β-reduct of $\mathsf{rec}\ \tau$, we have the following reductions, which are performed in a constant number of steps:

$$\mathsf{rec}_\tau\ \mathsf{o}\ u\ v \quad \to^6 \quad u \qquad \text{and} \qquad \mathsf{rec}_\tau\ (\mathsf{s}\ n)\ u\ v \quad \to^6 \quad v\ n\ (\mathsf{rec}_\tau\ n\ u\ v)$$ □

Functions defined by primitive recursion can also be directly coded in F^{rec}. Take for instance the addition and subtraction on Nat.

Example 2.10 (Addition of two natural numbers)

$$\begin{aligned}\mathsf{plus} := (&\mathsf{letrec}_{\mathsf{Nat}\to\mathsf{Nat}\to\mathsf{Nat}}\ plus = \lambda x : \mathsf{Nat}.\ \lambda y : \mathsf{Nat}.\\ &\quad \mathsf{case}_{\mathsf{Nat}}\ x\ \mathsf{of}\ \{\ \mathsf{o} \Rightarrow y\\ &\qquad\qquad\qquad \mid \mathsf{s} \Rightarrow \lambda x' : \mathsf{Nat}.\ \mathsf{s}\ (plus\ x'\ y)\ \}\\ ) :&\quad \mathsf{Nat} \to \mathsf{Nat} \to \mathsf{Nat}\end{aligned}$$ □

Example 2.11 (Subtraction of natural numbers)

$$\begin{aligned}\mathsf{minus} := (&\mathsf{letrec}_{\mathsf{Nat}\to\mathsf{Nat}\to\mathsf{Nat}}\ ms = \lambda x : \mathsf{Nat}.\ \lambda y : \mathsf{Nat}.\\ &\mathsf{case}_{\mathsf{Nat}}\ x\ \mathsf{of}\ \{\ \mathsf{o} \Rightarrow x\\ &\qquad \mid \mathsf{s} \Rightarrow \lambda x' : \mathsf{Nat}.\ \mathsf{case}_{\mathsf{Nat}}\ y\ \mathsf{of}\ \{\ \mathsf{o} \Rightarrow x\\ &\qquad\qquad\qquad\qquad\qquad \mid \mathsf{s} \Rightarrow \lambda y' : \mathsf{Nat}.\ ms\ x'\ y'\}\\ &\qquad \}\\ ) :&\quad \mathsf{Nat} \to \mathsf{Nat} \to \mathsf{Nat}\end{aligned}$$ □

Since general fixpoints are allowed, we can also give definitions where recursive calls are not performed on structurally smaller terms. This is the case of the Euclidean division on natural numbers. We will see in Sect. 3 that this function terminates provably with typed-based termination.

Example 2.12 (Euclidean division). This program for the Euclidean division depends on the function minus. It is not typable in systems with a syntactic guard predicate, as, syntactically, (minus x' y) is not properly structurally smaller than x in the program below.

$$\begin{aligned}\mathsf{div} := (&\mathsf{letrec}_{\mathsf{Nat}\to\mathsf{Nat}\to\mathsf{Nat}}\ div = \lambda x : \mathsf{Nat}.\ \lambda y : \mathsf{Nat}.\\ &\mathsf{case}_{\mathsf{Nat}}\ x\ \mathsf{of}\ \{\ \mathsf{o} \Rightarrow \mathsf{o}\\ &\qquad \mid \mathsf{s} \Rightarrow \lambda x' : \mathsf{Nat}.\ \mathsf{s}\ (div\ (\mathsf{minus}\ x'\ y)\ y)\ \}\\ ) :&\quad \mathsf{Nat} \to \mathsf{Nat} \to \mathsf{Nat}\end{aligned}$$ □

Polymorphic datatypes. System F^{rec} features polymorphic datatypes, such as polymorphic lists whose constructors, nil and cons, are typed as follows:

$$\mathsf{nil} : \Pi X.\ \mathsf{List}\ X \qquad\qquad \mathsf{cons} : \Pi X.\ X \to \mathsf{List}\ X \to \mathsf{List}\ X$$

Formally, the datatype of lists is defined as follows:

$$\textbf{Datatype}\ \ \mathsf{List}\ X\ \ :=\ \ \mathsf{nil} : \mathsf{List}\ X\ \mid\ \mathsf{cons} : X \to \mathsf{List}\ X \to \mathsf{List}\ X$$

List are eliminated using case-analysis, along a pattern similar to that of natural numbers. The case-analysis of polymorphic lists is performed on one particular instantiation of the datatype:

$$(\text{case})\ \frac{\Gamma \vdash e\ :\ \mathsf{List}\ \tau \qquad \Gamma \vdash e_{\mathsf{nil}}\ :\ \sigma \qquad \Gamma \vdash e_{\mathsf{cons}}\ :\ \tau \to \mathsf{List}\ \tau \to \sigma}{\Gamma \vdash \mathsf{case}_\sigma\ e\ \mathsf{of}\ \{\mathsf{nil} \Rightarrow e_{\mathsf{nil}} \mid \mathsf{cons} \Rightarrow e_{\mathsf{cons}}\}\ :\ \sigma}$$

This means that nil τ can be the subject of case-analysis, while nil can not. Accordingly, the branches of the case-analysis must be typable with the corresponding instantiation of the polymorphic type: e_{cons} takes an argument of type

$\mathsf{List}\,\tau$, but not of type $\Pi X.\ \mathsf{List}\,X$. The reduction rules are similar to that of natural numbers:

$$\begin{array}{rcl} \mathsf{case}_\sigma\ (\mathsf{nil}\ \tau)\ \mathsf{of}\ \{\mathsf{nil} \Rightarrow e_{\mathsf{nil}} \mid \mathsf{cons} \Rightarrow e_{\mathsf{cons}}\} & \to & e_{\mathsf{nil}} \\ \mathsf{case}_\sigma\ (\mathsf{cons}\ \tau\ x\ xs)\ \mathsf{of}\ \{\mathsf{nil} \Rightarrow e_{\mathsf{nil}} \mid \mathsf{cons} \Rightarrow e_{\mathsf{cons}}\} & \to & e_{\mathsf{cons}}\ x\ xs \end{array}$$

Here are two basic functions on lists, namely the concatenation of two lists and the map function.

Example 2.13 (The concatenation of two lists)

$$\begin{array}{l} \mathsf{app} := \Lambda X.\ (\mathsf{letrec}_{\mathsf{List}\,X \to \mathsf{List}\,X \to \mathsf{List}\,X}\ app = \lambda x : \mathsf{List}\ X.\ \lambda y : \mathsf{List}\ X. \\ \qquad \mathsf{case}_{\mathsf{List} X}\ x\ \mathsf{of}\ \{\ \mathsf{nil} \Rightarrow y \\ \qquad\qquad\qquad \mid \mathsf{cons} \Rightarrow \lambda z : X.\ \lambda x' : \mathsf{List}\ X.\ \ \mathsf{cons}\ X\ z\ (app\ x'\ y) \\ \qquad\qquad\qquad \} \\ \quad) : \quad \Pi X.\ \mathsf{List}\ X \to \mathsf{List}\ X \to \mathsf{List}\ X \end{array}$$ □

Example 2.14 (The map function on a list)

$$\begin{array}{l} \mathsf{map} := \Lambda X.\ \Lambda Y.\ \lambda f : X \to Y.\ \ (\mathsf{letrec}_{\mathsf{List}\,X \to \mathsf{List}\,Y}\ map = \lambda x : \mathsf{List}\,X. \\ \qquad \mathsf{case}_{\mathsf{List}\,Y}\ x\ \mathsf{of}\ \{\ \mathsf{nil} \Rightarrow \mathsf{nil} \\ \qquad\qquad\qquad \mid \mathsf{cons} \Rightarrow \lambda z : X.\ \ \lambda x' : \mathsf{List}\,X.\ \mathsf{cons}\ Y\ (f\ z)\ (map\ f\ x') \\ \qquad\qquad\qquad \} \\ \quad) : \quad \Pi X.\ \Pi Y.\ (X \to Y) \to \mathsf{List}\ X \to \mathsf{List}\ Y \end{array}$$ □

We can also define the concatenation of a list of lists. In F^{rec} the polymorphic type of lists of lists is $\Pi X.\ \mathsf{List}\ (\mathsf{List}\ X)$. The concatenation of a list of lists is therefore of type $\Pi X.\ \mathsf{List}\ (\mathsf{List}\ X) \to \mathsf{List}\ X$.

Example 2.15 (The concatenation of a list of lists)

$$\begin{array}{l} \mathsf{conc} := \Lambda X.\ (\mathsf{letrec}_{\mathsf{List}\,(\mathsf{List}\,X) \to \mathsf{List}\,X}\ conc = \lambda x : \mathsf{List}\,(\mathsf{List}\,X). \\ \quad \mathsf{case}_{\mathsf{List}\,X}\ x\ \mathsf{of}\ \{\ \mathsf{nil} \Rightarrow \mathsf{nil} \\ \qquad\qquad\qquad \mid \mathsf{cons} \Rightarrow \lambda z : \mathsf{List}\,X.\ \lambda x' : \mathsf{List}\,(\mathsf{List}\,X).\ \mathsf{app}\ X\ z\ (conc\ x') \\ \qquad\qquad\qquad \} \\ \quad) : \quad \Pi X.\ \mathsf{List}\ (\mathsf{List}\ X) \to \mathsf{List}\ X \end{array}$$ □

An other interesting polymorphic type is that of polymorphic finitely branching trees. These trees are composed of leaves, with one token of information, and of inner nodes, with one token of information and a list of successor subtrees. These two kinds of nodes are represented by the same constructor:

$$\mathsf{node} : \Pi X.\ X \to \mathsf{List}\ (\mathsf{Tree}\ X) \to \mathsf{Tree}\ X$$

For instance, the types of trees of natural numbers is $\mathsf{Tree\ Nat}$, and a leave with token n is represented by $\mathsf{node\ Nat}\ n\ (\mathsf{nil}\ (\mathsf{Tree\ Nat}))$. The important point with this type is that the recursive argument of $\mathsf{node}\,\tau$, which is a list of trees of τ, is not directly of type $\mathsf{Tree}\,\tau$ but of type $\mathsf{List}\,(\mathsf{Tree}\,\tau)$. This allows to encode trees where each node can have a different, but finite, arity.

Like natural numbers and lists, trees are eliminated by case-analysis. Since this type has only one constructor, the scheme of elimination essentially performs the projection of that constructor:

$$(\text{case})\ \frac{\Gamma \vdash e\ :\ \mathsf{List}\ \tau \qquad \Gamma \vdash e_{\mathsf{node}}\ :\ \tau \to \mathsf{List}\ (\mathsf{Tree}\ \tau) \to \sigma}{\Gamma \vdash \mathsf{case}_\sigma\ e\ \mathsf{of}\ \{\mathsf{node} \Rightarrow e_{\mathsf{node}}\}\ :\ \sigma}$$

The reduction rule is as follows:

$$\mathsf{case}_\sigma\ (\mathsf{node}\,\tau\,x\,l)\ \mathsf{of}\ \{\mathsf{node} \Rightarrow e_{\mathsf{node}}\} \quad \to \quad e_{\mathsf{node}}\,x\,l$$

For instance, the first projection is typed as

$$\frac{\Gamma \vdash e\ :\ \mathsf{List}\ \tau \qquad \Gamma \vdash \lambda x : \tau.\ \lambda l : \mathsf{List}\ (\mathsf{Tree}\ \tau).\ x\ :\ \tau \to \mathsf{List}\ (\mathsf{Tree}\ \tau) \to \tau}{\Gamma \vdash \mathsf{case}_\tau\ e\ \mathsf{of}\ \{\mathsf{node} \Rightarrow \lambda x : \tau.\ \lambda l : \mathsf{List}\ (\mathsf{Tree}\ \tau).\ x\}\ :\ \tau}$$

and we have $\mathsf{case}_\tau\ (\mathsf{node}\ \tau\ x\ l)\ \mathsf{of}\ \{\mathsf{node} \Rightarrow \lambda x : \tau.\ \lambda l : \mathsf{List}\ (\mathsf{Tree}\ \tau).\ x\} \to^3 x$.

The following example treats the flattening of finitely branching trees.

Example 2.16 (Flattening of finitely branching trees). This program depends on map, defined in Ex. 2.14 and on conc, defined in Ex. 2.15. Similarly to div, it is not typable in systems with a syntactic guard predicate.

$$\begin{array}{l}\mathsf{flatten} := \Lambda X.\ (\mathsf{letrec}_{\mathsf{Tree}\ X \to \mathsf{List}\ X}\ \mathit{flat} = \lambda t : \mathsf{Tree}\, X.\ \mathsf{case}_{\mathsf{List}\ X}\ t\ \mathsf{of}\ \{\\ \qquad\qquad \mathsf{node} \Rightarrow \lambda x : X.\ \lambda l : \mathsf{List}\ (\mathsf{Tree}\ X).\ \mathsf{cons}\ x\ (\mathsf{conc}\ (\mathsf{map}\ \mathit{flat}\ l))\\ \qquad\qquad \}\\ \qquad\quad) :\quad \Pi X.\ \mathsf{Tree}\ X \to \mathsf{List}\ X\end{array}$$

For readability, we have left the instantiation of polymorphic types implicit at the term level. □

Higher-order datatypes. Up to now, we only have presented first order datatypes, i.e. datatypes whose inhabitants represent particular forms of finitely branching trees.

There can in fact be much more powerful datatypes, representing infinitely branching trees, that we call higher-order datatypes. One of them is the type Ord of *Brouwer ordinals*. It is defined as follows:

$$\textbf{Datatype}\ \mathsf{Ord}\ := \mathsf{o} : \mathsf{Ord}\ \mid\ \mathsf{s} : \mathsf{Ord} \to \mathsf{Ord}\ \mid\ \mathsf{lim} : (\mathsf{Nat} \to \mathsf{Ord}) \to \mathsf{Ord}$$

Thanks to the constructors $\mathsf{o} : \mathsf{Ord}$ and $\mathsf{s} : \mathsf{Ord} \to \mathsf{Ord}$, Brouwer ordinals contain natural numbers. This is represented by the canonical injection $\mathsf{inj} : \mathsf{Nat} \to \mathsf{Ord}$ defined as follows:

$$\begin{array}{l}\mathsf{inj} := (\mathsf{letrec}_{\mathsf{Nat} \to \mathsf{Ord}}\ \mathit{inj} = \lambda x : \mathsf{Nat}.\\ \qquad\qquad \mathsf{case}_{\mathsf{Nat}}\ x\ \mathsf{of}\ \{\ \mathsf{o} \Rightarrow \mathsf{o}\\ \qquad\qquad\qquad\qquad\qquad \mid \mathsf{s} \Rightarrow \lambda x' : \mathsf{Nat}.\ \mathsf{s}\ (\mathit{inj}\ x')\}\\ \qquad\ ) :\quad \mathsf{Nat} \to \mathsf{Ord}\end{array}$$

For all $p \in \mathbb{N}$, we have $\mathsf{inj}\ (\mathsf{s}^p\,\mathsf{o}) \;\;\rightarrow\;\; \mathsf{s}^p\,\mathsf{o}$. Moreover, ordinals also feature the higher-order constructor $\mathsf{lim} : (\mathsf{Nat} \rightarrow \mathsf{Ord}) \rightarrow \mathsf{Ord}$. The expression $\mathsf{lim}\ f$ represents the supremum of the countable list of ordinals represented by $f : \mathsf{Nat} \rightarrow \mathsf{Ord}$. For instance, $\mathsf{lim}\ \mathsf{inj}$ is a term-level representation of the set of natural numbers.

Addition of ordinals can easily be defined in F^{rec}.

Example 2.17 (The addition of two ordinals)

$$
\begin{array}{l}
\mathsf{add} := (\mathsf{letrec}_{\mathsf{Ord}\rightarrow\mathsf{Ord}\rightarrow\mathsf{Ord}}\ \mathit{add} = \lambda x : \mathsf{Ord}.\ \lambda y : \mathsf{Ord}.\\
\qquad\quad \mathsf{case}_{\mathsf{Ord}}\ x\ \mathsf{of}\ \{\ \mathsf{o} \Rightarrow y\\
\qquad\qquad\qquad\qquad \mid \mathsf{s} \Rightarrow \lambda x' : \mathsf{Ord}.\ \mathsf{s}\ (\mathit{add}\ x'\ y)\\
\qquad\qquad\qquad\qquad \mid \mathsf{lim} \Rightarrow \lambda f : \mathsf{Nat} \rightarrow \mathsf{Ord}.\ \ \mathsf{lim}\ (\lambda z : \mathsf{Nat}.\ \mathit{add}\ (f\ z)\ y)\\
\qquad\qquad\qquad\qquad \}\\
\qquad) : \quad \mathsf{Ord} \rightarrow \mathsf{Ord} \rightarrow \mathsf{Ord}
\end{array}
$$

The addition of $\mathsf{lim}\ f$ and o is the limit for $n : \mathsf{Nat}$ of the addition of each $f\ n$ and o. For instance, $\mathsf{add}\ (\mathsf{lim}\ \mathsf{inj})\ \mathsf{o} \;\;\rightarrow^*\;\; \mathsf{lim}\ (\lambda x : \mathsf{Nat}.\ \mathsf{add}\ (\mathsf{inj}\ x)\ \mathsf{o})$. □

Formal definition. Now that we have presented the main features of F^{rec}, we can give its formal definition.

At the type level, F^{rec} extends System F with datatypes, which have names taken in a set $\mathcal{D}$ of datatypes identifiers. Moreover, each datatype has a fixed number of parameters. Hence we assume that each datatype identifier $d \in \mathcal{D}$ comes equipped with an arity $\mathsf{ar}(d)$.

Example 2.18. We have $\mathsf{ar}(\mathsf{Nat}) = 0$ and $\mathsf{ar}(\mathsf{List}) = \mathsf{ar}(\mathsf{Tree}) = 1$. □

Formally, the types of F^{rec} extend that of System F as follows:

$$\mathcal{T}\ ::=\ \ldots\ \mid\ \mathcal{D}\ \vec{\mathcal{T}}$$

where in $\mathcal{D}\ \vec{\mathcal{T}}$, it is assumed that the length of the vector $\vec{\mathcal{T}}$ is exactly the arity of the datatype.

We now turn to datatype declarations. Each datatype $d \in \mathcal{D}$ has a fixed set of *constructors* $\mathcal{C}(d)$, and each constructor $c \in \mathcal{C}(d)$ is assigned a closed type of the form

$$\Pi \boldsymbol{X}.\ \theta_1 \rightarrow \ldots \rightarrow \theta_p \rightarrow d\ \boldsymbol{X}$$

Note that the arity condition on d imposes that $\boldsymbol{X}$ has the same length for all $c \in \mathcal{C}(d)$. We let $\mathcal{C} =_{\mathrm{def}} \bigcup\{\mathcal{C}(d) \mid d \in \mathcal{D}\}$. The declaration of a datatype, which gathers its parameters, its constructors and their types, is performed in a *datatype definition* of the form:

$$\textbf{Datatype}\ \ d\,\boldsymbol{X}\ :=\ c_1 : \sigma_1\ \mid\ \ \ldots\ \ \mid c_n : \sigma_n$$

where $\mathcal{C}(d) = \{c_1, \ \ldots\ , c_n\}$ and each σ_k is of the form $\boldsymbol{\theta}_k \rightarrow d\,\boldsymbol{X}$. Given $k \in \{1, \ldots, k\}$, we write $c_k : \Pi \boldsymbol{X}.\ \boldsymbol{\theta}_k \rightarrow d\,\boldsymbol{X}$.

Example 2.19. We review here the datatypes that we have already seen. All these datatypes represent a form of well-founded trees. We call them *inductive*, and come back on this notion in Sect. 2.3. Moreover, we give an example of a non-well founded datatype, noted D.

(i) The inductive datatype of natural number is defined as

$$\textbf{Datatype}\ \mathsf{Nat}\ :=\ \mathsf{o} : \mathsf{Nat}\ \mid\ \mathsf{s} : \mathsf{Nat} \to \mathsf{Nat}$$

(ii) The inductive datatype of polymorphic lists is defined as

$$\textbf{Datatype}\ \mathsf{List}\ X\ :=\ \mathsf{nil} : \mathsf{List}\ X\ \mid\ \mathsf{cons} : X \to \mathsf{List}\ X \to \mathsf{List}\ X$$

(iii) The inductive datatype of polymorphic finitely branching trees is

$$\textbf{Datatype}\ \mathsf{Tree}\ X\ :=\ \mathsf{node} : X \to \mathsf{List}\ (\mathsf{Tree}\ X) \to \mathsf{Tree}\ X$$

(iv) The inductive datatype of Brouwer ordinals is defined as

$$\textbf{Datatype}\ \mathsf{Ord}\ :=\ \mathsf{o} : \mathsf{Ord}\ \mid\ \mathsf{s} : \mathsf{Ord} \to \mathsf{Ord}\ \mid\ \mathsf{lim} : (\mathsf{Nat} \to \mathsf{Ord}) \to \mathsf{Ord}$$

(v) The following datatype is not well-founded. We will see in Ex. 2.22 that it allows to build a non-terminating term of type $\bot$.

$$\textbf{Datatype}\ \mathsf{D}\ :=\ \mathsf{c} : (\mathsf{D} \to \bot) \to \mathsf{D}$$ □

The terms of System F^{rec} extend those of the Church's style System F with constructors, case-expressions and recursive definitions:

$$\mathcal{E}\ ::=\ \ldots\ \mid\ \mathcal{C}\ \mid\ \mathsf{case}_{\mathcal{T}}\ \mathcal{E}\ \mathsf{of}\ \{\mathcal{C} \Rightarrow \mathcal{E}\}\ \mid\ (\mathsf{letrec}_{\mathcal{T}}\ \mathcal{V}_{\mathcal{E}} = \mathcal{E})$$

The reduction calculus extends β-reduction with ι-reduction for case analysis and μ-reduction for unfolding recursive definitions. Formally,

- ι-reduction $\to_\iota$ is defined as the compatible closure of

$$\mathsf{case}_\sigma\ (c_i\ \boldsymbol{\tau}\ \boldsymbol{a})\ \mathsf{of}\ \{c_1 \Rightarrow e_1 \mid \ldots \mid c_n \Rightarrow e_n\}\quad \succ_\iota \quad e_i\ \boldsymbol{a}$$

- μ-reduction $\to_\mu$ is defined as the compatible closure of

$$(\mathsf{letrec}_\tau\ f = e)\ \succ_\mu\ e[f := (\mathsf{letrec}_\tau\ f = e)]$$

Then, $\beta\iota\mu$-reduction, written $\to_{\beta\iota\mu}$, is $\to_\beta \cup \to_\iota \cup \to_\mu$. The relation $\to_{\beta\iota\mu}$ is confluent.

The type system is standard. The typing relation $\Gamma \vdash e\ :\ \tau$ extends that of System F with the rules given in Fig. 2, where in the rules for (cons) and (case) it is assumed that $\mathcal{C}(d) = \{c_1, \ldots, c_n\}$, and that the type $\boldsymbol{\theta_k} \to d\,\boldsymbol{X}$ of the constructor c_k is given by the datatype declaration.

System F^{rec} enjoys subject reduction.

Theorem 2.20 (Subject reduction). *If $\Gamma \vdash e\ :\ \tau$ and $e \to_{\beta\iota\mu} e'$, then $\Gamma \vdash e'\ :\ \tau$.*

$$\text{(cons)}\ \frac{}{\Gamma \vdash c_k \ :\ \Pi \boldsymbol{X}.\, \boldsymbol{\theta_k} \to d\, \boldsymbol{X}} \qquad \text{(rec)}\ \frac{\Gamma, f : \tau \vdash e \ :\ \tau}{\Gamma \vdash (\mathsf{letrec}_\tau\ f = e)\ :\ \tau}$$

$$\text{(case)}\ \frac{\Gamma \vdash e \ :\ d\,\boldsymbol{\tau} \qquad \Gamma \vdash e_k \ :\ \boldsymbol{\theta_k}[\boldsymbol{X} := \boldsymbol{\tau}] \to \sigma \qquad (1 \le k \le n)}{\Gamma \vdash \mathsf{case}_\sigma\ e\ \mathsf{of}\ \{c_1 \Rightarrow e_1 \mid \cdots \mid c_n \Rightarrow e_n\}\ :\ \sigma}$$

Fig. 2. Typing rules for F^{rec}

Non-termination and incoherence. In this paragraph, we show that although convenient for computing, System F^{rec} lacks two of the most important properties of System F, namely termination and coherence. These problems are due to the presence of general recursion and non well-founded datatypes. We recall two independent examples, one involving unrestricted recursion and the other involving the non well-founded datatype D of Ex. 2.19.(v). Both examples provide a non-terminating *incoherent* term, that is, a non-terminating closed term of type $\bot$.

Example 2.21 (Recursion). The typing rule (rec) can be instantiated as follows:

$$\frac{f : \bot \vdash f \ :\ \bot}{\vdash (\mathsf{letrec}_\bot\ f = f)\ :\ \bot}$$

The closed term $(\mathsf{letrec}_\bot\ f = f)$ of type $\bot$ is non-terminating:

$$(\mathsf{letrec}_\bot\ f = f) \quad \to_\mu \quad (\mathsf{letrec}_\bot\ f = f) \quad \to_\mu \quad \ldots \qquad \square$$

The second well-known example shows how to write a non-normalizing term using case-analysis on the non well-founded datatype D of Ex. 2.19.(v). Note that it involves no recursion.

Example 2.22 (Non well-founded datatypes [14]). Consider the non well-founded datatype D of Ex. 2.19.(v). Recall that $\mathsf{c} : (\mathsf{D} \to \bot) \to \mathsf{D}$ and let

$$\mathsf{p} \ :=\ \lambda x : \mathsf{D}.\ \mathsf{case}_{\mathsf{D}\to\bot}\ x\ \mathsf{of}\ \{\mathsf{c} \Rightarrow \lambda y : \mathsf{D} \to \bot.\ y\}$$

We can derive

$$\frac{\dfrac{x : \mathsf{D} \vdash x \ :\ \mathsf{D} \qquad x : \mathsf{D} \vdash \lambda y : \mathsf{D} \to \bot.\ y \ :\ (\mathsf{D} \to \bot) \to (\mathsf{D} \to \bot)}{x : \mathsf{D} \vdash \mathsf{case}_{\mathsf{D}\to\bot}\ x\ \mathsf{of}\ \{\mathsf{c} \Rightarrow \lambda y : \mathsf{D} \to \bot.\ y\} \ :\ \mathsf{D} \to \bot}}{\vdash \lambda x : \mathsf{D}.\ \mathsf{case}_{\mathsf{D}\to\bot}\ x\ \mathsf{of}\ \{\mathsf{c} \Rightarrow \lambda y : \mathsf{D} \to \bot.\ y\} \ :\ \mathsf{D} \to (\mathsf{D} \to \bot)}$$

That is $p : \mathsf{D} \to (\mathsf{D} \to \bot)$. Furthermore, let $\omega_{\mathsf{D}} := \lambda x : \mathsf{D}.\ \mathsf{p}\ x\ x : \mathsf{D} \to \bot$. We then have $\mathsf{c}\ \omega_{\mathsf{D}} : \mathsf{D}$, hence $\mathsf{p}\ (\mathsf{c}\ \omega_{\mathsf{D}})\ (\mathsf{c}\ \omega_{\mathsf{D}}) : \bot$. This incoherent term is non-terminating:

$$\mathsf{p}\ (\mathsf{c}\ \omega_{\mathsf{D}})\ (\mathsf{c}\ \omega_{\mathsf{D}}) \ \to^*_{\beta\iota}\ (\lambda x : \mathsf{D}.\ \mathsf{p}\ x\ x)\ (\mathsf{c}\ \omega_{\mathsf{D}}) \ \to_{\beta\iota}\ \mathsf{p}\ (\mathsf{c}\ \omega_{\mathsf{D}})\ (\mathsf{c}\ \omega_{\mathsf{D}}) \ \to_{\beta\iota}\ \ldots \ \square$$

These two examples show that to achieve termination and coherence, we must restrict the formation of both recursive definitions and datatypes.

2.3 Inductive Datatypes

The standard means to rule out pathological cases such as the ones above is to focus on inductive datatypes. Intuitively, inductive datatypes are datatypes that can be constructed as the least fixed point of a monotonic operator. This is formalized using the notion of positivity.

Definition 2.23 (Positivity). *Let* σ nocc τ *if* σ *does not occur in* τ. *The predicate* σ pos τ *(resp.* σ neg τ*), stating that all occurrences of* σ *in* τ *are positive (resp. negative), is inductively defined in Fig. 3.*

Example 2.24. In the following types, the occurrences of τ are positive and the occurrences of σ are negative:

$$\tau \qquad\qquad \sigma \to \tau \qquad\qquad (\tau \to \sigma) \to \tau$$

In particular, Nat pos Nat, $\mathsf{Tree}\ X$ pos $\mathsf{List}\ (\mathsf{Tree}\ X)$ and Ord pos $(\mathsf{Nat} \to \mathsf{Ord})$, but *not* D pos $(\mathsf{D} \to \bot)$. □

$$\frac{}{\sigma\ \mathsf{pos}\ \sigma}$$

$$\frac{\sigma\ \mathsf{nocc}\ \tau}{\sigma\ \mathsf{pos}\ \tau} \qquad\qquad \frac{\sigma\ \mathsf{nocc}\ \tau}{\sigma\ \mathsf{neg}\ \tau}$$

$$\frac{\sigma\ \mathsf{neg}\ \tau_2 \qquad \sigma\ \mathsf{pos}\ \tau_1}{\sigma\ \mathsf{pos}\ \tau_2 \to \tau_1} \qquad\qquad \frac{\sigma\ \mathsf{pos}\ \tau_2 \qquad \sigma\ \mathsf{neg}\ \tau_1}{\sigma\ \mathsf{neg}\ \tau_2 \to \tau_1}$$

$$\frac{\sigma\ \mathsf{pos}\ \tau}{\sigma\ \mathsf{pos}\ \Pi X.\ \tau} \qquad\qquad \frac{\sigma\ \mathsf{neg}\ \tau}{\sigma\ \mathsf{neg}\ \Pi X.\ \tau}$$

$$\frac{\sigma\ \mathsf{pos}\ \tau_i \qquad (1 \le i \le \mathsf{ar}(d))}{\sigma\ \mathsf{pos}\ d\,\boldsymbol{\tau}} \qquad\qquad \frac{\sigma\ \mathsf{neg}\ \tau_i \qquad (1 \le i \le \mathsf{ar}(d))}{\sigma\ \mathsf{neg}\ d\,\boldsymbol{\tau}}$$

Fig. 3. Positivity and negativity of a type occurrence

Inductive datatypes are datatypes $d \in \mathcal{D}$ in which d and its parameters occur only positively in the type of their constructors.

Definition 2.25 (Inductive datatypes)

(i) An inductive datatype definition *is a datatype declaration*

$$\textbf{Datatype}\ \ d\,\boldsymbol{X}\ := c_1 : \sigma_1 \mid \ \ldots \ \mid c_n : \sigma_n$$

where for all $k \in \{1, \ldots, n\}$, σ_k *is of the form* $\boldsymbol{\theta}_k \to d\,\boldsymbol{X}$ *with* $\boldsymbol{X}$ pos $\boldsymbol{\theta}_k$ *and* $d\,\boldsymbol{X}$ pos $\boldsymbol{\theta}_k$. *Inductive datatypes definitions are written*

$$\textbf{Inductive}\ \ d\,\boldsymbol{X}\ := c_1 : \sigma_1 \mid \ \ldots \ \mid c_n : \sigma_n$$

(ii) An environment is a sequence of datatype definitions $I_1 \ldots I_n$ in which constructors of the datatype definition I_k only use datatypes introduced by $I_1 \ldots I_k$.

In the remainder of this tutorial, we implicitly assume given an environment in which every $d \in \mathcal{D}$ is an inductive datatype.

Example 2.26. Nat, List, Tree and Ord are inductive, but D is not. □

2.4 Guarded Reduction for Strong Normalization

The μ-reduction is inherently non strongly normalizing. Since

$$(\mathsf{letrec}_\tau\ f = e) \quad \rightarrow_\mu \quad e[f := (\mathsf{letrec}_\tau\ f = e)]$$

there are infinite μ-reductions starting from every expression ($\mathsf{letrec}\ f = e$) such that f occurs free in e. As a first step towards normalization, we restrict the typing and reduction rules of fixpoints. First, we require that fixpoints are only used to defined functions whose domain is a datatype, i.e. instead of the rule (rec) of Fig. 2, we will restrict to the following typing rule:

$$\frac{\Gamma, f : d\,\boldsymbol{\tau} \rightarrow \theta \vdash e \ :\ d\,\boldsymbol{\tau} \rightarrow \theta}{\Gamma \vdash (\mathsf{letrec}_{d\,\boldsymbol{\tau} \rightarrow \theta}\ f = e) \ :\ d\,\boldsymbol{\tau} \rightarrow \theta} \tag{1}$$

Note that all examples on natural numbers, lists, trees and ordinals presented in Sect. 2.2 can by typed with this rule.

Then we replace μ-reduction with a notion of *guarded* γ-reduction $\rightarrow_\gamma$ defined as the compatible closure of:

$$(\mathsf{letrec}_{d\,\boldsymbol{\tau} \rightarrow \theta}\ f = e)\ (c\ \boldsymbol{\tau}\ \boldsymbol{a}) \quad \succ_\gamma \quad e[f := (\mathsf{letrec}_{d\,\boldsymbol{\tau} \rightarrow \theta}\ f = e)]\ (c\ \boldsymbol{\tau}\ \boldsymbol{a})$$

Definition 2.27 (Guarded reduction). *The relation $\rightarrow$ is defined as*

$$\rightarrow \quad =_{def} \quad \rightarrow_\beta\ \cup\ \rightarrow_\iota\ \cup\ \rightarrow_\gamma$$

The relation $\rightarrow$ is confluent.

These restrictions do not rule out non-terminating and incoherent expressions.

Example 2.28 (Non-termination and incoherence). We can derive

$$\frac{f : \mathsf{Nat} \rightarrow \bot \vdash f \ :\ \mathsf{Nat} \rightarrow \bot}{\vdash (\mathsf{letrec}_{\mathsf{Nat} \rightarrow \bot}\ f = f) \ :\ \mathsf{Nat} \rightarrow \bot}$$

and we have $(\mathsf{letrec}_{\mathsf{Nat} \rightarrow \bot}\ f = f)\ \mathsf{o} : \bot$ with

$$(\mathsf{letrec}_{\mathsf{Nat} \rightarrow \bot}\ f = f)\ \mathsf{o} \quad \rightarrow \quad (\mathsf{letrec}_{\mathsf{Nat} \rightarrow \bot}\ f = f)\ \mathsf{o} \quad \rightarrow \quad \ldots$$ □

To obtain strong normalization, we must require that fixpoints must be functions defined by induction on an inductive datatype. This is the purpose of the criterion defined in the next section.

2.5 Syntactic Termination Criteria

Termination of recursive definitions can be enforced by adopting the guarded reduction rule of Definition 2.27 and by restricting the rule for recursive definitions so that e is a λ-abstraction, and the body of e is guarded by x, which stands for the recursive argument of the function. Formally, this is achieved by the rule:

$$\frac{\Gamma, f : d\boldsymbol{\tau} \to \sigma \vdash \lambda x : d\boldsymbol{\tau}.\ a\ :\ d\boldsymbol{\tau} \to \sigma \qquad \mathcal{G}^x_f(\emptyset, a)}{\Gamma \vdash (\mathsf{letrec}\ f = \lambda x : d\boldsymbol{\tau}.\ a)\ :\ d\boldsymbol{\tau} \to \sigma}$$

where the guard predicate $\mathcal{G}$ is defined to ensure that the calls to f are performed over expressions that are structurally smaller than x. Informally, a recursive definition is guarded by destructors, i.e. satisfies $\mathcal{G}$, if all occurrences of f in e are protected by a case analysis on x and are applied to a subcomponent of x. The notion of subcomponent is defined as the smallest transitive relation such that the variables that are introduced in the branches of a case analysis are subcomponents of the expression being matched. Barthe *et al* [5] provide a formal definition of the guard predicate for a simply typed λ-calculus and show that the resulting type system can be embedded in the simply typed fragment of System $F^{\frown}$ that we introduce in the next section.

Example 2.29. The addition on natural numbers, which we recall from Sect. 2.2:

$$\begin{array}{l} \mathsf{plus} := (\mathsf{letrec}_{\mathsf{Nat}\to\mathsf{Nat}\to\mathsf{Nat}}\ plus = \lambda x : \mathsf{Nat}.\ \lambda y : \mathsf{Nat}. \\ \qquad\qquad \mathsf{case}_{\mathsf{Nat}}\ x\ \mathsf{of}\ \{\ \mathsf{o} \Rightarrow y \\ \qquad\qquad\qquad\qquad\qquad\quad \mid \mathsf{s} \Rightarrow \lambda x' : \mathsf{Nat}.\ \mathsf{s}\ (plus\ x'\ y)\ \} \\ \qquad\quad) : \quad \mathsf{Nat} \to \mathsf{Nat} \to \mathsf{Nat} \end{array}$$

is guarded, since the only application of *plus* is protected by a case analysis on x, the formal argument of *plus*. The argument of this application is the pattern variable n, which is a component of x.

While syntactic criteria are widely used, they suffer from several weaknesses. A first weakness is that the syntactic criterion must consider all constructs of the language, and can only be applied if the body of the recursive definition is completely known. Thus, the approach is not compatible with separate compilation.

A second weakness of the approach is that the guard predicate is very sensitive to syntax; for example, the function

$$\begin{array}{l} (\mathsf{letrec}\ always\_zero = \lambda x : \mathsf{Nat}.\, \mathsf{case}\ x\ \mathsf{of}\ \{\mathsf{o} \Rightarrow \mathsf{o} \\ \qquad\qquad\qquad\qquad\qquad\qquad\quad \mid \mathsf{s} \Rightarrow \lambda n : \mathsf{Nat}.((\lambda f : \mathsf{Nat} \to \mathsf{Nat}.\, f)\ always\_zero)\ n\ \} \\ ) : \quad \mathsf{Nat} \to \mathsf{Nat} \end{array}$$

is not accepted by the guard predicate of [5], because f is passed as an argument to the identity function. It is tempting to extend the definition of the guard predicate with the rule of the form

$$\frac{\mathcal{G}^x_f(V, a') \qquad a \mapsto a'}{\mathcal{G}^x_f(V, a)}$$

where $\mapsto$ is a subset of the reduction relation. However, checking termination of recursive definitions in large developments may become prohibitive, because of the necessity to reduce the body of recursive definitions for checking the guard condition. Worse, an inappropriate choice of $\mapsto$ may lead to allow non-terminating expressions in the type system. For example, allowing $\mapsto$ to include reductions of the form $(\lambda x : A.\, a)\ a' \to a$ when x does not appear in a leads to non-terminating expressions, because it fails to impose any condition on a' which may then contain recursive calls that are not well-founded [5].

3 The System $F^{\frown}$ of Type-Based Termination

This section presents the system $F^{\frown}$ of type-based termination. This system has been published in [6], and is an extension of the system $\lambda^{\frown}$ of [5].

3.1 Semantical Ideas for a Type-Based Termination Criterion

In this section, we present some intuitions underlying type-based termination. To keep things as simple as possible, we focus on *weak termination*. Recall that an expression e is weakly terminating if and only if it has a normal form. Consider the definition of a recursive function over natural numbers:

$$\frac{f : \mathsf{Nat} \to \theta \vdash e \ :\ \mathsf{Nat} \to \theta}{\vdash (\mathsf{letrec}\ f = e) \ :\ \mathsf{Nat} \to \theta}$$

This function will be computed using the evaluation rules:

$$\begin{array}{rcl} (\mathsf{letrec}\ f = e)\ \mathsf{o} & \to_\gamma & e[f := (\mathsf{letrec}\ f = e)]\ \mathsf{o} \\ (\mathsf{letrec}\ f = e)\ (\mathsf{s}\, n) & \to_\gamma & e[f := (\mathsf{letrec}\ f = e)]\ (\mathsf{s}\, n) \end{array}$$

In order to make sure that the evaluation terminates, we have to ensure that something decreases during the computation. Think of $F =_{\mathrm{def}} (\mathsf{letrec}\ f = e)$ as being a function defined using successive approximations $F_0, \ldots, F_p, \ldots$. Now, assume that we want to evaluate $F(\mathsf{s}\, n)$. If there is some p such that the result of that evaluation can be computed using only $F_0, \ldots, F_{p+1}$, with

$$F_{k+1}(\mathsf{s}\, n) \quad \to_\gamma \quad e[f := F_k]\ (\mathsf{s}\, n) \qquad \text{for all} \quad k \leq p\ ,$$

then the evaluation of $F(\mathsf{s}\, n)$ terminates.

To express a notion of function approximation, we rely on a notion of approximation of *inductive datatype*. Roughly speaking, the type Nat of natural numbers can be drawn as

$$[\![\mathsf{Nat}]\!] \ = \ \{\mathsf{o}, \mathsf{s}\,\mathsf{o}, \ldots, \mathsf{s}^p\mathsf{o}, \ldots\}$$

Let $[\![\mathsf{Nat}]\!](0) =_{\mathrm{def}} \{\mathsf{o}\}$ and $[\![\mathsf{Nat}]\!](p+1) =_{\mathrm{def}} [\![\mathsf{Nat}]\!](p) \cup \{\mathsf{s}\, e \mid e \in [\![\mathsf{Nat}]\!](p)\}$ for all $p \in \mathbb{N}$. Now, the set $[\![\mathsf{Nat}]\!]$ is the limit of its approximations

$$[\![\mathsf{Nat}]\!](0) \ \subseteq\ [\![\mathsf{Nat}]\!](1) \ \subseteq\ \ldots\ \subseteq\ [\![\mathsf{Nat}]\!](p) \ \subseteq\ \ldots$$

These approximations of the type of natural numbers can be used to define functions as the limit of their approximants. More precisely, a total function $F : [\![\mathsf{Nat}]\!] \to \theta$ can be seen as the limit of its finite approximants $F_p : [\![\mathsf{Nat}]\!](p) \to \theta$ for $p \in \mathbb{N}$. Indeed, if $\mathsf{s}\,n$ is the representation of a natural number $p+1$, then $F(\mathsf{s}\,n)$ can by computed by evaluating $F_{p+1}(\mathsf{s}\,n)$. Conversely, in order to ensure that F is the limit of its approximants $(F_p)_{p\in\mathbb{N}}$, we can proceed by induction on $p \in \mathbb{N}$, and force F_{p+1} to be defined only in terms of F_p, as follows:

$$\frac{\forall p \in \mathbb{N} \qquad F_p : [\![\mathsf{Nat}]\!](p) \to \theta \vdash F_{p+1} \; : \; [\![\mathsf{Nat}]\!](p+1) \to \theta}{\vdash F \; : \; [\![\mathsf{Nat}]\!] \to \theta} \text{ if } F = \bigcup_{p\in\mathbb{N}} F_p \quad (2)$$

The basic idea of type-based termination is to use a type system to convey these notions of approximations. Each $[\![\mathsf{Nat}]\!](p)$ can be represented in the type system by an annotated type Nat^p. In such a system, the typing rule for s is

$$\frac{\vdash n \; : \; \mathsf{Nat}^p}{\vdash \mathsf{s}\,n \; : \; \mathsf{Nat}^{p+1}}$$

In addition, we introduce a type Nat^∞ to capture the datatype of natural numbers (corresponding to the datatype Nat of system F^{rec}). These types are naturally ordered by a subtyping relation, expressed by the subsumption rules:

$$\frac{\vdash n \; : \; \mathsf{Nat}^p}{\vdash n \; : \; \mathsf{Nat}^{p+1}} \qquad\qquad \frac{\vdash n \; : \; \mathsf{Nat}^p}{\vdash n \; : \; \mathsf{Nat}^\infty}$$

Now, the requirement expressed by (2) can be represented by the typing rule

$$\frac{\forall p \in \mathbb{N} \qquad f : \mathsf{Nat}^p \to \theta \vdash e \; : \; \mathsf{Nat}^{p+1} \to \theta}{\vdash (\mathsf{letrec}\; f = e) \; : \; \mathsf{Nat}^\infty \to \theta} \quad (3)$$

The only remaining issue is to type o. The obvious candidate

$$\frac{}{\vdash \mathsf{o} \; : \; \mathsf{Nat}^0}$$

is unfortunately unsound, both for termination and for coherence: Ex. 2.28 can be easily adapted.

Example 3.1. Assume that $\mathsf{o} : \mathsf{Nat}^0$. Then by subsumption we have $\mathsf{o} : \mathsf{Nat}^p$ for all $p \in \mathbb{N}$, and thus, using (3),

$$\frac{\forall p \in \mathbb{N} \qquad f : \mathsf{Nat}^p \to \bot \vdash \lambda x : \mathsf{Nat}.\; f\,\mathsf{o} \; : \; \mathsf{Nat}^{p+1} \to \bot}{\vdash (\mathsf{letrec}\; f = \lambda x : \mathsf{Nat}.\; f\,\mathsf{o}) \; : \; \mathsf{Nat}^\infty \to \bot}$$

Since $\vdash \mathsf{o} \; : \; \mathsf{Nat}^\infty$, we have a closed term $(\mathsf{letrec}\; f = \lambda x : \mathsf{Nat}.\; f\,\mathsf{o})\,\mathsf{o}$ of type $\bot$, which is moreover non-terminating:

$$(\mathsf{letrec}\; f = \lambda x : \mathsf{Nat}.\; f\,\mathsf{o})\,\mathsf{o} \;\to\; (\lambda x : \mathsf{Nat}.\; (\mathsf{letrec}\; f = \lambda x : \mathsf{Nat}.\; f\,\mathsf{o})\,\mathsf{o})\,\mathsf{o} \;\to \ldots \square$$

A solution is to assume that o belongs to all $[\![\mathsf{Nat}]\!](p+1)$ with $p \in \mathbb{N}$, but not to $[\![\mathsf{Nat}]\!](0)$, which leads to the interpretation of inductive datatypes detailed in Sect. 3.4. This is reflected by the typing rule

$$\frac{}{\vdash \mathsf{o} \ : \ \mathsf{Nat}^{p+1}}$$

Hence, the expression $\mathsf{s}^p\mathsf{o}$ has size $p+1$.

3.2 Formal Definition

Stages. Generalizing the discussion of the previous section, every datatype d is replaced by a family of approximations indexed over a set of *stages*, which are used to record a bound on the "depth" of values. Stages expression are build from a set $\mathcal{V}_{\mathcal{S}} = \{\imath, \jmath, \kappa, \dots\}$ of stage variables. They use the successor operation $\widehat{\cdot}$ and the constant ∞ denoting the greatest stage.

Definition 3.2 (Stages). *The set* $\mathcal{S} = \{s, r, \dots\}$ *of* stage expressions *is given by the abstract syntax:*

$$\mathcal{S} \ ::= \ \mathcal{V}_{\mathcal{S}} \mid \infty \mid \widehat{\mathcal{S}}$$

The substitution $s[\imath := r]$ *of the stage variable* $\imath$ *for* r *in* s *is defined in the obvious way.*

The inclusions $[\![\mathsf{Nat}]\!](0) \subseteq \dots \subseteq [\![\mathsf{Nat}]\!](p) \subseteq \mathsf{Nat}(p+1) \subseteq \dots \subseteq [\![\mathsf{Nat}]\!](\infty)$ will hold for each datatype $d \in \mathcal{D}$. This is reflected by a subtyping relation, which is derived from a substage relation $s \leq r$.

Definition 3.3 (Substage relation). *The* substage relation *is the smallest relation* $\leq \subseteq \mathcal{S} \times \mathcal{S}$ *closed under the rules*

$$(\mathit{refl})\ \frac{}{s \leq s} \qquad (\mathit{trans})\ \frac{s \leq r \quad r \leq p}{s \leq p} \qquad (\mathit{succ})\ \frac{}{s \leq \widehat{s}} \qquad (\mathit{sup})\ \frac{}{s \leq \infty}$$

Types. The approximations $(d^s)_{s \in \mathcal{S}}$ of datatypes are directly represented in the syntax of types. Therefore, the types of $F^{\frown}$ are the types of F^{rec} where datatype identifiers $d \in \mathcal{D}$ are annotated by size expressions $s \in \mathcal{S}$.

Definition 3.4 (Sized types). *The set* $\overline{\mathcal{T}}$ *of* sized types *is given by the following abstract syntax:*

$$\overline{\mathcal{T}} \ ::= \ \mathcal{V}_{\mathcal{T}} \mid \overline{\mathcal{T}} \rightarrow \overline{\mathcal{T}} \mid \Pi \mathcal{V}_{\mathcal{T}}.\, \overline{\mathcal{T}} \mid \mathcal{D}^{\mathcal{S}}\, \overline{\mathcal{T}}$$

where in the clause for datatypes, it is assumed that the length of the vector $\overline{\mathcal{T}}$ *is exactly the arity of the datatype.*

Sized types are denoted by lower-case over lined Greek letters $\overline{\tau}, \overline{\theta}, \overline{\sigma}, \dots$.

The subtyping relation $\overline{\tau} \sqsubseteq \overline{\sigma}$ is directly inherited from the substage relation. The subtyping rule for datatypes

$$\text{(data)}\ \frac{s \leq r \qquad \overline{\boldsymbol{\tau}} \sqsubseteq \overline{\boldsymbol{\sigma}}}{d^s \overline{\boldsymbol{\tau}} \sqsubseteq d^r \overline{\boldsymbol{\sigma}}}$$

expresses two things. First, it specifies that datatypes are covariant w.r.t. their parameters (an assumption made for the sake of simplicity). For instance we have $\mathsf{List}^{\infty}\,\mathsf{Nat}^{s} \sqsubseteq \mathsf{List}^{\infty}\,\mathsf{Nat}^{\widehat{s}}$. Second, it reflects inclusions of datatypes approximations:

$$\frac{e : d^s\,\overline{\boldsymbol{\tau}} \qquad s \leq r}{e : d^r\,\overline{\boldsymbol{\tau}}}$$

The substage relation imposes that ∞ is the greatest stage of the system. Hence, we have $\mathsf{Nat}^s \sqsubseteq \mathsf{Nat}^{\infty}$ for all stage s. This means that the type Nat^{∞} has no information on the size of its inhabitants. Therefore, it corresponds to the type Nat of system F^{rec}.

Notation 3.5. *Given a datatype identifier d, we write $d\,\overline{\boldsymbol{\tau}}$ to mean $d^{\infty}\,\overline{\boldsymbol{\tau}}$.*

Definition 3.6 (Subtyping). *The* subtyping relation *is the smallest relation $\overline{\tau} \sqsubseteq \overline{\sigma}$, where $\overline{\tau}, \overline{\sigma} \in \overline{\mathfrak{T}}$, such that*

$$\textit{(var)}\ \frac{}{X \sqsubseteq X} \qquad\qquad \textit{(func)}\ \frac{\overline{\tau'} \sqsubseteq \overline{\tau} \quad \overline{\sigma} \sqsubseteq \overline{\sigma'}}{\overline{\tau} \to \overline{\sigma} \sqsubseteq \overline{\tau'} \to \overline{\sigma'}}$$

$$\textit{(prod)}\ \frac{\overline{\tau} \sqsubseteq \overline{\sigma}}{\Pi X.\,\overline{\tau} \sqsubseteq \Pi X.\,\overline{\sigma}} \qquad\qquad \textit{(data)}\ \frac{s \leq r \quad \overline{\boldsymbol{\tau}} \sqsubseteq \overline{\boldsymbol{\sigma}}}{d^s \overline{\boldsymbol{\tau}} \sqsubseteq d^r \overline{\boldsymbol{\sigma}}}$$

We denote by $|.| : \overline{\mathfrak{T}} \to \mathfrak{T}$ the erasure function from sized types to types, which forgets the size information represented in a type of $F^{\frown}$. Erasure is defined inductively as follows:

$$|X| = X \qquad |\overline{\tau} \to \overline{\theta}| = |\overline{\tau}| \to |\overline{\theta}| \qquad |\Pi X.\,\overline{\tau}| = \Pi X.\,|\overline{\tau}| \qquad |d^s\,\overline{\boldsymbol{\tau}}| = d\,|\overline{\boldsymbol{\tau}}|$$

Sized inductive datatypes. We now turn to datatype definitions. In Def. 2.25, we have defined inductive datatypes definitions for F^{rec} as declarations of the form

$$\textbf{Inductive}\ d\,\boldsymbol{X} := c_1 : \sigma_1 \mid \ldots \mid c_n : \sigma_n$$

where for all $k \in \{1, \ldots, n\}$, σ_k is of the form $\boldsymbol{\theta}_k \to d\,\boldsymbol{X}$ with $\boldsymbol{X}$ pos $\boldsymbol{\theta}_k$ and $d\,\boldsymbol{X}$ pos $\boldsymbol{\theta}_k$.

The inductive datatypes of $F^{\frown}$ are annotated versions of inductive datatypes of F^{rec}. Each occurrence of $d' \neq d$ in $\overline{\boldsymbol{\theta}}_k$ is annotated with ∞, and each occurrence of d in $\boldsymbol{\theta}_k$ is annotated with the stage variable $\imath$. Then, the annotated type of c_k is $\Pi \boldsymbol{X}.\,\overline{\boldsymbol{\theta}}_k \to d^{\widehat{\imath}}\,\boldsymbol{X}$. Definitions of sized inductive datatypes are like definitions of inductive datatypes in F^{rec}, excepted that constructors are now given their sized type. For instance, sized natural numbers are declared as follows:

$$\textbf{Inductive}\ \mathsf{Nat} := \mathsf{o} : \mathsf{Nat}^{\widehat{\imath}} \mid \mathsf{s} : \mathsf{Nat}^{\imath} \to \mathsf{Nat}^{\widehat{\imath}}$$

In words, the constructor o always build an expression with at least one constructor, hence of size $\widehat{0}$. Since stages record upper-bound on sizes, we have o of stage $\widehat{p}$ for all stages p. On the other hand, s turns an expression of stage p into one of stage $\widehat{p}$.

We now turn to the formal definition.

Definition 3.7 (Sized inductive datatypes)
(i) A sized inductive datatype definition *is a declaration*

$$\textbf{Inductive}\ d\ \boldsymbol{X}\ :=\ c_1 : \overline{\sigma}_1\ \mid\ \ldots\ \mid\ c_n : \overline{\sigma}_n$$

such that

- *its erased form* **Inductive** $d\ \boldsymbol{X}\ :=\ c_1 : |\overline{\sigma}_1|\ \mid\ \ldots\ \mid\ c_n : |\overline{\sigma}_n|$ *is an inductive datatype definition in* F^{rec}, *and*
- *for all* $k \in \{1, \ldots, n\}$, *the sized type* $\overline{\sigma}_k$ *is of the form* $\overline{\boldsymbol{\theta}}_k \to d^{\widehat{\imath}}\ \boldsymbol{X}$ *where each occurrence of* $d' \neq d$ *in* $\overline{\boldsymbol{\theta}}_k$ *is annotated with* ∞, *and each occurrence of* d *in* $\boldsymbol{\theta}_k$ *is annotated with the stage variable* $\imath$.

For all $k \in \{1, \ldots, n\}$, *we write* $c_k : \Pi \boldsymbol{X}.\ \overline{\boldsymbol{\theta}}_k \to d^{\widehat{\imath}}\ \boldsymbol{X}$.

(ii) A sized environment *is a sequence of sized inductive datatype definitions* $I_1 \ldots I_n$ *in which constructors of the sized inductive datatype definition* I_k *only use datatypes introduced by* $I_1 \ldots I_k$.

Note that our definition of inductive datatypes types rules out heterogeneous and mutually inductive datatypes. This is only a matter of simplicity.

Besides, the positivity requirement for $d^{\imath}\boldsymbol{X}$ is necessary to guarantee strong normalization. Also, the positivity requirement for $\boldsymbol{X}$ is added to guarantee the soundness of the subtyping rule (data) for datatypes, and to avoid considering polarity, as in e.g. [17].

Example 3.8 (Sized datatypes definitions)

(i) The sized inductive datatype of polymorphic lists is defined as

$$\textbf{Inductive}\ \mathsf{List}\ X\ :=\ \mathsf{nil} : \mathsf{List}^{\widehat{\imath}}\ X\ \mid\ \mathsf{cons} : X \to \mathsf{List}^{\imath}\ X \to \mathsf{List}^{\widehat{\imath}}\ X$$

The minimal stage of a list is its length, with the nil list being of stage at least $\widehat{\imath}$. For instance, leaving implicit the type argument of constructors, we have $\mathsf{cons}\ n\ \mathsf{nil} : \mathsf{List}^{\widehat{\widehat{\imath}}}\ \mathsf{Nat}$ and $\mathsf{cons}\ n_1(\ldots(\mathsf{cons}\ n_p\ \mathsf{nil})\ldots) : \mathsf{List}^{\widehat{\imath}^{p+1}}\ \mathsf{Nat}$.

(ii) The sized inductive datatype of polymorphic finitely branching trees is

$$\textbf{Inductive}\ \mathsf{Tree}\ X\ :=\ \mathsf{node} : X \to \mathsf{List}\ (\mathsf{Tree}^{\imath}\ X) \to \mathsf{Tree}^{\widehat{\imath}}\ X$$

The minimal stage of a tree is its depth. The least tree contains just one leave $\mathsf{node}\, n\, \mathsf{nil}$ and is of stage at least $\widehat{\imath}$. Consider p trees $t_1, \ldots, t_p$ of respective types $\mathsf{Tree}^{s_1}\ \mathsf{Nat}, \ldots, \mathsf{Tree}^{s_p}\ \mathsf{Nat}$, and let $l\ :=\ \mathsf{cons}\ t_1(\ldots(\mathsf{cons}\ t_p\ \mathsf{nil})\ldots)$. For all stage s greater than each s_k, we have $l : \mathsf{List}^{\widehat{\imath}^{p+1}}\ (\mathsf{Tree}^{s}\ \mathsf{Nat})$, hence $\mathsf{node}\, n\, l : \mathsf{Tree}^{\widehat{s}}\ \mathsf{Nat}$. Therefore, the least stage of $\mathsf{node}\, n\, l$ is the strict supremum of the stages of the trees in l. Moreover, the stage of l as a list has been forgotten in the stage of $\mathsf{node}\, n\, l$.

(iii) The sized inductive datatype of Brouwer ordinals is defined as

$$\textbf{Inductive}\ \mathsf{Ord} := \mathsf{o} : \mathsf{Ord}^{\widehat{\imath}} \mid \mathsf{s} : \mathsf{Ord}^{\imath} \to \mathsf{Ord}^{\widehat{\imath}} \mid \mathsf{lim} : (\mathsf{Nat} \to \mathsf{Ord}^{\imath}) \to \mathsf{Ord}^{\widehat{\imath}}$$

As with finitely branching trees, the least stage of $\mathsf{lim}\, f$ is the strict supremum of the stages of $f\, n$ for $n \in \mathsf{Nat}$. □

In the remaining of this tutorial, we implicitly assume given a sized environment in which every $d \in \mathcal{D}$ is a sized inductive datatype.

Terms and reductions. The terms of $F^{\frown}$ are those of F^{rec}, defined in Sect. 2.2. The reduction relation of $F^{\frown}$ is the rewrite relation $\to$ defined in Def. 2.27.

Remark 3.9 (Stages in terms). Note that the types appearing in terms are those of F^{rec}: they do not carry stage expressions. As shown in [6], subject reduction would have failed if terms conveyed stage expressions. However, it is often useful to write these annotations in examples. For instance, we may write $\lambda x : \mathsf{Nat}^{\imath}.\ x$ to denote the term $\lambda x : \mathsf{Nat}.\ x$.

Typing rules. The typing rule for fixpoints uses a predicate $\imath \ \mathsf{pos}\ \overline{\sigma}$ that is used to ensure that a stage variable occurs positively in the codomain of the type of a recursive definition. Its definition is similar to that of the predicate $\tau\ \mathsf{pos}\ \sigma$ of Sect. 2.3.

Definition 3.10 (Positivity). *Given two stage expressions s and r, let $s\ \mathsf{occ}\ r$ (resp. $s\ \mathsf{nocc}\ r$) if and only if s occurs in r (resp. does not occurs in r). Moreover, let $s\ \mathsf{nocc}\ \overline{\tau}$ if the stage expression s does not occur in the sized type $\overline{\tau}$.*

The predicate $s\ \mathsf{pos}\ \overline{\tau}$ (resp. $s\ \mathsf{neg}\ \overline{\tau}$), stating that all occurrences of s in $\overline{\tau}$ are positive (resp. negative), is inductively defined in Fig. 4.

The typing rules follow [6].

Definition 3.11 (Typing). *A* sized context *is a map $\overline{\Gamma} : \mathcal{V}_{\mathcal{E}} \to \overline{\mathcal{T}}$ of finite domain. The* typing relation *is the smallest relation $\overline{\Gamma} \vdash e : \overline{\tau}$ which is closed under the rules of Fig. 5, page 128.*

All rules but (cons), (case), (rec) and (sub) do not mention stages. They are therefore the same as in F^{rec}. The rule (cons) for constructors simply says that a constructor can be given any possible stage instance of its type specified in a datatype definition.

In order to understand the rule (case), we look at it for natural numbers:

$$\frac{\overline{\Gamma} \vdash e : \mathsf{Nat}^{\widehat{s}} \qquad \overline{\Gamma} \vdash e_{\mathsf{o}} : \overline{\sigma} \qquad \overline{\Gamma} \vdash e_{\mathsf{s}} : \mathsf{Nat}^{s} \to \overline{\sigma}}{\overline{\Gamma} \vdash \mathsf{case}_{|\overline{\sigma}|}\ e\ \mathsf{of}\ \{0 \Rightarrow e_{\mathsf{o}} \mid \mathsf{s} \Rightarrow e_{\mathsf{s}}\} : \overline{\sigma}}$$

The important point, which makes the difference with the rule of F^{rec}, is that the type of the expression e subject to case analysis must have a stage of the form $\widehat{s}$. Note that this is always possible thanks to subtyping. Now, assume that e is of the form $\mathsf{s}\, n$. The rule (case) says that the term e_{s} sees n as an expression of stage s. Indeed, we have

$$\mathsf{case}_{|\overline{\sigma}|}\ (\mathsf{s}\, n)\ \mathsf{of}\ \{0 \Rightarrow e_{\mathsf{o}} \mid \mathsf{s} \Rightarrow e_{\mathsf{s}}\} \ \to_{\iota}\ e_{\mathsf{s}}\, n \qquad \text{with} \qquad \overline{\Gamma} \vdash e_{\mathsf{s}}\ :\ \mathsf{Nat}^{s} \to \overline{\sigma}$$

We now discuss the typing rule (rec) for fixpoints, in the case of natural numbers, and assuming that $\imath$ does not occur in $\overline{\theta}$:

$$(\text{rec})\ \frac{\overline{\Gamma}, f\ :\ \mathsf{Nat}^{\imath} \to \overline{\theta} \vdash e\ :\ \mathsf{Nat}^{\widehat{\imath}} \to \overline{\theta}}{\overline{\Gamma} \vdash (\mathsf{letrec}_{\mathsf{Nat}\to|\overline{\theta}|}\ f = e)\ :\ \mathsf{Nat}^{s} \to \overline{\theta}}\ \text{if } \imath \notin \overline{\Gamma}, \overline{\tau}$$

As explained in Sect. 3.1, typing $\mathsf{fix} := (\mathsf{letrec}_{\mathsf{Nat}\to|\overline{\theta}|}\ f = e)$ with type $\mathsf{Nat}^{\infty} \to \overline{\theta}$ requires showing that the body e turns an approximation of fix of type $\mathsf{Nat}^{\imath} \to \overline{\theta}$ into its next approximation, which is of type $\mathsf{Nat}^{\widehat{\imath}} \to \overline{\theta}$. As discussed in Sect 3.4, such recursive functions are terminating and, despite its simplicity, this mechanism is powerful enough to capture course-of-value recursion.

Notation 3.12. *When writing examples of typings of fixpoints, it is convenient to write at the term level the stage annotations corresponding to fixpoint variables. For instance, given a derivation of the form*

$$(\textit{rec})\ \frac{f : \mathsf{Nat}^{\imath} \to \overline{\theta} \vdash e\ :\ \mathsf{Nat}^{\widehat{\imath}} \to \overline{\theta}}{\vdash (\mathsf{letrec}_{\mathsf{Nat}\to|\overline{\theta}|}\ f = e)\ :\ \mathsf{Nat}^{s} \to \overline{\theta}}$$

where $\imath \notin \overline{\theta}$, *it is convenient to write* $(\mathsf{letrec}\ f\ :\ \mathsf{Nat}^{\imath} \to \overline{\theta} = e)\ :\ \mathsf{Nat}^{s} \to \overline{\theta}$ *to mean that using* $f\ :\ \mathsf{Nat}^{\imath} \to \overline{\theta}$, *we must have* $e\ :\ \mathsf{Nat}^{\widehat{\imath}} \to \overline{\theta}$. *We use a similar notation when* $\imath \in \overline{\theta}$.

The following example, taken from [2], shows that strong normalization may fail if the positivity condition is not met. However, there are finer conditions on the occurrences of $\imath$ in $\overline{\theta}$ than positivity that nevertheless preserve strong normalization, see [3,2].

Example 3.13 (Counter-example for the positivity condition [2]). Consider the terms

$$\begin{aligned}
\mathsf{shift} &:= \lambda f : \mathsf{Nat} \to \mathsf{Nat}^{\widehat{\widehat{\imath}}}.\ \lambda x : \mathsf{Nat}.\ \mathsf{case}_{\mathsf{Nat}}\ \overbrace{f\,(\mathsf{s}\,x)}^{\mathsf{Nat}^{\widehat{\widehat{\imath}}}}\ \mathsf{of}\ \{\ \mathsf{o} \Rightarrow \mathsf{o} \\
&\qquad\qquad\qquad\qquad\qquad\qquad\qquad\qquad\quad \mid \mathsf{s} \Rightarrow \lambda y : \mathsf{Nat}^{\widehat{\imath}}.\ y\ \} \\
\mathsf{plus_2} &:= \lambda x : \mathsf{Nat}.\ \mathsf{s}\,(\mathsf{s}\,x)
\end{aligned}$$

of type respectively $\mathsf{Nat} \to \mathsf{Nat}^{\widehat{\widehat{\imath}}}$ and $\mathsf{Nat} \to \mathsf{Nat}^{\widehat{\imath}}$. Note that $\mathsf{shift}\ \mathsf{plus\_2} \to^{*} \mathsf{plus\_2}$. Consider now the following fixpoint:

$$\frac{s\ \mathsf{nocc}\ \overline{\tau}}{s\ \mathsf{pos}\ \overline{\tau}} \qquad \frac{s\ \mathsf{pos}\ \overline{\tau}_i \quad (1 \leq i \leq \mathsf{ar}(d))}{s\ \mathsf{pos}\ d^r\ \overline{\tau}}$$

$$\frac{s\ \mathsf{pos}\ \overline{\tau}}{s\ \mathsf{pos}\ \Pi X.\ \overline{\tau}} \qquad \frac{s\ \mathsf{neg}\ \overline{\tau}_2 \qquad s\ \mathsf{pos}\ \overline{\tau}_1}{s\ \mathsf{pos}\ \overline{\tau}_2 \rightarrow \overline{\tau}_1}$$

$$\frac{s\ \mathsf{nocc}\ \overline{\tau}}{s\ \mathsf{neg}\ \overline{\tau}} \qquad \frac{s\ \mathsf{neg}\ \overline{\tau}_i \quad (1 \leq i \leq \mathsf{ar}(d))}{s\ \mathsf{neg}\ d^r\ \overline{\tau}}$$

$$\frac{s\ \mathsf{neg}\ \overline{\tau}}{s\ \mathsf{neg}\ \Pi X.\ \overline{\tau}} \qquad \frac{s\ \mathsf{pos}\ \overline{\tau}_2 \qquad s\ \mathsf{neg}\ \overline{\tau}_1}{s\ \mathsf{neg}\ \overline{\tau}_2 \rightarrow \overline{\tau}_1}$$

Fig. 4. Positivity and negativity of a stage occurrence

$$
\begin{array}{l}
\mathsf{loop} := (\mathsf{letrec}\ \mathit{loop} : \mathsf{Nat}^{\imath} \rightarrow (\mathsf{Nat} \rightarrow \mathsf{Nat}^{\widehat{\imath}}) \rightarrow \mathsf{Nat} = \lambda x : \mathsf{Nat}^{\widehat{\imath}}.\ \lambda f : \mathsf{Nat} \rightarrow \mathsf{Nat}^{\widehat{\widehat{\imath}}}.\\
\quad \mathsf{case}_{\mathsf{Nat}}\ (f\ x)\ \mathsf{of}\ \{\mathsf{o} \Rightarrow \mathsf{o}\\
\qquad\qquad \mid \mathsf{s} \Rightarrow \lambda x' : \mathsf{Nat}^{\widehat{\imath}}.\ \mathsf{case}\ x'\ \mathsf{of}\ \{\\
\qquad\qquad\qquad \mid \mathsf{o} \Rightarrow \mathsf{o}\\
\qquad\qquad\qquad \mid \mathsf{s} \Rightarrow \lambda y' : \mathsf{Nat}^{\imath}.\ \mathit{loop}\ y'\ (\mathsf{shift}\ f)\\
\qquad\qquad\qquad \}\\
\qquad\qquad \}\\
\quad) : \quad \mathsf{Nat}^{s} \rightarrow (\mathsf{Nat} \rightarrow \mathsf{Nat}^{\widehat{s}}) \rightarrow \mathsf{Nat}
\end{array}
$$

The stage variable $\imath$ occurs negatively in the type $(\mathsf{Nat} \rightarrow \mathsf{Nat}^{\widehat{\imath}}) \rightarrow \mathsf{Nat}$. Therefore, the expression loop would be typable in $F^{\frown}$ without the condition $\imath$ pos $\overline{\theta}$ in the rule (rec). But then it would also be possible to type the term loop o plus_2 which is non normalizing

$$\mathsf{loop\ o\ plus\_2} \rightarrow^* \mathsf{loop\ o\ (shift\ plus\_2)} \rightarrow^* \mathsf{loop\ o\ plus\_2} \rightarrow \ldots \qquad \square$$

Examples. We now review some examples of functions presented in Sect. 2.2. We begin with the minus and div functions on natural numbers.

*Example 3.14 (*minus *and* div*).* In F^{rec}, minus and div are defined as follows:

$$
\begin{array}{l}
\mathsf{minus} := (\mathsf{letrec}_{\mathsf{Nat} \rightarrow \mathsf{Nat} \rightarrow \mathsf{Nat}}\ \mathit{ms} = \lambda x : \mathsf{Nat}.\ \lambda y : \mathsf{Nat}.\\
\quad \mathsf{case}_{\mathsf{Nat}}\ x\ \mathsf{of}\ \{\ \mathsf{o} \Rightarrow x\\
\qquad\qquad \mid \mathsf{s} \Rightarrow \lambda x' : \mathsf{Nat}.\ \mathsf{case}\ y\ \mathsf{of}\ \{\ \mathsf{o} \Rightarrow x\\
\qquad\qquad\qquad\qquad \mid \mathsf{s} \Rightarrow \lambda y' : \mathsf{Nat}.\ \mathit{ms}\ x'\ y'\ \}\\
\qquad\qquad \}\\
\quad) : \quad \mathsf{Nat} \rightarrow \mathsf{Nat} \rightarrow \mathsf{Nat}
\end{array}
$$

$$
\begin{array}{l}
\mathsf{div} := (\mathsf{letrec}_{\mathsf{Nat} \rightarrow \mathsf{Nat} \rightarrow \mathsf{Nat}}\ \mathit{div} = \lambda x : \mathsf{Nat}.\ \lambda y : \mathsf{Nat}.\\
\quad \mathsf{case}_{\mathsf{Nat}}\ x\ \mathsf{of}\ \{\ \mathsf{o} \Rightarrow \mathsf{o}\\
\qquad\qquad \mid \mathsf{s} \Rightarrow \lambda x' : \mathsf{Nat}.\ \mathsf{s}\ (\mathit{div}\ (\mathsf{minus}\ x'\ y)\ y)\ \}\\
\quad) : \quad \mathsf{Nat} \rightarrow \mathsf{Nat} \rightarrow \mathsf{Nat}
\end{array}
$$

For minus, in $\overline{\Gamma'} =_{\mathrm{def}} ms : \mathsf{Nat}^{\imath} \to \mathsf{Nat} \to \mathsf{Nat}^{\imath}, x : \mathsf{Nat}^{\widehat{\imath}}, y : \mathsf{Nat}, x' : \mathsf{Nat}^{\imath}$ we have

$$\frac{\overline{\Gamma'} \vdash y \ : \ \mathsf{Nat}^{\widehat{\infty}} \qquad \overline{\Gamma'} \vdash x \ : \ \mathsf{Nat}^{\widehat{\imath}} \qquad \overline{\Gamma'} \vdash \lambda y' : \mathsf{Nat}.\ ms\, x'\, y' \ : \ \mathsf{Nat}^{\infty} \to \mathsf{Nat}^{\widehat{\imath}}}{\overline{\Gamma'} \vdash \mathsf{case}_{\mathsf{Nat}}\ y\ \mathsf{of}\ \{\mathsf{o} \Rightarrow x \mid \mathsf{s} \Rightarrow \lambda y' : \mathsf{Nat}.\ ms\, x'\, y'\} \ : \ \mathsf{Nat}^{\widehat{\imath}}}$$

We deduce that

$$\frac{\overline{\Gamma} \vdash x \ : \ \mathsf{Nat}^{\widehat{\imath}} \qquad \overline{\Gamma} \vdash x \ : \ \mathsf{Nat}^{\widehat{\imath}} \qquad \overline{\Gamma} \vdash \lambda x' : \mathsf{Nat}.\ e_{\mathsf{s}} \ : \ \mathsf{Nat}^{\imath} \to \mathsf{Nat}^{\widehat{\imath}}}{\overline{\Gamma} \vdash \mathsf{case}_{\mathsf{Nat}}\ x\ \mathsf{of}\ \{\mathsf{o} \Rightarrow x \mid \mathsf{s} \Rightarrow \lambda x' : \mathsf{Nat}.\ e_{\mathsf{s}}\} \ : \ \mathsf{Nat}^{\widehat{\imath}}}$$

where $e_{\mathsf{s}} := \mathsf{case}_{\mathsf{Nat}}\ y\ \mathsf{of}\ \{\mathsf{o} \Rightarrow x \mid \mathsf{s} \Rightarrow \lambda y' : \mathsf{Nat}.\ ms\, x'\, y'\}$ and $\overline{\Gamma}$ is the typing context $ms : \mathsf{Nat}^{\imath} \to \mathsf{Nat} \to \mathsf{Nat}^{\imath}, x : \mathsf{Nat}^{\widehat{\imath}}, y : \mathsf{Nat}$. Using (rec), for all stages s we get

$$\frac{ms : \mathsf{Nat}^{\imath} \to \mathsf{Nat} \to \mathsf{Nat}^{\imath} \vdash \lambda x : \mathsf{Nat}.\ \lambda y : \mathsf{Nat}.\ e_{\mathsf{minus}} \ : \ \mathsf{Nat}^{\widehat{\imath}} \to \mathsf{Nat} \to \mathsf{Nat}^{\widehat{\imath}}}{\vdash (\mathsf{letrec}\ ms = \lambda x : \mathsf{Nat}.\ \lambda y : \mathsf{Nat}.\ e_{\mathsf{minus}}) \ : \ \mathsf{Nat}^{s} \to \mathsf{Nat} \to \mathsf{Nat}^{s}}$$

where $e_{\mathsf{minus}} := \mathsf{case}_{\mathsf{Nat}}\ x\ \mathsf{of}\ \{\mathsf{o} \Rightarrow x \mid \mathsf{s} \Rightarrow \lambda x' : \mathsf{Nat}.\ e_{\mathsf{s}}\}$. Hence, system $F^{\frown}$ is powerful enough to express that the size of ($\mathsf{minus}\ n\ m$) is at most the size of n. This information is essential for the typing of div. In the computation of ($\mathsf{div}\,(\mathsf{s}\,n)\,m$), the recursive call to div is performed on the argument ($\mathsf{minus}\ n\ m$) which is not a subterm of ($\mathsf{s}\,n$). It can even be syntactically arbitrarily bigger! However, with stages we have the information that if ($\mathsf{s}\,n$), as a natural number, is of size at most $\widehat{p}$, then ($\mathsf{minus}\ n\ m$) is of size at most p. The termination argument relies on this decreasing from $\widehat{p}$ to p.

Formally, using (rec), for all stages s we obtain $\mathsf{div} : \mathsf{Nat}^{s} \to \mathsf{Nat} \to \mathsf{Nat}^{s}$ from the judgment

$$\begin{array}{l} \qquad div : \mathsf{Nat}^{\imath} \to \mathsf{Nat} \to \mathsf{Nat}^{\imath} \vdash \\ \lambda x : \mathsf{Nat}.\ \lambda y : \mathsf{Nat}.\ \mathsf{case}_{\mathsf{Nat}}\ x\ \mathsf{of}\ \{\ \mathsf{o} \Rightarrow \mathsf{o} \\ \qquad\qquad\qquad\qquad\qquad\qquad \mid \mathsf{s} \Rightarrow \lambda x' : \mathsf{Nat}.\ \mathsf{s}\ \underbrace{(div\ \underbrace{(\mathsf{minus}\ x'\ y)}_{\mathsf{Nat}^{\imath}}\ y)}_{\mathsf{Nat}^{\imath}} \\ \qquad\qquad\qquad\qquad\qquad \}\ :\ \mathsf{Nat}^{\widehat{\imath}} \to \mathsf{Nat} \to \mathsf{Nat}^{\widehat{\imath}} \end{array}$$

□

Example 3.15 (Ordinals). In F^{rec}, the addition on ordinals is defined as

$$\begin{array}{l} \mathsf{add} := (\mathsf{letrec}_{\mathsf{Ord} \to \mathsf{Ord} \to \mathsf{Ord}}\ add = \lambda x : \mathsf{Ord}.\ \lambda y : \mathsf{Ord}. \\ \qquad\quad \mathsf{case}_{\mathsf{Ord}}\ x\ \mathsf{of}\ \{\mathsf{o} \Rightarrow y \\ \qquad\qquad\qquad\qquad\quad \mid \mathsf{s} \Rightarrow \lambda x' : \mathsf{Ord}.\ \mathsf{s}\ (add\ x'\ y) \\ \qquad\qquad\qquad\qquad\quad \mid \mathsf{lim} \Rightarrow \lambda f : \mathsf{Nat} \to \mathsf{Ord}.\ \ \mathsf{lim}\ (\lambda z : \mathsf{Nat}.\ add\ (f\ z)\ y)\} \\ \qquad)\ :\quad \mathsf{Ord} \to \mathsf{Ord} \to \mathsf{Ord} \end{array}$$

Therefore, we have $\mathsf{add}\ (\mathsf{lim}\ f)\ e \to^{*} \mathsf{lim}\ (\lambda z : \mathsf{Nat}.\ \mathsf{add}\ (f\ z)\ e)$. The difficulty here is that $f\,z$ is not a subterm of $\mathsf{lim}\,f$. However, this example is handled by the syntactic termination criterion described in Sect. 2.5. In $F^{\frown}$, add is typed as follows:

$$
\begin{array}{l}
\mathsf{add} := (\mathsf{letrec}\ add : \mathsf{Ord}^{\imath} \to \mathsf{Ord} \to \mathsf{Ord} = \lambda x : \mathsf{Ord}^{\widehat{\imath}}.\ \lambda y : \mathsf{Ord}. \\
\qquad \mathsf{case}_{\mathsf{Ord}}\ x\ \mathsf{of}\ \{\mathsf{o} \Rightarrow y \\
\qquad\qquad \mid \mathsf{s} \Rightarrow \lambda x' : \mathsf{Ord}^{\imath}.\ \mathsf{s}\ (add\ x'\ y) \\
\qquad\qquad \mid \mathsf{lim} \Rightarrow \lambda f : \mathsf{Nat} \to \mathsf{Ord}^{\imath}.\ \mathsf{lim}\ (\lambda z : \mathsf{Nat}.\ add\ \underbrace{(f\ z)}_{\mathsf{Ord}^{\imath}}\ y)\} \\
\quad) : \quad \mathsf{Ord}^{s} \to \mathsf{Ord} \to \mathsf{Ord}
\end{array}
$$

We now come back to the discussion of Ex. 3.8.(iii), about the stage of lim inj, where inj : Nat → Ord is the canonical injection of natural numbers into ordinals. In $F^{\frown}$, it is defined as follows:

$$
\begin{array}{l}
\mathsf{inj} := (\mathsf{letrec}\ inj : \mathsf{Nat}^{\imath} \to \mathsf{Ord}^{\imath} = \lambda x : \mathsf{Nat}^{\widehat{\imath}}. \\
\qquad \mathsf{case}_{\mathsf{Nat}}\ x\ \mathsf{of}\ \{\mathsf{o} \Rightarrow \mathsf{o} \\
\qquad\qquad \mid \mathsf{s} \Rightarrow \lambda x' : \mathsf{Nat}^{\imath}.\ \mathsf{s}\ (inj\ x')\} \\
\quad) : \quad \mathsf{Nat}^{s} \to \mathsf{Ord}^{s}
\end{array}
$$

Note that this definition uses the same stage variable $\imath$ to annotate both Nat and Ord. Moreover, for all $p \in \mathbb{N}$ we have $\mathsf{inj}\,(\mathsf{s}^p\,\mathsf{o}) \ \to^* \ (\mathsf{s}^p\,\mathsf{o})$. The only way to apply inj to lim is to instantiate their sized types as $\mathsf{Nat}^{\infty} \to \mathsf{Ord}^{\infty}$ and $(\mathsf{Nat}^{\infty} \to \mathsf{Ord}^{\infty}) \to \mathsf{Ord}^{\infty}$ respectively. We thus get $\mathsf{lim\,inj} : \mathsf{Ord}^{\infty}$, and ∞ is the best possible approximation of the size of lim inj expressible in the system. □

Example 3.16 (Concatenations of lists). The function app concatenates two lists. Therefore, if l_1 and l_2 are of respective size s_1 and s_2, then app $l_1\,l_2$ is of size $s_1 + s_2$. But system $F^{\frown}$ does not feature stage addition. Hence the precise size of app $l_1\,l_2$ is not expressible in the system, and we have app $l_1\,l_2 : \mathsf{List}^{\infty}\,X$. Since recursion is performed only on the first argument of app, the size of the second one is not relevant, and for all stages s we have $\mathsf{app} : \Pi X.\ \mathsf{List}^{s}\,X \to \mathsf{List}\,X \to \mathsf{List}\,X$. The function app is defined as follows:

$$
\begin{array}{l}
\mathsf{app} := \Lambda X.\ (\mathsf{letrec}\ app : \mathsf{List}^{\imath}\,X \to \mathsf{List}\,X \to \mathsf{List}\,X = \lambda x : \mathsf{List}^{\widehat{\imath}}\,X.\ \lambda y : \mathsf{List}\,X. \\
\qquad \mathsf{case}_{\mathsf{List}X}\ x\ \mathsf{of}\ \{\mathsf{nil} \Rightarrow y \\
\qquad\qquad \mid \mathsf{cons} \Rightarrow \lambda z : X.\ \lambda x' : \mathsf{List}^{\imath}\,X.\ \ \mathsf{cons}\ z\ (app\ x'\ y) \\
\qquad\qquad \} \\
\quad) : \quad \Pi X.\ \mathsf{List}^{s}\,X \to \mathsf{List}\,X \to \mathsf{List}\,X
\end{array}
$$

The function conc concatenates a list of lists. As for app, we cannot express its precise typing in $F^{\frown}$, and for all stage s we have $\mathsf{conc} : \Pi X.\ \mathsf{List}^{s}\,(\mathsf{List}\,X) \to \mathsf{List}\,X$. The function conc is defined as follows:

$$
\begin{array}{l}
\mathsf{conc} := \Lambda X.\ \ (\mathsf{letrec}\ conc : \mathsf{List}^{\imath}\,(\mathsf{List}\,X) \to \mathsf{List}\,X = \lambda x : \mathsf{List}^{\widehat{\imath}}\,(\mathsf{List}\,X). \\
\qquad \mathsf{case}_{\mathsf{List}\,(\mathsf{List}\,X)}\ x\ \mathsf{of}\ \{\mathsf{nil} \Rightarrow \mathsf{nil} \\
\qquad\qquad \mid \mathsf{cons} \Rightarrow \lambda z : \mathsf{List}\,X.\ \ \lambda x' : \mathsf{List}^{\imath}\,(\mathsf{List}\,X).\ \mathsf{app}\ z\ (conc\ x') \\
\qquad\qquad \} \\
\quad) : \quad \Pi X.\ \mathsf{List}^{s}\,(\mathsf{List}\,X) \to \mathsf{List}\,X
\end{array}
$$

□

Example 3.17 (The map function on a list). The function $\mathsf{map}\, f\, l$ applies the function f to each element of the list l and produces the corresponding list. Hence $\mathsf{map}\, f\, l$ evaluates to a list of the same size as l. This is expressible in $F^{\frown}$ by $\mathsf{map} : \Pi X.\ \Pi Y.\ (X \to Y) \to \mathsf{List}^{s}\, X \to \mathsf{List}^{s}\, Y$. The function map is defined as follows:

$$\begin{array}{l} \mathsf{map} := \Lambda X.\ \Lambda Y.\ \lambda f : X \to Y.\ (\mathsf{letrec}\ \mathit{map} : \mathsf{List}^{\imath}\, X \to \mathsf{List}^{\imath}\, Y = \lambda x : \mathsf{List}^{\hat{\imath}}\, X. \\ \qquad \mathsf{case}_{\mathsf{List}\, X}\ x\ \mathsf{of}\ \{\mathsf{nil} \Rightarrow \mathsf{nil} \\ \qquad\qquad\qquad \mid \mathsf{cons} \Rightarrow \lambda z : X.\ \ \lambda x' : \mathsf{List}^{\imath}\, X.\ \underbrace{\mathsf{cons}\ (f\ z)\ \underbrace{(\mathit{map}\ f\ x')}_{\mathsf{List}^{\imath}\, Y}}_{\mathsf{List}^{\hat{\imath}}\, Y} \\ \qquad\qquad\qquad \} \\ \quad) : \quad \Pi X.\ \Pi Y.\ (X \to Y) \to \mathsf{List}^{s}\, X \to \mathsf{List}^{s}\, Y \qquad \square \end{array}$$

Example 3.18 (Flattening of finitely branching trees). System $F^{\frown}$ is able to prove the termination of flatten, even if the recursive call is made through a call to map. However, as for app and conc, the system $F^{\frown}$ cannot express the precise typing of the flattening of finitely branching trees flatten. The function flatten is defined by induction on the depth of its argument. We thus have

$$\begin{array}{l} \mathsf{flatten} := \Lambda X.\ (\mathsf{letrec}\ \mathit{flat} : \mathsf{Tree}^{\imath}\, X \to \mathsf{List}\, X = \lambda t : \mathsf{Tree}^{\hat{\imath}}\, X.\ \mathsf{case}_{\mathsf{Tree}\ X}\ t\ \mathsf{of}\ \{ \\ \qquad\quad \mathsf{node} \Rightarrow \lambda x : X.\ \lambda xs : \mathsf{List}\ (\mathsf{Tree}^{\imath}\ X).\ \mathsf{cons}\ x\ \underbrace{(\mathsf{conc}\ \underbrace{(\mathsf{map}\ \mathit{flat}\ xs)}_{\mathsf{List}\ (\mathsf{List}\ X)})}_{\mathsf{List}\ X} \\ \qquad\quad \} \\ \quad) : \quad \Pi X.\ \mathsf{Tree}^{s}\, X \to \mathsf{List}\ X \qquad \square \end{array}$$

3.3 Some Important Properties

We now state some important properties of system $F^{\frown}$. They are the properties underlined in Sect. 2.1 for system F, namely subject reduction, strong normalizability of typable terms, and coherence of the type system.

Subject reduction. The proof of this property is easily adapted from the proof for $\lambda^{\frown}$ presented in [5].

Theorem 3.19 (Subject reduction). *If $\overline{\Gamma} \vdash e\ :\ \overline{\tau}$ and $e \to e'$, then also $\overline{\Gamma} \vdash e'\ :\ \overline{\tau}$.*

With respect to stage annotations, subject reduction says that the size approximations represented by stages are preserved by reduction, and moreover that they can be retrieved by the type system after a reduction step.

Strong normalization and coherence. System $F^{\frown}$ enjoys the two crucial properties that fail for F^{rec}, namely strong normalizability of typable terms and coherence. Proofs are sketched in the next section, respectively in Cor. 3.29 and

$$\text{(var)}\ \frac{}{\overline{\Gamma}, x : \overline{\sigma} \vdash x : \overline{\sigma}} \qquad \text{(sub)}\ \frac{\overline{\Gamma} \vdash e : \overline{\sigma} \quad \overline{\sigma} \sqsubseteq \overline{\tau}}{\overline{\Gamma} \vdash e : \overline{\tau}}$$

$$\text{(abs)}\ \frac{\overline{\Gamma}, x : \overline{\tau} \vdash e : \overline{\sigma}}{\overline{\Gamma} \vdash \lambda x : |\overline{\tau}|.\, e : \overline{\tau} \to \overline{\sigma}} \qquad \text{(app)}\ \frac{\overline{\Gamma} \vdash e : \overline{\tau} \to \overline{\sigma} \quad \overline{\Gamma} \vdash e' : \overline{\tau}}{\overline{\Gamma} \vdash e\, e' : \overline{\sigma}}$$

$$\text{(T-abs)}\ \frac{\overline{\Gamma} \vdash e : \overline{\sigma}}{\overline{\Gamma} \vdash \Lambda X.\, e : \Pi X.\, \overline{\sigma}}\ \text{if } X \notin \overline{\Gamma} \qquad \text{(T-app)}\ \frac{\overline{\Gamma} \vdash e : \Pi X.\, \overline{\sigma}}{\overline{\Gamma} \vdash e\, |\overline{\tau}| : \overline{\sigma}[X := \overline{\tau}]}$$

$$\text{(cons)}\ \frac{}{\overline{\Gamma} \vdash c_k : \Pi \boldsymbol{X}.\, \overline{\boldsymbol{\theta}}_{\boldsymbol{k}} \to d^{\hat{\imath}}\, \boldsymbol{X}}\ \text{if } c_k \in \mathcal{C}(d) \text{ for some } d$$

$$\text{(case)}\ \frac{c_k : \Pi \boldsymbol{X}.\, \overline{\boldsymbol{\theta}}_{\boldsymbol{k}} \to d^{\hat{\imath}}\, \boldsymbol{X} \qquad \overline{\Gamma} \vdash e : d^{\hat{s}}\, \overline{\boldsymbol{\tau}} \quad \overline{\Gamma} \vdash e_k : \overline{\boldsymbol{\theta}}_{\boldsymbol{k}}[\boldsymbol{X} := \overline{\boldsymbol{\tau}}, \imath := s] \to \overline{\sigma} \quad (1 \leq k \leq n)}{\overline{\Gamma} \vdash \mathsf{case}_{|\overline{\sigma}|}\ e \text{ of } \{c_1 \Rightarrow e_1 \mid \cdots \mid c_n \Rightarrow e_n\} : \overline{\sigma}}$$
$$\text{if } \mathcal{C}(d) = \{c_1, \ldots, c_n\}$$

$$\text{(rec)}\ \frac{\overline{\Gamma}, f : d^{\imath}\overline{\boldsymbol{\tau}} \to \overline{\theta} \vdash e : d^{\hat{\imath}}\overline{\boldsymbol{\tau}} \to \overline{\theta}[\imath := \hat{\imath}] \qquad \imath \text{ pos } \overline{\theta}}{\overline{\Gamma} \vdash (\mathsf{letrec}_{d|\overline{\boldsymbol{\tau}}| \to |\overline{\theta}|}\ f = e) : d^{s}\overline{\boldsymbol{\tau}} \to \overline{\theta}[\imath := s]}\ \text{if } \imath \notin \overline{\Gamma}, \overline{\boldsymbol{\tau}}$$

Fig. 5. Typing rules for $F^{\frown}$

in Cor. 3.30. They both rely on a reducibility interpretation of $F^{\frown}$ by saturated sets [11,18]. Let SN be the set of strongly normalizing terms. Hence SN is the least set of terms such that

$$\forall e. \quad (\forall e'. \quad e \to_{\beta\iota\gamma} e' \quad \Longrightarrow \quad e' \in \mathsf{SN}) \quad \Longrightarrow \quad e \in \mathsf{SN}$$

Theorem 3.20 (Strong normalization). *If $\overline{\Gamma} \vdash e : \overline{\tau}$ then $e \in \mathsf{SN}$.*

Theorem 3.21 (Coherence). *There is no term e such that $\vdash e : \bot$.*

3.4 A Reducibility Interpretation

In this section, we sketch the correctness proof of a reducibility semantics for $F^{\frown}$. Our semantics is based on a variant of reducibility [12] called Tait's saturated sets [18], and will be used to prove both the strong normalization of typable terms and the coherence of the type system. We begin by the interpretation of stages, and turn to the model construction. We then state its correctness, from which we deduce strong normalization and coherence.

In the whole section, if f is a map from A to B, $a \in A$ and $b \in B$, then $f(a := b) : A \to B$ maps a to b and is equal to f everywhere else.

The stage model. Stages are interpreted by the ordinals used to build the interpretation of inductive types. While first-order inductive types can be interpreted by induction on $\mathbb{N}$, higher-order inductive types may require an induction on countable ordinals. Recall that $(\Omega, \leq_\Omega)$ denote the well-ordered set of countable ordinals and by $+_\Omega$ the usual ordinal addition on Ω.

Let $\widehat{\Omega} =_{\mathrm{def}} \Omega \cup \{\Omega\}$. For all $\alpha \in \Omega$ and all $\beta \in \widehat{\Omega}$, let $\alpha < \beta$ iff ($\beta = \Omega$ or $\alpha <_\Omega \beta$).

Definition 3.22 (Interpretation of stages). *A* stage valuation *is a map* π *from* $\mathcal{V}_{\mathcal{S}}$ *to* $\widehat{\Omega}$*, and is extended to a* stage interpretation $(\!|.|\!)_\pi : \mathcal{S} \to \widehat{\Omega}$ *as follows:*

$$(\!|\iota|\!)_\pi = \pi(\iota) \qquad (\!|0|\!)_\pi = 0 \qquad (\!|\infty|\!)_\pi = \Omega \qquad (\!|\widehat{s}|\!)_\pi = \begin{cases} (\!|s|\!)_\pi + 1 & \text{if } (\!|s|\!)_\pi < \Omega \\ \Omega & \text{if } (\!|s|\!)_\pi = \Omega \end{cases}$$

Type interpretation. In this section, we define the type interpretation and prove its correctness. Our proof follows the pattern of [1]. We interpret types by saturated sets. It is convenient to define them by means of *elimination contexts*:

$$E[\,] \;::=\; [\,] \mid E[\,]\,e \mid E[\,]\,|\tau| \mid \mathsf{case}_{|\tau|}\, E[\,] \;\mathsf{of}\; \{\mathbf{c} \Rightarrow \mathbf{e}\}$$

Note that the hole $[\,]$ of $E[\,]$ never occurs under a binder. Thus $E[\,]$ can be seen as a term with one occurrence of a special variable $[\,]$. Therefore, we can define $E[e]$ as $E[\,][[\,] := e]$. The relation of *weak head* $\beta\iota\gamma$*-reduction* is defined as $E[e] \to_{\mathrm{wh}} E[e']$ if and only if $e \succ_{\beta\iota\gamma} e'$.

Definition 3.23 (Saturated sets)
A set $S \subseteq \mathsf{SN}$ *is* saturated *(*$S \in \mathsf{SAT}$*) if*

(SAT1) $E[x] \in S$ *for all* $E[\,] \in \mathsf{SN}$ *and all* $x \in \mathcal{V}_{\mathcal{E}}$,
(SAT2) *if* $e \in \mathsf{SN}$ *and* $e \to_{wh} e'$ *for some* $e' \in S$ *then* $e \in S$.

One can easily show that $\mathsf{SN} \in \mathsf{SAT}$ and that $\bigcap \mathcal{Y}, \bigcup \mathcal{Y} \in \mathsf{SAT}$ for all non-empty $\mathcal{Y} \subseteq \mathsf{SAT}$. One can also check that the *function space* on SAT, defined for $X, Y \in \mathsf{SAT}$ as:

$$X \to Y \;=_{\mathrm{def}}\; \{e \mid \forall e'.\, e' \in X \implies e\,e' \in Y\}$$

returns a saturated set.

Because saturated sets are closed under non-empty intersections, one can define for each $X \subseteq \mathsf{SN}$ the smallest saturated set containing X, written $\overline{X}$. We let $\bot =_{\mathrm{def}} \overline{\emptyset}$; it is easy to show that $\bot$ is the smallest element of SAT. The following properties precisely characterizes the membership of an expression to a saturated set.

Lemma 3.24
(i) $\bot = \{e \in \mathsf{SN} \mid \exists E[\,], x.\;\; e \to^*_{wh} E[x]\}$.
(ii) If $X \subseteq \mathsf{SN}$ *then* $\overline{X} = \bot \cup \{e \in \mathsf{SN} \mid e \to^*_{wh} X\}$.

The interpretation of types is defined in two steps. We first define the interpretation scheme of types, given an interpretation of datatypes. We then define the interpretation of datatypes.

Definition 3.25. *An* interpretation of datatypes *is a family* $(\mathcal{I}_d)_{d\in\mathcal{D}}$ *of functions* $\mathcal{I}_d : \mathsf{SAT}^{\mathsf{ar}(d)} \times \widehat{\Omega} \to \mathsf{SAT}$ *for each* $d \in \mathcal{D}$*. Given an interpretation of datatypes* $\mathcal{I}$*, a stage valuation* π *and a* type valuation $\xi : \mathcal{V}_{\mathcal{T}} \to \mathsf{SAT}$*, the* type interpretation $[\![.]\!]^{\mathcal{I}}_{\pi,\xi} : \underline{\mathcal{T}} \to \mathsf{SAT}$ *is defined by induction on types as follows*

$$\begin{aligned}
[\![X]\!]^{\mathcal{I}}_{\pi,\xi} &= \xi(X)\\
[\![\tau \to \sigma]\!]^{\mathcal{I}}_{\pi,\xi} &= [\![\tau]\!]^{\mathcal{I}}_{\pi,\xi} \to [\![\sigma]\!]^{\mathcal{I}}_{\pi,\xi}\\
[\![\Pi X.\, \tau]\!]^{\mathcal{I}}_{\pi,\xi} &= \left\{e \mid \forall |\sigma| \in |\mathcal{T}|,\ \forall S \in \mathsf{SAT},\quad e\,|\sigma| \in [\![\tau]\!]^{\mathcal{I}}_{\pi,\xi(X:=S)}\right\}\\
[\![d^s \boldsymbol{\tau}]\!]^{\mathcal{I}}_{\pi,\xi} &= \mathcal{I}_d([\![\boldsymbol{\tau}]\!]^{\mathcal{I}}_{\pi,\xi}, (\![s]\!)_\pi)
\end{aligned}$$

We now define the interpretation of inductive datatypes. Recall that they are defined in an ordered list $I_1, \ldots, I_n$ of declarations (see Def. 2.25). Let us say that k is the *rank* of d if d is defined in I_k. The interpretation $(\mathcal{I}_d)_{d\in\mathcal{D}}$ is defined by induction on the rank, and for each $d \in \mathcal{D}$, the map $\mathcal{I}_d : \mathsf{SAT}^{\mathsf{ar}(d)} \times \widehat{\Omega} \to \mathsf{SAT}$ is defined by induction on $\widehat{\Omega}$.

Definition 3.26. *For all* $d \in \mathcal{D}$*, all* $\boldsymbol{S} \in \mathsf{SAT}^{\mathsf{ar}(d)}$ *and all* $\alpha \in \widehat{\Omega}$*, we define* $\mathcal{I}_d(\boldsymbol{S}, \alpha)$ *by induction on pairs* (k, α) *ordered by* $(<,<)_{lex}$*, where* k *is the rank of* d*, as follows:*

$$\begin{aligned}
\mathcal{I}_d(\boldsymbol{S}, 0) &= \bot\\
\mathcal{I}_d(\boldsymbol{S}, \alpha+1) &= \bigcup\{c\,[\![\overline{\boldsymbol{\theta}}]\!]^{\mathcal{I}}_{\iota:=\alpha, \boldsymbol{X}:=\boldsymbol{S}} \mid c \in \mathcal{C}(d) \wedge \mathsf{Type}(c) = \Pi \boldsymbol{X}.\, \overline{\boldsymbol{\theta}} \to d^{\iota}\boldsymbol{X}\}\\
\mathcal{I}_d(\boldsymbol{S}, \lambda) &= \bigcup\{\mathcal{I}_d(\boldsymbol{S}, \alpha) \mid \alpha < \lambda\} \qquad\qquad \textit{if } \lambda \textit{ is a limit ordinal}
\end{aligned}$$

where $c\,\boldsymbol{S} =_{def} \overline{\{c\,|\boldsymbol{\tau}|\,\boldsymbol{a} \mid \boldsymbol{a} \in \boldsymbol{S} \ \wedge\ |\boldsymbol{\tau}| \in |\mathcal{T}|\}}$ *for all* $\boldsymbol{S} \in \mathsf{SAT}$.

Note that $\mathcal{I}_d(\boldsymbol{S}, \alpha+1)$ only uses $c[\![\overline{\boldsymbol{\theta}}]\!]^{\mathcal{I}}_{\iota:=\alpha, \boldsymbol{X}:=\boldsymbol{S}}$ with $c \in \mathcal{C}(d)$, which in turn only uses $\mathcal{I}_d(\boldsymbol{U}, \beta)$ with $(p, \beta)\,(<,<)_{\mathrm{lex}}\,(k, \alpha+1)$, where k (resp. p) is the rank of d (resp. d').

Now that we have an interpretation of inductive datatypes $(\mathcal{I}_d)_{d\in\mathcal{D}}$, we can interpret types as in Def. 3.25 using this interpretation of datatypes. It is convenient to denote $[\![.]\!]^{\mathcal{I}}_{\pi,\xi}$ by $[\![.]\!]_{\pi,\xi}$.

We gather in Fig. 6 some properties of $(\![.]\!)_\pi$ and $[\![.]\!]_{\pi,\xi}$. The following Proposition states that each inductive datatype can be interpreted by a countable ordinal. This is crucial in order to deal with the rule (cons) in the proof of Thm. 3.28. The key-point is that for every *countable* $S \subseteq \Omega$, there is $\beta \in \Omega$ such that $\alpha < \beta$ for all $\alpha \in S$ [9].

Proposition 3.27. *For all* $d \in \mathcal{D}$ *and all* $\boldsymbol{S} \in \mathsf{SAT}^{\mathsf{ar}(d)}$*, there is an ordinal* $\alpha < \Omega$ *such that* $\mathcal{I}_d(\boldsymbol{S}, \alpha) = \mathcal{I}_d(\boldsymbol{S}, \beta)$ *for all* β *such that* $\alpha \leq \beta \leq \Omega$*.*

Correctness of the interpretation. As usual, soundness is shown by induction on typing derivations. Given $\pi : \mathcal{V}_{\mathcal{S}} \to \widehat{\Omega}$, $\xi : \mathcal{V}_{\mathcal{T}} \to \mathsf{SAT}$ and $\rho : (\mathcal{V}_{\mathcal{E}} \to \mathcal{E}) \uplus (\mathcal{V}_{\mathcal{T}} \to |\mathcal{T}|)$, we let $(\pi, \xi, \rho) \models \Gamma$ if and only if $\rho(x) \in [\![\Gamma(x)]\!]_{\pi,\xi}$ for all $x \in \mathsf{dom}(\Gamma)$.

Substitution	$(\!\|p[\iota := s]\|\!)_\pi$	$=$	$(\!\|p\|\!)_{\pi(\iota := (\!\|s\|\!)_\pi)}$
	$[\![\overline{\tau}[\iota := s]]\!]_{\pi,\xi}$	$=$	$[\![\overline{\tau}]\!]_{\pi(\iota := (\!\|s\|\!)_\pi),\xi}$
	$[\![\overline{\tau}[X := \overline{\sigma}]]\!]_{\pi,\xi}$	$=$	$[\![\overline{\tau}]\!]_{\pi,\xi(X := [\![\overline{\sigma}]\!]_{\pi,\xi})}$
Stage monotony	$\alpha \leq \beta$	$\Rightarrow$	$\mathcal{I}_d(\boldsymbol{S}, \alpha) \subseteq \mathcal{I}_d(\boldsymbol{S}, \beta)$
	$\alpha \leq \beta \ \wedge \ \iota \ \mathsf{pos} \ \theta$	$\Rightarrow$	$[\![\theta]\!]_{\pi(\iota := \alpha),\xi} \subseteq [\![\theta]\!]_{\pi(\iota := \beta),\xi}$
	$\alpha \leq \beta \ \wedge \ \iota \ \mathsf{neg} \ \theta$	$\Rightarrow$	$[\![\theta]\!]_{\pi(\iota := \beta),\xi} \subseteq [\![\theta]\!]_{\pi(\iota := \alpha),\xi}$
Substage soundness	$s \leq p$	$\Rightarrow$	$(\!\|s\|\!)_\pi \leq (\!\|p\|\!)_\pi$
Subtyping soundness	$\overline{\tau} \sqsubseteq \overline{\sigma}$	$\Rightarrow$	$[\![\overline{\tau}]\!]_{\pi,\xi} \subseteq [\![\overline{\sigma}]\!]_{\pi,\xi}$

Fig. 6. Properties of the type interpretation

Theorem 3.28 (Typing soundness). *If $\overline{\Gamma} \vdash e : \overline{\tau}$, then $e\rho \in [\![\overline{\tau}]\!]_{\pi,\xi}$ for all π, ξ, ρ such that $(\pi, \xi, \rho) \models \overline{\Gamma}$.*

We deduce the strong normalization of typable terms and the coherence of the system.

Corollary 3.29 (Strong normalization). *If $\overline{\Gamma} \vdash e : \overline{\tau}$ then $e \in \mathsf{SN}$.*

Proof. Apply Thm. 3.28 with any π and ξ, and with the identity substitution for ρ. We thus have $(\pi, \xi, \rho) \models \overline{\Gamma}$, hence $e = e\rho \in [\![\overline{\tau}]\!]_{\pi,\xi} \subseteq \mathsf{SN}$. □

Corollary 3.30 (Coherence). *There is no term e such that $\vdash e : \Pi X.\ X$.*

Proof. Assume that $\vdash e : \Pi X.\ X$. Note that e must be a closed term, i.e. $\mathsf{FV}_{\mathcal{E}}(e) = \emptyset$. By Thm. 3.28, we have $e \in [\![\Pi X.\ X]\!]$. Therefore, for all $\tau \in \mathcal{T}$, we have $e\,\tau \in \bot$. By Lem. 3.24.(i), $e\,\tau$ reduces to a term of the form $E[x]$ for some $x \in \mathcal{V}_{\mathcal{E}}$. But $E[x]$ is an open term, which contradicts the fact that $e\,\tau$ is closed. □

4 Type Inference

The purpose of this section is to present a sound and complete algorithm that infers size annotations for $F\widehat{\ }$. One particularity of our algorithm is to return concise results, in the form of constrained types (C, τ) where τ is a sized type and C is a set of stage inequalities. Restricting such constrained types is beneficial for two reasons: first of all, sets of stage inequalities are always satisfiable (by mapping all stage variables to ∞), hence a term e is typable whenever the inference algorithm does not return an error. Second of all, the algorithm avoids the use of disjunction, which makes satisfiability of constraints complex. Disjunctive typings are avoided by requiring recursive definitions to carry tags that identify which positions are meant to carry a size annotation related to the size of the recursive argument. Consider the following expression:

$$(\mathsf{letrec}_{\mathsf{Nat} \to \mathsf{Nat}}\ f = \lambda x : \mathsf{Nat}.\ \mathsf{o})$$

It may be given the types $\mathsf{Nat}^{\imath} \to \mathsf{Nat}^{\imath}$ and $\mathsf{Nat}^{\imath} \to \mathsf{Nat}^{\widehat{\jmath}}$. If we restrict to conjunctive constrained types as discussed above, it is impossible to obtain a more general type that subsumes both types. In order to achieve more general types without using disjunctive constrained types, we tag positions whose size must use the same base size variable as the recursive argument with a special symbol $\star$. These tags will be used by the inference algorithm to separate between stage variables that must pertain to the same hierarchy as the stage variable of the recursive arguments, and those that must not. In effect, the inference algorithm will produce the following results:

$$(\mathsf{letrec}_{\mathsf{Nat}^\star \to \mathsf{Nat}^\star}\ f = \lambda x : \mathsf{Nat}.\ \mathsf{o}) : \mathsf{Nat}^{\imath} \to \mathsf{Nat}^{\imath}$$
$$(\mathsf{letrec}_{\mathsf{Nat}^\star \to \mathsf{Nat}}\ f = \lambda x : \mathsf{Nat}.\ \mathsf{o}) : \mathsf{Nat}^{\imath} \to \mathsf{Nat}^{\widehat{\jmath}}$$

For clarity, the inference algorithm is defined together with a checking algorithm, that takes as additional argument a candidate type and verifies that it is a correct instance of the computed type. Since we start from terms that do not carry size annotations, both algorithms must generate size variables that are used to build the size annotations that decorate the inferred or checked types. In order to guarantee that they only introduce fresh size variables, the algorithms take an auxiliary parameter V, that represents the set of size variables that have been used elsewhere, and return an extended set V' that includes V and the new stage variables that were used for the expression under evaluation. Therefore,

- the type inference algorithm $\mathtt{Infer}(V, \overline{\Gamma}, e)$ takes as input a context $\overline{\Gamma}$, an expression e and a set of size variables V s.t. $\mathsf{FV}(\overline{\Gamma}) \subseteq V$, and returns a tuple $(V', C, \overline{\tau})$ where $\overline{\tau}$ is an annotated type, C is a constraint, and V' is a set of size variables s.t. $\mathsf{FV}(C, \overline{\tau}) \cup V \subseteq V'$;
- the type checking algorithm takes as additional input a candidate type $\overline{\tau}$; then $\mathtt{Check}(V, \overline{\Gamma}, e, \overline{\tau})$ returns a pair (V', C) s.t. $\mathsf{FV}(C, \overline{\tau}) \cup V \subseteq V'$ and ensuring that e has type $\rho\overline{\tau}$ in environment $\overline{\Gamma}$ provided that ρ is a solution for C.

The algorithm is sound and complete.

Proposition 4.1 (Soundness and completeness of Check and Infer)

- *Soundness:*
  (i) If $\mathtt{Check}(V, \overline{\Gamma}, e, \overline{\tau}) = (V', C)$ *then* $\rho(\overline{\Gamma}) \vdash e : \rho(\overline{\tau})$ *for all* ρ *s.t.* $\rho \models C$.
  (ii) If $\mathtt{Infer}(V, \overline{\Gamma}, e) = (V', C, \overline{\tau})$ *then* $\rho(\overline{\Gamma}) \vdash e : \rho(\overline{\tau})$ *for all* ρ *s.t.* $\rho \models C$.
- *Completeness:*
  (i) If $\rho(\overline{\Gamma}) \vdash e : \rho\overline{\tau}$ *and* $\mathsf{FV}_{\jmath}(\overline{\Gamma}, \overline{\tau}) \subseteq V$ *then there exist* V', C, ρ' *such that* $\mathtt{Check}(V, \overline{\Gamma}, e, \overline{\tau}) = (V', C)$ *and* $\rho' \models C$ *and* $\rho =_V \rho'$.
  (ii) If $\rho(\overline{\Gamma}) \vdash e : \overline{\theta}$ *and* $\mathsf{FV}_{\jmath}(\overline{\Gamma}) \subseteq V$ *there exist* $V', C, \overline{\tau}, \rho'$ *such that* $\mathtt{Infer}(V, \overline{\Gamma}, e) = (V', C, \overline{\tau})$ *and* $\rho' \models C$ *and* $\rho'(\overline{\tau}) \sqsubseteq \overline{\theta}$ *and* $\rho' =_V \rho$
  where $\rho =_V \rho'$ *means that* $\rho(\alpha) = \rho'(\alpha)$ *for all* $\alpha \in V$.

Note that every conjunctive constraint has a solution. Therefore, if the inference algorithm is successful on input $(\overline{\Gamma}, e)$, i.e. $\mathtt{Infer}(\overline{\Gamma}, e) = (C, \tau)$, one can find ρ such that $\rho \models C$. Therefore, by soundness $\rho\overline{\Gamma} \vdash e : \rho\tau$.

The crux of the algorithm is the rule for recursive definitions, which must check the existence of solutions for more elaborate constraints, in which one can also declare that a stage variable $\imath$ can only be interpreted as itself (in effect it amounts to restrict ourselves to substitutions ρ such that $\rho(\imath) = \imath$), and that a stage s cannot be in the same hierarchy as a fixed stage variable $\imath$. For such systems, the existence of a solution is not always guaranteed, and we shall therefore device a dedicated algorithm to verify whether a solution exists.

Outline. Type inference is presented step by step. We begin by recalling the straightforward type inference algorithm of system F in Sect. 4.1. Then, in Sect. 4.2, we discuss the effect of adding sized inductive datatypes, with subtyping and case analysis but without recursion. We concentrate on the subtyping relation and the necessity to infer stage annotations for λ-abstractions, type applications and case analysis. At this level, we do not need to be precise about freshness conditions. Its is sufficient to work with

- the judgment $C\ ;\ \overline{\Gamma} \vdash e \uparrow \overline{\tau}$, which stands for $\texttt{Infer}(\overline{\Gamma}, e) = (C, \overline{\tau})$, and
- the judgment $C\ ;\ \overline{\Gamma} \vdash e \downarrow \overline{\tau}$, which stands for $\texttt{Check}(\overline{\Gamma}, e, \overline{\tau}) = C$.

In Sect. 4.3, we informally discuss the way we handle recursive definitions. The main point is an auxiliary algorithm called `RecCheck`, which is informally presented and justified. Finally, in Sect. 4.4 we discuss the full type inference algorithm of $F^{\frown}$, as presented in [6] and using the functions $\texttt{Infer}(V, \overline{\Gamma}, e)$ and $\texttt{Check}(V, \overline{\Gamma}, e, \overline{\tau})$.

4.1 Preliminaries: Type Inference in System F

In the Church style system F, as presented in Sect. 2.1, type inference is trivial, because the typing derivation of a term is uniquely determined by the shape of a term. Hence, the type inference algorithm is directly given by the typing rules read bottom-up:

- The type of x in the context Γ is $\Gamma(x)$ if and only if $x \in \mathsf{dom}(\Gamma)$.
- The type of $\lambda x : \tau.\ e$ in Γ is $\tau \to \sigma$ if and only if the type of e in $\Gamma, x : \tau$ is σ;
- The type of $e\,e'$ in Γ is σ if and only if there is a (necessarily unique) type τ such that the type of e (resp. e') in Γ is $\tau \to \sigma$ (resp. τ).
- The type of $\Lambda X.\ e$ in Γ is $\Pi X.\ \tau$ if and only if the type of e in Γ is τ and $X \notin \Gamma$.
- The type of $e\,\tau$ in Γ is $\sigma[X := \tau]$ if and only if the type of e in Γ is $\Pi X.\ \sigma$.

4.2 Adding Sized Inductive Datatypes

We present type inference in system F enriched with the sized typing rules for constructors, case analysis, and subtyping. Recall that sized types, defined in Def. 3.4, are given by the abstract syntax:

$$\overline{\mathcal{T}} ::= \mathcal{V}_{\mathcal{T}} \mid \overline{\mathcal{T}} \to \overline{\mathcal{T}} \mid \Pi\mathcal{V}_{\mathcal{T}}.\ \overline{\mathcal{T}} \mid \mathcal{D}^{\mathcal{S}}\,\overline{\mathcal{T}}$$

and that the typing rule (cons), (case) and (sub) are the following:

$$\text{(cons)}\ \frac{}{\overline{\Gamma} \vdash c_k\ :\ \Pi \boldsymbol{X}.\, \overline{\boldsymbol{\theta}}_{\boldsymbol{k}} \to d^{\widehat{\imath}}\, \boldsymbol{X}}\ \text{if } c_k \in \mathcal{C}(d) \text{ for some } d \qquad \text{(sub)}\ \frac{\overline{\Gamma} \vdash e\ :\ \overline{\sigma} \qquad \overline{\sigma} \sqsubseteq \overline{\tau}}{\overline{\Gamma} \vdash e\ :\ \overline{\tau}}$$

$$\text{(case)}\ \frac{\begin{array}{c} c_k : \Pi \boldsymbol{X}.\, \overline{\boldsymbol{\theta}}_{\boldsymbol{k}} \to d^{\widehat{\imath}}\, \boldsymbol{X} \\ \overline{\Gamma} \vdash e\ :\ d^{\widehat{s}}\, \overline{\boldsymbol{\tau}} \quad \overline{\Gamma} \vdash e_k\ :\ \overline{\boldsymbol{\theta}}_{\boldsymbol{k}}[\boldsymbol{X} := \overline{\boldsymbol{\tau}}, \imath := s] \to \overline{\sigma} \quad (1 \leq k \leq n) \end{array}}{\overline{\Gamma} \vdash \mathsf{case}_{|\overline{\sigma}|}\ e \text{ of } \{c_1 \Rightarrow e_1 \mid \cdots \mid c_n \Rightarrow e_n\}\ :\ \overline{\sigma}}\ \text{if } \mathcal{C}(d) = \{c_1, \ldots, c_n\}$$

In this section, it is not mandatory for the informal discussion to be very precise on freshness conditions. Moreover, we work step by step, and progressively introduce the features of the type inference algorithm. Therefore, instead of using $\mathtt{Infer}(\overline{\Gamma}, e)$ and $\mathtt{Check}(\overline{\Gamma}, e, \overline{\tau})$, we start with two simple unconstrained judgments $\overline{\Gamma} \vdash e \uparrow \overline{\tau}$ for type inference and $\overline{\Gamma} \vdash e \downarrow \overline{\tau}$ for type-checking. we will then introduce constraints, which lead us to

- the judgment $C\ ;\ \overline{\Gamma} \vdash e \uparrow \overline{\tau}$, which stands for $\mathtt{Infer}(\overline{\Gamma}, e) = (C, \overline{\tau})$, and
- the judgment $C\ ;\ \overline{\Gamma} \vdash e \downarrow \overline{\tau}$, which stands for $\mathtt{Check}(\overline{\Gamma}, e, \overline{\tau}) = C$.

Inference of size annotations. We now discuss the case of λ-abstractions. The natural inference rule would be

$$\frac{\overline{\Gamma}, x\ :\ \overline{\tau} \vdash e \uparrow \overline{\sigma}}{\overline{\Gamma} \vdash \lambda x : |\overline{\tau}|.\ e \uparrow \overline{\tau} \to \overline{\sigma}} \tag{4}$$

That is, we infer the type $\overline{\tau} \to \overline{\sigma}$ for $\lambda x : |\overline{\tau}|.\ e$ if we can infer the type $\overline{\sigma}$ for e in a context where the variable x is given the type $\overline{\tau}$. In other words, we have to infer the type $\overline{\tau}$ from its erasure $|\overline{\tau}|$. The difficulty is that the type $\overline{\tau}$ may depend on e. For instance, with

$$\overline{\Gamma} =_{\text{def}} f : \mathsf{Nat}^{\imath} \to \mathsf{Nat}^{\imath}, g : \mathsf{Nat}^{\jmath} \to \mathsf{Nat}^{\jmath}$$

we have

$$\frac{\overline{\Gamma}, x\ :\ \mathsf{Nat}^{\imath} \vdash f\, x\ :\ \mathsf{Nat}^{\imath}}{\overline{\Gamma} \vdash \lambda x : \mathsf{Nat}.\ f\, x\ :\ \mathsf{Nat}^{\imath} \to \mathsf{Nat}^{\imath}} \quad \text{and} \quad \frac{\overline{\Gamma}, x\ :\ \mathsf{Nat}^{\jmath} \vdash g\, x\ :\ \mathsf{Nat}^{\imath}}{\overline{\Gamma} \vdash \lambda x : \mathsf{Nat}.\ g\, x\ :\ \mathsf{Nat}^{\jmath} \to \mathsf{Nat}^{\imath}}$$

where the typing of $\lambda x : \mathsf{Nat}.\ f\, x$ and $\lambda x : \mathsf{Nat}.\ g\, x$ require two different annotations of Nat. A solution is to proceed similarly as in Hindley-Milner type inference for ML-like languages. We perform type inference in a system whose stage expressions feature *inference stage variables* $\mathcal{V}_{\mathcal{I}} = \{\alpha, \beta, \ldots\}$.

Definition 4.2 (Inference stages). *The set* $\mathcal{S}_{\mathcal{I}} = \{s, r, \ldots\}$ *of* inference stage expressions *is given by the abstract syntax:*

$$\mathcal{S}_{\mathcal{I}}\ ::=\ \mathcal{V}_{\mathcal{S}} \mid \mathcal{V}_{\mathcal{I}} \mid \widehat{\mathcal{S}_{\mathcal{I}}} \mid \infty$$

The substitution $s[\alpha := r]$ *of the inference stage variable* α *for* r *in* s *is defined in the obvious way.*

Then, each type $\sigma \in \mathcal{T}$ can be systematically annotated with inference variables. This is performed by a function Annot satisfying the following specification. If V is a set of inference stage variables and $\sigma \in \mathcal{T}$ is a type, then $\mathtt{Annot}(\sigma, V)$ returns a pair $(\overline{\sigma}, V')$ such that

- $|\overline{\sigma}| = \sigma$,
- each occurrence of an inductive datatype in $\overline{\sigma}$ is annotated with a distinct inference stage variable $\alpha \notin V$ (so that α occurs at most once in $\overline{\sigma}$),
- $V' = V \cup \mathsf{FV}_{\mathcal{I}}(\overline{\sigma})$.

For instance, $\mathtt{Annot}(\mathsf{Nat} \to \mathsf{Nat}, \{\alpha_1, \alpha_2\}) = (\mathsf{Nat}^{\alpha_3} \to \mathsf{Nat}^{\alpha_4}, \{\alpha_1, \alpha_2, \alpha_3, \alpha_4\})$. For the moment, we do not use the set of variables V' produced by Annot. If we add these systematic annotations to the rule (4), we obtain

$$(\text{abs})\ \frac{(\overline{\tau}, V) := \mathtt{Annot}(\tau, \mathsf{FV}_{\mathcal{I}}(\overline{\Gamma})) \qquad \overline{\Gamma}, x : \overline{\tau} \vdash e \uparrow \overline{\sigma}}{\overline{\Gamma} \vdash \lambda x : \tau.\ e \uparrow \overline{\tau} \to \overline{\sigma}}$$

In such system, the intended semantics of type inference and type checking can be phrased by the property that for all substitution $\rho : \mathcal{V}_{\mathcal{I}} \to \mathcal{S}_{\mathcal{I}}$ we have

$$\begin{array}{lcl} \Gamma \vdash e \uparrow \overline{\tau} & \Longrightarrow & \Gamma\rho \vdash e : \overline{\tau}\rho \\ \Gamma \vdash e \downarrow \overline{\tau} & \Longrightarrow & \Gamma\rho \vdash e : \overline{\tau}\rho \end{array}$$

Checking subtyping derivations. Type inference with a rule like the above does not work directly: we have to take subtyping into account more seriously. Let us look at the type inference derivation of $\lambda x : \mathsf{Nat}.\ f\,x$ in the context $f : \mathsf{Nat}^{\imath} \to \mathsf{Nat}^{\infty}$. We would have a derivation of the form

$$\frac{f : \mathsf{Nat}^{\imath} \to \mathsf{Nat}^{\infty}, x : \mathsf{Nat}^{\alpha} \vdash f\,x \uparrow ? \qquad (\mathsf{Nat}^{\alpha}, V) = \mathtt{Annot}(\mathsf{Nat}, \emptyset)}{f : \mathsf{Nat}^{\imath} \to \mathsf{Nat}^{\infty} \vdash \lambda x : \mathsf{Nat}.\ f\,x \uparrow ?} \qquad (5)$$

but we get stuck because this would require $\mathsf{Nat}^{\alpha} \sqsubseteq \mathsf{Nat}^{\imath}$, which does not hold.

In other words, once we generate sized types featuring stage inference variables, we have to adapt our way of handling subtyping. In Sect. 3.2, we have seen that the substage relation $s \leq r$ (defined in Def. 3.3) leads to the subtyping relation $\overline{\tau} \sqsubseteq \overline{\sigma}$ (defined in Def. 3.6). For type checking, we go the other way: starting from a subtyping assertion $\overline{\tau} \sqsubseteq \overline{\sigma}$, we generate a conjunction of substage assertions $s_1 \leq r_1, \ldots, s_n \leq r_n$, which holds if and only if $\overline{\tau} \sqsubseteq \overline{\sigma}$ is derivable.

Definition 4.3 (Constraints)

(i) A constraint *is either the false constraint* $\bot$ *or a set of inference stage expressions inequalities* $\{s_1 \leq r_1, \ldots, s_n \leq r_n\}$.

(ii) A substitution $\rho : \mathcal{V}_{\mathcal{I}} \to \mathcal{S}_{\mathcal{I}}$ *satisfies a constraint* C*, notation* $\rho \models C$*, if and only if* $C \neq \bot$ *and* $s\rho \leq r\rho$ *is derivable using the rules of Def. 3.3 for all* $s \leq r \in C$.

(iii) A subtyping assertion $\overline{\tau} \sqsubseteq \overline{\sigma}$ *generates a constraint* $(\!|\overline{\tau} \sqsubseteq \overline{\sigma}|\!)$ *defined as follows*

$$
\begin{array}{lll}
(\!|X \sqsubseteq X|\!) & =_{def} & \emptyset \\
(\!|\overline{\tau}_2 \rightarrow \overline{\tau}_1 \sqsubseteq \overline{\sigma}_2 \rightarrow \overline{\sigma}_1|\!) & =_{def} & (\!|\overline{\sigma}_2 \sqsubseteq \overline{\tau}_2|\!) \cup_\bot (\!|\overline{\tau}_1 \sqsubseteq \overline{\sigma}_1|\!) \\
(\!|\Pi X.\, \overline{\tau} \sqsubseteq \Pi X.\, \overline{\sigma}|\!) & =_{def} & (\!|\overline{\tau} \sqsubseteq \overline{\sigma}|\!) \\
(\!|d^s\, \overline{\boldsymbol{\tau}} \sqsubseteq d^r\, \overline{\boldsymbol{\sigma}}|\!) & =_{def} & \{s \leq r\} \cup_\bot (\!|\overline{\boldsymbol{\tau}} \sqsubseteq \overline{\boldsymbol{\sigma}}|\!) \\
(\!|\overline{\tau} \sqsubseteq \overline{\sigma}|\!) & =_{def} & \bot \qquad \textit{in all other cases}
\end{array}
$$

where

$$
C_1 \cup_\bot C_2 \quad =_{def} \quad \begin{cases} \bot & \textit{if } C_1 = \bot \textit{ or } C_2 = \bot \\ C_1 \cup C_2 & \textit{otherwise} \end{cases}
$$

We write $s_1 \leq r_1, \ldots, s_n \leq r_n$ instead of $\{s_1 \leq r_1, \ldots, s_n \leq r_n\}$. Note that we have $\rho \models \emptyset$ for all $\rho : \mathcal{V}_\jmath \rightarrow \mathcal{S}_\jmath$, and that the empty substitution does not satisfies the false constraint $\bot$. The satisfaction of constraints generated by subtyping assertions corresponds exactly to the derivability of subtyping judgments.

Proposition 4.4. $\rho \models (\!|\overline{\tau} \sqsubseteq \overline{\sigma}|\!)$ *if and only if* $\overline{\tau}\rho \sqsubseteq \overline{\sigma}\rho$.

Example 4.5.
(i) The assertion $\mathsf{Nat}^\infty \sqsubseteq \mathsf{Bool}^\infty$ generates the constraint $\bot$. It follows that $\mathsf{Nat}^\infty \sqsubseteq \mathsf{Bool}^\infty$ is not derivable.
(ii) The assertion $\mathsf{Nat}^\imath \sqsubseteq \mathsf{Nat}^\infty$ generates the constraint $\{\imath \leq \infty\}$. The inequality $\imath \leq \infty$ is derivable, hence $\mathsf{Nat}^\imath \sqsubseteq \mathsf{Nat}^\infty$ is also derivable.
(iii) The assertion $\mathsf{Nat}^\imath \sqsubseteq \mathsf{Nat}^\jmath$ generates the constraint $\{\imath \leq \jmath\}$. The inequality $\imath \leq \jmath$ is not derivable, hence $\mathsf{Nat}^\imath \sqsubseteq \mathsf{Nat}^\jmath$ is not derivable. □

Inference rules. We have to adapt type inference to take into account the constraints generated by subtyping. We now consider judgments of the form

$$
C\,;\overline{\Gamma} \vdash e \uparrow \overline{\tau} \qquad \text{and} \qquad C\,;\overline{\Gamma} \vdash e \downarrow \overline{\tau}
$$

where C is a constraint. The constraints are generated by subtyping

$$
(\text{sub})\ \frac{C\,;\overline{\Gamma} \vdash e \uparrow \overline{\tau}}{C \cup_\bot (\!|\overline{\tau} \sqsubseteq \overline{\sigma}|\!)\,;\overline{\Gamma} \vdash e \downarrow \overline{\sigma}}
$$

and transmitted by the other rules. In all rules, constraints have to be read top-bottom. The system is presented in Fig. 7, and its correctness is stated the following Proposition. The rule (cons) and (case) are commented in the next paragraph.

Proposition 4.6 (Correctness)
(i) If $C\,;\overline{\Gamma} \vdash e \uparrow \overline{\tau}$ *and* $\rho \models C$ *then* $\overline{\Gamma}\rho \vdash e : \overline{\tau}\rho$
(ii) If $C\,;\overline{\Gamma} \vdash e \downarrow \overline{\tau}$ *and* $\rho \models C$ *then* $\overline{\Gamma}\rho \vdash e : \overline{\tau}\rho$

Let us now look at the derivation (5). We have

$$\frac{\emptyset \; ; \; f : \mathsf{Nat}^{\imath} \to \mathsf{Nat}^{\infty}, x : \mathsf{Nat}^{\alpha} \vdash x \uparrow \mathsf{Nat}^{\alpha}}{\alpha \leq \imath \; ; \; f : \mathsf{Nat}^{\imath} \to \mathsf{Nat}^{\infty}, x : \mathsf{Nat}^{\alpha} \vdash x \downarrow \mathsf{Nat}^{\imath}}$$

and it follows that

$$\frac{\alpha \leq \imath \; ; \; f : \mathsf{Nat}^{\imath} \to \mathsf{Nat}^{\infty}, x : \mathsf{Nat}^{\alpha} \vdash f\, x \uparrow \mathsf{Nat}^{\infty} \qquad (\mathsf{Nat}^{\alpha}, V) = \mathtt{Annot}(\mathsf{Nat}, \emptyset)}{\alpha \leq \imath \; ; \; f : \mathsf{Nat}^{\imath} \to \mathsf{Nat}^{\infty} \vdash \lambda x : \mathsf{Nat}.\; f\, x \uparrow \mathsf{Nat}^{\alpha} \to \mathsf{Nat}^{\infty}}$$

By Prop. 4.6.(i), we get $f : \mathsf{Nat}^{\imath} \to \mathsf{Nat}^{\infty} \vdash \lambda x : \mathsf{Nat}.\; f\, x \; : \; \mathsf{Nat}^{\imath} \to \mathsf{Nat}^{\infty}$.

Inductive datatypes. We now focus on the type inference rules (cons) and (case) that correspond respectively to the introduction and to the elimination of inductive datatypes. The only particular feature of the type inference rule for constructors is that it introduces a fresh inference stage variable:

$$(\text{cons}) \; \frac{c_k : \Pi \boldsymbol{X}.\, \overline{\boldsymbol{\theta}_k} \to d^{\widehat{\imath}}\, \boldsymbol{X}}{\emptyset \; ; \; \overline{\Gamma} \vdash c_k \uparrow \Pi \boldsymbol{X}.\, \overline{\boldsymbol{\theta}_k}[\imath := \alpha] \to d^{\widehat{\alpha}}\, \boldsymbol{X}} \; \text{if } \alpha \notin \mathcal{V}_{\mathcal{I}}(\overline{\Gamma}) \text{ and } c_k \in \mathcal{C}(d) \text{ for some } d$$

Consider now the type inference rule (case) for case-analysis:

$$\frac{\begin{array}{lll} C \; ; \; \overline{\Gamma} \vdash e \uparrow d^{s}\, \overline{\boldsymbol{\tau}} & \alpha \notin \mathcal{V}_{\mathcal{I}}(\overline{\Gamma}) & (\overline{\sigma}, V) = \mathtt{Annot}(\sigma, \mathcal{V}_{\mathcal{I}}(\overline{\Gamma}) \cup \{\alpha\}) \\ c_k : \Pi \boldsymbol{X}.\, \overline{\boldsymbol{\theta}_k} \to d^{\widehat{\imath}}\, \boldsymbol{X} & C_k \; ; \; \overline{\Gamma} \vdash e_k \downarrow \overline{\boldsymbol{\theta}_k}[\boldsymbol{X} := \overline{\boldsymbol{\tau}}, \imath := \alpha] \to \overline{\sigma} & (1 \leq k \leq n) \end{array}}{\{s \leq \widehat{\alpha}\} \cup_{\perp} C \cup_{\perp} (\bigcup_{\perp} C_k) \; ; \; \overline{\Gamma} \vdash \mathsf{case}_{\sigma}\; e \;\mathsf{of}\; \{c_1 \Rightarrow e_1 \mid \cdots \mid c_n \Rightarrow e_n\} \uparrow \overline{\sigma}}$$

where $\mathcal{C}(d) = \{c_1, \ldots, c_n\}$

For simplicity, we consider a simple case where the output type σ does not contain any datatype (hence $\overline{\sigma} = \sigma$) and where the datatype d subject of the case-analysis is the type of natural numbers. Assume that we want to infer the type of $\mathsf{case}_{\sigma}\; e \;\mathsf{of}\; \{0 \Rightarrow e_{\mathsf{o}} \mid \mathsf{s} \Rightarrow e_{\mathsf{s}}\}$ in the context $\overline{\Gamma}$. First, we infer the type of the subject e of the case-analysis, and we get a constraint C such that $C \; ; \; \overline{\Gamma} \vdash e \uparrow \mathsf{Nat}^{s}$. Now, recall the typing rule case imposes that the subject can be typed with a stage of the form $\widehat{r}$, and that in our case, the branch e_{s} corresponding to the constructor s has type $\mathsf{Nat}^{r} \to \sigma$:

$$\frac{\overline{\Gamma} \vdash e \; : \; \mathsf{Nat}^{\widehat{r}} \qquad \overline{\Gamma} \vdash e_{\mathsf{o}} \; : \; \sigma \qquad \overline{\Gamma} \vdash e_{\mathsf{s}} \; : \; \mathsf{Nat}^{r} \to \sigma}{\overline{\Gamma} \vdash \mathsf{case}_{\sigma}\; e \;\mathsf{of}\; \{0 \Rightarrow e_{\mathsf{o}} \mid \mathsf{s} \Rightarrow e_{\mathsf{s}}\} \; : \; \sigma}$$

We express this by using a fresh stage variable α together with a constraint $s \leq \widehat{\alpha}$, and we typecheck the branch e_{s} against the type $\mathsf{Nat}^{\alpha} \to \sigma$. This gives:

$$\frac{C \; ; \; \overline{\Gamma} \vdash e \uparrow \mathsf{Nat}^{s} \qquad C_{\mathsf{o}} \; ; \; \overline{\Gamma} \vdash e_{\mathsf{o}} \downarrow \sigma \qquad C_{\mathsf{s}} \; ; \; \overline{\Gamma} \vdash e_{\mathsf{s}} \downarrow \mathsf{Nat}^{\alpha} \to \sigma}{\{s \leq \widehat{\alpha}\} \cup_{\perp} C \cup_{\perp} C_{\mathsf{o}} \cup_{\perp} C_{\mathsf{s}} \; ; \; \overline{\Gamma} \vdash \mathsf{case}_{\sigma}\; e \;\mathsf{of}\; \{0 \Rightarrow e_{\mathsf{o}} \mid \mathsf{s} \Rightarrow e_{\mathsf{s}}\} \uparrow \sigma}$$

where $\alpha \notin \mathcal{V}_{\mathcal{I}}(\overline{\Gamma})$

Example 4.7 Let us look at the following example, where $V \in \mathcal{V}_{\mathcal{T}}$:

$$? \; ; v : V, \; f : \mathsf{Nat}^{\alpha} \to V, \; y : \mathsf{Nat}^{\beta} \vdash \mathsf{case}_V \; y \; \mathsf{of} \; \{0 \Rightarrow v \mid \mathsf{s} \Rightarrow \lambda z : \mathsf{Nat}. \; f \, z\} \uparrow ?$$

Since $\gamma \leq \alpha \; ; v : V, \; f : \mathsf{Nat}^{\alpha} \to V, \; y : \mathsf{Nat}^{\beta}, \; z : \mathsf{Nat}^{\gamma} \vdash f \, z \uparrow V$, we deduce

$$\gamma \leq \alpha, \, \alpha \leq \gamma \; ; v : V, \; f : \mathsf{Nat}^{\alpha} \to V, \; y : \mathsf{Nat}^{\beta} \vdash \lambda z : \mathsf{Nat}. \; f \, z \downarrow \mathsf{Nat}^{\alpha} \to V$$

It follows that

$$\begin{array}{l} \gamma \leq \alpha, \, \alpha \leq \gamma, \, \beta \leq \widehat{\alpha} \; ; \\ v : V, \; f : \mathsf{Nat}^{\alpha} \to V, \; y : \mathsf{Nat}^{\beta} \vdash \mathsf{case}_V \; y \; \mathsf{of} \; \{0 \Rightarrow v \mid \mathsf{s} \Rightarrow \lambda z : \mathsf{Nat}. \; f \, z\} \uparrow V \end{array}$$

There are two things to note about the constraint $\gamma \leq \alpha, \alpha \leq \gamma, \beta \leq \widehat{\alpha}$. First, it contains a variable γ that appears nowhere else in the sequent. It is in fact the inference stage variable that corresponds to the bound variable z. Hence, if the types recorded under abstractions were annotated by stages, we would have:

$$\begin{array}{l} \gamma \leq \alpha, \, \alpha \leq \gamma, \, \beta \leq \widehat{\alpha} \; ; \\ v : V, \; f : \mathsf{Nat}^{\alpha} \to V, \; y : \mathsf{Nat}^{\beta} \vdash \mathsf{case}_V \; y \; \mathsf{of} \; \{0 \Rightarrow v \mid \mathsf{s} \Rightarrow \lambda z : \mathsf{Nat}^{\gamma}. \; f \, z\} \uparrow V \end{array}$$

Second, this constraint implies $\alpha = \gamma$, hence the type inference judgment above can be simplified to

$$\beta \leq \widehat{\alpha} \; ; v : V, \; f : \mathsf{Nat}^{\alpha} \to V, \; y : \mathsf{Nat}^{\beta} \vdash \mathsf{case}_V \; y \; \mathsf{of} \; \{0 \Rightarrow v \mid \mathsf{s} \Rightarrow \lambda z : \mathsf{Nat}^{\alpha}. \; f \, z\} \uparrow V$$

Such notations are very convenient to write type inference judgments. □

4.3 Checking the Correctness of Recursive Definitions

We now discuss the typing rule of fixpoints. For the sake of simplicity, we assume that d is an inductive datatype without parameters and that $\imath \notin \overline{\theta}$. In this case, the typing rule of fixpoints becomes

$$(\mathrm{rec}) \; \frac{\overline{\Gamma}, f : d^{\imath} \to \overline{\theta} \vdash e \; : \; d^{\widehat{\imath}} \to \overline{\theta}}{\overline{\Gamma} \vdash (\mathsf{letrec}_{d \to |\overline{\theta}|} \; f = e) \; : \; d^{s} \to \overline{\theta}} \quad \text{if } \imath \notin \overline{\Gamma}, \overline{\theta}$$

Consider now that rule from the point of view of type inference. If we start from

$$? \; ; \overline{\Gamma} \vdash (\mathsf{letrec}_{d \to \theta} \; f = e) \uparrow ?$$

then we have to compute a constraint C^{Rec} and a type $d^{\alpha} \to \overline{\theta}$ such that $|\overline{\theta}| = \theta$ and

$$C^{\mathsf{Rec}} \; ; \overline{\Gamma} \vdash (\mathsf{letrec}_{d \to \theta} \; f = e) \uparrow d^{\alpha} \to \overline{\theta}$$

The constraint C^{Rec} must be computed from the constraint C generated by typechecking the body e of the recursive definition. By analogy with (rec), the inference rule can be written

$$\frac{C \; ; \overline{\Gamma}, f : d^{\alpha} \to \overline{\theta} \vdash e \downarrow d^{\widehat{\alpha}} \to \overline{\theta}}{C^{\mathsf{Rec}} \; ; \overline{\Gamma} \vdash (\mathsf{letrec}_{d \to \theta} \; f = e) \uparrow d^{\alpha} \to \overline{\theta}}$$

$$\text{(var)} \quad \frac{}{\emptyset\ ;\ \overline{\Gamma}, x : \overline{\sigma} \vdash x \uparrow \overline{\sigma}}$$

$$\text{(abs)} \quad \frac{(\overline{\tau}, V) := \mathtt{Annot}(\tau, \mathcal{V}_\jmath(\overline{\Gamma})) \qquad C\ ;\ \overline{\Gamma}, x : \overline{\tau} \vdash e \uparrow \overline{\sigma}}{C\ ;\ \overline{\Gamma} \vdash \lambda x : \tau.\ e \uparrow \overline{\tau} \to \overline{\sigma}}$$

$$\text{(app)} \quad \frac{C_1\ ;\ \overline{\Gamma} \vdash e \uparrow \overline{\tau} \to \overline{\sigma} \qquad C_2\ ;\ \overline{\Gamma} \vdash e' \downarrow \overline{\tau}}{C_1 \cup_\perp C_2\ ;\ \overline{\Gamma} \vdash e\ e' \uparrow \overline{\sigma}}$$

$$\text{(T-abs)} \quad \frac{C\ ;\ \overline{\Gamma} \vdash e \uparrow \overline{\sigma}}{C\ ;\ \overline{\Gamma} \vdash \Lambda X.\ e \uparrow \Pi X.\ \overline{\sigma}} \qquad \text{if } X \notin \overline{\Gamma}$$

$$\text{(T-app)} \quad \frac{C\ ;\ \overline{\Gamma} \vdash e \uparrow \Pi X.\ \overline{\sigma} \qquad (\overline{\tau}, V) = \mathtt{Annot}(\tau, \mathcal{V}_\jmath(\overline{\Gamma}))}{C\ ;\ \overline{\Gamma} \vdash e\ \tau \uparrow \overline{\sigma}[X := \overline{\tau}]}$$

$$\text{(cons)} \quad \frac{c_k : \Pi \boldsymbol{X}.\ \overline{\boldsymbol{\theta}}_{\boldsymbol{k}} \to \widehat{d^\imath}\ \boldsymbol{X}}{\emptyset\ ;\ \overline{\Gamma} \vdash c_k \uparrow \Pi \boldsymbol{X}.\ \overline{\boldsymbol{\theta}}_{\boldsymbol{k}}[\imath := \alpha] \to d^{\widehat{\alpha}}\ \boldsymbol{X}} \ \text{if } \alpha \notin \mathcal{V}_\jmath(\overline{\Gamma})$$

where $\mathcal{C}(d) = \{c_1, \ldots, c_n\}$ for some d

$$\text{(case)} \quad \frac{\begin{array}{lll} C\ ;\ \overline{\Gamma} \vdash e \uparrow d^s\, \overline{\boldsymbol{\tau}} & \alpha \notin \mathcal{V}_\jmath(\overline{\Gamma}) & (\overline{\sigma}, V) = \mathtt{Annot}(\sigma, \mathcal{V}_\jmath(\overline{\Gamma}) \cup \{\alpha\}) \\ c_k : \Pi \boldsymbol{X}.\ \overline{\boldsymbol{\theta}}_{\boldsymbol{k}} \to \widehat{d^\imath}\ \boldsymbol{X} & C_k\ ;\ \overline{\Gamma} \vdash e_k \downarrow \overline{\boldsymbol{\theta}}_{\boldsymbol{k}}[\boldsymbol{X} := \overline{\boldsymbol{\tau}}, \imath := \alpha] \to \overline{\sigma} & (1 \le k \le n) \end{array}}{\{s \le \widehat{\alpha}\} \cup_\perp C \cup_\perp \left(\bigcup_\perp C_k\right)\ ;\ \overline{\Gamma} \vdash \mathsf{case}_\sigma\ e\ \mathsf{of}\ \{c_1 \Rightarrow e_1 \mid \cdots \mid c_n \Rightarrow e_n\} \uparrow \overline{\sigma}}$$

where $\mathcal{C}(d) = \{c_1, \ldots, c_n\}$

$$\text{(sub)} \quad \frac{C\ ;\ \overline{\Gamma} \vdash e \uparrow \overline{\tau}}{C \cup_\perp (\!|\overline{\tau} \sqsubseteq \overline{\sigma}|\!)\ ;\ \overline{\Gamma} \vdash e \downarrow \overline{\sigma}}$$

Fig. 7. Type inference with constraints

To guarantee correctness, as stated in Prop. 4.6, we want that $\rho \models C^{\mathsf{Rec}}$ entails

$$\overline{\Gamma}\rho \vdash (\mathsf{letrec}_{d \to \theta}\ f = e)\ :\ d^{\rho(\alpha)} \to \overline{\theta}\rho$$

For the above judgment to be derivable, it must be the case (applying inversion) that the premises of the rule (rec) must hold, and there must exist a substitution ρ' such that $\overline{\Gamma}\rho' = \overline{\Gamma}\rho'$, $\rho' \models C$, $\rho'(\alpha) = \imath$ and

$$\overline{\Gamma}\rho', f : d^\imath \to \overline{\theta}\rho' \vdash e\ :\ \widehat{d^\imath} \to \overline{\theta}\rho' \qquad \text{with} \quad \imath \notin \overline{\Gamma}\rho'$$

We explain how to define C^{Rec} by considering two examples of fixpoints definitions:

$$\begin{array}{lll} \mathsf{fix}_1 & := & (\mathsf{letrec}_{\mathsf{Nat} \to \mathsf{Nat}}\ f = \lambda x : \mathsf{Nat}.\ \mathsf{o}) \\ \mathsf{fix}_2 & := & (\mathsf{letrec}_{\mathsf{Nat} \to \mathsf{Nat}}\ f = \lambda x : \mathsf{Nat}.\ (f\ \mathsf{o})) \end{array}$$

Note that $\mathsf{fix}_1\,\mathsf{o}$ terminates while $\mathsf{fix}_2\,\mathsf{o}$ does not. Hence, fix_1 must be typable while fix_2 must be rejected by the type inference algorithm. Let us now inspect the typechecking derivations of the bodies of these two functions.

- For the body of fix_1, we have

$$\frac{\emptyset\ ;\ f : \mathsf{Nat}^{\alpha} \rightarrow \mathsf{Nat}^{\beta}, x : \mathsf{Nat}^{\gamma} \vdash \mathsf{o} \uparrow \mathsf{Nat}^{\widehat{\delta}}}{\emptyset\ ;\ f : \mathsf{Nat}^{\alpha} \rightarrow \mathsf{Nat}^{\beta} \vdash \lambda x : \mathsf{Nat}.\ \mathsf{o} \uparrow \mathsf{Nat}^{\gamma} \rightarrow \mathsf{Nat}^{\widehat{\delta}}}$$

  Since $(\!|\mathsf{Nat}^{\gamma} \rightarrow \mathsf{Nat}^{\widehat{\delta}} \sqsubseteq \mathsf{Nat}^{\widehat{\alpha}} \rightarrow \mathsf{Nat}^{\beta}|\!) = \widehat{\alpha} \le \gamma, \widehat{\delta} \le \beta$, it follows that

$$\widehat{\alpha} \le \gamma, \widehat{\delta} \le \beta\ ;\ f : \mathsf{Nat}^{\alpha} \rightarrow \mathsf{Nat}^{\beta} \vdash \lambda x : \mathsf{Nat}.\ \mathsf{o} \downarrow \mathsf{Nat}^{\widehat{\alpha}} \rightarrow \mathsf{Nat}^{\beta}$$

- For the body of fix_2, we have

$$\frac{\emptyset\ ;\ f : \mathsf{Nat}^{\alpha} \rightarrow \mathsf{Nat}^{\beta}, x : \mathsf{Nat}^{\gamma} \vdash \mathsf{o} \uparrow \mathsf{Nat}^{\widehat{\delta}}}{\widehat{\delta} \le \alpha\ ;\ f : \mathsf{Nat}^{\alpha} \rightarrow \mathsf{Nat}^{\beta}, x : \mathsf{Nat}^{\gamma} \vdash \mathsf{o} \downarrow \mathsf{Nat}^{\alpha}}$$

  Hence

$$\frac{\widehat{\delta} \le \alpha\ ;\ f : \mathsf{Nat}^{\alpha} \rightarrow \mathsf{Nat}^{\beta}, x : \mathsf{Nat}^{\gamma} \vdash f\ \mathsf{o} \uparrow \mathsf{Nat}^{\beta}}{\widehat{\delta} \le \alpha\ ;\ f : \mathsf{Nat}^{\alpha} \rightarrow \mathsf{Nat}^{\beta} \vdash \lambda x : \mathsf{Nat}.\ (f\ \mathsf{o}) \uparrow \mathsf{Nat}^{\gamma} \rightarrow \mathsf{Nat}^{\beta}}$$

  It follows that

$$\widehat{\delta} \le \alpha, \widehat{\alpha} \le \gamma\ ;\ f : \mathsf{Nat}^{\alpha} \rightarrow \mathsf{Nat}^{\beta} \vdash \lambda x : \mathsf{Nat}.\ (f\ \mathsf{o}) \downarrow \mathsf{Nat}^{\widehat{\alpha}} \rightarrow \mathsf{Nat}^{\beta}$$

We arrive at these two derivations

$$\frac{\widehat{\alpha} \le \gamma, \widehat{\delta} \le \beta\ ;\ f : \mathsf{Nat}^{\alpha} \rightarrow \mathsf{Nat}^{\beta} \vdash \lambda x : \mathsf{Nat}.\ \mathsf{o} \downarrow \mathsf{Nat}^{\widehat{\alpha}} \rightarrow \mathsf{Nat}^{\beta}}{C_1^{\mathsf{Rec}}\ ; \vdash (\mathsf{letrec}_{\mathsf{Nat}\rightarrow\mathsf{Nat}}\ f = \lambda x : \mathsf{Nat}.\ \mathsf{o}) \uparrow \mathsf{Nat}^{\widehat{\alpha}} \rightarrow \mathsf{Nat}^{\beta}}\ (\mathsf{fix}_1)$$

$$\frac{\widehat{\delta} \le \alpha, \widehat{\alpha} \le \gamma\ ;\ f : \mathsf{Nat}^{\alpha} \rightarrow \mathsf{Nat}^{\beta} \vdash \lambda x : \mathsf{Nat}.\ (f\ \mathsf{o}) \downarrow \mathsf{Nat}^{\widehat{\alpha}} \rightarrow \mathsf{Nat}^{\beta}}{C_2^{\mathsf{Rec}}\ ; \vdash (\mathsf{letrec}_{\mathsf{Nat}\rightarrow\mathsf{Nat}}\ f = \lambda x : \mathsf{Nat}.\ (f\ \mathsf{o})) \uparrow \mathsf{Nat}^{\widehat{\alpha}} \rightarrow \mathsf{Nat}^{\beta}}\ (\mathsf{fix}_2)$$

where

C_1^{Rec}	is computed from	C_1	$=_{\mathsf{def}}\ \widehat{\alpha} \le \gamma, \widehat{\delta} \le \beta$
C_2^{Rec}	is computed from	C_2	$=_{\mathsf{def}}\ \widehat{\delta} \le \alpha, \widehat{\alpha} \le \gamma$

The constraints C_1^{Rec} and C_2^{Rec} must satisfy different properties:

- We want fix_1 to be typable. Hence, C_1^{Rec} must be satisfiable, and moreover, for all substitution ρ such that $\rho \models C_1^{\mathsf{Rec}}$, there must be a substitution ρ' and a stage variable $\imath$ such that $\imath \notin \mathsf{codom}(\rho)$, $\rho'(\alpha) = \imath$, $\rho'(\beta) = \rho(\beta)$ and $\rho' \models \widehat{\alpha} \le \gamma, \widehat{\delta} \le \beta$.
- C_2^{Rec} must be unsatisfiable because fix_2 is not typable since it does not terminate. C_2^{Rec} will actually be the false constraint $\bot$.

These properties are provided by an algorithm called `RecCheck`, which we describe below. To ease the explanations, we introduce some terminology. Recall that stage expressions $s \in \mathcal{S}$ are either of the form $\widehat{\imath}^n$ with $\imath \in \mathcal{V}_\mathcal{S}$ or of the form $\widehat{\infty}^n$. Hence, any stage expression s has at most one occurrence of a unique stage variable $\imath \in \mathcal{V}_\mathcal{S}$. We call this stage variable the *base stage* of s, and write it $\lfloor s \rfloor$. Furthermore, consider a fixpoint $(\mathsf{letrec}_{d \to \theta}\ f = e)$ such that

$$C\ ;\ \overline{\Gamma}, f\ :\ d^{\alpha} \to \overline{\theta} \vdash e \downarrow d^{\widehat{\alpha}} \to \overline{\theta} \qquad \text{with} \quad \alpha \notin \overline{\Gamma}, \overline{\theta} \tag{6}$$

We say that α is the *fixpoint inference stage variable* of $(\mathsf{letrec}_{d \to \theta}\ f = e)$.

Example 4.8 The fixpoint stage variable of both fix_1 and fix_2 is α. □

Consider an instance of the judgment (6) for substitution ρ. In order to apply the rule (rec) with that instance as premise, the fixpoint inference stage variable α must be mapped to a fresh stage variable $\imath$. Moreover, we must have $\imath \notin \overline{\Gamma}\rho, \overline{\theta}\rho$. This imposes that no inference stage variable occurring in $\overline{\Gamma}, \overline{\theta}$ can be mapped to a stage expression with base stage $\imath$. Let $V^{\neq} =_{\text{def}} \mathcal{V}_\mathcal{I}(\overline{\Gamma}, \overline{\theta})$.

The algorithm works on a representation of C as a graph whose nodes are inference stages variables and ∞, and whose edges are integers. Each constraint in C is of the form $\infty \le \widehat{\beta}^n$, or $\widehat{\alpha}_1^{n_1} \le \widehat{\alpha}_2^{n_2}$. In the first case, one adds an edge from β to ∞ labeled with 0, in the second case one adds an edge from α_2 to α_1 labeled with $n_2 - n_1$. We do not represent edges for constraints of the form $\widehat{\beta}^n \le \widehat{\beta}^n$.

Example 4.9 The graphs representing C_1 and C_2 are depicted in Fig. 8. □

Before explaining the algorithm, let us make an important remark on the graph of constraints. It may happen that the graph contains a negative cycle, i.e. a cycle where the sum of the edges is strictly negative. Such cycles imply $\widehat{\beta}^{k+1} \le \beta$, or equivalently $\infty \le \beta$, for the variable β in the cycle. Hence, every variable in a negative cycle *must* be mapped to ∞. Therefore, at some stage in the algorithm, it is necessary to compute negative cycles. This can be done using Bellman's algorithm, which runs n^2, where n is number of edges of the graph, hence the number of inference stage variables in C.

The algorithm runs in two phases. The first phase ensures that the fixpoint inference stage variable α can be mapped to $\imath$, and the second phase ensures that no variable in $V^{\neq}$ must be mapped to a stage expression with base stage $\imath$.

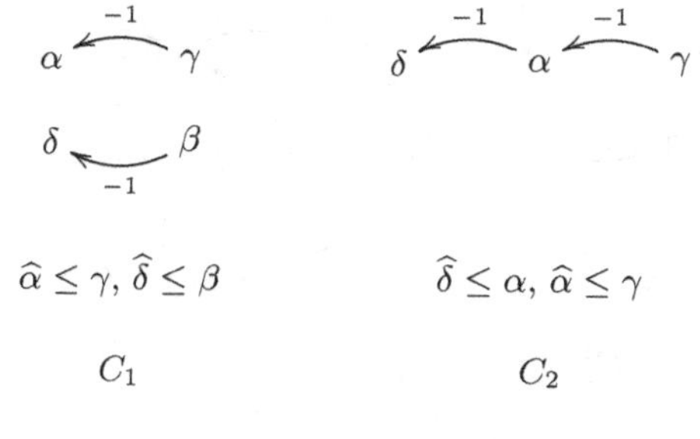

Fig. 8. The graphs of the constraints C_1 and C_2

First phase: variables that must be mapped to $\imath$. First, note that the constraint $\widehat{\delta} \leq \alpha$, $\widehat{\alpha} \leq \gamma$ of fix_2 cannot be satisfied by a substitution which sends α to the stage variable $\imath$. Indeed, the constraint $\widehat{\delta} \leq \alpha$ would lead to a stage inequality of the form $\widehat{s} \leq \imath$, which is derivable for no stage expression s.

We briefly indicate how to detect this kind of situation. Observe that constraints of the form $\widehat{\beta}^n \leq \widehat{\alpha}^m$ force β to be mapped to a stage expression with base stage $\imath$. This is the case of the variable δ in the constraint C_2. So, we define $S^\imath$, the set of inference stage variable that must be mapped to a stage expression with base stage $\imath$, as the downward closure of $\{\alpha\}$:

$$\alpha \in S^\imath \qquad \text{and} \qquad \beta \in S^\imath \quad \text{if} \quad \widehat{\beta}^n \leq \widehat{\gamma}^m \in C \quad \text{with} \quad \gamma \in S^\imath$$

Example 4.10 For fix_1 we have $S^\imath = \{\alpha\}$ and for fix_2 we have $S^\imath = \{\alpha, \delta\}$. □

Note that if $\beta \in S^\imath$ is mapped to a s depending on $\imath$, then we must have $\imath \leq s$. We represent this by computing a new set of constraints

$$C^1 \;=_{\text{def}}\; C \cup \{\alpha \leq \beta \mid \beta \in S^\imath\}$$

Example 4.11 These constraints for fix_1 and fix_2, denoted respectively C_1^1 and C_2^1, are depicted in Fig. 9. We have $C_1^1 = C_1$. On the other hand, the graph of C_2^1 contains a negative cycle which forces α to be mapped to ∞. Hence α cannot be mapped to $\imath$. □

Therefore, we now have to check for negative cycles in the graph of C^1. For each such cycle starting from β, we compute the set $V_{\beta\leq}$ of variables greater or equal to β, remove all inequalities about variables in $V_{\beta\leq}$ and add the constraints $\infty \leq \gamma$ for $\gamma \in V_{\beta\leq}$. Hence, we get a new set of constraints C^2 that does not contain cycles.

Example 4.12 The sets C_1^2 and C_2^2 for fix_1 and fix_2 are depicted on Fig. 10. The negative cycle involving α in C_2^1 implies that C_2^2 forces α to be mapped to ∞, which makes impossible to map α to $\imath$. Therefore, we can already discard fix_2 at this point, and put $C_2^{\mathsf{Rec}} =_{\text{def}} \perp$. On the other hand, the constraint C_1^2 poses no problem. □

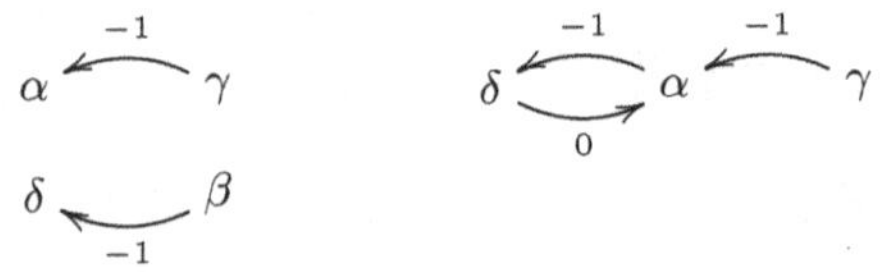

$\widehat{\alpha} \leq \gamma$, $\widehat{\delta} \leq \beta$ $\qquad\qquad$ $\widehat{\delta} \leq \alpha$, $\widehat{\alpha} \leq \gamma$, $\alpha \leq \delta$

C_1^1 $\qquad\qquad$ C_2^1

Fig. 9. The graphs of the constraints C_1^1 and C_2^1

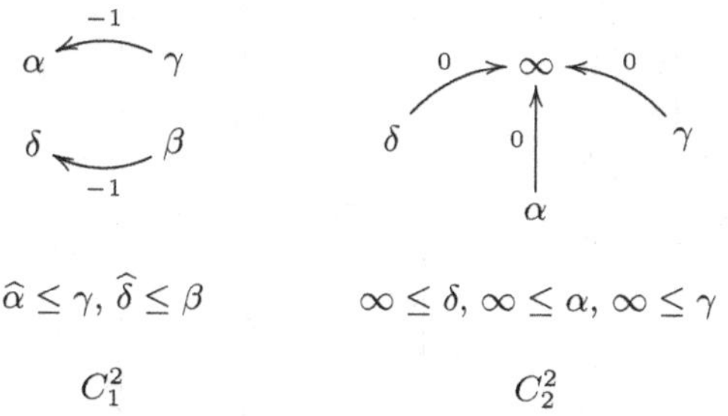

Fig. 10. The graphs of the constraints C_1^2 and C_2^2

Second phase: ensuring that $\imath \notin \overline{\Gamma}\rho, \overline{\theta}\rho$. Since we must have $\imath \notin \overline{\Gamma}\rho, \overline{\theta}\rho$, no inference stage variables occurring in $\overline{\Gamma}, \overline{\theta}$ can be mapped by ρ to a stage expression with base stage $\imath$. Moreover, if β is such a variable and $\widehat{\beta}^n \leq \widehat{\delta}^m$ is derivable from C^2 (i.e. if there is a path from δ to β in the graph of C^2), then δ cannot be mapped to a stage expression with base stage $\imath$. Indeed, $s \leq \widehat{\imath}^p$ implies that s is of the form $\widehat{\imath}^q$. Hence, mapping δ to $\widehat{\imath}^p$ for some p forces to map β to $\widehat{\imath}^q$ some q. Therefore, we let $S^{\neg\imath}$, the set of variables that cannot be mapped to a stage expression with base stage $\imath$, be the upward closure of $V^{\neq}$:

$$V^{\neq} \subseteq S^{\neg\imath} \qquad \text{and} \qquad \delta \in S^{\neg\imath} \ \text{ if } \ \widehat{\beta}^n \leq \widehat{\delta}^m \in C^2 \ \text{ with } \ \beta \in S^{\neg\imath}$$

(recall that $V^{\neq} = \mathcal{V}_{\mathfrak{I}}(\overline{\Gamma}, \overline{\theta})$).

Example 4.13 For fix_1 and fix_2 we have $S_1^{\neg\imath} = S_2^{\neg\imath} = \{\beta\} = V_1^{\neq} = V_2^{\neq}$. □

Now, assume that there is in C^2 a path from a variable $\delta \in S^{\neg\imath}$ to a variable $\beta \in S^{\imath}$ (hence that $\widehat{\beta}^n \leq \widehat{\delta}^m$ is derivable from C^2). Since β must be mapped to an expression with base stage $\imath$, there are two possibilities for δ: it must be mapped either to a stage expression with base stage $\imath$ or to ∞. But δ cannot be mapped to a stage expression with base stage $\imath$. It must therefore be mapped to ∞, which is expressed by the constraint $\infty \leq \delta$. Now, it may happen that such new constraints force a variable $\gamma \in S^{\imath}$ to be mapped to ∞ (see for instance Ex. 4.14 below). In this case the algorithm fails, otherwise it succeeds.

Formally, we proceed as follows.

1. We compute the upward closed set $S^{\imath\leq}$ of stage variables that must be mapped to ∞ or to a stage expression with base stage $\imath$:

$$S^{\imath} \subseteq S^{\imath\leq} \qquad \text{and} \qquad \delta \in S^{\imath\leq} \ \text{ if } \ \widehat{\beta}^n \leq \widehat{\delta}^m \in C^2 \ \text{ with } \ \beta \in S^{\imath\leq}$$

   For fix_1, we have $S_1^{\imath\leq} = \{\alpha, \gamma\}$.
2. Proceeding as for computing C^2, we set all variables $\beta \in S^{\neg\imath} \cap S^{\imath\leq}$ to ∞. This generates a new set of constraints C^3. For fix_1, we have $S_1^{\neg\imath} \cap S_1^{\imath\leq} = \emptyset$, hence $C_1^3 = C_1^2$.

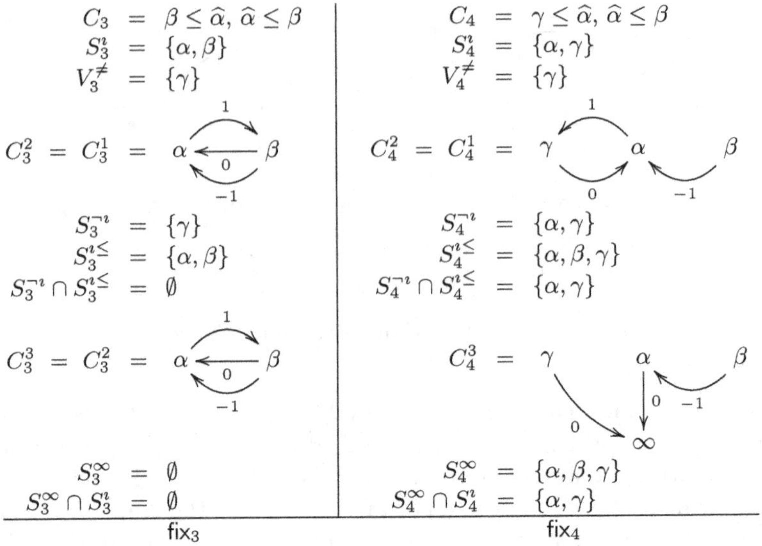

Fig. 11. Runs of `RecCheck` on fix_3 and fix_4 of Ex. 4.14

3. We compute the upward closed set S^∞ of stage variables that must be mapped to ∞:

$$\beta \in S^\infty \qquad \text{if} \qquad \infty \leq \widehat{\beta}^k \in C^3 \quad \text{or} \quad \left(\widehat{\delta}^n \leq \widehat{\beta}^m \in C^3 \quad \text{with} \quad \delta \in S^\infty\right)$$

Now, if $S^\imath \cap S^\infty = \emptyset$, then the algorithm succeeds and we put $C^{\mathsf{Rec}} := C^3$, otherwise it fails and we put $C^{\mathsf{Rec}} := \bot$.

This second phase succeeds for fix_1. On the other hand, the failure of the algorithm for fix_2 was already known at the end of the first phase. In Ex. 4.14 below, we give an expression for which the algorithm succeeds on the first phase and fails on the second.

In the case of fix_1, the algorithm succeeds and we have $C_1^{\mathsf{Rec}} = C_1^2 = C_1^1 = C_1$. We arrive at the following inference derivation:

$$\frac{\widehat{\alpha} \leq \gamma,\, \widehat{\delta} \leq \beta \;;\; f : \mathsf{Nat}^\alpha \to \mathsf{Nat}^\beta \vdash \lambda x : \mathsf{Nat}.\ \mathsf{o} \downarrow \mathsf{Nat}^{\widehat{\alpha}} \to \mathsf{Nat}^\beta}{\widehat{\alpha} \leq \gamma,\, \widehat{\delta} \leq \beta \;;\; \vdash (\mathsf{letrec}_{\mathsf{Nat}\to\mathsf{Nat}}\ f = \lambda x : \mathsf{Nat}.\ \mathsf{o}) \uparrow \mathsf{Nat}^\alpha \to \mathsf{Nat}^\beta}$$

We check that the constraint C_1^{Rec} allows applying the rule (rec):

$$(\mathrm{rec})\ \frac{f : \mathsf{Nat}^\imath \to \mathsf{Nat}^r \vdash \lambda x : \mathsf{Nat}.\ \mathsf{o} \ :\ \mathsf{Nat}^{\widehat{\imath}} \to \mathsf{Nat}^r}{\vdash (\mathsf{letrec}_{\mathsf{Nat}\to\mathsf{Nat}}\ f = \lambda x : \mathsf{Nat}.\ \mathsf{o}) \ :\ \mathsf{Nat}^s \to \mathsf{Nat}^r} \quad \text{if } \imath \notin r$$

Let ρ such that $\widehat{\rho(\alpha)} \leq \rho(\gamma)$ and $\widehat{\rho(\delta)} \leq \rho(\beta)$. Moreover, let $s =_{\mathrm{def}} \rho(\alpha)$ and $r =_{\mathrm{def}} \rho(\beta)$. Let $\imath \notin \rho(\beta), \rho(\delta)$ and define ρ' such that

$$\rho'(\alpha) = \imath \qquad \rho'(\gamma) = \widehat{\imath} \qquad \rho'(\beta) = \rho(\beta) \qquad \rho'(\delta) = \rho(\delta)$$

We thus have $\widehat{\rho'(\alpha)} \leq \rho'(\gamma)$ and $\widehat{\rho'(\delta)} \leq \rho'(\beta)$. It follows that

$$f : \mathsf{Nat}^{\imath} \to \mathsf{Nat}^{r} \vdash \lambda x : \mathsf{Nat}.\ \mathsf{o}\ :\ \mathsf{Nat}^{\widehat{\imath}} \to \mathsf{Nat}^{r}$$

Since $\imath \notin r$, by (rec) deduce that

$$\vdash (\mathsf{letrec}_{\mathsf{Nat}\to\mathsf{Nat}}\ f = \lambda x : \mathsf{Nat}.\ \mathsf{o})\ :\ \mathsf{Nat}^{s} \to \mathsf{Nat}^{r}$$

hence $\vdash (\mathsf{letrec}_{\mathsf{Nat}\to\mathsf{Nat}}\ f = \lambda x : \mathsf{Nat}.\ \mathsf{o})\ :\ \mathsf{Nat}^{\rho(\alpha)} \to \mathsf{Nat}^{\rho(\beta)}$.

Example 4.14 (The second phase of `RecCheck`*)* Consider the expressions:

$$\begin{aligned}\mathsf{fix}_3 &:= \lambda v : V.\ \lambda y : \mathsf{Nat}.\ (\mathsf{letrec}\ f = \lambda x : \mathsf{Nat}.\\ &\qquad \mathsf{case}_V\ x\ \mathsf{of}\ \{\mathsf{o} \Rightarrow v \mid \mathsf{s} \Rightarrow \lambda z : \mathsf{Nat}.\ f\,z\})\end{aligned}$$

$$\begin{aligned}\mathsf{fix}_4 &:= \lambda v : V.\ \lambda y : \mathsf{Nat}.\ (\mathsf{letrec}\ f = \lambda x : \mathsf{Nat}.\\ &\qquad \mathsf{case}_V\ y\ \mathsf{of}\ \{\mathsf{o} \Rightarrow v \mid \mathsf{s} \Rightarrow \lambda z : \mathsf{Nat}.\ f\,z\})\end{aligned}$$

Forgetting stages, fix_3 and fix_4 would have type $V \to \mathsf{Nat} \to \mathsf{Nat} \to V$, hence

$$v : V \vdash \mathsf{fix}_3\ v\ (\mathsf{s}\ \mathsf{o})\ \mathsf{o}\ :\ V \qquad \text{and} \qquad v : V \vdash \mathsf{fix}_4\ v\ (\mathsf{s}\ \mathsf{o})\ \mathsf{o}\ :\ V$$

The only difference between fix_3 and fix_4 is the variable subject to the case-analysis: in fix_3, this is the variable x, bound inside the fixpoint, while in fix_4, this is the variable y, bound outside the fixpoint. This leads to very different behaviors: $\mathsf{fix}_3\,v\,(\mathsf{s}\,\mathsf{o})\,\mathsf{o}$ is strongly normalizing and reduces to v, whereas $\mathsf{fix}_4\,v\,(\mathsf{s}\,\mathsf{o})\,\mathsf{o}$ has no normal form. Indeed, we have $\mathsf{fix}_4\,v\,(\mathsf{s}\,\mathsf{o})\,\mathsf{o} \ \to^*\ \mathsf{fix}'_4\mathsf{o}$ and

$$\mathsf{fix}'_4\ \mathsf{o}\ \to^*\ \mathsf{case}_V\ (\mathsf{s}\,\mathsf{o})\ \mathsf{of}\ \{\mathsf{o} \Rightarrow v \mid \mathsf{s} \Rightarrow \lambda z : \mathsf{Nat}.\ \mathsf{fix}'_4\,z\}\ \to\ \mathsf{fix}'_4\ \mathsf{o}\ \to\ \ldots$$

where $\mathsf{fix}'_4\ :=\ (\mathsf{letrec}\ f = \lambda x : \mathsf{Nat}.\ \mathsf{case}_V\ (\mathsf{s}\,\mathsf{o})\ \mathsf{of}\ \{\mathsf{o} \Rightarrow v \mid \mathsf{s} \Rightarrow \lambda z : \mathsf{Nat}.\ f\,z\})$. Let us have a look at the constraints generated during the typechecking of fix_3 and fix_4. Reasoning as in Ex. 4.7 (and doing the same simplifications), we obtain the following judgment for fix_3:

$$\begin{aligned}&\beta \leq \widehat{\alpha}\ ;\ v : V,\ y : \mathsf{Nat}^{\gamma},\ f : \mathsf{Nat}^{\alpha} \to V,\ x : \mathsf{Nat}^{\beta} \vdash\\ &\qquad\qquad \mathsf{case}_V\ x\ \mathsf{of}\ \{0 \Rightarrow v \mid \mathsf{s} \Rightarrow \lambda z : \mathsf{Nat}^{\alpha}.\ f\,z\} \uparrow V\end{aligned}$$

and for fix_4:

$$\begin{aligned}&\gamma \leq \widehat{\alpha}\ ;\ v : V,\ y : \mathsf{Nat}^{\gamma},\ f : \mathsf{Nat}^{\alpha} \to V,\ x : \mathsf{Nat}^{\beta} \vdash\\ &\qquad\qquad \mathsf{case}_V\ y\ \mathsf{of}\ \{0 \Rightarrow v \mid \mathsf{s} \Rightarrow \lambda z : \mathsf{Nat}^{\alpha}.\ f\,z\} \uparrow V\end{aligned}$$

This leads to the following premises for the inference rule (rec): for fix_3, we have

$$\begin{aligned}&\beta \leq \widehat{\alpha},\ \widehat{\alpha} \leq \beta\ ;\ v : V,\ y : \mathsf{Nat}^{\gamma},\ f : \mathsf{Nat}^{\alpha} \to V \vdash\\ &\qquad \lambda x : \mathsf{Nat}^{\beta}.\ \mathsf{case}_V\ x\ \mathsf{of}\ \{0 \Rightarrow v \mid \mathsf{s} \Rightarrow \lambda z : \mathsf{Nat}^{\alpha}.\ f\,z\} \downarrow \mathsf{Nat}^{\widehat{\alpha}} \to V\end{aligned}$$

and for fix_4, we have

$$\gamma \leq \widehat{\alpha},\, \widehat{\alpha} \leq \beta\,;\, v : V,\, y : \mathsf{Nat}^{\gamma},\, f : \mathsf{Nat}^{\alpha} \to V \vdash$$
$$\lambda x : \mathsf{Nat}^{\beta}.\ \mathsf{case}_V\ y\ \mathsf{of}\ \{0 \Rightarrow v \mid \mathsf{s} \Rightarrow \lambda z : \mathsf{Nat}^{\alpha}.\ f\, z\} \downarrow \mathsf{Nat}^{\widehat{\alpha}} \to V$$

Let $C_3 =_{\mathrm{def}} \beta \leq \widehat{\alpha}, \widehat{\alpha} \leq \beta$ and $C_4 =_{\mathrm{def}} \gamma \leq \widehat{\alpha}, \widehat{\alpha} \leq \beta$. In both cases, when checking the body of the recursive definition, α is the fixpoint stage variable (i.e. it must be mapped to $\imath$), while γ cannot be mapped to a stage expression with base stage $\imath$. The variable β must normally not appear as an annotation of Nat under the λ-abstraction; we write it just for convenience. We have $V_3^{\neq} = V_4^{\neq} = \{\gamma\}$, hence there is *a priori* no restriction on β. The constraint C_4 impose γ to be mapped to $\imath$, and the algorithm will fail on fix_4 for this reason. We display on Fig.11 the runs of the algorithm on fix_3 and fix_4. The algorithm succeeds on fix_3. On fix_4, the first phase succeeds but the second fails. □

4.4 Type Inference in System $F^{\frown}$

We now turn to the formal and precise description of the type inference algorithm for $F^{\frown}$. Our presentation follows [6], where more details can be found.

System $F^{\frown\star}$. When we discussed the typing rule of fixpoint in the last section (Sect. 4.3), we silenced one issue concerning the types appearing as tags in terms. Consider the typing rule (rec)

$$(\mathrm{rec})\ \frac{\overline{\Gamma}, f : d^{\imath}\overline{\tau} \to \overline{\theta} \vdash e : \widehat{d^{\imath}}\overline{\tau} \to \overline{\theta}[\imath := \widehat{\imath}] \qquad \imath\ \mathsf{pos}\ \overline{\theta}}{\overline{\Gamma} \vdash (\mathsf{letrec}_{d|\overline{\tau}| \to |\overline{\theta}|}\ f = e) : d^{s}\overline{\tau} \to \overline{\theta}[\imath := s]}\ \text{if } \imath \notin \overline{\Gamma}, \overline{\tau}$$

In the general case, the stage variable may appear in $\overline{\theta}$. But when inferring the type of a fixpoint $? \,;\, \overline{\Gamma} \vdash (\mathsf{letrec}_{d\,\overline{\tau} \to \theta}\ f = e) \uparrow ?$ we have *a priori* no indication on how the θ should be decorated. Therefore, type inference is performed in a system $F^{\frown\star}$ such that the type appearing in fixpoints convey an indication, symbolized by the tag $\star$, of the positions at which the fixpoint stage variable must appear. Such types are called *position types* and are given by the abstract syntax:

$$\mathcal{T}^{\star} \ ::=\ \mathcal{V}_{\mathcal{T}} \mid \mathcal{T}^{\star} \to \mathcal{T}^{\star} \mid \Pi\mathcal{V}_{\mathcal{T}}.\, \mathcal{T}^{\star} \mid \mathcal{D}^{\star}\, \vec{\mathcal{T}^{\star}} \mid \mathcal{D}\, \vec{\mathcal{T}^{\star}}$$

where in the clause for datatypes, it is assumed that the length of the vector $\vec{\mathcal{T}^{\star}}$ is exactly the arity of the datatype. We let $|.| : \mathcal{T}^{\star} \to \mathcal{T}$ be the obvious erasure map from $\mathcal{T}^{\star}$ to $\mathcal{T}$.

The terms of $F^{\frown\star}$ are those of $F^{\frown}$, excepted that fixpoints are now of the form $(\mathsf{letrec}_{\tau^{\star}}\ f = e)$ where $\tau^{\star} \in \mathcal{T}^{\star}$ is a position type. The typing rules of $F^{\frown\star}$ are those of $F^{\frown}$, excepted that the typing rule (rec) of fixpoints is now

$$\frac{\overline{\Gamma}, f : d^{\imath}\overline{\tau} \to \overline{\theta} \vdash e : \widehat{d^{\imath}}\overline{\tau} \to \overline{\theta}[\imath := \widehat{\imath}]}{\overline{\Gamma} \vdash (\mathsf{letrec}_{\tau^{\star}}\ f = e) : d^{s}\overline{\tau} \to \overline{\theta}[\imath := s]}\ \text{if} \begin{cases} \imath \notin \overline{\Gamma}, \overline{\tau} \text{ and } \imath\ \mathsf{pos}\ \overline{\theta} \\ \tau^{\star} \text{ is } \imath\text{-compatible with } d^{\imath}\overline{\tau} \to \overline{\theta} \end{cases}$$

where we say that a position type $\sigma^\star$ is *$\imath$-compatible* with a sized type $\overline{\sigma}$ if $\sigma^\star$ can be obtained from $\overline{\sigma}$ by replacing all stage annotations containing $\imath$ by $\star$ and by erasing all other size annotations. For instance, $\mathsf{Nat}^\imath \to \mathsf{Nat}^\jmath \to \mathsf{Nat}^{\widehat{\imath}}$ is $\imath$-compatible with $\mathsf{Nat}^\star \to \mathsf{Nat} \to \mathsf{Nat}^\star$, while $\mathsf{Nat}^\imath \to \mathsf{Nat}^\imath \to \mathsf{Nat}^{\widehat{\imath}}$ is not.

Remark 4.15 (The shape of $\tau^\star$) Note that the conjunction of the conditions $\imath \notin \overline{\boldsymbol{\tau}}$ and $\tau^\star$ $\imath$-compatible with $d^\imath\overline{\boldsymbol{\tau}} \to \overline{\theta}$ implies that $\tau^\star$ is of the form $d^\star\boldsymbol{\tau} \to \theta^\star$, where $\boldsymbol{\tau}$ are not position types (i.e. they convey no tag $\star$).

The annotation of a position type $\tau^\star$ is performed by a function $\mathtt{Annot}^\star$, which is similar to $\mathtt{Annot}$ but takes as input a position type instead of a bare type. Intuitively, if V is a set of inference stage variables and $\sigma^\star \in \mathcal{T}^\star$ is a position type, then $\mathtt{Annot}^\star(\sigma^\star, V)$ returns a tuple $(\overline{\sigma}, V', V^\star)$ such that $|\sigma^\star| = |\overline{\sigma}|$ and:

- as with $\mathtt{Annot}$, each occurrence of an inductive datatype (tagged or not) in $\sigma^\star$ is annotated with a distinct inference stage variable $\alpha \notin V$ (so that α occurs at most once in $\sigma^\star$), and $V' = V \cup \mathcal{V}_{\mathcal{I}}(\overline{\sigma})$,
- $V^\star$ is the set of inference stages variables occurring in $\overline{\sigma}$ at positions that where tagged in σ.

E.g., $\mathtt{Annot}^\star(\mathsf{Nat}^\star \to \mathsf{Nat}, \{\alpha_1, \alpha_2\}) = (\mathsf{Nat}^{\alpha_3} \to \mathsf{Nat}^{\alpha_4}, \{\alpha_1, \alpha_2, \alpha_3, \alpha_4\}, \{\alpha_3\})$. Therefore, the inference rule for fixpoints will have the following shape:

$$\frac{C\ ;\ \overline{\Gamma}, f : d^\alpha\overline{\boldsymbol{\tau}} \to \overline{\theta} \vdash e \downarrow d^{\widehat{\alpha}}\overline{\boldsymbol{\tau}} \to \overline{\theta} \qquad (d^\alpha\overline{\boldsymbol{\tau}} \to \overline{\theta}, V', V^\star) = \mathtt{Annot}^\star(d^\star\boldsymbol{\tau} \to \theta^\star, V)}{C^{\mathsf{Rec}}\ ;\ \overline{\Gamma} \vdash (\mathsf{letrec}_{d^\star\boldsymbol{\tau} \to \theta^\star}\ f = e) \uparrow d^\alpha\overline{\boldsymbol{\tau}} \to \overline{\theta}}$$

where C^{Rec} is computed by $\mathtt{RecCheck}$ and $V = \mathcal{V}_{\mathcal{I}}(\overline{\Gamma})$. Before giving the formal definition of $\mathtt{RecCheck}$, let us stress some important points. Recall that there must be a fresh stage variable $\imath$ such that the variables $\beta \in V^\star$ must all be mapped to a stage expression of base stage $\imath$, and moreover the fixpoint variable α, which belongs to $V^\star$, must be mapped to $\imath$. Note that $V^\star \setminus \{\alpha\}$ contains exactly the set of inference variables occurring in $\overline{\theta}$ that must be mapped to a stage expression with base stage $\imath$. Therefore, the variables $\beta \in V \setminus V^\star$ are annotations of untagged datatypes occurrences in $\tau^\star$, and cannot be mapped to stage expressions depending on $\imath$. Moreover the typing rule of fixpoint imposes that for all substitution ρ, all occurrences of $\imath$ in $\overline{\theta}\rho$ must be positive. It follows that all occurrences of $\beta \in V^\star \setminus \{\alpha\}$ in $\overline{\theta}$ must be positive. The type inference algorithm checks this by encoding positivity tests in constraints.

Lemma 4.16 $\imath\ \mathsf{pos}\ \overline{\tau}$ *if and only if* $\overline{\tau} \sqsubseteq \overline{\tau}[\imath := \widehat{\imath}]$.

Note that by definition of $\mathtt{Annot}^\star$, the fixpoint variable α does not occur in $\overline{\theta}$. Hence the positivity test for the occurrences of variables $\beta \in V^\star$ in $\overline{\theta}$ can be coded by the constraint $(\!|\overline{\theta} \sqsubseteq \widehat{\theta}|\!)$ where $\widehat{\theta}$ is defined as $\widehat{\theta} =_{\mathrm{def}} \overline{\theta}[\beta := \widehat{\beta}]_{\beta \in V^\star}$. Therefore, in addition to the constraint C^{Rec} computed by $\mathtt{RecCheck}$, the type inference rule of fixpoints produces a constraint $(\!|\overline{\theta} \sqsubseteq \widehat{\theta}|\!)$:

$$\frac{C\ ;\ \overline{\Gamma}, f : d^\alpha\overline{\boldsymbol{\tau}} \to \overline{\theta} \vdash e \downarrow d^{\widehat{\alpha}}\overline{\boldsymbol{\tau}} \to \overline{\theta} \qquad (d^\alpha\overline{\boldsymbol{\tau}} \to \overline{\theta}, V', V^\star) = \mathtt{Annot}^\star(d^\star\boldsymbol{\tau} \to \theta^\star, V)}{C^{\mathsf{Rec}} \cup_\perp (\!|\overline{\theta} \sqsubseteq \widehat{\theta}|\!)\ ;\ \overline{\Gamma} \vdash (\mathsf{letrec}_{d^\star\boldsymbol{\tau} \to \theta^\star}\ f = e) \uparrow d^\alpha\overline{\boldsymbol{\tau}} \to \overline{\theta}}$$

where $V = \mathcal{V}_{\mathcal{I}}(\overline{\Gamma})$.

The RecCheck algorithm. We now turn to the computation of RecCheck. This algorithm is at the core of guaranteeing termination. As we have in Sect.4.3, it takes as input the set of constraints that has been inferred for the body of the recursive definition, and either returns an error if the definition is unsound w.r.t. the type system, or the set of constraints for the recursive definition, if the definition is sound w.r.t. the type system. The formal definition of the function is given below. Let us look at its signature. Starting from $(d^{\alpha}\overline{\tau} \to \overline{\theta}, V, V^{\star}) :=$ $\texttt{Annot}^{\star}(d^{\star}\tau \to \theta^{\star}, \mathcal{V}_{\mathcal{J}}(\overline{\Gamma}))$, we have

- an inference fixpoint variable α which must be mapped to a fresh stage variable $\imath$,
- a set of inference stage variables $V^{\star}$, containing α, which must be mapped to a stage expression with base stage $\imath$,
- and a set $V \setminus V^{\star}$ which cannot be mapped to stage expressions with base stage $\imath$.

This corresponds to the first three arguments of RecCheck. The last one is the constraint C generated by typechecking the body of the recursive definition. Formally, the function RecCheck takes as input a tuple $(\alpha, V^{\star}, V^{\neq}, C)$, where

- α is the fixpoint inference stage variable of the recursive definition ; it must be mapped to a fresh base stage $\imath$;
- $V^{\star}$ is a set of inference stage variables that must be mapped to a stage expression with the same base stage as α. The set $V^{\star}$ is determined by the position types in the tag of the recursive definition. In particular, we have $\alpha \in V^{\star}$;
- $V^{\neq}$ is a set of inference stage variables that must be mapped to a stage expression with a base stage different from $\imath$;
- C is the constraint inferred by typechecking the body of the recursive definition.

The algorithm $\texttt{RecCheck}(\alpha, V^{\star}, V^{\neq}, C)$ returns $\perp$ or a set of constraints subject to conditions that will be presented later.

We now turn to the computation of $\texttt{RecCheck}(\alpha, V^{\star}, V^{\neq}, C)$. Assuming that we intend to map α to a fresh stage variable $\imath$, the computation proceeds as follows:

1. it computes the downwards closed set $S^{\imath}$ of stage variables that must be mapped to a stage expression with base stage $\imath$. The rules are $V^{\star} \subseteq S^{\imath}$, and if $\alpha_1 \in S^{\imath}$ and $\widehat{\alpha}_2^{n_2} \leq \widehat{\alpha}_1^{n_1} \in C$ then $\alpha_2 \in S^{\imath}$;
2. the algorithm must enforce that α is the smallest variable in $S^{\imath}$. It does so by adding to C the constraints $\alpha \leq S^{\imath}$. Let $C_1 = C \cup \alpha \leq S^{\imath}$;
3. the algorithm checks for negative cycles in the graph representation of C_1. Each time it finds such a cycle starting from β, the algorithm computes the set $V_{\sqsupseteq\beta}$ of variables greater or equal to β, removes all inequalities about variables in $V_{\sqsupseteq\beta}$ and adds the constraints $\infty \leq V_{\sqsupseteq\beta}$. At the end of this step there are no more negative cycles in the graph, and we get a new set of constraints C_2;

4. the algorithm computes the upwards closed set $S^{\imath\leq}$ of stage variables that must be mapped to ∞ or to a stage expression with base stage $\imath$. The rules are $S^{\imath} \subseteq S^{\imath\leq}$ and if $\alpha_1 \in S^{\imath\leq}$ and $\widehat{\alpha}_1^{n_1} \leq \widehat{\alpha}_2^{n_2} \in C_2$ then $\alpha_2 \in S^{\imath\leq}$;
5. the algorithm computes the upwards closed set $S^{\neg\imath}$ of stage variables that cannot be mapped to a stage expression with base stage $\imath$. The rules are $V^{\neq} \subseteq S^{\neg\imath}$ and if $\alpha_1 \in S^{\neg\imath}$ and $\widehat{\alpha}_1^{n_1} \leq \widehat{\alpha}_2^{n_2} \in C_2$ then α_2 is in $S^{\neg\imath}$;
6. the algorithm sets all variables $\beta \in S^{\neg\imath} \cap S^{\imath\leq}$ to ∞ (as in Step 3). At the end of this step we get a new set of constraints C_3;
7. the algorithm computes the upwards closed set S^{∞} of stage variables that must be mapped to ∞. If $\infty \leq \widehat{\beta}^k \in C_3$ then β is in S^{∞}, and if $\alpha_1 \in S^{\infty}$ and $\widehat{\alpha}_1^{n_1} \leq \widehat{\alpha}_2^{n_2} \in C_3$ then α_2 is in S^{∞}.
8. if $S^{\infty} \cap S^{\imath} = \emptyset$ the algorithm returns the new set of constraints, else it fails.

We have already explained this algorithm in Sect. 4.3. Note that at the end of step 3, the algorithm can already stop and fail if $C_2 \vdash \infty \leq \alpha$.

The inference algorithm. We now turn to the formal definition of the inference algorithm. Contrary to what we have done up to now, it is not presented by inference rules. The cause is that we want to have a very precise control on the fresh variables introduced during type inference. The defect of the presentation by inference rules can be seen on the inference rule (app) for the application:

$$(\text{app})\ \frac{C_1 \,;\, \overline{\Gamma} \vdash e \uparrow \overline{\tau} \to \overline{\sigma} \qquad C_2 \,;\, \overline{\Gamma} \vdash e' \downarrow \overline{\tau}}{C_1 \cup_{\perp} C_2 \,;\, \overline{\Gamma} \vdash e\ e' \uparrow \overline{\sigma}}$$

Assume that the derivation of $C_1 \,;\, \overline{\Gamma} \vdash e \uparrow \overline{\tau} \to \overline{\sigma}$ has generated fresh inference variables $\boldsymbol{\alpha}$ occurring in C_1 but not in $\overline{\Gamma}$. If we need fresh inference variables in the derivation of $C_2 \,;\, \overline{\Gamma} \vdash e' \downarrow \overline{\tau}$, then we must ensure that these variables are not taken among $\boldsymbol{\alpha}$. Hence, we have to transmit the current set of non-fresh inference variable along the derivations of type inference. The easiest to do this is to use two functions `Infer` and `Check` such that

- `Infer` takes as input a tuple $(V, \overline{\Gamma}, e)$, where V is a set of already used inference variables such that $\mathcal{V}_{\mathfrak{I}}(\overline{\Gamma}) \subseteq V$. It returns a tuple $(V', C, \overline{\tau})$ such that $C \,;\, \overline{\Gamma} \vdash e \uparrow \overline{\tau}$ and $\mathcal{V}_{\mathfrak{I}}(C, \overline{\tau}) \cup V \subseteq V'$.
- `Check` takes as input a tuple $(V, \overline{\Gamma}, e)$, where V is a set of already used inference variables such that $\mathcal{V}_{\mathfrak{I}}(\overline{\Gamma}, \overline{\tau}) \subseteq V$. It returns a tuple (V', C) such that $C \,;\, \overline{\Gamma} \vdash e \downarrow \overline{\tau}$ and $\mathcal{V}_{\mathfrak{I}}(C, \overline{\tau}) \cup V \subseteq V'$.

For instance, the inference rule for the application now becomes:

$$\begin{array}{rcl} \texttt{Infer}(V, \overline{\Gamma}, e_1\, e_2) & = & (V_2, C_1 \cup C_2, \overline{\tau}) \\ & & \text{where } (V_1, C_1, \overline{\tau}_2 \to \overline{\tau}) := \texttt{Infer}(V, \overline{\Gamma}, e_1) \\ & & (V_2, C_2) := \texttt{Check}(V_1, \overline{\Gamma}, e_2, \overline{\tau}_2) \end{array}$$

Hence, if the derivation of $C_1 \,;\, \overline{\Gamma} \vdash e \uparrow \overline{\tau} \to \overline{\sigma}$ uses stage variables in V_1, then no fresh variable used in the derivation of $C_2 \,;\, \overline{\Gamma} \vdash e' \downarrow \overline{\tau}$ belongs to V_1. The whole inference algorithm is presented in Fig. 12.

$$
\begin{array}{lcl}
\mathtt{Check}(V,\overline{\Gamma},e,\overline{\tau}) & = & (V_e,(C_e \cup_\perp \llparenthesis \overline{\tau}_e \sqsubseteq \overline{\tau} \rrparenthesis)) \\
 & & \text{where } (V_e,C_e,\overline{\tau}_e) := \mathtt{Infer}(\overline{\Gamma},e) \\
\mathtt{Infer}(V,\overline{\Gamma},x) & = & (V,\emptyset,\overline{\Gamma}(x)) \\
\mathtt{Infer}(V,\overline{\Gamma},\lambda x:\tau_1.\, e) & = & (V_e,C_e,\overline{\tau}_1 \to \overline{\tau}_2) \\
 & & \text{where } (V_1,\overline{\tau}_1) := \mathtt{Annot}(V,\tau_1) \\
 & & \qquad (V_e,C_e,\overline{\tau}_2) := \mathtt{Infer}(V_1,\overline{\Gamma},x:\overline{\tau}_1,e) \\
\mathtt{Infer}(V,\overline{\Gamma},\Lambda A.\, e) & = & (V_e,C_e,\Pi A.\,\overline{\tau}) \\
 & & \text{where } (V_e,C_e,\overline{\tau}) := \mathtt{Infer}(V,\overline{\Gamma},e) \\
 & & \text{if } A \text{ does not occur in } \overline{\Gamma} \\
\mathtt{Infer}(V,\overline{\Gamma},e_1\, e_2) & = & (V_2,(C_1 \cup_\perp C_2),\overline{\tau}) \\
 & & \text{where } (V_1,C_1,\overline{\tau}_2 \to \overline{\tau}) := \mathtt{Infer}(V,\overline{\Gamma},e_1) \\
 & & \qquad (V_2,C_2) := \mathtt{Check}(V_1,\overline{\Gamma},e_2,\overline{\tau}_2) \\
\mathtt{Infer}(V,\overline{\Gamma},e\,\tau) & = & (V_e,C_e,\overline{\tau}_e[A := \overline{\tau}]) \\
 & & \text{where } (V_1,\overline{\tau}) := \mathtt{Annot}(V,\tau) \\
 & & \qquad (V_e,C_e,\Pi A.\,\overline{\tau}_e) := \mathtt{Infer}(V_1,\overline{\Gamma},e) \\
\mathtt{Infer}(V,\overline{\Gamma},c) & = & ((V \cup \{\alpha\}),\emptyset,\mathsf{Type}(c,\alpha)) \\
 & & \text{with } \alpha \notin V \\
\mathtt{Infer}(V,\overline{\Gamma},\mathsf{case}_\theta\ e \ \mathsf{of}\ \{\boldsymbol{c} \Rightarrow \boldsymbol{e}\}) & = & (V_n,(\{s \le \widehat{\alpha}\} \cup_\perp C_e \cup_\perp \bigcup_{i=1}^n C_i),\overline{\theta}) \\
 & & \text{where } \alpha \notin V \\
 & & \qquad (V_\theta,\overline{\theta}) := \mathtt{Annot}(V \cup \{\alpha\},\theta) \\
 & & \qquad (V_0,C_e,d^s\overline{\boldsymbol{\tau}}) := \mathtt{Infer}(V_\theta,\overline{\Gamma},e) \\
 & & \qquad (V_i,C_i) := \mathtt{Check}(V_{i-1},\overline{\Gamma},e_i,\mathsf{Inst}(c_i,\alpha,\overline{\boldsymbol{\tau}},\overline{\theta})) \\
 & & \text{if } \mathcal{C}(d) = \{c_1,\ldots,c_n\} \\
\mathtt{Infer}(V,\overline{\Gamma},(\mathsf{letrec}_{d^\star\boldsymbol{\tau}\to\theta}\ f = e)) & = & (V_e,C_f,d^\alpha\overline{\boldsymbol{\tau}} \to \overline{\theta}) \\
 & & \text{where } (V_1,V^\star,d^\alpha\overline{\boldsymbol{\tau}} \to \overline{\theta}) := \mathtt{Annot}^\star(V,d^\star\boldsymbol{\tau} \to \theta) \\
 & & \qquad \widehat{\theta} := \overline{\theta}[\alpha_i := \widehat{\alpha_i}]_{\alpha_i \in V^\star} \\
 & & (V_e,C_e) := \mathtt{Check}(V_1,\overline{\Gamma},f : d^\alpha\overline{\boldsymbol{\tau}} \to \overline{\theta},e,d^{\widehat{\alpha}}\overline{\boldsymbol{\tau}} \to \widehat{\theta}) \\
 & & \qquad C_f := \mathtt{RecCheck}(\alpha,V^\star,V_1 \backslash V^\star,C_e \cup_\perp \llparenthesis \overline{\theta} \sqsubseteq \widehat{\theta} \rrparenthesis)
\end{array}
$$

Fig. 12. Inference algorithm

We end the description of the type inference algorithm by the following observation about constraints.

Remark 4.17 The principal type returned by the inference algorithm may not be represented in its most compact form: for example, the inference algorithm will infer for the usual definition of addition the unconstrained type $\mathsf{Nat}^\imath \to \mathsf{Nat}^\jmath \to \mathsf{Nat}^\infty$ whereas it would be more readable to use the equivalent type $\mathsf{Nat}^\infty \to \mathsf{Nat}^\infty \to \mathsf{Nat}^\infty$. Formally, we can define a notion of equivalence between pairs of types and constraint: we say $(C,\overline{\tau}) \preceq (C',\overline{\tau'})$ iff for every ρ s.t. $\rho \models C$ there exists ρ' s.t. $\rho' \models C'$ and $\rho'\overline{\tau'} \sqsubseteq \rho\overline{\tau}$. Then, we define $(C,\overline{\tau}) \simeq (C',\overline{\tau'})$ iff $(C,\overline{\tau}) \preceq (C',\overline{\tau'})$ and $(C',\overline{\tau'}) \preceq (C,\overline{\tau})$. Now, we can define a set of heuristics that transform a pair $(C,\overline{\tau})$ into simpler ones. For example, one can replace by ∞ all size variables that only occur in negative positions in the type component of such pairs. One can also perform simplifications in the constraint, in the spirit of the rules that are used in the algorithm that checks the correctness of recursive definitions. We do not formalize the notion of simplification, but it is possible to define a notion of canonical form and provide a set of rules that transform every such pair to an equivalent, canonical one.

The soundness and completeness of the algorithm, which is stated in Proposition 4.1, is proved by induction on derivations, and relies on a proof that the algorithm `RecCheck` is itself sound and complete.

5 Further Reading

The material presented in this paper is based on the research papers [5,6]; the first paper introduces $\lambda^{\widehat{}}$, a simply typed fragment of the $F^{\widehat{}}$, and shows that it enjoys strong normalization, whereas the second paper introduces $F^{\widehat{}}$ and presents the inference algorithm.

Type-based termination has its origins in Mendler's formulation of recursion in the style of fixpoints [14]. Mendler's ideas were further developed in a series of works, including [7,19], and adapted to reactive programming by Pareto, Hughes, and Sabry [13], and to type theory by Giménez [10]. Abel [2] and Barthe *et al* provide a more detailed account of related work in the area of type-based termination. Coquand and Dybjer [8] provide an historical account of inductive definitions in type theory, whereas Aczel [4] provides an introduction to inductive definitions in a set-theoretical setting.

References

1. Abel, A.: Termination Checking with Types. RAIRO – Theoretical Informatics and Applications 38(4), 277–319 (2004); Special Issue (FICS 2003)
2. Abel, A.: Type-Based Termination. A Polymorphic Lambda-Calculus with Sized Higher-Order Types. PhD thesis, LMU University, Munich (2006)
3. Abel, A.: Semi-Continuous Sized Types and Termination. LMCS 4(2-3) (2008)
4. Aczel, P.: An Introduction to Inductive Definitions. In: Barwise, J. (ed.) Handbook of mathematical logic. Studies in Logic and the Foundations of Mathematics, vol. 90, pp. 739–782. North-Holland, Amsterdam (1977)
5. Barthe, G., Frade, M.J., Giménez, E., Pinto, L., Uustalu, T.: Type-Based Termination of Recursive Definitions. Mathematical Structures in Computer Science 14(1), 97–141 (2004)
6. Barthe, G., Grégoire, B., Pastawski, F.: Practical Inference for Type-Based Termination in a Polymorphic Setting. In: Urzyczyn, P. (ed.) TLCA 2005. LNCS, vol. 3461, pp. 71–85. Springer, Heidelberg (2005)
7. Chin, W.-N., Khoo, S.-C.: Calculating Sized Types. Higher-Order and Symbolic Computation 14(2-3), 261–300 (2001)
8. Coquand, T., Dybjer, P.: Inductive Definitions and Type Theory: an Introduction (Preliminary Version). In: Thiagarajan, P.S. (ed.) FSTTCS 1994. LNCS, vol. 880, pp. 60–76. Springer, Heidelberg (1994)
9. Gallier, J.H.: What's So Special About Kruskal's Theorem and the Ordinal Γ_0? A Survey of Some Results in Proof Theory. Annals of Pure and Applied Logic 53(3), 199–260 (1991)

10. Giménez, E.: Structural Recursive Definitions in Type Theory. In: Larsen, K.G., Skyum, S., Winskel, G. (eds.) ICALP 1998. LNCS, vol. 1443, pp. 397–408. Springer, Heidelberg (1998)
11. Girard, J.-Y.: Interprétation Fonctionnelle et Élimination des Coupures de l'Arithmétique d'Ordre Supérieur. PhD thesis, Université Paris 7 (1972)
12. Girard, J.-Y., Lafont, Y., Taylor, P.: Proofs and Types. Cambridge Tracts in Theoretical Computer Science. Cambridge University Press, Cambridge (1989)
13. Hughes, J., Pareto, L., Sabry, A.: Proving the Correctness of Reactive Systems Using Sized Types. In: Proceedings of POPL 1996, pp. 410–423. ACM, New York (1996)
14. Mendler, N.P.: Recursive Types and Type Constraints in Second Order Lambda-Calculus. In: Proceedings of LiCS 1987, pp. 30–36. IEEE Computer Society, Los Alamitos (1987)
15. Parigot, M.: On the Representation of Data in Lambda-Calculus. In: Börger, E., Kleine Büning, H., Richter, M.M. (eds.) CSL 1989. LNCS, vol. 440, pp. 309–321. Springer, Heidelberg (1990)
16. Spławski, Z., Urzyczyn, P.: Type Fixpoints: Iteration vs. Recursion. In: Proceedings of ICFP 1999, pp. 102–113. ACM, New York (1999)
17. Steffen, M.: Polarized Higher-order Subtyping. PhD thesis, Department of Computer Science, University of Erlangen (1997)
18. Tait, W.W.: A Realizability Interpretation of the Theory of Species. In: Parikh, R. (ed.) Logic Colloquium. LNCS, vol. 453, pp. 240–251. Springer, Heidelberg (1975)
19. Xi, H.: Dependent Types for Program Termination Verification. Higher-Order and Symbolic Computation 15(1), 91–131 (2002)

Structural Abstract Interpretation: A Formal Study Using Coq*

Yves Bertot

INRIA Sophia-Méditerranée

Abstract. Abstract interpreters are tools to compute approximations for behaviors of a program. These approximations can then be used for optimisation or for error detection. In this paper, we show how to describe an abstract interpreter using the type-theory based theorem prover Coq, using inductive types for syntax and structural recursive programming for the abstract interpreter's kernel. The abstract interpreter can then be proved correct with respect to a Hoare logic for the programming language.

1 Introduction

Higher-order logic theorem provers provide a description language that is powerful enough to describe programming languages. Inductive types can be used to describe the language's main data structure (the syntax) and recursive functions can be used to describe the behavior of instructions (the semantics). Recursive functions can also be used to describe tools to analyse or modify programs. In this paper, we will describe such a collection of recursive function to analyse programs, based on abstract interpretation [7].

1.1 An Example of Abstract Interpretation

We consider a small programming language with loop statements and assignments. Loops are written with the keywords `while`, `do` and `done`, assignments are written with `:=`, and several instructions can be grouped together, separating them with a semi-column. The instructions grouped using a semi-column are supposed to be executed in the same order as they are written. Comments are written after two slashes `//`.

We consider the following simple program:

```
x:= 0;              // line 1
While x < 10 do    // line 2
  x := x + 1       // line 3
done               // line 4
```

We want to design a tool that is able to gather information about the value of the variable x at each position in the program. For instance here, we know that

* This work was partially supported by ANR contract Compcert, ANR-05-SSIA-0019.

A. Bove et al. (Eds.): LerNet ALFA Summer School 2008, LNCS 5520, pp. 153–194, 2009.

after executing the first line, x is always in the interval [0,0]; we know that before executing the assignment on the third line, x is always smaller than 10 (because the test `x < 10` was just satisfied). With a little thinking, we can also guess that x increases as the loop executes, so that we can infer that before the third line, x is always in the interval [0,9]. On the other hand, after the third line, x is always in the interval [1, 10]. Now, if execution exits the loop, we can also infer that the test `x < 10` failed, so that we know that x is larger than or equal to 10, but since it was at best in [0,10] before the test, we can guess that x is exactly 10 after executing the program. So we can write the following new program, where the only difference is the information added in the comments:

```
// Nothing is known about x on this line
x := 0;                 // 0 <= x <= 0
while x < 10 do
                        // 0 <= x <= 9
  x := x + 1            // 1 <= x <= 10
done
                        // 10 <= x <= 10
```

We want to produce a tool that performs this analysis and produces the same kind of information for each line in the program. Our tool will do slightly more: first it will also be able to take as input extra information about variables before entering the program, second it will produce information about variables after executing the program, third it will associate an *invariant* property to all while loops in the program. Such an invariant is a property that is true *before and after* all executions of the loop body (in our example the loop body is `x := x+1`). A fourth feature of our tool is that it will be able to detect occasions when we can be sure that some code is never executed. In this case, it will mark the program points that are never reached with a `false` statement meaning "when this point of the program is reached, the `false` statement can be proved (in other words, this cannot happen)".

Our tool will also be designed in such a way that it is guaranteed to terminate in reasonable time. Such a tool is called a *static* analysis tool, because the extra information can be obtained without running the program: in this example, executing the program requires at least a thousand operations, but our reasoning effort takes less than ten steps.

Tools of this kind are useful, for example to avoid bugs in programs or as part of efficient compilation techniques. For instance, the first mail-spread virus exploited a programming error known as a buffer overflow (an array update was operating outside the memory allocated for that array), but buffer overflows can be detected if we know over which interval each variable is likely to range.

1.2 Formal Description and Proofs

Users should be able to trust the information added in programs by the analysers. Program analysers are themselves programs and we can reason about their correctness. The program analysers we study in this paper are based on abstract interpretation [7] and we use the Coq system [13,3] to reason on its correctness. The development described in this paper is available on the net at the following address (there are two versions, compatible with the latest stable release of Coq —V8.1pl3— and with the upcoming version —V8.2).

`http://hal.inria.fr/inria-00329572`

This paper has 7 more sections. Section 2 gives a rough introduction to the notion of abstract interpretation. Section 3 describes the programming language that is used as our playground. The semantics of this programming language is described using a weakest pre-condition calculus. This weakest pre-condition calculus is later used to argue on the correctness of abstract interpreters. In particular, abstract interpretation returns an annotated instruction and an abstract state, where the abstract state is used as a post-condition and the annotations in the instruction describe the abstract state at the corresponding point in the program. Section 4 describes a first simple abstract interpreter, where the main ideas around abstractly interpreting assignments and sequences are covered, but while loops are not treated. In Section 4, we also show that the abstract interpreter can be formally proved correct. In Section 5, we address while loops in more detail and in particular we show how tests can be handled in abstract interpretation, with applications to dead-code elimination. In Section 6, we observe that abstract interpretation is a general method that can be applied to a variety of abstract domains and we recapitulate the types, functions, and properties that are expected from each abstract domain. In Section 7, we show how the main abstract interpreter can be instantiated for a domain of intervals, thus making the analysis presented in the introduction possible. In Section 8, we give a few concluding remarks.

2 An Intuitive View of Abstract Interpretation

Abstract interpretation is a technique for the static analysis of programs. The objective is to obtain a tool that will take programs as data, perform some symbolic computation, and return information about all executions of the input programs. One important aspect is that this tool should always terminate (hence the adjective *static*). The tool can then be used either directly to provide information about properties of variables in the program (as in the Astree tool [8]), or as part of a compiler, where it can be used to guide optimization. For instance, the kind of interval-based analysis that we describe in this paper can be used to avoid runtime array-bound checking in languages that impose this kind of discipline like Java.

The central idea of abstract interpretation is to replace the values normally manipulated in a program by sets of values, in such a way that all operations still make sense.

For instance, if a program manipulates integer values and performs additions, we can decide to take an abstract point of view and only consider whether values are odd or even. With respect to addition, we can still obtain meaningful results, because we know, for instance, that adding an even and an odd value returns an odd value. Thus, we can decide to run programs with values taken in a new type that contains values `even` and `odd`, with an addition that respects the following table:

$$\begin{aligned} \texttt{odd} + \texttt{even} &= \texttt{odd} \\ \texttt{even} + \texttt{odd} &= \texttt{odd} \\ \texttt{odd} + \texttt{odd} &= \texttt{even} \\ \texttt{even} + \texttt{even} &= \texttt{even}. \end{aligned}$$

When defining abstract interpretation for a given abstract domain, all operations must be updated accordingly. The behavior of control instructions is also modified, because abstract values may not be precise enough to decide how a given decision should be taken.

For instance, if we know that the abstract value for a variable `x` is `odd`, then we cannot tell which branch of a conditional statement of the following form will be taken:

```
if x < 10 then x := 0 else x := 1.
```

After the execution of this conditional statement, the abstract value for `x` cannot be `odd` or `even`. This example also shows that the domain of abstract values must contain an abstract value that represents the whole set of values, or said differently, an abstract value that represents the absence of knowledge. This value will be called `top` later in the paper.

There must exist a connection between abstract values and concrete values for abstract interpretation to work well. This connection has been studied since [7] and is known as a Galois connection. For instance, if the abstract values are `even`, `odd`, and `top`, and if we can infer that a value is in $\{0, 2\}$, then correct choices for the abstract value are `top` or `even`, but obviously the abstract interpreter will work better if the more precise `even` is chosen.

Formal proofs of correctness for abstract interpretation were already studied before, in particular in [11]. The approach taken in this paper is different, in that it follows directly the syntax of a simple structured programming language, while traditional descriptions are tuned to studying a control-flow graph language. The main advantage of our approach is that it supports a very concise description of the abstract interpreter, with very simple verifications that it is terminating.

3 The Programming Language

In this case study, we work with a very small language containing only assignments, sequences, and while loops. The right-hand sides for assignments are expressions made of numerals, variables, and addition. The syntax of the programming language is as follows:

- variable names are noted x, y, x_1, x', etc.
- integers are noted n, n_1, n', etc.

- Arithmetic expressions are noted e, e_1, e', etc. For our case study, these expressions can only take three forms:

$$e ::= n \mid x \mid e_1 + e_2$$

- boolean expressions are noted b, b_1, b', etc. For our case study, these expressions can only take one form:

$$b ::= e_1 < e_2$$

- instructions are noted i, i_1, i', etc. For our case study, these instructions can only take three forms:

$$i ::= x{:=}e \mid i_1{;}i_2 \mid \texttt{while}\ b\ \texttt{do}\ i\ \texttt{done}$$

For the Coq encoding, we use pre-defined strings for variable names and integers for the numeric values. Thus, we use unbounded integers, which is contrary to usual programming languages, but the question of using bounded integers or not is irrelevant for the purpose of this example.

3.1 Encoding the Language

In our Coq encoding, the description of the various kinds of syntactic components is given by inductive declarations.

```
Require Import String ZArith List.
Open Scope Z_scope.

Inductive aexpr : Type :=
 anum (x:Z) | avar (s:string) | aplus (e1 e2:aexpr).

Inductive bexpr : Type := blt (e1 e2 : aexpr).

Inductive instr : Type :=
 assign (x:string)(e:expr)
| seq (i1 i2:instr)
| while (b:bexpr)(i:instr).
```

The first two lines instruct Coq to load pre-defined libraries and to tune the parsing mechanism so that arithmetic formulas will be understood as formulas concerning integers by default.

The definition for `aexpr` states that expressions can only have the three forms `anum`, `avar`, and `aplus`, it also expresses that the names `anum`, `avar`, and `aplus` can be used as function of type, `Z -> aexpr`, `string -> aexpr`, and `aexpr -> aexpr -> aexpr`, respectively. The definition of `aexpr` as an inductive type also implies that we can write recursive functions on this type. For instance, we will use the following function to evaluate an arithmetic expression, given a *valuation* function `g`, which maps every variable name to an integer value.

```
Fixpoint af (g:string->Z)(e:aexpr) : Z :=
 match e with
   anum n => n
 | avar x => g x
 | aplus e1 e2 => af g e1 + af g e2
 end.
```

This function is defined by pattern-matching. There is one pattern for each possible form of arithmetic expression. The third line indicates that when the input `e` has the form `anum n`, then the value `n` is the result. The fourth line indicates that when the input has the form `avar x`, then the value is obtained by applying the function `g` to `x`. The fifth line describes the computation that is done when the expression is an addition. There are two recursive calls to the function `af` in the expression returned for the addition pattern. The recursive calls are made on direct subterms of the initial instruction, this is known as *structural recursion* and guarantees that the recursive function will terminate on all inputs.

A similar function `bf` is defined to describe the boolean value of a boolean expression.

3.2 The Semantics of the Programming Language

To describe the semantics of the programming language, we simply give a *weakest pre-condition calculus* [9]. We describe the conditions that are necessary to ensure that a given logical property is satisfied at the end of the execution of an instruction, when this execution terminates. This weakest pre-condition calculus is defined as a pair of functions whose input is an instruction annotated with logical information at various points in the instruction. The output of the first function call `pc` is a condition that should be satisfied by the variables at the beginning of the execution (this is the *pre-condition* and it should be as easy to satisfy as possible, hence the adjective *weakest*); the output of the second function, called `vc`, is a collection of logical statements. When these statements are valid, we know that every execution starting from a state that satisfies the pre-condition will make the logical annotation satisfied at every point in the program and make the post-condition satisfied if the execution terminates.

Annotating programs. We need to define a new data-type for instructions annotated with assertions at various locations. Each assertion is a quantifier-free logical formula where the variables of the program can occur. The intended meaning is that the formula is guaranteed to hold for every execution of the program that is consistent with the initial assertion.

The syntax for assertions is described as follows:

```
Inductive assert : Type :=
  pred (p:string)(l:list aexpr)
 | a_b (b:bexpr)
 | a_conj (a1 a2:assert)
 | a_not (a: assert)
```

```
| a_true
| a_false.
```

This definition states that assertions can have six forms: the first form represents the application of a predicate to an arbitrary list of arithmetic expressions, the second represents a boolean test: this assertion holds when the boolean test evaluates to `true`, the third form is the conjunction of two assertions, the fourth form is the negation of an assertion, the fifth and sixth forms give two constant assertions, which are always and never satisfied, respectively. In a minimal description of a weakest pre-condition calculus, as in [2], the last two constants are not necessary, but they will be useful in our description of the abstract interpreter.

Logical annotations play a central role in our case study, because the result of abstract interpretation will be to add information about each point in the program: this new information will be described by assertions.

To consider whether an assertion holds, we need to know what meaning is attached to each predicate name and what value is attached to each variable name. We suppose the meaning of predicates is given by a function `m` that maps predicate names and list of integers to propositional values and the value of variables is given by a valuation as in the function `af` given above. Given such a meaning for predicates and such a valuation function for variables, we describe the computation of the property associated to an assertion as follows:

```
Fixpoint ia (m:string->list Z->Prop)(g:string->Z)
  (a:assert) : Prop :=
 match a with
  pred s l => m s (map (af g) l)
 | a_b b => bf g b = true
 | a_conj a1 a2 => (ia m g a1) /\ (ia m g a2)
 | a_not a => not (ia m g a)
 | a_true => True
 | a_false => False
 end.
```

The type of this function exhibits a specificity of type theory-based theorem proving: propositions are described by *types*. The Coq system also provides a type of types, named `Prop`, whose elements are the types that are intended to be used as propositions. Each of these types contains the proofs of the proposition they represent. This is known as the *Curry-Howard isomorphism*. For instance, the propositions that are unprovable are represented by empty types. Here, assertions are data, their interpretation as propositions are types, which belongs to the `Prop` type. More details about this description of propositions as types is given in another article on type theory in the same volume.

Annotated instructions are in a new data-type, named `a_instr`, which is very close to the `instr` data-type. The two modifications are as follows: first an extra operator `pre` is added to make it possible to attach assertions to any instruction, second `while` loops are mandatorily annotated wih an *invariant* assertion.

In concrete syntax, we will write { a } i for the instruction i carrying the assertion a (noted pre a i in the Coq encoding).

```
Inductive a_instr : Type :=
 pre (a:assert)(i:a_instr)
| a_assign (x:string)(e:aexpr)
| a_seq (i1 i2:a_instr)
| a_while (b:bexpr)(a:assert)(i:a_instr).
```

Reasoning on assertions. We can reason on annotated programs, because there are logical reasons for programs to be consistent with assertions. The idea is to compute a collection of logical formulas associated to an annotated program and a final logical formula, the *post-condition*. When this collection of formulas holds, there exists an other logical formula, the *pre-condition* whose satisfiability before executing the program is enough to guarantee that the post-condition holds after executing the program.

Annotations added to an instruction (with the help of the pre construct) must be understood as formulas that hold just before executing the annotated instruction. Assertions added to while loops must be understood as *invariants*, they are meant to hold at the beginning and the end every time the inner part of the while loop is executed.

When assertions are present in the annotated instruction, they are taken for granted. For instance, when the instruction is {x = 3} x := x + 1 , the computed pre-condition is x = 3, whatever the post-condition is.

When the instruction is a plain assignment, one can find the pre-condition by substituting the assigned variable with the assigned expression in the post-condition. For instance, when the post condition is x = 4 and the instruction is the assignement x := x + 1, it suffices that the pre-condition x + 1 = 4 is satisfied before executing the assignment to ensure that the post-condition is satisfied after executing it.

When the annotated instruction is a while loop, the pre-condition simply is the invariant for this while loop. When the annotated instruction is a sequence of two instructions, the pre-condition is the pre-condition computed for the first of the two instructions, but using the pre-condition of the second instruction as the post-condition for the first instruction.

Coq encoding for pre-condition computation. To encode this pre-condition function in Coq, we need to describe functions that perform the substitution of a variable with an arithmetic expression in arithmetic expressions, boolean expressions, and assertions. These substitution functions are given as follows:

```
Fixpoint asubst (x:string) (s:aexpr) (e:aexpr) : aexpr :=
 match e with
  anum n => anum n
 | avar x1 => if string_dec x x1 then s else e
 | aplus e1 e2 => aplus (asubst x s e1) (asubst x s e2)
 end.
```

```
Definition bsubst (x:string) (s:aexpr) (b:bexpr) : bexpr :=
 match b with
  blt e1 e2 => blt (asubst x s e1) (asubst x s e2)
 end.

Fixpoint subst (x:string) (s:aexpr) (a:assert) : assert :=
 match a with
  pred p l => pred p (map (asubst x s) l)
 | a_b b => a_b (bsubst x s b)
 | a_conj a1 a2 => a_conj (subst x s a1) (subst x s a2)
 | a_not a => a_not (subst x s a)
 | any => any
 end.
```

In the definition of asubst, the function string_dec compares two strings for equality. The value returned by this function can be used in an if-then-else construct, but it is not a boolean value (more detail can be found in [3]). The rest of the code is just a plain traversal of the structure of expressions and assertions. Note also that the last pattern-matching rule in subst is used for both a_true and a_false.

Once we know how to substitute a variable with an expression, we can easily describe the computation of the pre-condition for an annotated instruction and a post-condition. This is given by the following simple recursive procedure:

```
Fixpoint pc (i:a_instr) (post : assert) : assert :=
 match i with
  pre a i => a
 | a_assign x e => subst x e post
 | a_seq i1 i2 => pc i1 (pc i2 post)
 | a_while b a i => a
 end.
```

A verification condition generator. When it receives an instruction carrying an annotation, the function pc simply returns the annotation. In this sense, the pre-condition function takes the annotation for granted. To make sure that an instruction is consistent with its pre-condition, we need to check that the assertion really is strong enough to ensure the post-condition.

For instance, when the post-condition is x < 10 and the instruction is the annotated assigment { x = 2 } x := x + 1, satisfying x = 2 before the assignment is enough to ensure that the post-condition is satisfied. On the other hand, if the annotated instruction was {x < 10 } x := x + 1, there would be a problem because there are cases where x < 10 holds before executing the assignment and x < 10 does not hold after.

In fact, for assigments that are not annotated with assertions, the function pc computes the best formula, the *weakest pre-condition*. Thus, in presence of an annotation, it suffices to verify that the annotation does imply the weakest pre-condition. We are now going to describe a function that collects all the verifications that need to be done. More precisely, the new function will compute conditions that are sufficient to ensure that the pre-condition from the previous section is strong enough to guarantee that the post-condition holds after executing the program, when the program terminates.

The verification that an annotated instruction is consistent with a post-condition thus returns a sequence of implications between assertions. When all these implications are logically valid, there is a guarantee that satisfying the pre-condition before executing the instruction is enough to ensure that the post-condition will also be satisfied after executing the instruction. This guarantee is proved formally in [2].

When the instruction is a plain assignment without annotation, there is no need to verify any implication because the computed pre-condition is already good enough. When the instruction is an annotated instruction `{` A `}` i and the post-condition is P, we can first compute the pre-condition P' and a list of implications l for the instruction i and the post-condition P. We then only need to add $A \Rightarrow P'$ to l to get the list of conditions for the whole instruction.

For instance, when the post-condition is `x=3` and the instruction is the assignment `x := x+1`, the pre-condition computed by `pc` is `x + 1 = 3` and this is obviously good enough for the post-condition to be satisfied. On the other hand, when the instruction is an annotated instruction, `{`P`}` `x := x+1`, we need to verify that $P \Rightarrow \mathtt{x} + 1 = 3$ holds.

If we look again at the first example in this section, concerning an instruction `{x < 10} x := x+1` and a post-condition `x < 10`, there is a problem, because a value of 9 satisfies the pre-condition, but execution leads to a value of 10, which does not satisfy the post-condition The condition generator constructs a condition of the form `x < 10` $\Rightarrow$ `x + 1 < 10`. The fact that this logical formula is actually unprovable relates to the fact that the triplet composed of the pre-condition, the assignment, and the post-condition is actually inconsistent.

When the instruction is a sequence of two instructions i_1`;`i_2 and the post-condition is P, we need to compute lists of conditions for both sub-components i_1 and i_2. The list of conditions for i_2 is computed for the post-condition for the whole construct P, while the list of conditions of i_1 is computed taking as post-condition the pre-condition of i_2 for P. This is consistent with the intuitive explanation that it suffices that the pre-condition for an instruction holds to ensure that the post-condition will hold after executing that instruction. If we want P to hold after executing i_2, we need the pre-condition of i_2 for P to be satisfied and it is the responsibility of the instruction i_1 to guarantee this. Thus, the conditions for i_1 can be computed with this assertion as a post-condition.

When the instruction is a while loop, of the form `while` b `do {` A `}` i `done` we must remember that the assertion A should be an invariant during the loop execution. This is expressed by requiring that A is satisfied before executing i should be enough to guarantee that A is also satisfied after executing i. However, this is needed only in the cases where the loop test b is also satisfied, because when b is not satisfied the inner instruction of the while loop is not executed. At the end of the execution, we can use the information that the invariant A is satisfied and the information that we know the loop has been executed because the test eventually failed. The program is consistent when these two logical properties are enough to imply the initial post-condition P. Thus, we must first compute the pre-condition A' for the inner instruction i and the post-condition A, compute the list of conditions for i with A as post-condition, add the condition $A \wedge b \Rightarrow A'$, and add the condition $A \wedge \neg b \Rightarrow P$.

Coq encoding of the verification condition generator. The verification conditions always are implications. We provide a new data-type for these implications:

```
Inductive cond : Type := imp (a1 a2:assert).
```

The computation of verification conditions is then simply described as a plain recursive function, which follows the structure of annotated instructions.

```
Fixpoint vc (i:a_instr)(post : assert) : list cond :=
 match i with
  pre a i => (imp a (pc i post))::vc i post
 | a_assign _ _ => nil
 | a_seq i1 i2 => vc i1 (pc i2 post)++vc i2 post
 | a_while b a i =>
  (imp (a_conj a (a_b b)) (pc i a))::
  (imp (a_conj a (a_not (a_b b))) post)::
  vc i a
 end.
```

Describing the semantics of programming language using a verification condition generator is not the only approach that can be used to describe the language. In fact, this approach is partial, because it describes properties of inputs and outputs when instruction execution terminates, but it gives no information about termination. More precise descriptions can be given using operational or denotational semantics and the consistency of this verification condition generator with such a complete semantics can also be verified formally. This is done in [2], but it is not the purpose of this article.

When reasoning about the correctness of a given annotated instruction, we can use the function `vc` to obtain a list of conditions. It is then necessary to reason on the validity of this list of conditions. What we want to verify is that the implications hold for every possible instantiation of the program variables. This is described by the following function.

```
Fixpoint valid (m:string->list Z ->Prop) (l:list cond) : Prop :=
 match l with
  nil => True
 | c::tl =>
  (let (a1, a2) := c in forall g, ia m g a1 -> ia m g a2)
   /\ valid m tl
 end.
```

An annotated program i is consistent with a given post-condition p when the property `valid` (`vc` i p) holds. This means that the post-condition is guaranteed to hold after executing the instruction if the computed pre-condition was satisfied before the execution and the execution of the instruction terminates.

3.3 A Monotonicity Property

In our study of an abstract interpreter, we will use a property of the condition generator.

Theorem 1. *For every annotated instruction i, if p_1 and p_2 are two post-conditions such that p_1 is stronger than p_2, if the pre-condition for i and p_1 is satisfied and all the verification conditions for i and the post-condition p_1 are valid, then the pre-condition for i and p_2 is also satisfied and the verification conditions for i and p_2 are also valid.*

Proof. This proof is done in the context of a given mapping from predicate names to actual predicates, m. The property is proved by induction on the structure of the instruction i. The statement p_1 is stronger than p_2 when the implication $p_1 \Rightarrow p_2$ is valid. In other words, for every assignment of variables g, the logical value of p_1 implies the logical value of p_2.

If the instruction is an assignment, we can rely on a lemma: the value of any assertion `subst` x e p in any valuation g is equal to the value of the assertion p in the valuation g' that is equal to g on every variable but x, for which it returns the value of e in the valuation g. Thus, the precondition for the assignment $x := e$ for p_i is `subst` x e p_i and the the validity of `subst` x e $p_1 \Rightarrow$ `subst` x e p_2 simply is an instance of the validity of $p_1 \Rightarrow p_2$, which is given by hypothesis. Also, when the instruction is an assignment, there is no generated verification condition and the second part of the statement holds.

If the instruction is a sequence $i_1;i_2$, then we know by induction hypothesis that the pre-condition p'_1 for i_2 and p_1 is stronger than the pre-condition p'_2 for i_2 and p_2 and all the verification conditions for that part are valid; we can use an induction hypothesis again to obtain that the pre-condition for i_1 and p'_1 is stronger than the pre-condition for i_1 and p'_2, and the corresponding verification conditions are all valid. The last two pre-conditions are the ones we need to compare, and the whole set of verification conditions is the union of the sets which we know are valid.

If the instruction is an annotated instruction $\{a\}i$, the two pre-conditions for p_2 and p_1 alre always a, so the first part of the statement trivially holds. Moreover, we know by induction hypothesis that the pre-condition p'_1 for i and p_1 is stronger that the pre-condition p'_2 for i and p_2. The verification conditions for the whole instruction and p_1 (resp. p_2) are the same as for the sub-instruction, with the condition $a \Rightarrow p'_1$ (resp. $a \Rightarrow p'_2$) added. By hypothesis, $a \Rightarrow p'_1$ holds, by induction hypothesis $p'_1 \Rightarrow p'_2$, we can thus deduce that $a \Rightarrow p'_2$ holds.

If the instruction is a loop `while` b `do`$\{a\}$ i `done`, most verification conditions and generated pre-conditions only depend on the loop invariant. The only thing that we need to check is the verification condition containing the invariant, the negation of the test and the post-condition. By hypothesis, $a \wedge \neg b \Rightarrow p_1$ and $p_1 \Rightarrow p_2$ are valid. By transitivity of implication we obtain $a \wedge \neg b \Rightarrow p_2$ easily.

In Coq, we first prove a lemma that expresses that the satisfiability of an assertion `a` where a variable `x` is substituted with an arithmetic expression `e'` for a valuation `g` is the same as the satisfiability of the assertion `a` without substitution, but for a valuation that maps `x` to the value of `e'` in `g` and coincides with `g` for all other variables.

```
Lemma subst_sound :
 forall m g a x e',
  ia m g (subst x e' a) =
  ia m (fun y => if string_dec x y then af g e' else g y) a.
```

This lemma requires similar lemmas for arithmetic expressions, boolean expressions, and lists of expressions. All are proved by induction on the structure of expressions.

An example proof for substitution. For instance, the statement for the substitution in arithmetic expressions is as follows:

```
Lemma subst_sound_a :
 forall g e x e',
  af g (asubst x e' e) =
  af (fun y => if string_dec x y then af g e' else g y) e.
```

The proof can be done in Coq by an induction on the expression `e`. This leads the system to generate three cases, corresponding to the three constructors of the `aexpr` type. The combined tactic we use is as follows:

```
intros g e x e'; induction e; simpl; auto.
```

The tactic `induction e` generates three goals and the tactics `simpl` and `auto` are applied to all of them. One of the cases is the case for the `anum` constructor, where both instances of the `af` function compute to the value carried by the constructor, thus `simpl` forces the computation and leads to an equality where both sides are equal. In this case, `auto` solves the goal. Only the other two goals remain.

The first other goal is concerned with the `avar` construct. In this case the expression has the form `avar s` and the expression `subst x e' (avar s)` is transformed into the following expression by the `simpl` tactic.

```
if string_dec x s then e' else (avar s)
```

For this case, the system displays a goal that has the following shape:

```
g : string -> Z
s : string
x : string
e' : aexpr
============================
 af g (if string_dec x s then e' else avar s) =
 (if string_dec x s then af g e' else g s)
```

In Coq goals, the information that appears above the horizontal bar is data that is known to exist, the information below the horizontal bar is the expression that we need to prove. Here the information that is known only corresponds to typing information.

We need to reason by cases on the values of the expression `string_dec x s`. The tactic `case ...` is used for this purposes. It generate two goals, one corresponding to the case where `string_dec x s` has an affimative value and one corresponding to the case where `string_dec x s` has a negative value. In each the goal, the `if-then-else` constructs are reduced accordingly. In the goal where `string_dec x s` is affirmative, both sides of the equality reduce to `af g e'`; in the other goal, both sides of the equality reduce to `g x`. Thus in both cases, the proof becomes easy. This reasoning step is easily expressed with the following combined tactic:

```
case (string_dec x s); auto.
```

There only remains a goal for the last possible form of arithmetic expression, `aplus e1 e2`. The induction tactic provides *induction hypotheses* stating that the property we want to prove already holds for `e1` and `e2`. After symbolic computation of the functions `af` and `asubst`, as performed by the `simpl` tactic, the goal has the following shape:

```
 ...
 IHe1 : af g (asubst x e' e1) =
      af (fun y : string =>
         if string_dec x y then af g e' else g y) e1
 IHe2 : af g (asubst x e' e2) =
      af (fun y : string =>
         if string_dec x y then af g e' else g y) e2
 ============================
  af g (asubst x e' e1) + af g (asubst x e' e2) =
  af (fun y : string =>
     if string_dec x y then af g e' else g y) e1 +
  af (fun y : string =>
     if string_dec x y then af g e' else g y) e2
```

This proof can be finished by rewriting with the two equalities named `IHe1` and `IHe2` and then recognizing that both sides of the equality are the same, as required by the following tactics.

```
rewrite IHe1, IHe2; auto.
Qed.
```

We can now turn our attention to the main result, which is then expressed as the following statement:

```
Lemma vc_monotonic :
 forall m i p1 p2, (forall g, ia m g p1 -> ia m g p2) ->
  valid m (vc i p1) ->
  valid m (vc i p2) /\
  (forall g, ia m g (pc i p1) -> ia m g (pc i p2)).
```

To express that this proof is done by induction on the structure of instructions, the first tactic sent to the proof system has the form:

```
intros m; induction i; intros p1 p2 p1p2 vc1.
```

The proof then has four cases, which are solved in about 10 lines of proof script.

4 A First Simple Abstract Interpreter

We shall now define two abstract interpreters, which run instructions symbolically, updating an abstract state at each step. The abstract state is then transformed into a logical expression which is added to the instructions, thus producing an annotated instruction. The abstract state is also returned at the end of execution, in one of two forms. In the first simple abstract interpreter, the final abstract state is simply returned. In the seccond abstract interpreter, only an optional abstract state will be returned, a `None` value being used when the abstract interpreter can detect that the program can never terminate: the second abstract interpreter will also perform dead code detection.

For example, if we give our abstract interpreter an input state stating that `x` is even and `y` is odd and the instruction `x:= x+y; y:=y+1`, the resulting value will be:

```
({even x /\ odd y} x:=x+y; {odd x /\ odd y} y:= y+1,
 (x, odd)::(y,even)::nil)
```

We suppose there exists a data-type A whose elements will represent abstract values on which instructions are supposed to compute. For instance, the data-type `A` could be the type containing three values `even`, `odd`, and `top`. Another traditional example of abstract data-type is the type of intervals, that are either of the form $[m, n]$, with $m \leq n$, $[-\infty, n]$, $[m, +\infty]$, or $[-\infty, +\infty]$.

The data-type of abstract values should come with a few elements and functions, which we will describe progresssively.

4.1 Using Galois Connections

Abstract values represent specific sets of concrete values. There is a natural order on sets : set inclusion. Similarly, we can consider an order on abstract values, which mimics the order between the sets they represent. The traditional approach to describe this correspondance between the order on sets of values and the order on abstract values is to consider that the type of abstract values is given with a pair of functions α and γ, where $\alpha : \mathcal{P}(\mathbb{Z}) \rightarrow A$ and $\gamma : A \rightarrow \mathcal{P}(\mathbb{Z})$. The function γ maps any abstract value to the set of concrete values it represents. The function α maps any set of concrete values to the smallest abstract value whose interpretation as a set contains the input. Written in a mathematical formula where $\sqsubseteq$ denotes the order on abstract values, the two functions and the orders on sets of concrete values and on abstract values are related by the following statement:

$$\forall a \in A, \forall b \in \mathcal{P}(\mathbb{Z}).b \subset \gamma(a) \Leftrightarrow \alpha(b) \sqsubseteq a.$$

When the functions α and γ are given with this property, one says that there is a *Galois connection.*

In our study of abstract interpretation, the functions α and γ do not appear explicitly. In a sense, γ will be represented by a function `to_pred` mapping abstract values to assertions depending on arithmetic expressions. However, it is useful to keep these functions in mind when trying to figure out what properties are expected for the various components of our abstract interpreters, as we will see in the next section.

4.2 Abstract Evaluation of Arithmetic Expressions

Arithmetic expressions contain integer constants and additions, neither of which are concerned with the data-type of abstract values. To be able to associate an abstract value to an arithmetic expression, we need to find ways to establish a correspondance between concrete values and abstract values. This is done by supposing the existence of two functions and a constant, which are the first three values axiomatized for the data-type of abstract values (but there will be more later):

- `from_Z : Z -> A`, this is used to associate a relevant abstract value to any concrete value,
- `a_add : A -> A -> A`, this is used to add two abstract values,
- `top : A`, this is used to represent the abstract value that carries no information.

In terms of Galois connections, the function `from_Z` corresponds to the function α, when applied to singletons. The function `a_add` must be designed in such a way that the following property is satisfied:

$$\forall v_1\ v_2, \{x+y | x \in (\gamma(v_1)), y \in (\gamma(v_2))\} \subset \gamma(\texttt{a\_add}\ v_1\ v_2).$$

With this constraint, a function that maps any pairs of abstract values to `top` would be acceptable, however it would be useless. It is better if `a_add` v_1 v_2 is the least satisfactory abstract value such that the above property is satisfied.

The value `top` is the maximal element of A, the image of the whole $\mathbb{Z}$ by the function α.

4.3 Handling Abstract States

When computing the value of a variable, we suppose that this value is given by looking up in a state, which actually is a list of pairs of variables and abstract values.

```
Definition state := list(string*A).

Fixpoint lookup (s:state) (x:string) : A :=
  match s with
    nil => top
  | (y,v)::tl => if string_dec x y then v else lookup tl x
  end.
```

As we see in the definition of lookup, when a value is not defined in a state, the function behaves as if it was defined with top as abstract value. The computation of abstract values for arithmetic expressions is then described by the following function.

```
Fixpoint a_af (s:state)(e:aexpr) : A :=
 match e with
  avar x => lookup s x
 | anum n => from_Z n
 | aplus e1 e2 => a_add (a_af s e1) (a_af s e2)
 end.
```

When executing assignments abstractly, we are also supposed to modify the state. If the state contained no previous information about the assigned variable, a new pair is created. Otherwise, the first existing pair must be updated. This is done with the following function.

```
Fixpoint a_upd(x:string)(v:A)(l:state) : state :=
 match l with
  nil => (x,v)::nil
 | (y,v')::tl =>
  if string_dec x y then (y, v)::tl else (y,v')::a_upd x v tl
 end.
```

Later in this paper, we define a function that generates assertions from states. For this purpose, it is better to update by modifying existing pairs of a variable and a value rather than just inserting the new pair in front.

4.4 The Interpreter's Main Function

When computing abstract interpretation on instructions we want to produce a final abstract state and an annotated instruction. We will need a way to transform an abstract value into an assertion. This is given by a function with the following type:

- to_pred : A -> aexpr -> assert this is used to express that that the value of the arithmetic expression in a given valuation will belong to the set of concrete values represented by the given abstract value. So to_pred is axiomatized in the same sense as from_Z, a_add, top.

Relying on the existence of to_pred, we can define a function that maps states to assertions:

```
Fixpoint s_to_a (s:state) : assert :=
 match s with
  nil => a_true
 | (x,a)::tl => a_conj (to_pred a (avar x)) (s_to_a tl)
 end.
```

This function is implemented in a manner that all pairs present in the state are transformed into assertions. For this reason, it is important that a_upd works by modifying existing pairs rather than hiding them.

Our first simple abstract interpreter only implements a trivial behavior for while loops. Basically, this says that no information can be gathered for while loops (the result is nil, and the while loop's invariant is also nil).

```
Fixpoint ab1 (i:instr)(s:state) : a_instr*state :=
 match i with
  assign x e =>
  (pre (s_to_a s) (a_assign x e), a_upd x (a_af s e) s)
 | seq i1 i2 =>
  let (a_i1, s1) := ab1 i1 s in
  let (a_i2, s2) := ab1 i2 s1 in
   (a_seq a_i1 a_i2, s2)
 | while b i =>
  let (a_i, _) := ab1 i nil in
    (a_while b (s_to_a nil) a_i, nil)
 end.
```

In this function, we see that the abstract interpretation of sequences is simply described as composing the effect on states and recombining the instruction obtained from each component of the sequence.

4.5 Expected Properties for Abstract Values

To prove the correctness of the abstract interpreter, we need to know that the various functions and values provided around the type A satisfy a collection of properties. These are gathered as a set of hypotheses.

One value that we have not talked about yet is the mapping from predicate names to actual predicates on integers, which is necessary to interpret the assertions generated by to_pred. This is given axiomatically, like top and the others:

- m : string -> list Z -> Prop, maps all predicate names used in to_pred to actual predicates on integers.

The first hypothesis expresses that top brings no information.

```
Hypothesis top_sem : forall e, (to_pred top e) = a_true.
```

The next two hypotheses express that the predicates associated to each abstract value are *parametric* with respect to the arithmetic expression they receive. Their truth does not depend on the exact shape of the expressions, but only on the concrete value such an arithmetic expression may take in the current valuation. Similarly, substitution basically affects the arithmetic expression part of the predicate, not the part that depends on the abstract value.

```
Hypothesis to_pred_sem :
 forall g v e, ia m g (to_pred v e) =
```

```
  ia m g (to_pred v (anum (af g e))).
Hypothesis subst_to_pred :
 forall v x e e', subst x e' (to_pred v e) =
   to_pred v (asubst x e' e).
```

For instance, if the abstract values are intervals, it is natural that the `to_pred` function will map an abstract value `[3,10]` and an arithmetic expression `e` to an assertion `between(3, e, 10)`. When evaluating this assertion with respect to a given valuation `g`, the integers `3` and `10` will not be affected by `g`. Similarly, substitution will not affect these integers.

The last two hypotheses express that the interpretation of the associated predicates for abstract values obtained through `from_Z` and `a_add` are consistent with the concrete values computed for immediate integers and additions. The hypothesis `from_Z_sem` actually establishes the correspondence between `from_Z` and the abstraction function α of a Galois connection. The hypothesis `a_add_sem` expresses the condition which we described informally when introducing the function `a_add_sem`.

```
Hypothesis from_Z_sem :
 forall g x, ia m g (to_pred (from_Z x) (anum x)).
Hypothesis a_add_sem : forall g v1 v2 x1 x2,
 ia m g (to_pred v1 (anum x1)) ->
 ia m g (to_pred v2 (anum x2)) ->
 ia m g (to_pred (a_add v1 v2) (anum (x1+x2))).
```

4.6 Avoiding Duplicates in States

The way `s_to_a` and `a_upd` are defined is not consistent: `s_to_a` maps every pair occuring in a state to an assertion fragment, while `a_upd` only modifies the first pair occuring in the state.

For instance, when the abstract interpretation computes with intervals, `s` is `("x", [1,1])::("x",[1,1])::nil`, and the instruction is `x := x + 1`, the resulting state is `("x",[2,2])::("x",[1,1])::nil` and the resulting annotated instruction is `{` $1 \leq$ `x` $\leq 1 \wedge 1 \leq$ `x` ≤ 1`}` `x:= x+1`. The post-condition corresponding to the resulting state is $2 \leq$ `x` $\leq 2 \wedge 1 \leq$ `x` ≤ 1. It is contradictory and cannot be satisfied when executing from valuations satisfying the pre-condition, which is not contradictory.

To cope with this difficulty, we need to express that the abstract interpreter works correctly only with states that contain no duplicates. We formalize this with a predicate `consistent`, which is defined as follows:

```
Fixpoint mem (s:string)(l:list string): bool :=
 match l with
  nil => false
 | x::l => if string_dec x s then true else mem s l
 end.
```

```
Fixpoint no_dups (s:state)(l:list string) :bool :=
 match s with
  nil => true
 | (s,_)::tl => if mem s l then false else no_dups tl (s::l)
 end.
```

```
Definition consistent (s:state) := no_dups s nil = true.
```

The function no_dups actually returns true when the state s contains no duplicates and no element from the exclusion list l. We prove, by induction on the of structure of s, that updating a state that satisfies no_dups for an exclusion list l, using a_upd for a variable x outside the exclusion list returns a new state that still satisfies no_dups for l. The statement is as follows:

```
Lemma no_dups_update :
 forall s l x v, mem x l = false ->
  no_dups s l = true -> no_dups (a_upd x v s) l = true.
```

The proof of this lemma is done by induction on s, making sure that the property that is established for every s is universally quantified over l: the induction hypothesis is actually used for a different value of the the exclusion list.

The corollary from this lemma corresponding to the case where l is instantiated with the empty list expresses that a_upd preserves the consistent property.

```
Lemma consistent_update :
 forall s x v, consistent s -> consistent (a_upd x v s).
```

4.7 Proving the Correctness of This Interpreter

When the interpreter runs on an instruction i and a state s and returns an annotated instruction i' and a new state s', the correctness of the run is expressed with three properties:

- The assertion s_to_a s is stronger than the pre-condition pc i' (s_to_a s'),
- All the verification conditions in vc i' (s_to_a s') are valid,
- The annotated instruction i' is an annotated version of the input i.

In the next few sections, we will prove that all runs of the abstract interpreter are correct.

4.8 Soundness of Abstract Evaluation for Expressions

When an expression e evaluates abstractly to an abstract value a and concretely to an integer z, z should satisfy the predicate associated to the value a. Of course, the evaluation of e can only be done using a valuation that takes care of providing values for all variables occuring in e. This valuation must be consistent with the abstract state that is used for the abstract evaluation leading to a. The fact that a valuation is consistent with an abstract state is simply expressed by saying that the interpretation of the corresponding assertion for this valuation has to hold. Thus, the soundness of abstract evaluation is expressed with a lemma that has the following shape:

```
Lemma a_af_sound :
 forall s g e, ia m g (s_to_a s) ->
  ia m g (to_pred (a_af s e) (anum (af g e))).
```

This lemma is proved by induction on the expression `e`. The case where `e` is a number is a direct application of the hypothesis `from_Z_sem`, the case where `e` is an addition is a consequence of `a_add_sem`, combined with induction hypotheses. The case where `e` is a variable relies on another lemma:

```
Lemma lookup_sem : forall s g, ia m g (s_to_a s) ->
 forall x, ia m g (to_pred (lookup s x) (anum (g x))).
```

This other lemma is proved by induction on `s`. In the base case, `s` is empty, `lookup s x` is `top`, and the hypothesis `top_sem` makes it possible to conclude; in the step case, if `s` is `(y,v)::s'` then the hypothesis

```
ia m g (s_to_a s)
```

reduces to

```
to_pred v (avar y) /\ ia m g (s_to_a s')
```

We reason by cases on whether `x` is `y` or not. If `x` is equal to `y` then `to_pred v (avar y)` is the same as `to_pred v (anum (g x))` according to `to_pred_sem` and `lookup s x` is the same as `v` by definition of `lookup`, this is enough to conclude this case. If `x` and `y` are different, we use the induction hypothesis on `s'`.

4.9 Soundness of Update

In the weakest pre-condition calculus, assignments of the form `x := e` are taken care of by substituting all occurrences of the assigned variable `x` with the arithmetic expression `e` in the post-condition to obtain the weakest pre-condition. In the abstract interpreter, assignment is taken care of by updating the first instance of the variable in the state. There is a discrepancy between the two approaches, where the first approach acts on all instances of the variable and the second approach acts only on the first one. This discrepancy is resolved in the conditions of our experiment, where we work with abstract states that contain only one binding for each variable: in this case, updating the first variable is the same as updating all variables. We express this with the following lemmas:

```
Lemma subst_no_occur :
 forall s x l e,
  no_dups s (x::l) = true -> subst x e (s_to_a s) = (s_to_a s).
```

```
Lemma subst_consistent :
  forall s g v x e, consistent s -> ia m g (s_to_a s) ->
   ia m g (to_pred v (anum (af g e))) ->
   ia m g (subst x e (s_to_a (a_upd x v s))).
```

Both lemmas are proved by induction on s and the second one uses the first in the case where the substituted variable x is the first variable occuring in s. This proof also relies on the hypothesis subst_to_pred.

4.10 Relating Input Abstract States and Pre-conditions

For the correctness proof we consider runs starting from an instruction i and an initial abstract state s and obtaining an annotated instruction i' and a final abstract state s'. We are then concerned with the verification conditions and the pre-condition generated for the post-condition corresponding to s' and the annotated instruction i'. The pre-condition we obtain is either the assertion corresponding to s or the assertion a_true, when the first sub-instruction in i is a while loop. In all cases, the assertion corresponding to s is stronger than the pre-condition. This is expressed with the following lemma, which is easily proved by induction on i.

```
Lemma ab1_pc :
 forall i i' s s', ab1 i s = (i', s') ->
  forall g a, ia m g (s_to_a s) -> ia m g (pc i' a).
```

This lemma is actually stronger than needed, because the post-condition used for computing the pre-condition does not matter, since the resulting annotated instruction is heavily annotated with assertions and the pre-condition always comes from one of the annoations.

4.11 Validity of Generated Conditions

The main correctness statement only concerns states that satisfy the consistent predicate, that is, states that contain at most one entry for each variable. The statement is proved by induction on instructions. As is often the case, what we prove by induction is a stronger statement; Such a stronger statement also means stronger induction hypotheses. Here we add the information that the resulting state is also consistent.

Theorem 2. *If s is a consistent state and running the abstract interpreter* ab1 *on i from s returns a new annotated instruction i' and afinal state s', then all the verification conditions generated for i' and the post-condition associated to s' are valid. Moreover, the state s' is consistent.*

The Coq encoding of this theorem is as follows:

```
Theorem ab1_correct : forall i i' s s',
 consistent s -> ab1 i s = (i', s') ->
  valid m (vc i' (s_to_a s')) /\ consistent s'.
```

This statement is proved by induction on `i`. Three cases arise, corresponding to the three instructions in the language.

1. When `i` is an assignment `x := e`, this is the base case. `ab1 i s` computes to

   `(pre (s_to_a s) (a_assign x e), a_upd x (a_af s e) s)`

   From the lemma `a_af_sound` we obtain that the concrete value of `e` in any valuation `g` that satisfies `ia m g (s_to_a s)` satisfies the following property:

   `ia m g (to_pred (a_af s e) (anum (af g e)))`

   The lemma `subst_consistent` can then be used to obtain the validity of the following condition.

   `imp (s_to_a s) (subst x e (s_to_a (a_upd x (a_af s e) s)))`

   This is the single verification condition generated for this instruction. The second part is taken care of by `consistent_update`.
2. When the instruction `i` is a sequence `seq i1 i2`, the abstract interpreter first processes `i1` with the state `s` as input to obtain an annotated instruction `a_i1` and an output state `s1`, it then processes `i2` with `s1` as input to obtain an annotated instruction `a_i2` and a state `s2`. The state `s2` is used as the output state for the whole instruction. We then need to verify that the conditions generated for `a_seq a_i1 a_i2` using `s_to_a a2` as post-condition are valid and `s2` satisfies the `consistent` property. The conditions can be split in two parts. The second part is `vc a_i2 (s_to_a a2)`. the validity of these conditions is a direct consequence of the induction hypotheses. The first part is `vc a_i1 (pc a_i2 (s_to_a s2))`. This is not a direct consequence of the induction hypothesis, which only states `vc a_i1 (s_to_a s1)`. However, the lemma `ab1_pc` applied on `a_i2` states that `s_to_a s1` is stronger than `pc (s_to_a s2)` and the lemma `vc_monotonic` makes it possible to conclude. With respect to the `consistent` property, it is recursively transmitted from `s` to `s1` and from `s1` to `s2`.
3. When the instruction is a while loop, the body of the loop is recursively processed with the `nil` state, which is always satisfied. Thus, the verification conditions all conclude to `a_true` which is trivially true. Also, the `nil` state also trivially satisfies the `consistent` property.

4.12 The Annotated Instruction

We also need to prove that the produced annotated instruction really is an annotated version of the initial instruction. To state this new lemma, we first define a simple function that forgets the annotations in an annotated instruction:

```
Fixpoint cleanup (i: a_instr) : instr :=
 match i with
  pre a i => cleanup i
 | a_assign x e => assign x e
 | a_seq i1 i2 => seq (cleanup i1) (cleanup i2)
 | a_while b a i => while b (cleanup i)
 end.
```

We then prove a simple lemma about the abstract interpreter and this function.

```
Theorem ab1_clean : forall i i' s s',
  ab1 i s = (i', s') -> cleanup i' = i.
```

The proof of this lemma is done by induction on the structure of `i`.

4.13 Instantiating the Simple Abstract Interpreter

We can instantiate this simple abstract interpreter on a data-type of odd-even values, using the following inductive type and functions:

```
Inductive oe : Type := even | odd | oe_top.

Definition oe_from_Z (n:Z) : oe :=
 if Z_eq_dec (Zmod n 2) 0 then even else odd.

Definition oe_add (v1 v2:oe) : oe :=
 match v1,v2 with
   odd, odd => even
 | even, even => even
 | odd, even => odd
 | even, odd => odd
 | _, _ => oe_top
 end.
```

The abstract values can then be mapped into assertions in the obvious way using a function `oe_pred` which we do not describe here for the sake of conciseness. Running this simple interpreter on a small example, representing the program

```
x := x + y; y := y + 1
```

for the state `("x", odd)::("y", even)::nil` is represented by the following dialog:

```
Definition ab1oe := ab1 oe oe_from_Z oe_top oe_add oe_to_pred.

Eval vm_compute in
 ab1oe (seq (assign "x" (aplus (avar "x") (avar "y")))
        (assign "y" (aplus (avar "y") (anum 1))))
  (("x",even)::("y",odd)::nil).
   = (a_seq
      (pre
       (a_conj (pred "even" (avar "x" :: nil))
         (a_conj (pred "odd" (avar "y" :: nil)) a_true))
       (a_assign "x" (aplus (avar "x") (avar "y"))))
      (pre
       (a_conj (pred "odd" (avar "x" :: nil))
         (a_conj (pred "odd" (avar "y" :: nil)) a_true))
```

```
    (a_assign "y" (aplus (avar "y") (anum 1)))),
  ("x", odd) :: ("y", even) :: nil)
: a_instr * state oe
```

5 A Stronger Interpreter

More precise results can be obtained for while loops. For each loop we need to find a state whose interpretation as an assertion will be an acceptable invariant for the loop. We want this invariant to take into account any information that can be extracted from the boolean test in the loop: when entering inside the loop, we know that the test succeeded; when exiting the loop we know that the test failed. It turns out that this information can help us detect cases where the body of a loop is never executed and cases where a loop can never terminate. To describe non-termination, we change the type of values returned by the abstract interpreter: instead of returning an annotated instruction and a state, our new abstract interpreter returns an annotated instruction and an optional state: the optional value is `None` when we have detected that execution cannot terminate. This detection of guaranteed non-termination is conservative: when the analyser cannot guarantee that an instruction loops, it returns a state as usual. The presence of optional states will slightly complexify the structure of our static analysis.

We assume the existence of two new functions for this purpose.

- `learn_from_success : state -> bexpr -> option state`, this is used to encode the information learned when the test succeeded. For instance if the environment initially contains an interval `[0,10]` for the variable `x` and the test is `x < 6`, then we can return the environment so that the value for `x` becomes `[0, 5]`. Sometimes, the initial environment is so that the test can never be satisfied, in this case a value `None` is returned instead of an environment.
- `learn_from_failure : state -> bexpr -> option state`, this is used to compute information about a state knowing that a test failed.

The body of a while loop is often meant to be run several times. In abstract interpretation, this is also true. At every run, the information about each variable at each location of the instruction needs to be updated to take into account more and more concrete values that may be reached at this location. In traditional approaches to abstract interpretation, a binary operation is applied at each location, to combine the information previously known at this location and the new values discovered in the current run. This is modeled by a binary operation.

- `join : A -> A -> A`, this function takes two abstract values and returns a new abstract value whose interpretation as a set is larger than the two inputs.

The theoretical description of abstract interpretation insists that the set `A`, together with the values `join` and `top` should constitute an upper semi-lattice. In fact, We will use only part of the properties of such a structure in our proofs about the abstract interpreter.

When the functions `learn_from_success` and `learn_from_failure` return a `None` value, we actually detect that some code will never be executed. For instance, if `learn_from_success` returns `None`, we can know that the test at the entry of a loop will never be satisfied and we can conclude that the body of the loop is not executed. In this condition, we can mark this loop body with a false assertion. We provide a function for this purpose:

```
Fixpoint mark (i:instr) : a_instr :=
 match i with
  assign x e => pre a_false (a_assign x e)
 | seq i1 i2 => a_seq (mark i1) (mark i2)
 | while b i => a_while b a_false (mark i)
 end.
```

Because it marks almost every instruction, this function makes it easy to recognize at first glance the fragments of code that are dead code. A more lightweight approach could be to mark only the sub-instructions for which an annotation is mandatory: while loops.

5.1 Main Structure of Invariant Search

In general, finding the most precise invariant for a while loop is an undecidable problem. Here we are describing a static analysis tool. We will trade preciseness for guaranteed termination. The approach we will describe will be as follows:

1. Run the body of the loop abstractly for a few times, progressively widening the sets of values for each variable at each run. If this process stabilizes, we have reached an invariant,
2. If no invariant was reached, try taking over-approximations of the values for some variables and run again the loop for a few times. This process may also reach an invariant,
3. If no invariant was reached by progressive widening, pick an abstract state that is guaranteed to be an invariant (as we did for the first simple interpreter: take the *top* state that gives no information about any variable),
4. Invariants that were obtained by over-approximation can then be improved by a *narrowing* process: when run through the loop again, even if no information about the state is given at the beginning of the loop, we may still be able to gather some information at the end of executing the loop. The state that gathers the information at the end of the loop and the information before entering the loop is most likely to be an invariant, which is more precise (narrower) than the top state. Again this process may be run several times.

We shall now review the operations involved in each of these steps.

5.2 Joining States Together

Abstract states are finite list of pairs of variable names and abstract values. When a variable does not occur in a state, the associated abstract value is `top`. When joining two states together every variable that does not occur in one of the two states should receive the `top` value, and every variable that occurs in both states should receive the join of the two values found in each state. We describe this by writing a function that studies all the variables that occur in one of the lists: it is guaranteed to perform the right behavior for all the variables in both lists, it naturally associates the `top` value to the variables that do not occur in the first list (because no pair is added for these variables), and it naturally associates the `top` value to the variables that do not occur in the second list, because `top` is the value found in the second list and `join` preserves `top`.

```
Fixpoint join_state (s1 s2:state) : state :=
 match s1 with
  nil => nil
 | (x,v)::tl => a_upd x (join v (lookup s2 x)) (join_state tl s2)
 end.
```

Because we sometimes detect that some instruction will not be executed we occasionally have to consider situation were we are not given a state after executing a while loop. In this case, we have to combine together a state and the absence of a state. But because the absence of state corresponds to a false assertion, the other state is enough to describe the required invariant. We encode this in an auxiliary function.

```
Definition join_state' (s: state)(s':option state) : state :=
  match s' with
   Some s' => join_state s s'
  | None => s
  end.
```

5.3 Running the Body a Few Times

In our general description of the abstract interpretation of loops, we need to execute the body of loops in two different modes: one mode is a *widening* mode the other is a *narrowing* mode. In the narrowing mode, after executing the body of the loop needs to be joined with the initial state before executing the body of the loop, so that the result state is less precise than both the state before executing the body of the loop and the state after executing the body of the loop. In the *narrowing* mode, we start the execution with an environment that is guaranteed to be large enough, hoping to narrow this environment to a more precise value. In this case, the `join` operation must not be done with the state that is used to start the execution, but with another state which describes the information known about variables before considering the loop. To accomodate these two modes of abstract execution, we use a function that takes two states as input: the first state is the one with which the result must be joined, the second state is the one with which execution must start. In this function, the argument `ab` is the function that describes the abstract interpretation on the instruction inside the loop, the argument `b` is the test of the loop. The function `ab` returns an optional state and an annotated instruction. The optional state is None when the abstract interpreter can detect that the execution of the program from the input state will never terminate. When putting all elements together, the argument ab will be instantiated with the recursive call of the abstract interpreter on the loop body.

```
Definition step1 (ab: state -> a_instr * option state)
 (b:bexpr) (init s:state) : state :=
 match learn_from_success s b with
   Some s1 => let (_, s2) := ab s1 in join_state' init s2
 | None => s
 end.
```

We then construct a function that repeats step1 a certain number of times. This number is denoted by a natural number n. In this function, the constant 0 is a natural number and we need to make it precise to Coq's parser, by expressing that the value must be interpreted in a parsing scope for natural numbers instead of integers, using the specifier %nat.

```
Fixpoint step2 (ab: state -> a_instr * option state)
 (b:bexpr) (init s:state) (n:nat) : state :=
 match n with
   0%nat => s
 | S p => step2 ab b init (step1 ab b init s) p
 end.
```

The complexity of these functions can be improved: there is no need to compute all iterations if we can detect early that a fixed point was reached. In this paper, we prefer to keep the code of the abstract interpreter simple but potentially inefficient to make our formal verification work easier.

5.4 Verifying That a State Is More Precise Than Another

To verify that we have reached an invariant, we need to check for a state s, so that running this state through step1 ab b s s returns a new state that is not less precise than s. For this, we assume that there exist a function that makes it possible to compare two abstract values:

- thinner : A -> A -> bool, this function returns true when the first abstract value gives more precise information than the second one.

Using this basic function on abstract values, we define a new function on states:

```
Fixpoint s_stable (s1 s2 : state) : bool :=
 match s1 with
   nil => true
 | (x,v)::tl => thinner (lookup s2 x) v && s_stable tl s2
 end.
```

This function traverses the first state to check that the abstract value associated to each variable is less precise than the information found in the second state. This function is then easily used to verify that a given state is an invariant through the abstract interpretation of a loop's test and body.

```
Definition is_inv (ab:state-> a_instr * option state)
  (s:state)(b:bexpr):bool := s_stable s (step1 ab b s s).
```

5.5 Narrowing a State

The `step2` function receives two arguments of type `state`. The first argument is solely used for join operations, while the second argument is used to start a sequence of abstract states that correspond to iterated interpretations of the loop test and body. When the start state is not stable through interpretation, the resulting state is larger than both the first argument and the start argument. When the start state is stable through interpretation, there are cases where the resulting state is smaller than the start state.

For instance, in the cases where the abstract values are `even` and `odd`, if the first state argument maps the variable `y` to `even` and the variable `z` to `odd`, the start state maps `y` and `z` to the top abstract value (the abstract value that gives no information) and the while loop is the following:

```
while (x < 10) do x := x + 1; z:= y + 1; y := 2 done
```

Then, after abstractly executing the loop test and body once, we obtain a state where `y` has the value `even` and `z` has the top abstract value. This state is more precise than the start state. After abstractly executing the loop test and body a second time, we obtain a state where `z` has the value `odd` and `y` has the value `even`. This state is more precise than the one obtained only after the first abstract run of the loop test and body.

The example above shows that over-approximations are improved by running the abstract interpreter again on them. This phenomenon is known as *narrowing*. It is worth forcing a narrowing phase after each phase that is likely to produce an over-approximation of the smallest fixed-point of the abstract interpreter. This is used in the abstract interpreter that we describe below.

5.6 Allowing for Over-Approximations

In general, the finite amount of abstract computation performed in the `step2` function is not enough to reach the smallest stable abstract state. This is related to the undecidability of the halting problem: it is often possible to write a program where a variable will receive a precise value exactly when some other program terminates. If we were able to compute the abstract value for this variable in a finite amount of time, we would be able to design a program that solves the halting problem.

Even if we are facing a program where finding the smallest state can be done in a finite amount of time, we may want to accelerate the process by taking over-approximations. For instance, if we consider the following loop:

```
while x < 10 do x := x + 1 done
```

If the abstract values we are working with are intervals and we start with the interval [0,0], after abstractly interpreting the loop test and body once, we obtain that the value for x should contain at least [0,1], after abstractly interpreting 9 times, we obtain that the value for x should contain at least [0,9]. Until these 9 executions, we have not seen a stable state. At the 10th execution, we obtain that the value for x should contain at least [0, 10] and the 11th execution shows that this value actually is stable.

At any time before a stable state is reached, we may choose to replace the current unstable state with a state that is "larger". For instance, we may choose to replace [0,3] with [0,100]. When this happens, the abstract interpreter can discover that the resulting state after starting with the one that maps x to [0,100] actually maps x to [0,10], thus [0,100] is stable and is good candidate to enter a narrowing phase. This narrowing phase actually converges to a state that maps x to [0,10].

The choice of over-approximations is arbitrary and information may actually be lost in the process, because over-approximated states are less precise, but this is compensated by the fact that the abstract interpreter gives quicker answers. The termination of the abstract interpreter can even be guaranteed if we impose that a guaranteed over-approximation is taken after a finite amount of steps. An example of a guaranteed over-approximation is a state that maps every variable to the top abstract value. In our Coq encoding, such a state is represented by the nil value.

The choice of over-approximation strategies varies from one abstract domain to the other. In our Coq encoding, we chose to let this over-approximation be represented by a function with the following signature:

- over_approx : nat -> state -> state -> state When applied to n, s, and s', this function computes an over approximation of s'. The value s is supposed to be a value that comes before s' in the abstract interpretation and can be used to choose the over-approximation cleverly, as it gives a sense of direction to the current evolution of successive abstract values. The number n should be used to fine-tune the coarseness of the over-approximation: the lower the value of n, the coarser the approximation.

For instance, when considering the example above, knowing that $s = [0, 1]$ and $s' = [0, 2]$ are two successive unstable values reached by the abstract interpreter for the variable x can suggest to choose an over-approximation where the upper bound changes but the lower bound remains unchanged. In this case, we expect the function over_approx to return [0,+∞], for example.

5.7 The Main Invariant Searching Function

We can now describe the function that performs the process described in section 5.1. The code of this function is as follows:

```
Fixpoint find_inv ab b init s i n : state :=
 let s' := step2 ab b init s (choose_1 s i) in
 if is_inv ab s' b then s' else
  match n with
   0%nat => nil
  | S p => find_inv ab b init (over_approx p s s') i p
  end.
```

The function choose_1 is provided at the same time as all other functions that are specific to the abstract domain A, such as join, a_add, etc.

The argument function ab is supposed to be the function that performs the abstract interpretation of the loop inner instruction i (also called the loop body), the boolean expression b is supposed to be the loop test. The state init is supposed to be the initial input state at the first invocation of find_inv on this loop and s is supposed to be the current over-approximation of init, n is the number of over-approximations that are still allowed before the function should switch to the nil state, which is a guaranteed over-approximation. This function systematically runs the abstract interpreter on the inner instruction an arbitrary number of times (given by the function choose_1) and then tests whether the resulting state is an invariant. Narrowing steps actually take place if the number of iterations given by choose_1 is large enough. If the result of the iterations is an invariant, then it is returned. When the result state is not an invariant, the function find_inv is called recursively with a larger approximation computed by over_approx. When the number of allowed recursive calls is reached, the nil value is returned.

5.8 Annotating the Loop Body with Abstract Information

The find_inv function only produces a state, while the abstract interpreter is also supposed to produce an annotated version of the instruction. Once we know the invariant, we can annotate the while loop with this invariant and obtain an annotated version of the loop body by re-running the abstract interpreter on this instruction. This is done with the following function:

```
Definition do_annot (ab:state-> a_instr * option state)
 (b:bexpr) (s:state) (i:instr) : a_instr :=
 match learn_from_success s b with
  Some s' => let (ai, _) := ab s' in ai
 | None => mark i
 end.
```

In this function, ab is supposed to compute the abstract interpretation of the loop body. When the function learn_from_success returns a None value, this means that the loop body is never executed and it is marked as dead code by the function mark.

5.9 The Abstract Interpreter's Main Function

With the function find_inv, we can now design a new abstract interpreter. Its main structure is about the same as for the naive one, but there are two important differences. First, the abstract interpreter now uses the find_inv function to compute an invariant state for the while loop. Second, this abstract interpreter can detect cases where instructions are guaranteed to not terminate. This is a second part of dead code detection: when a good invariant is detected for the while loop, a comparison between this invariant and the loop test may give the information that the loop test can never be falsified. If this is the case, no state is returned and the instructions following this while loop in sequences must be marked as dead code. This is handled by the fact that the abstract interpreter now returns an optional state and an annotated instruction. The case for the sequence is modified to make sure instruction are marked as dead code when receiving no input state.

```
Fixpoint ab2 (i:instr)(s:state) : a_instr*option state :=
 match i with
  assign x e =>
  (pre (s_to_a s) (a_assign x e), Some (a_upd x (a_af s e) s))
 | seq i1 i2 =>
  let (a_i1, s1) := ab2 i1 s in
   match s1 with
    Some s1' =>
    let (a_i2, s2) := ab2 i2 s1' in
      (a_seq a_i1 a_i2, s2)
   | None => (a_seq a_i1 (mark i2), None)
   end
 | while b i =>
  let inv := find_inv (ab2 i) b s s i (choose_2 s i) in
    (a_while b (s_to_a inv)
       (do_annot (ab2 i) b inv i),
    learn_from_failure inv b)
 end.
```

This function relies on an extra numeric function choose_2 to decide the number of times find_inv will attempt progressive over-approximations before giving up and falling back on the nil state. Like choose_1 and over_approx, this function must be provided at the same time as the type for abstract values.

6 Proving the Correctness of the Abstract Interpreter

To prove the correctness of our abstract interpreter, we adapt the correctness statements that we already used for the naive interpreter. The main change is that the resulting state is optional, with a None value corresponding to non-termination. This means that when a None value is obtained we can take the post-condition as the false assertion. This is expressed with the following function, mapping an optional state to an assertion.

```
Definition s_to_a' (s':option state) : assert :=
 match s' with Some s => s_to_a s | None => a_false end.
```

The main correctness statement thus becomes the following one:

```
Theorem ab2_correct : forall i i' s s', consistent s ->
 ab2 i s = (i', s') -> valid m (vc i' (s_to_a' s')).
```

By comparison with the similar theorem for ab1, we removed the part about the final state satisfying the consistent. This part is actually proved in a lemma beforehand. The reason why we chose to establish the two results at the same time for ab1 and in two stages for ab2 is anecdotal.

As for the naive interpreter this theorem is paired with a lemma asserting that cleaning up the resulting annotated instruction i' yields back the initial instruction i. We actually need to prove two lemmas, one for the mark function (used to mark code as dead code) and one for ab2 itself.

```
Lemma mark_clean : forall i, cleanup (mark i) = i.

Theorem ab2_clean : forall i i' s s',
  ab2 i s = (i', s') -> cleanup i' = i.
```

These two lemmas are proved by induction on the structure of the instruction i.

6.1 Hypotheses about the Auxiliary Functions

The abstract interpreter relies on a collection of functions that are specific to the abstract domain being handled. In our Coq development, this is handled by defining the function inside a section, where the various components that are specific to the abstract domain of interpretation are given as section variables and hypotheses. When the section is closed, the various functions defined in the section are abstracted over the variables that they use. Thus, the function ab2 becomes a 16-argument function. The extra twelve arguments are as follows:

1. A : Type, the type containing the abstract values,
2. from_Z : Z -> A, a function mapping integer values to abstract values,
3. top : A, an abstract value representing lack of information,
4. a_add : A -> A -> A, an addition operation for abstract values,
5. to_pred : A -> aexpr -> assert, a function mapping abstract values to their interpretations as assertions on arithmetic expressions,
6. learn_from_success : state A -> bexpr -> state A, a function that is able to improve a state, knowing that a boolean expression's evaluation returns true,
7. learn_from_failure : state A -> bexpr -> state A, similar to the previous one, but using the knowledge that the boolean expression's evaluation returns false,
8. join : A -> A -> A, a binary function on abstract values that returns an abstract value that is coarser than the two inputs,
9. thinner : A -> A -> bool, a comparison function that succeeds when the first argument is more precise than the second,

10. `over_approx : nat -> state A -> state A -> state A`, a function that implements heuristics to find over-approximations of its arguments,
11. `choose_1 : state A -> instr -> nat`, a function that returns the number of times a loop body should be executed with a given start state before testing for stabilisation,
12. `choose_2 : state A -> instr -> nat`, a function that returns the number of times over-approximations should be attempted before giving up and using the coarsest state.

Most of these functions must satisfy a collection of properties to ensure that the correctness statement will be provable. There are fourteen such properties, which can be sorted in the following way:

1. Three properties are concerned with the assertions created by `to_pred`, with respect to their logical interpretation and to substitution.
2. Two properties are concerned with the consistency of interpretation of abstract values obtained through `from_Z` and `a_add` as predicates over integers.
3. Two properties are concerned with the logical properties of abstract states computed with the help of `learn_from_success` and `learn_from_failure`.
4. Four properties are concerned with ensuring that `over_approx`, `join`, and `thinner` do return or detect over-approximations correctly,
5. Three properties are concerned with ensuring that the `consistent` properties is preserved through `learn_from...` and `over_approx`.

6.2 Maintaining the `consistent` Property

For this abstract interpreter, we need again to prove that it maintains the property that all states are duplication-free. It is first established for the `join_state` operation. Actually, since the `join_state` operation performs repetitive updates from the `nil` state, the result is duplication-free, regardless of the duplications in the inputs. This is easily obtained with a proof by induction on the first argument. For once, we show the full proof script.

```
Lemma join_state_consistent :
 forall s1 s2, consistent (join_state s1 s2).
intros s1 s2; induction s1 as [ | [x v] s1 IHs1]; simpl; auto.
apply consistent_update; auto.
Qed.
```

The first two lines of this Coq excerpt give the theorem statement. The line `intros ...` explains that a proof by induction should be done. This proof raises two cases, and the as ... fragment states that in the step case (the second case), one should consider a list whose tail is named `s1` and whose first pair contains a variable `x` and an abstract value `v`, and we have an induction hypothesis, which should be named `IHs1`: this induction hypothesis states that `s1` already satisfies the `consistent` property. The `simpl` directive expresses that the recursive function should be simplified if possible, and `auto` attempts to solve the goals that are generated. Actually, the computation of recursive functions leads to proving `true = true` in the base case and `auto` takes care of this. For the step case, we simply need to rely on the theorem `consistent_update` (see section 4.6). The premise of this theorem actually is `IHs1` and `auto` finds it.

6.3 Relating Input Abstract States and Pre-conditions

Similarly to what was done for the naive abstract interpreter, we want to ensure that the interpretation of the input abstract state as a logical formula implies the pre-condition for the generated annotated instruction and the generated post-condition. For the while loop, this relies on the fact that the selected invariant is obtained after repetitive joins with the input state. We first establish two monotonicity properties for the `join_state` function, we show only the first one:

```
Lemma join_state_safe_1 : forall g s1 s2,
 ia m g (s_to_a s1) -> ia m g (s_to_a (join_state s1 s2)).
```

Then, we only need to propagate the property up from the `step1` function. Again, we show only the first one but there are similar lemmas for `step2`, `find_inv`; and we conclude with the property for `ab2`:

```
Lemma step1_pc : forall g ab b s s',
 ia m g (s_to_a s) -> ia m g (s_to_a s') ->
 ia m g (s_to_a (step1 ab b s s')).
```

```
Lemma ab2_pc :
 forall i i' s s', ab2 i s = (i', s') ->
  forall g a, ia m g (s_to_a s) -> ia m g (pc i' a).
```

The proof for `step1_pc` is a direct consequence of the definition and the properties of `join_state`. The proofs for `step2` and `find_inv` are done by induction on `n`. The proof for `ab2` is an easy induction on the instruction `i`. In particular, the two state arguments to the function `find_inv` are both equal to the input state in the case of `while` loops.

6.4 Validity of the Generated Conditions

The main theorem is about ensuring that all verification conditions are provable. A good half of this problem is already taken care of when we prove the theorem `ab2_pc`, which expresses that at each step the state is strong enough to ensure the validity of the pre-condition for the instruction that follows. The main added difficulty is to verify that the invariant computed for each while loop actually is invariant. This difficulty is taken care of by the structure of the function `find_inv`, which actually invokes the function `is_inv` on its expected output before returning it. Thus, we only need to prove that `is_inv` correctly detects states that are invariants:

```
Lemma is_inv_correct :
 forall ab b g s s' s2 ai,
  is_inv ab s b = true -> learn_from_success s b = Some s' ->
  ab s' = (ai, s2) -> ia m g (s_to_a' s2) -> ia m g (s_to_a s).
```

We can then deduce that find_inv is correct: the proof proceeds by showing that the value this function returns is either verified using is_inv or the nil state. The correctness statement for find_inv has the following form:

```
Lemma find_inv_correct : forall ab b g i n init s s' s2 ai,
 learn_from_success (find_inv ab b init s i n) b = Some s' ->
 ab s' = (s2, ai) -> ia m g (s_to_a' s2) ->
 ia m g (s_to_a (find_inv ab b init s i n)).
```

This can then be combined with the assumptions that learn_from_success and learn_from_failure correctly improve the information given in abstract state to show that the value returned for while loops in ab2 is correct. These assumptions have the following form (the hypothesis for the learn_from_failure has a negated third assumption).

```
Hypothesis learn_from_success_sem :
 forall s b g, consistent s ->
   ia m g (s_to_a s) -> ia m g (a_b b) ->
   ia m g (s_to_a' (learn_from_success s b)).
```

7 An Interval-Based Instantiation

The abstract interpreters we have described so far are generic and are ready to be instantiated on specific abstract domains. In this section we describe an instantiation on an abstract domain to represent intervals. This domain of intervals contains intervals with finite bounds and intervals with infinite bounds. The interval with two infinite bounds represents the whole type of integers. We describe these intervals with an inductive type that has four variants:

```
Inductive interval : Type :=
 above : Z -> interval
| below : Z -> interval
| between : Z -> Z -> interval
| all_Z : interval.
```

For instance, the interval containing all values larger than or equal to 10 is represented by above 10 and the whole type of integers is represented by all_Z.

The interval associated to an integer is simply described as the interval with two finite bounds equal to this integer.

```
Definition i_from_Z (x:Z) := between x x.
```

When adding two intervals, it suffices to add the two bounds, because addition preserves the order on integers. Coping with all the variants of each possible input yields a function with many cases.

```
Definition i_add (x y:interval) :=
 match x, y with
   above x, above y => above (x+y)
 | above x, between y z => above (x+y)
 | below x, below y => below (x+y)
 | below x, between y z => below (x+z)
 | between x y, above z => above (x+z)
 | between x y, below z => below (y+z)
 | between x y, between z t => between (x+z) (y+t)
 | _, _ => all_Z
 end.
```

The assertions associated to each abstract value can rely on only one, as we can re-use the same comparison predicate for almost all variants. This is described in the to_pred function.

```
Definition i_to_pred (x:interval) (e:aexpr) : assert :=
 match x with
   above a => pred "leq" (anum a::e::nil)
 | below a => pred "leq" (e::anum a::nil)
 | between a b => a_conj (pred "leq" (anum a::e::nil))
             (pred "leq" (e::anum b::nil))
 | all_Z => a_true
 end.
```

Of course, the meaning attached to the string "leq" must be correctly fixed in the corresponding instantiation for the m parameter:

```
Definition i_m (s : string) (l: list Z) : Prop :=
 if string_dec s "leq" then
  match l with x::y::nil => x <= y | _ => False end
 else False.
```

7.1 Learning from Comparisons

The functions i_learn_from_success and i_learn_from_failure used when processing while loops can be made arbitrarily complex. For the sake of conciseness, we have only designed a pair of functions that detect the case where the boolean test has the form x < e, where e is an arbitrary arithmetic expression. In this case, the function i_learn_from_success updates only the value associated to x: the initial interval associated with x is intersected with the interval of all values that are less than the upper bound of the interval computed for e. An impossibility is detected when the lowest possible value for x is larger than or equal to the upper bound for e. Even this simple strategy yields a function with many cases, of which we show only the cases where both x and e have interval values with finite bounds:

```
Definition i_learn_from_success s b :=
 match b with
  blt (avar x) e =>
   match a_af _ i_from_Z all_Z i_add s e,
      lookup _ all_Z s x with
   ...
   | between _ n, between m p =>
      if Z_le_dec n m then None else
      if Z_le_dec n p
      then Some (a_upd _ x (between m (n-1)) s)
      else Some s
  ...
   end
 | _ => Some s
 end.
```

In the code of this function, the functions `a_af`, `lookup`, and `a_upd` are parameterized by the functions from the datatype of intervals that they use: `i_from_Z`, `all_Z` and `i_add` for `a_af`, `all_Z` for `lookup`, etc.

The function `i_learn_from_failure` is designed similarly, looking at upper bounds for x and lower bounds for e instead.

7.2 Comparing and Joining Intervals

The treatement of loops also requires a function to find upper bounds of pairs of intervals and a function to compare two intervals. These functions are simply defined by pattern-matching on the kind of intervals that are encountered and then comparing the upper and lower bounds.

```
Definition i_join (i1 i2:interval) : interval :=
 match i1, i2 with
  above x, above y =>
   if Z_le_dec x y then above x else above y
 ...
 | between x y, between z t =>
   let lower := if Z_le_dec x z then x else z in
   let upper := if Z_le_dec y t then t else y in
   between lower upper
 | _, _ => all_Z
 end.

Definition i_thinner (i1 i2:interval) : bool :=
 match i1, i2 with
```

```
  above x, above y => if Z_le_dec y x then true else false
 | above _, all_Z => true
 ...
 | between x _, above y => if Z_le_dec y x then true else false
 | between _ x, below y => if Z_le_dec x y then true else false
 | _, all_Z => true
 ...
 end.
```

7.3 Finding Over-Approximations

When the interval associated to a variable does not stabilize, an over-approximation must be found for this interval. We implement an approach where several steps of over-approximation can be taken one after the other. For intervals, finding over-approximations can be done by pushing one of the bounds of each interval to infinity. We use the fact that the generic abstract interpreter calls the over-approximation with two values to choose the bound that should be pushed to infinity: in a first round of over-approximation, only the bound that does not appear to be stable is modified. This strategy is particularly well adapted for loops where one variable is increased or decreased by a fixed amount at each execution of the loop's body.

The strategy is implemented in two functions, the first function over-approximates an interval, the second function applies the first to all the intervalles found in a state.

```
Definition open_interval (i1 i2:interval) : interval :=
 match i1, i2 with
  below x, below y => if Z_le_dec y x then i1 else all_Z
 | above x, above y => if Z_le_dec x y then i1 else all_Z
 | between x y, between z t =>
  if Z_le_dec x z then if Z_le_dec t y then i1 else above x
  else if Z_le_dec t y then below y else all_Z
 | _, _ => all_Z
 end.
```

```
Definition open_intervals (s s':state interval) : state interval :=
 map (fun p:string*interval =>
     let (x, v) := p in
      (x, open_interval v (lookup _ all_Z s' x))) s.
```

The result of `open_interval i1 i2` is expected to be an over-approximation of `i1`. The second argument `i2` is only used to choose which of the bounds of `i1` should be modified.

The function `i_over_approx` receives a numeric parameter to indicate the strength of over-approximation that should be applied. Here, there are only two strengths: at the first try (when the level is larger than 0), the function applies open_intervals; at the second try, it simply returns the nil state, which corresponds to the top value in the domain of abstract states.

```
Definition i_over_approx n s s' :=
 match n with
   S _ => open_intervals s s'
 | _ => nil
 end.
```

The abstract interpreter also requires two functions that compute the number of attempts at each level of repetitive operation. We define these two functions as constant functions:

```
Definition i_choose_1 (s:state interval) (i:instr) := 2%nat.
Definition i_choose_2 (s:state interval) (i:instr) := 3%nat.
```

Once the type interval and the various functions are provided we obtain an abstract interpreter for computing with intervals.

```
Definition abi :=
 ab2 interval i_from_Z all_Z i_add i_to_pred
   i_learn_from_success i_learn_from_failure
   i_join i_thinner i_over_approx i_choose_1 i_choose_2.
```

We can already run this instantiated interpreter inside the Coq system. For instance, we can run the interpreter on the instruction:

```
while x < 10 do x := x + 1 done
```

This gives the following dialog (where the answer of the Coq system is written in italics):

```
Eval vm_compute in
  abi (while (blt (avar "x") (anum 10))
        (assign "x" (aplus (avar "x") (anum 1))))
    (("X", between 0 0)::nil).
   = (a_while (blt (avar "x") (anum 10))
     (a_conj
       (a_conj (pred "leq" (anum 0 :: avar "x" :: nil))
         (pred "leq" (avar "x" :: anum 10 :: nil))) a_true)
     (pre
       (a_conj
         (a_conj (pred "leq" (anum 0 :: avar "x" :: nil))
           (pred "leq" (avar "x" :: anum 9 :: nil))) a_true)
       (a_assign "x" (aplus (avar "x") (anum 1))))),
    Some (("x", between 10 10) :: nil))
   : a_instr * option (state interval)
```

8 Conclusion

This paper describes how the functional language present in a higher-order theorem prover can be used to encode a tool to perform a static analysis on an arbitrary programming language. The example programming language is chosen to be extremely simple, so that the example can be described precisely in this tutorial paper. The static analysis tool that we described is inspired by the approach of abstract interpretation. However this work is not a comprehensive introduction to abstract interpretation, nor does it cover all the aspects of encoding abstract interpretation inside a theorem prover. Better descriptions of abstract interpretation and its formal study are given in [11,5,12].

The experiment is performed with the Coq system. More extensive studies of programming languages using this system have been developed over the last years. In particular, experiments by the Compcert team show that not only static analysis but also efficient compilation can be described and proved correct [4,10,6]. Coq is also used extensively for the study of functional programming languages, in particular to study the properties of type systems and there are a few Coq-based solutions to the general landmark objective known as POPLMark [1].

The abstract interpreter we describe here is inefficient in many respects: when analysing the body of a loop, this loop needs to be executed abstractly several times, the annotations computed each time are forgotten, and then when an invariant is discovered, the whole process needs to be done again to produce the annotated instruction. A more efficient interpreter could be designed where computed annotations are kept in memory long enough to avoid recomputation when the invariant is found. We did not design the abstract interpreter with this optimisation, thinking that the sources of inefficiency could be calculated away through systematic transformation of programs, as studied in another paper in this volume. The abstract interpreter provided with the paper [2] contains some of these optimisations.

An important remark is that program analyses can be much more efficient when they consider the relations between several variables at a time, as opposed to the experiment described here where the variables are considered independently of each other. More precise work where relations between variables can be tracked is possible, on the condition that abstract values are used to describe complete states, instead of single variables as in [4], where the result of the analysis is used as a basis for a compiler optimisation known as *common subexpression elimination.*

We have concentrated on a very simple while language in this paper, for didactical purposes. However, abstract interpreters have been applied to much more complete programming languages. For instance, the Astree [8] analyser covers most of the C programming language. On the other hand, the foundational papers describe abstract interpretation in terms of analyses on control flow graphs. The idea of abstract interpretation is general enough that it should be possible to apply it to any form of programming language.

References

1. Aydemir, B., Bohannon, A., Fairbairn, M., Foster, J., Pierce, B., Sewell, P., Vytiniotis, D., Washburn, G., Weirich, S., Zdancewic, S.: Mechanized metatheory for the masses: The POPLmark challenge. In: Hurd, J., Melham, T. (eds.) TPHOLs 2005. LNCS, vol. 3603, pp. 50–65. Springer, Heidelberg (2005)
2. Bertot, Y.: Theorem proving support in programming language semantics. Technical Report 6242, INRIA (2007); to appear in a book in memory of Gilles Kahn
3. Bertot, Y., Castéran, P.: Interactive Theorem Proving and Program Development, Coq'Art: the Calculus of Inductive Constructions. Springer, Heidelberg (2004)
4. Bertot, Y., Grégoire, B., Leroy, X.: A structured approach to proving compiler optimizations based on dataflow analysis. In: Filliâtre, J.-C., Paulin-Mohring, C., Werner, B. (eds.) TYPES 2004. LNCS, vol. 3839, pp. 66–81. Springer, Heidelberg (2006)
5. Besson, F., Jensen, T., Pichardie, D.: Proof-carrying code from certified abstract interpretation and fixpoint compression. Theoretical Computer Science 364(3), 273–291 (2006)
6. Blazy, S., Dargaye, Z., Leroy, X.: Formal verification of a C compiler front-end. In: Misra, J., Nipkow, T., Sekerinski, E. (eds.) FM 2006. LNCS, vol. 4085, pp. 460–475. Springer, Heidelberg (2006)
7. Cousot, P., Cousot, R.: Abstract interpretation: a unified lattice model for static analysis of programs by construction or approximation of fixpoints. In: Conference Record of the Fourth ACM Symposium on Principles of Programming Languages, POPL 1977, pp. 238–252. ACM Press, New York (1977)
8. Cousot, P., Cousot, R., Feret, J., Miné, A., Mauborgne, L., Monniaux, D., Rival, X.: The ASTREÉ analyzer. In: Sagiv, M. (ed.) ESOP 2005, vol. 3444, pp. 21–30. Springer, Heidelberg (2005)
9. Dijkstra, E.W.: A discipline of Programming. Prentice Hall, Englewood Cliffs (1976)
10. Leroy, X.: Formal certification of a compiler back-end, or: programming a compiler with a proof assistant. In: 33rd symposium Principles of Programming Languages, pp. 42–54. ACM Press, New York (2006)
11. Pichardie, D.: Interprétation abstraite en logique intuitionniste : extraction d'analyseurs Java certifiés. PhD thesis, Université Rennes 1 (2005) (in French)
12. Pichardie, D.: Building certified static analysers by modular construction of well-founded lattices. In: Proc. of the 1st International Conference on Foundations of Informatics, Computing and Software (FICS 2008). Electronic Notes in Theoretical Computer Science (2008)
13. The Coq development team. The coq proof assistant (2008), `http://coq.inria.fr`

Extended Static Checking by Calculation Using the Pointfree Transform

José N. Oliveira

CCTC, Universidade do Minho, 4700-320 Braga, Portugal
jno@di.uminho.pt

Abstract. The pointfree transform offers to the predicate calculus what the Laplace transform offers to the differential/integral calculus: the possibility of changing the underlying mathematical space so as to enable agile algebraic calculation. This paper addresses the foundations of the transform and its application to a calculational approach to extended static checking (ESC) in the context of abstract modeling. In particular, a calculus is given whose rules help in breaking the complexity of the proof obligations involved in static checking arguments. The close connection between such calculus and that of weakest pre-conditions makes it possible to use the latter in ESC proof obligation discharge, where pointfree notation is again used, this time to calculate with invariant properties to be maintained.

A connection with the *"everything is a relation"* lemma of Alloy is established, showing how close to each other the pointfree and Alloy notations are. The main advantage of this connection is that of complementing pen-and-paper pointfree calculations with model checking support wherever validating sizable abstract models.

Keywords: Theoretical foundations, formal methods, proof obligations, extended static checking.

> *"Certaines personnes ont [l'affectation] d'éviter en apparence toute espèce de calcul, en traduisant par des phrases fort longues ce qui s'exprime très brièvement par l'algèbre, et ajoutant ainsi à la longueur des opérations, les longueurs d'un langage qui n'est pas fait pour les exprimer. Ces personnes-là sont en arrière de cent ans."*
>
> Evariste Galois (1831)

1 Introduction

Much of our programming effort goes into making sure that a number of *"good" relationships* hold among the software artifacts we build. There are two main ways of ensuring that such good things happen. According to the first, the intended relationship is first *postulated* as a logic statement and then *verified*. We shall refer to this as the "invent & verify" way. Alternatively, one may try and *calculate* the intended relationship out of other valid relationships using an algebra, or theory of relationships. This will be referred to as the "correct by construction" approach.

A. Bove et al. (Eds.): LerNet ALFA Summer School 2008, LNCS 5520, pp. 195–251, 2009.

Let us illustrate the contrast between these two approaches with examples. Whenever Haskell programmers declare function types, eg.

$$\underbrace{f}_{function} \ :: \ \underbrace{a \rightarrow b}_{type} \tag{1}$$

they are postulating a *"is of type"* relationship involving two kinds of artifact: functions (λ-expressions) and types (τ-expressions). It is quite common to declare $f :: a \rightarrow b$ first, write the body of f afterwards and then wait for the interpreter's reaction (type checker) when verifying the consistency of both declarations.

Clearly, this is an *invent & verify* approach to writing type correct functional code. What about the *correct by construction* alternative? It goes the other way round: one writes the body of f first and lets the interpreter *calculate* (by polymorphic type inference) its principal type, which can be instantiated later, if convenient.

Note that absence of type errors in the *invent & verify* approach does not ensure associating a function to its most generic type: the programmer's guess (invention) may happen to be stronger, implicitly reducing the scope of application of the function being declared. This is also a danger of *invent & verify* applied to *extended typed checking* as in, for instance, typing code using Hoare triples:

$$\{p\}P\{q\}$$

This postulate about piece of code P captures relationship *"is such that pre-condition p ensures post-condition q"*. So it could be alternatively written as

$$\underbrace{P}_{program} \ :: \ \underbrace{p \rightarrow q}_{predicative\ type} \tag{2}$$

involving, as artifacts, programs (imperative code) and pre/post conditions (predicates). The *invent & verify* way of handling Hoare triples consists of writing P, inventing p and q and finally proving that $\{p\}P\{q\}$ holds. The *correct by construction* equivalent consists of writing two of the ingredients q, P and p and calculating the third. Typically, one will calculate the weakest pre-condition (*wp*) for q to hold upon execution of P. Again, the calculated pre-condition p may be strengthened at a later stage, if convenient.

Our third and last example, in the area of discrete maths, is perhaps the most eloquent in contrasting verification against calculation. Think of how to postulate that a given function f is a bijection: one may prove f injective, total and surjective or, in typical *invent & verify* mode, guess its converse f° and then prove the two cancellations $\langle \forall\ x\ ::\ f^\circ(f\ x) = x \rangle$ and $\langle \forall\ y\ ::\ f(f^\circ y) = y \rangle$. By contrast, a constructive, calculational alternative will go as follows: using relation algebra, one calculates f°, which in general is a relation, not a function; both f and f° will be bijective iff a function f° is obtained. The approach is constructive (f° is calculated, not guessed) and simpler.

From the examples above it can be observed that "traditional thinking" in maths and software design tends to follow the *invent & verify* reasoning style. This paper is devoted to the alternative, constructive approach to building correct code. In particular, it focuses on a calculational approach to discharging proof obligations involved in writing type correct software, a discipline which can be framed into the wider topic of *extended static type checking* (ESC) [24].

Our starting point is the observation that thinking constructively requires a "turn of mind". And this raises the question: are the logics and calculi we traditionally rely upon up-to-date for such a turn of mind? In an excellent essay on the history of scientific technology, Russo [55] writes:

> *The immense usefulness of exact science consists in providing models of the real world within which there is a guaranteed method for telling false statements from true. (...) Such models, of course, allow one to describe and predict natural phenomena, by translating them to the theoretical level via correspondence rules, then solving the "exercises" thus obtained and translating the solutions obtained back to the real world.*

The verdict is that disciplines unable to build themselves around *exercises* should be regarded as *pre-scientific*.

This fits neatly into the current paper's overall message. Our idea is to invest in a scientific theory for software development whereby code is obtained by solving exercises whose solutions are the artifacts one wants to produce. So, the formulæ and equations involved in such exercises should range over programs and properties of programs (assertions, specifications, etc) and not over the particular data values handled (stored, retrieved etc) by such programs. This identifies a first challenge: to devise a way of abstracting from program control/data structures. A second challenge consists in finding a single notation unifying properties of programs, program data, the programs themselves (or models thereof) and their "desirable" relationships.

Fortunately, such a unified notation exists already and does not need to be (re)invented: it is the notation of the pointfree relation calculus [60,13,7]. The link between conventional point-level logic and such a relation calculus is a transformation which abstracts from quantifiers and bound variables (points) found in predicates and converts these to formulæ involving binary relations only. In this *pointfree transform* (PF-transform for short) [60,50] variables are removed from program descriptions in the same way Backus develops his algebra of programs [10]. The main difference stays in the fact that one is transforming logical formulæ while Backus does so for functional terms only[1].

Structure of the paper. The remainder of this paper is organized as follows: sections 2 to 5 are concerned with motivation, background and related work. Extended static checking (ESC) is addressed in sections 6 and 7. The PF-transform and relational calculus, which are central to the whole paper, are given in sections 3, 9 and 12. PF-transformed ESC reasoning leads to the ESC/PF calculus for typing functions which is the subject of sections 8, 10 and 11. The generalization of this to relations is given in sections 14, 15 and 17. Sections 13 and 18 are concerned with case studies illustrating the use of the ESC/PF calculus. The second of these case studies, introduced in section16, is a real-life problem tackled in the context of the Verified Software Initiative. The connection with Alloy is addressed in sections 4 and 19. Conclusions and future work are given in sections 20 and 21, respectively. Annex A lists a number of laws of the Eindhoven quantifier calculus which are relevant to the PF-transform.

[1] See section 5 for more details on the pointfree notation and the origins of relational methods in computer science.

2 Motivation

Consider the following fragment of requirements put by a hypothetical telecom company:

> *(...) For each* list of calls *stored in the mobile phone (eg. numbers dialed, SMS messages, lost calls), the* store *operation should work in a way such that (a) the more recently a* call *is made the more accessible it should be; (b) no number appears twice in a list; (c) only the last 10 entries are stored in each list.*

It is not difficult to write a functional model for the required *store* operation on finite lists of calls,

$$store\; c\; l \;\triangleq\; take\; 10\; (c : [\, x \mid x \leftarrow l, x \neq c\,]) \tag{3}$$

where $c : l$ denotes list l prefixed by call number c and $take\; n\; l$ returns the prefix of l of length n, or l itself if $n > length\; l$, as in the Haskell notation and standard libraries [33]. However, how can one be sure that all requirements are properly met by (3)? Think of clause (b), for instance. Intuitively, missing $x \neq c$ in the list comprehension would compromise this property. But, is this enough? too strong?

Following the standard practice in formal methods, one first of all needs to formalize requirement (b) in the form of a predicate on lists of calls[2]:

$$noDuplicates\; l \;\triangleq\; \langle \forall\, i, j \;:\; 1 \leq i, j \leq length\; l :\; (l\; i) = (l\; j) \Rightarrow i = j \rangle \tag{4}$$

Next, we need to formulate and discharge the proof obligation which ensures that the *store* operation on lists of calls maintains property $noDuplicates$:

$$\langle \forall\, c, l \;:\; noDuplicates\; l :\; noDuplicates(store\; c\; l) \rangle \tag{5}$$

Desirable properties such as (4) which should be maintained by all operations of a given software application are known as *invariant* properties [32,31]. Our toy requirements include other such properties, for instance that corresponding to clause (c):

$$leq10\; l \;\triangleq\; length\; l \leq 10 \tag{6}$$

Ensuring that invariants are preserved by software operations entails the need for formal proofs. The complexity of such proofs grows dramatically with the complexity of the formal models of both invariant properties and operations. So, any effort to modularize such models and proofs is welcome. In the case of (3), for instance, it can be observed that *store* is the "pipeline" of three sub-operations: filtering c first, *cons*'ing it afterwards and finally taking 10 elements at most. This is nicely expressed by writing

$$store\; c \triangleq (take\; 10) \cdot (c\, :) \cdot filter(c \neq) \tag{7}$$

where $filter$ is the obvious list processing function and combinator "$\cdot$ " denotes function composition:

$$(f \cdot g)\, a \;\triangleq\; f\, (g\, a) \tag{8}$$

[2] We use notation $\langle \forall\, x \;:\; R :\; T \rangle$ to mean *for all x in range R it is the case that T holds.* Properties of this notation, known as the *Eindhoven quantifier notation* [7,4], are given in appendix A.

Note that (7) abstracts from input variable l (of type *list of calls*) thanks to (8) and to extensional functional equality:

$$f = g \;\Leftrightarrow\; \langle \forall\, a \,::\, f\, a = g\, a \rangle \tag{9}$$

Also note the use of sections $(take\ 10)$ and $(c\ :)$ in converting curried binary operators $take$ and $(:)$ into unary ones by "freezing" the first argument.

The main advantage of (7) when compared to (3) is that different invariants may happen to be maintained by different stages of the pipeline, reducing the overall complexity of proof obligations. For instance, $leq10$ has to do with lists not going beyond 10 elements: clearly, this is ensured by the outermost stage alone,

$$\langle \forall\, l \,::\, length(take\ 10\ l) \leq 10 \rangle \tag{10}$$

independently of how argument list l is built. Property (10) can in fact be shown to hold for function

$$\begin{aligned} take\ 0\ \_ &= [\,] \\ take\ \_\ [\,] &= [\,] \\ take\ (n+1)\ (x : xs) &= x : take\ n\ xs \end{aligned}$$

Clearly, proving (10) requires less effort that proving that $leq10$ is preserved by the whole function $store$:

$$\langle \forall\, c, l \,:\, length\, l \leq 10 :\, length(take\ 10\ (c : [\, x \mid x \leftarrow l, x \neq c\,])) \leq 10 \rangle \tag{11}$$

The use of notation (7) instead of (3) above is an example of PF-transformation: instead of writing $f(g\ a)$ such as in the right hand side of (8), one writes $f \cdot g$ and drops variable (point) a. This kind of transformation, which is not a privilege of functions, is introduced in the section which follows.

3 Overview of the PF-Transform

Composing relations. Functional composition (8) is a special case of *relational composition*,

$$b(R \cdot S)c \;\Leftrightarrow\; \langle \exists\, a \,::\, bRa \,\wedge\, aSc \rangle \tag{12}$$

where R, S are binary relations and notation yRx means "*y is related to x by R*".

No other concept traverses human knowledge more ubiquitously than that of a *relation*, from philosophy to mathematics, to information systems (think eg. of relational databases [38]), etc. Symbol R in yRx can stand for virtually any relationship we may think of: not only those expressed by the "::" symbol in type assertions (1,2) but also those expressing facts as simple as eg. `"a"` *prefix_of* `"ab"` among strings, $n \leq n+1$ among natural numbers, TRUE $\in$ {TRUE, FALSE} in the Booleans, etc. In particular, R can be a function f, in which case $y\ f\ x$ means that y is the output of f for input x.

Before going further, note the notation convention of writing outputs on the left hand side and inputs on the right hand side, as suggested by the usual way of declaring functions in ordinary mathematics, $y = f\ x$, where y ranges over outputs (cf. the vertical axis of the Cartesian plane) and x over inputs (cf. the other, horizontal axis).

This convention is adopted consistently throughout this text and is extended to relations, as already seen above.

Comparing relations. The main advantage of relational thinking lies in its powerful combinators and associated laws, of which composition (12) is among the most useful: it expresses data flow in maths formulæ in a natural, implicit way while dropping existential quantifiers. Removing quantifiers from formulæ makes these more amenable to calculation. For instance, the rule which introduces *relational inclusion*

$$R \subseteq S \;\Leftrightarrow\; \langle \forall\, b, a \,:\, b\, R\, a :\, b\, S\, a \rangle \tag{13}$$

can be regarded (if read from right to left) as a way of dropping a very common pattern of universal quantification. (Read $R \subseteq S$ as "R is at most S", meaning that S is either more defined or less deterministic than R.)

Relational equality is usually established by circular inclusion:

$$R = S \;\Leftrightarrow\; R \subseteq S \,\wedge\, S \subseteq R \tag{14}$$

A less obvious, but very useful way of calculating the equality of two relations is the method of *indirect equality* [1,13]:

$$R = S \;\Leftrightarrow\; \langle \forall\, X \,::\, (X \subseteq R \Leftrightarrow X \subseteq S) \rangle \tag{15}$$

The reader unaware of this way of indirectly setting algebraic equalities will recognize that the same pattern of indirection is used when establishing set equality via the membership relation, cf. $A = B \;\Leftrightarrow\; \langle \forall\, x \,::\, x \in A \Leftrightarrow x \in B \rangle$.

Dividing relations. It is easy to check that $R \cdot S$ (12) has a *multiplicative* flavour: it is associative (albeit not commutative), it distributes over the union of two relations $R \cup S$, defined by

$$b(R \cup S)a \;\triangleq\; bRa \vee bSa$$

and it has a unit element, the identity relation id defined in the obvious way: $b\ id\ a$ iff $b = a$. Given such a multiplicative flavour, one may question: is there any reasonable notion of *relation division*? It turns out that the following property holds, for all binary relations R, S and T

$$X \cdot R \subseteq S \Leftrightarrow X \subseteq S/R \tag{16}$$

where S/R is the relation whose pointwise meaning is

$$a(S/R)b \;\Leftrightarrow\; \langle \forall\, c \,:\, b\, R\, c :\, a\, S\, c \rangle \tag{17}$$

Again note the economy of notation S/R when compared to its pointwise expansion as a universal quantification. Expanding the whole of (16) will lead to formula

$$\langle \forall\, b, a \,:\, \langle \exists\, c \,:\, bXc :\, cRa \rangle :\, bSa \rangle \;\Leftrightarrow\; \langle \forall\, b, c \,:\, bXc :\, \langle \forall\, a \,:\, cRa \,:\, bSa \rangle \rangle$$

which expresses a trading rule between existential and universal quantification harder to parse and memorize.

Phrase *pointfree transform* (or *PF-transform* for short) will denote, throughout this paper, this process of transforming predicate calculus expressions into their equivalent relational combinator based representations.

Coreflexives. Given a binary predicate p, we will denote by R_p the binary relation such that $b\ R_p\ a \;\Leftrightarrow\; p(b,a)$ holds, for all suitably typed a and b. How does one transform a unary predicate $u\ a$ into a *binary* relation? We will see that this can be done in more than one way, for instance by building the relation Φ_u such that $b\ \Phi_u\ a$ means $(b = a) \wedge (u\ a)$. That is, Φ_u is the relation that maps every a which satisfies u (and only such a) onto itself. Clearly, such relation is a fragment of the identity relation: $\Phi_u \subseteq id$.

Relations at most id are referred to as *coreflexive* relations and those larger than id as *reflexive* relations. Coreflexives will be denoted by uppercase Greek letters (Φ, Ψ) as in the case of Φ_u.

Composition with coreflexives expresses pre-conditioning and post-conditioning in a natural way, cf. $R \cdot \Phi$ and $\Psi \cdot R$, respectively. Coreflexives also act as data *filters*. For instance, suppose we need to transform the following variant of the right hand side of (12), $\langle \exists\ a\ :\ u\ a :\ b\ R\ a\ \wedge\ a\ Sc \rangle$, where u shrinks the range of the quantification. It can be easily checked that $R \cdot \Phi_u \cdot S$ is the corresponding extension to (12)[3].

Arrow notation and diagrams. We will use arrows to depict relations. In general, arrow $B \xleftarrow{R} A$ denotes a binary relation with source type A and target type B. We will say that $B \longleftarrow A$ is the *type* of R and write $b\ R\ a$ to mean that pair (b,a) is in R. Type declarations $B \xleftarrow{R} A$ and $A \xrightarrow{R} B$ mean the same. Arrow notation makes it possible to explain relational formulæ in terms of diagrams. For instance,

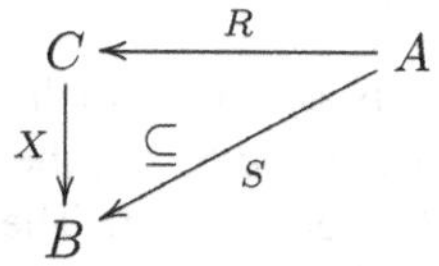

equivalent to

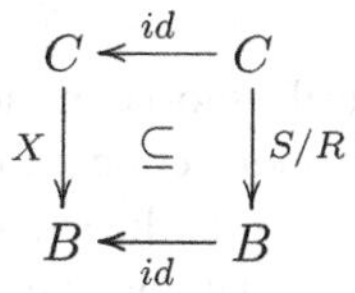

helps in understanding (16).

Galois connections. Properties such as (16) are known as *Galois connections* (GCs) [51] and prove very useful in problem understanding and reasoning, while bearing particular resemblance with school algebra: compare, for instance, (16) with a similar property defining integer division, for all $d, n, q \in I\!N$ $(d > 0)$[4]:

$$q \times d \leq n \Leftrightarrow q \leq n/d \qquad \begin{array}{c|c} n & d \\ \hline r & q \end{array} \tag{18}$$

By substituting $X := S/R$ in (16) we obtain $(S/R) \cdot R \subseteq S$ meaning that S/R approximates S once composed with R; by reading (16) from left to right, we obtain implication $X \cdot R \subseteq S \Rightarrow X \subseteq S/R$, which means that S/R is largest among all such approximations. So S/R is a supremum (as is quotient n/d).

---

3 See section 9 in the sequel for more about this important class of relations.

4 See [56] for a derivation of the algorithm of integer division from Galois connection (18) as an example of PF-calculation performed by the *Galculator*, the prototype of a proof assistant solely based on the algebra of Galois connections and PF-reasoning.

Table 1. Sample of PF-transform rules

Pointwise	Pointfree
$\langle \exists\, a :: b\, R\, a \wedge a\, S\, c \rangle$	$b(R \cdot S)c$
$\langle \forall\, x : x\, R\, b : x\, S\, a \rangle$	$b(R \setminus S)a$
$\langle \forall\, c : b\, R\, c : a\, S\, c \rangle$	$a(S\, /\, R)b$
$b\, R\, a \wedge c\, S\, a$	$(b, c)\langle R, S\rangle a$
$b\, R\, a \wedge d\, S\, c$	$(b, d)(R \times S)(a, c)$
$b\, R\, a \wedge b\, S\, a$	$b\,(R \cap S)\, a$
$b\, R\, a \wedge \neg b\, S\, a$	$b\,(R - S)\, a$
$b\, R\, a \vee b\, S\, a$	$b\,(R \cup S)\, a$
$(f\, b)\, R\, (g\, a)$	$b(f^{\circ} \cdot R \cdot g)a$
TRUE	$b \top a$
FALSE	$b \perp a$
$\langle \forall\, b, a : b\, R\, a : b\, S\, a \rangle$	$R \subseteq S$
$\langle \forall\, a :: a\, R\, a \rangle$	$id \subseteq R$

As example of other Galois connections bearing relationship with school algebra consider the following, which captures the operation which "subtracts" relations,

$$X - R \subseteq Y \;\Leftrightarrow\; X \subseteq Y \cup R \tag{19}$$

and is analogue of number subtraction:

$$x - n \leq y \;\Leftrightarrow\; x \leq y + n \tag{20}$$

Table 1 lists the most common relational operators associated to the PF-transform. $R \cap S$ denotes the intersection (or *meet*) of two relations R and S. $\top$ is the largest relation of its type. Its dual is $\perp$, the smallest such relation (the empty one). The following universal properties of relational *meet* and *join* are also Galois connections:

$$X \subseteq R \cap S \;\Leftrightarrow\; X \subseteq R \wedge X \subseteq S \tag{21}$$

$$R \cup S \subseteq X \;\Leftrightarrow\; R \subseteq X \wedge S \subseteq X \tag{22}$$

The two variants of division in table 1 arise from the fact that relation composition is not commutative, the Galois connection for $R \setminus S$ being similar to (16):

$$R \cdot X \subseteq S \Leftrightarrow X \subseteq R \setminus S \tag{23}$$

Converses. Every relation $A \xrightarrow{R} B$ has a converse, which is relation $A \xleftarrow{R^{\circ}} B$ such that

$$a(R^{\circ})b \Leftrightarrow b\, R\, a \tag{24}$$

holds. Two important properties of converse follow: it is an involution

$$(R^{\circ})^{\circ} = R \tag{25}$$

and it commutes with composition in a contravariant way:

$$(R \cdot S)^{\circ} = S^{\circ} \cdot R^{\circ} \tag{26}$$

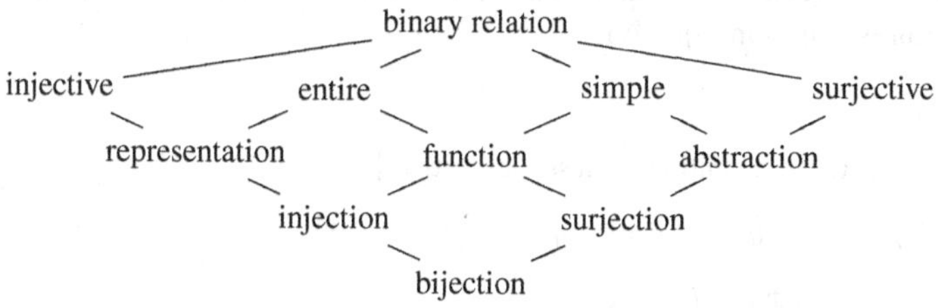

Fig. 1. Binary relation taxonomy

Functions. Lowercase symbols (f, g) stand for relations which are *functions*. The interplay between functions and relations is a rich part of the binary relation calculus [13]. From table 1 we single out rule

$$b(f^\circ \cdot R \cdot g)a \Leftrightarrow (f\ b)R(g\ a) \qquad \text{cf. diagram} \qquad \begin{array}{ccc} C & \xleftarrow{R} & D \\ {\scriptstyle f}\uparrow & & \uparrow{\scriptstyle g} \\ B & \xleftarrow[f^\circ \cdot R \cdot g]{} & A \end{array} \tag{27}$$

which involves two functions f, g and relation R and plays a special role in pushing variables out of relational expressions.

The exact characterization of functions as special cases of relations is achieved in terms of converse, which is in fact of paramount importance in establishing the whole taxonomy of binary relations depicted in figure 1. First, we define two important notions: the *kernel* of a relation R, $\mathsf{ker}\,R \triangleq R^\circ \cdot R$ and its dual, $\mathsf{img}\,R \triangleq R \cdot R^\circ$, the *image* of R[5].

From (25, 26) one immediately draws

$$\mathsf{ker}\,(R^\circ) = \mathsf{img}\,R \tag{28}$$

$$\mathsf{img}\,(R^\circ) = \mathsf{ker}\,R \tag{29}$$

Kernel and image lead to the four top criteria of the taxonomy of figure 1:

	Reflexive	*Coreflexive*
$\mathsf{ker}\,R$	entire R	injective R
$\mathsf{img}\,R$	surjective R	simple R

(30)

In words: a relation R is said to be *entire* (or total) iff its kernel is reflexive and to be *simple* (or functional) iff its image is coreflexive. Dually, R is *surjective* iff R° is entire, and R is *injective* iff R° is simple.

[5] As explained later on, These operators are relational extensions of two concepts familiar from set theory: the image of a function f, which corresponds to the set of all y such that $\langle \exists\ x\ ::\ y = f\ x \rangle$, and the kernel of f, which is the equivalence relation $b(\mathsf{ker}\,f)a \Leftrightarrow f\,b = f\,a$. (See exercise 3 later on.).

Let us check (30) with examples. First, we PF-transform the pointwise formula which captures function injectivity:

$$
\begin{array}{ll}
& f \text{ is injective} \\
\Leftrightarrow & \quad \{ \text{ recall definition from school maths } \} \\
& \langle \forall\, y, x \,:\, (f\ y) = (f\ x) :\ y = x \rangle \qquad (31) \\
\Leftrightarrow & \quad \{ \text{ introduce } id \text{ (twice) } \} \\
& \langle \forall\, y, x \,:\, (f\ y) id (f\ x) :\ y (id) x \rangle \\
\Leftrightarrow & \quad \{ \text{ (27) } \} \\
& \langle \forall\, y, x \,:\, y (f^{\circ} \cdot id \cdot f) x :\ y (id) x \rangle \\
\Leftrightarrow & \quad \{ \ id \text{ is the unit of composition; then go pointfree via (13) } \} \\
& f^{\circ} \cdot f \subseteq id \\
\Leftrightarrow & \quad \{ \text{ definition } \} \\
& \mathsf{ker}\, f \subseteq id
\end{array}
$$

Going the other way round, let us now see what $id \subseteq \mathsf{img}\, f$ means:

$$
\begin{array}{ll}
& id \subseteq \mathsf{img}\, f \\
\Leftrightarrow & \quad \{ \text{ definition } \} \\
& id \subseteq f \cdot f^{\circ} \\
\Leftrightarrow & \quad \{ \text{ relational inclusion (13) } \} \\
& \langle \forall\, y, x \,:\, y (id) x :\ y (f \cdot f^{\circ}) x \rangle \\
\Leftrightarrow & \quad \{ \text{ identity relation ; composition (12) } \} \\
& \langle \forall\, y, x \,:\, y = x :\ \langle \exists\, z \,::\, y\ f\ z \wedge z\ f^{\circ} x \rangle \rangle \\
\Leftrightarrow & \quad \{ \text{ converse (24) } \} \\
& \langle \forall\, y, x \,:\, y = x :\ \langle \exists\, z \,::\, y\ f\ z \wedge x\ f\ z \rangle \rangle \\
\Leftrightarrow & \quad \{ \ \forall\text{-one point rule (175) ; trivia ; function } f \ \} \\
& \langle \forall\, x \,::\, \langle \exists\, z \,::\, x = f\ z \rangle \rangle \\
\Leftrightarrow & \quad \{ \text{ recalling definition from school maths } \} \\
& f \text{ is surjective}
\end{array}
$$

The interested reader is welcome to convert the two remaining entries of (30) to pointwise notation.

Exercise 1. Resort to (28,29) and (30) to prove the following four rules of thumb:

– converse of *injective* is *simple* (and vice-versa)

- converse of *entire* is *surjective* (and vice-versa)
- smaller than injective (simple) is injective (simple)
- larger than entire (surjective) is entire (surjective) □

Exercise 2. Show that

$$R \cup S \text{ is injective } \Leftrightarrow R \text{ is injective } \wedge S \text{ is injective } \wedge R^\circ \cdot S \subseteq id \quad (32)$$

$$R \cup S \text{ is simple } \Leftrightarrow R \text{ is simple } \wedge S \text{ is simple } \wedge R \cdot S^\circ \subseteq id \quad (33)$$

Suggestion: resort to universal property (22). □

Exercise 3. Given a function $B \xleftarrow{f} A$, use (27) in the calculation of

$$b(\mathsf{ker}\, f)a \Leftrightarrow f\, b = f\, a \quad (34)$$

□

Constant functions. Quite often one needs to internalize particular constant values in PF-expressions. For instance, we may want to say that, given some x, there exists some z such that $x > z$ and $f\ z = c$, for some fixed value c. This requires the *"everywhere c"* constant function. In general, given a nonempty datatype C and $c \in C$, notation $\underline{c}$ denotes such a function:

$$\begin{array}{l} \underline{c} : A \longrightarrow C \\ \underline{c}\, a \triangleq c \end{array} \quad (35)$$

Thanks to (35) and (27) it can be easily checked that PF-term $> \cdot f^\circ \cdot \underline{c}$ asserts the requirement above.

Constant functions are also useful in PF-transforming particular relation pairs. For instance, it is easy to check that $\underline{b} \cdot \underline{c}^\circ$ is the singleton relation $\{(b, c)\}$. Then $\mathsf{img}\, \underline{c}$ is the singleton coreflexive $\{(c, c)\}$ which PF-transforms predicate $\lambda x.x = c$:

$$\Phi_{\lambda x.x=c} = \mathsf{img}\, \underline{c} \quad (36)$$

Thanks to (34), it is easy to show that $\top$ is the kernel of every constant function, $1 \xleftarrow{!} A$ included, where function ! — read "!" as "bang" — is the unique function of its type, where 1 denotes the singleton data domain.

Exercise 4. Check the meaning of relation $\underline{b}^\circ \cdot \underline{c}$. □

The Reynolds-Backhouse relation on functions. Consider two functions f and g related in the following way: if $y = f\ x$ holds then $y \leq g\ x$ holds, for a given ordering $\leq$ on the outputs of both f and g[6]. It is easy to see that this relationship between f and g PF-transforms to $f \subseteq \leq \cdot g$. Now suppose that g is such that $g \cdot \preceq \subseteq \leq \cdot g$, for $\preceq$ another ordering, this time on the input side. Back to points, this re-writes to $\langle \forall\, x, x' : x \preceq x' : g\, x \leq g\, x' \rangle$, meaning that g is monotonic.

[6] It is common to record this fact by writing $f \stackrel{.}{\leq} g$, the so-called pointwise ordering on functions.

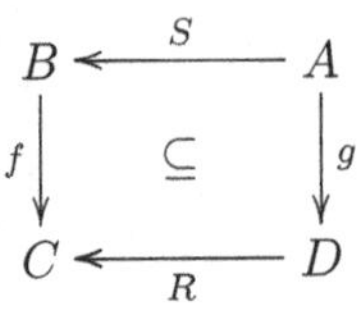

Once PF-transformed, the two situations just above are instances of the diagram aside, for suitable versions of relations R, S and functions f, g (these two, in particular, can be the same, as in the monotonicity condition). The diagram captures a very useful way of relating functions and relations (note the higher-order flavour) which was identified first by John Reynolds [54] and later treated in the pointfree style by Roland Backhouse [5,3].

We will refer to this as the relational "arrow combinator", to be written $R \leftarrow S$. Given R and S, $R \leftarrow S$ is a relation on functions f and g defined as follows:

$$f(R \leftarrow S)g \;\Leftrightarrow\; f \cdot S \subseteq R \cdot g \tag{37}$$

With points, $f(R \leftarrow S)g$ means $\langle \forall\, b, a \;:\; b\, S\, a : \; (f\, b) R (g\, a) \rangle$, that is, f and g produce R-related outputs $f\, b$ and $g\, a$ provided their inputs are S-related ($b\, S\, a$).

Properties and applications of this (PF) relational combinator can be found in eg. [3,12]. The special case $f(R \leftarrow S)f$ will suit our needs later on, and it will prove useful to write $R \xleftarrow{f} S$ to mean $f(R \leftarrow S)f$. Therefore, we will rely on equivalence

$$R \xleftarrow{f} S \;\Leftrightarrow\; f \cdot S \subseteq R \cdot f \tag{38}$$

The notation just introduced captures the view that types of functions can be regarded as relations. This is indeed the essence of the abstraction theorem [54] on type polymorphism which, as we shall see in section 11, plays its role in what is to come.

This important combinator closes our introduction to the relational combinators involved in the PF-transform. Before proceeding to the application of this transform to our topics of interest, let us frame it into a wider context.

4 Haskell and Alloy: Two PF-Flavoured Languages

As will become apparent throughout this paper, PF-notation will be regarded as a single, abstract (ie. technology free) unifying notation encompassing program specifications, implementations, program data and program properties. How far is such a notation from programming languages and notations available from the community?

Most commercially available programming languages are pointwise. But there are notations and languages which embody a pointfree subset. Functional programming languages with higher order functions have the power to define functional combinators and therefore make it possible to program in the pointfree style. Among these, some actually have pointfree constructs in their core syntax. Haskell [33] is one of these, as we have already seen in the motivating example of section 2. However, the artifacts one can build in Haskell do not go beyond partial functions, that is, simple relations.

Alloy [30] — a notation and associated model-checking tool which has been successful in *alloying* a number of disparate approaches to software modeling, namely model-orientation, object-orientation, etc. — is a rare example of a language where relations and their combinators are the standard way of doing things. In fact, the "everything is a relation" motto of Alloy matches perfectly with the view purported in the current paper. Quoting [30]:

(...) "*All structures are represented as relations, and structural properties are expressed with a few simple but powerful operators.* (...) *Sets are represented as relations with a single column, and scalars as singleton sets.* (...) *In the Alloy logic, all values are relations* [and] *the unification of sets and relations makes the syntax simpler, since there is no need to convert between sets and relations, or between scalars and sets.*" (...) *In Alloy, everything's a relation.*

It is interesting to note that Haskell and Alloy complement each other in a nice way: Haskell provides for models closer to implementations in the sense that they are reactive by construction: the idea is to evaluate typed λ-expressions which express the reaction of a system to input stimuli. However, there is no native syntax to express datatype invariants, pre and post-conditions and assertions. As a checking tool, Haskell invites the software designer to invent test cases and check for their behaviour[7].

Alloy is not functional, therefore it is a passive language. One writes uninterpreted data models and predicates about such models, as well as assertions about such predicates. The system runs checks for such assertions trying and finding counter-examples able to falsify such assertions. If no counter-example is found then the formula *may be* valid. Purists often regard model-checking as the poor relative to theorem proving. Experience tells, however, that many subtleties and design flaws can be unveiled by model checking. In other words: the checker does not prove things for certain but is of great help in improving what one wants to prove.

To catch a glimpse of the proximity between Alloy and the PF-notation adopted in the current paper, consider the Alloy pointwise definition of an injective relation R^8,

```
pred Injective {
    all x, y : A, z : B | z in x.R && z in y.R => x=y
}
```

and its PF-equivalent,

```
pred Injective' {
    R.~R in iden :> A
}
```

— recall $R^\circ \cdot R \subseteq id$ (30), for R° denoted by `~R` and id denoted by `iden :> A`. Also note that composition is written in reverse order.

5 Related Work

The idea of encoding predicates in terms of relations was initiated by De Morgan in the 1860s and followed by Peirce who, in the 1870s, found interesting equational laws of the calculus of binary relations [53]. The pointfree nature of the notation which emerged from this embryonic work was later further exploited by Tarski and his students [60]. In the 1980's, Freyd and Ščedrov [25] developed the notion of an *allegory*

[7] Tools such as QuickCheck [15] help in this respect.

[8] Note the transposed notation `x.R` meaning set $\{y \mid y\ R\ x\}$.

(a category whose homsets are partially ordered) which eventually accommodates the binary relation calculus as special case. In this context, a relation R is viewed as an arrow (morphism) $B \xleftarrow{R} A$ between objects B and A, respectively referred to as the target and source of R. Composition of such arrows corresponds to relational composition (12), identity is id, and relational expressions can be "type-checked" by drawing diagrams such as in category theory.

Such advances in mathematics were meanwhile captured by the Eindhoven computer science school in their development of program construction as a mathematical discipline [1,8,20,13,7] enhanced by judicious use of Galois connections, as already illustrated above.

Our view of this approach as a kind of *Laplace transform* [37] for logic was first expressed in [42]. Such a transform (the PF-transform) has henceforth been applied to several areas of the software sciences, namely relational database schema design [44,2,18], *hashing* [49], software components [11], coalgebraic reasoning [12], algorithmic refinement [50], data refinement [18,48] and separation logic [65].

The remainder of this paper will be devoted to yet another example of application of the PF-transform which we regard as a particularly expressive illustration of its power: extended static type checking (ESC) [24]. If performed at abstract model level, ESC includes what is commonly known as invariant preservation and satisfiability proof obligations in specification languages such as VDM [32,22] and Z [57]. Hoare triples [27] and weakest pre-condition calculus [19] are also related to ESC, as will be shown later. With notable exceptions (eg. [9,6]) these theories are available in the *pointwise* style, as most theories in computing are. Evidence will be provided not only of the unifying effect of the PF-transform in putting together different (but related) theories in programming but also of how it can be used and applied to real-sized (non trivial) case studies in connection with mechanical support provided by model checking [30] and theorem proving [26].

6 Extended Static Checking and Datatype Invariants

Type theory [52] is unanimously regarded as one of the most solid and relevant branches of computer science. Thanks to the concept of a *type*, the quality of code can be checked statically, ie. before execution. In programming languages such as Haskell, for instance, ill-typed programs simply don't compile, meaning that types are an effective way of controlling software robustness.

The ESC acronym for "extended static checking" was coined at Compaq SRC in their development of a tool for Java (ESC/Java) able to detect as many programming errors as possible at compile-time [24]:

> *Our group at the Systems Research Center has built and experimented with two realizations of a new program checking technology that we call extended static checking (ESC): "static" because the checking is performed without running the program, and "extended" because ESC catches more errors than are caught by conventional static checkers such as type checkers.*

If we look at the particular kinds of error which such a tool is able to catch — null dereferencing, array bounds errors, negative array indices, etc — we realize that these can be abstractly characterized by properties of particular datatypes which are violated by the running program, and/or a pre-condition of a given operation which is not ensured in some program trace. These two are related: the standard way of ensuring that a particular property of a datatype is maintained consists of adding pre-conditions to operations which may put such properties at risk.

However, adding arbitrary run-time checks for every property (a style often referred to as *defensive programming* [39]) may be counterproductive: one may write too many or much too strong checks. In the limit, the context may happen to ensure the properties one wants to maintain, thus rendering such checks useless and redundant.

Properties statically associated to datatypes are known as *invariants* [32] and as *state invariants* in case the particular datatypes embody the state of some state-based machine or system, often handled coalgebraically [31,12]. For instance, in a system for monitoring aircraft flight paths of in a controlled airspace [22], altitude, latitude and longitude cannot be specified simply as

$$Alt \;=\; Lat \;=\; Lon \;=\; \mathbb{R}$$

because altitudes cannot be negative, latitudes must range between $-90°$ and $90°$ and longitudes between $-180°$ and $180°$. Using traditional maths notation, one would write:

$$\begin{aligned} Alt &= \{a \in \mathbb{R} \mid a \geq 0\} \\ Lat &= \{x \in \mathbb{R} \mid -90 \leq x \leq 90\} \\ Lon &= \{y \in \mathbb{R} \mid -180 \leq y \leq 180\} \end{aligned} \tag{39}$$

Formal modeling notations such as VDM and Z cater specially for invariants. In the case of languages of the VDM family (eg. VDM-SL [22], VDM++ [23]) the standard notation is

$$\begin{aligned} &Alt \;=\; \mathbb{R} \\ &\textbf{inv}\ a \triangleq a \geq 0 \end{aligned}$$

for *Alt* (39) (and similarly for *Lat* and *Lon*), which implicitly defines a predicate

$$\begin{aligned} &\text{inv-}Alt : \mathbb{R} \to \mathbb{B} \\ &\text{inv-}Alt\ a \triangleq a \geq 0 \end{aligned}$$

known as the *invariant* of *Alt*. In general, given A and a predicate $p : A \to \mathbb{B}$, data type declaration

$$\begin{aligned} &T \;=\; A \\ &\textbf{inv}\ a \triangleq p\,a \end{aligned}$$

means the type whose extension is

$$T = \{x \in A \mid p\,x\}$$

Therefore, writing $a \in T$ means $a \in A \wedge p\,a$. Note that A itself can have its own invariant, so the process of finding which properties hold about a given datatype is inductive on the structure of types. (See more about this in section 17.)

7 Invariants Entail Proof Obligations

Static checking of formal models involving invariants is a complex process relying on generation and discharge of proof obligations, as pointed out more than two decades ago by Jones [32]:

> *The valid objects of Datec are those which (...) satisfy inv-Datec. This has a profound consequence for the type mechanism of the notation. (...) The inclusion of a sub-typing mechanism which allows truth-valued functions forces the type checking here to rely on proofs.*

The required proofs, which are known under the headings *invariant preservation* or *satisfiability* [32][9] belong clearly to the ESC family. Recalling the mobile phone toy requirements of section 2, it should be clear by now that predicates $noDuplicates$ (4) and $leq10$ (6) are components of the invariant of the list of calls datatype handled by $store$, say

$$\begin{array}{l} ListOfCalls = Call^{\star} \\ \mathbf{inv}\ l \triangleq noDuplicates\, l\ \wedge\ leq10\, l \end{array}$$

and that (5) and (11) express two proof obligations entailed by such an invariant, concerning the $store$ operation.

In general, given a function $A \xrightarrow{f} B$ where both A and B have invariants, extended static checking (ESC) of f means discharging proof obligation (PO)

$$\langle \forall\, a\ :\ \text{inv-}A\, a :\ \text{inv-}B(f\ a) \rangle \tag{40}$$

which ensures that f is invariant-preserving. The fact that invariants are intrinsic to datatypes is better captured by the following version of the above,

$$\langle \forall\, a\ :\ a \in A :\ (f\ a) \in B \rangle \tag{41}$$

where membership ($\in$) should be understood in the broad sense of encompassing all invariants. (Again we anticipate that this will be handled in precise terms later on in section 17.) Also note the following variant of (41),

$$\langle \forall\, a, b\ :\ a \in A\ \wedge\ b = f\ a :\ b \in B \rangle \tag{42}$$

which is granted by the $\forall$-one-point rule (175).

How does one handle ESC POs? The sheer complexity of such proofs in real-size problems calls for mechanical support and this can be essentially of three kinds: PO-generation, model-checking and theorem-proving.

Generating all proof obligations (POs) needed for checking a particular formal model is a mechanical process available from tool-sets such as eg. the VDMTools [17]. In practice, the number of generated POs is larger than expected because of the adoption of "rich types" such as sequences and finite mappings, which can be regarded as *simple* relations (30), as we shall see. Such types, in a sense, hide particularly common invariants which "turn up" at PO-level.

---

[9] This nuance will be explained in section 14.

The following situations can take place:

1. Independently of satisfying (42) or not, f is "semantically wrong" because it does not behave according to the requirements. This calls for manual tests, which may include running the model as a prototype, should an interpreter be available.
2. f survives all tests compiled in the previous step (including dynamic type checks) and yet testers are not aware that it does not satisfy (42). In this case, a model checker able to automatically generate counter-examples to (42) which could suggest how to improve f is welcome.
3. The model checker of the step just above finds no counter-examples. In this case a theorem prover is welcome to mechanically check (42).
4. Proof obligation (42) is too complex for the available theorem prover. In this situation, our ultimate hope is a pen-and-paper manual proof, or some kind of exercise able to decompose too complex POs into smaller sub-proofs.

The main purpose of this paper is to show the suitability of the PF-transform and relation calculus to carry out the pen-and-paper proofs (as exercises in the sense of [55]) mentioned in the last step. The idea is to regard such POs as "first class citizens" which are represented by arrows which, in turn, can be put together or decomposed in simpler ones using a suitable PO-calculus supported by the relational calculus.

8 PF-Transformed ESC

In [46] it is argued that the complexity of POs mentioned above is partly due to the pointwise notation itself, which does not scale up very well to complex models, leading to long, unreadable POs full of nested quantifications. Experience in PF-transforming such formulæ invariably leads to much shorter, sharp relation-level formulæ which (albeit more cryptic) convey the essence of the proof, which quite often has to do with particular relationships between data flows.

In this section we set ourselves the task of investigating PF-transformed ESC proof obligations. As we shall see, these include invariant preservation, satisfiability and Hoare triples. We begin with a very simple example: checking a function which doubles even numbers,

$$\begin{aligned} &twice : Even \to Even \\ &twice\ n \triangleq 2n \end{aligned}$$

where

$$\begin{aligned} Even &= I\!N_0 \\ \mathbf{inv}\ n &\triangleq \underbrace{\langle \exists\, k\ :\ k \in I\!N_0 : \ n = 2k \rangle}_{even\ n} \end{aligned} \tag{43}$$

Is $twice$ properly typed? To be so, the following instance of (42) telling that function $twice$ preserves even numbers

$$\langle \forall\, x, y\ :\ even\ x \wedge y = twice\ x :\ even\ y \rangle \tag{44}$$

should be discharged. According to our strategy, the first step consists in PF-transforming (44). We tackle the range of quantification (44) first,

$$
\begin{array}{ll}
& y = twice\ x\ \wedge\ even\ x \\
\Leftrightarrow & \quad \{\ \exists\text{-one-point (176)}\ \} \\
& \langle \exists\ z\ :\ z = x :\ y = twice\ z\ \wedge\ even\ z \rangle \\
\Leftrightarrow & \quad \{\ \exists\text{-trading (174) ; introduce coreflexive } \Phi_{even}\ \} \\
& \langle \exists\ z\ ::\ y = twice\ z\ \wedge\ \underbrace{z = x\ \wedge\ even\ z}_{z\ \Phi_{even}\ x} \rangle \\
\Leftrightarrow & \quad \{\ \text{composition (12)}\ \} \\
& y(twice \cdot \Phi_{even})x
\end{array}
$$

cf. diagram

$$
\begin{array}{ccc}
I\!N_0 & \xleftarrow{\Phi_{even}} & I\!N_0 \\
{\scriptstyle twice}\downarrow & & \\
I\!N_0 & &
\end{array}
$$

which expresses $twice$ pre-conditioned by $even$. Next, we proceed to the whole thing:

$$
\begin{array}{ll}
& \langle \forall\ x, y\ :\ y = twice\ x\ \wedge\ even\ x :\ even\ y \rangle \\
\Leftrightarrow & \quad \{\ \text{just above}\ \} \\
& \langle \forall\ x, y\ :\ y(twice \cdot \Phi_{even})x :\ even\ y \rangle \\
\Leftrightarrow & \quad \{\ \exists\text{-one-point (176)}\ \} \\
& \langle \forall\ x, y\ :\ y(twice \cdot \Phi_{even})x :\ \langle \exists\ z\ :\ z = y :\ even\ z \rangle \rangle \\
\Leftrightarrow & \quad \{\ \text{predicate calculus: } p\ \wedge\ \text{TRUE} = p\ \} \\
& \langle \forall\ x, y\ :\ y(twice \cdot \Phi_{even})x :\ \langle \exists\ z\ ::\ y = z\ \wedge\ even\ z\ \wedge\ \text{TRUE} \rangle \rangle \\
\Leftrightarrow & \quad \{\ \top \text{ is the topmost relation, cf. table 1}\ \} \\
& \langle \forall\ x, y\ :\ y(twice \cdot \Phi_{even})x :\ \langle \exists\ z\ ::\ y\ \Phi_{even}\ z\ \wedge\ z \top x \rangle \rangle \\
\Leftrightarrow & \quad \{\ \text{composition (12)}\ \} \\
& \langle \forall\ x, y\ :\ y(twice \cdot \Phi_{even})x :\ y(\Phi_{even} \cdot \top)x \rangle \\
\Leftrightarrow & \quad \{\ \text{go pointfree (13)}\ \} \\
& twice \cdot \Phi_{even}\ \subseteq\ \Phi_{even} \cdot \top
\end{array}
\qquad (45)
$$

Note that the two occurrences of unary predicate *even* in (44) are PF-transformed in two different but related ways: via coreflexive Φ_{even} on the lower side of (45) and via $\Phi_{even} \cdot \top$ on the upper side — a so-called (left) *condition*[10]. Coreflexives relate to

[10] For a detailed account of this duality see the *monotype-condition isomorphism* formalised in [20].

conditions in a number of ways, namely in what concerns pre/post restrictions:

$$R \cdot \Phi = R \cap \top \cdot \Phi \tag{46}$$

$$\Psi \cdot R = R \cap \Psi \cdot \top \tag{47}$$

This makes it possible to transform (45) even further:

$$\begin{array}{ll} & (45) \\ \Leftrightarrow & \{ \text{ (21), since } twice \cdot \Phi_{even} \subseteq twice \ \} \\ & twice \cdot \Phi_{even} \subseteq twice \cap \Phi_{even} \cdot \top \\ \Leftrightarrow & \{ \text{ (47) } \} \\ & twice \cdot \Phi_{even} \subseteq \Phi_{even} \cdot twice \\ \Leftrightarrow & \{ \text{ (38) } \} \\ & \Phi_{even} \xleftarrow{twice} \Phi_{even} \end{array} \tag{48}$$

cf. diagram

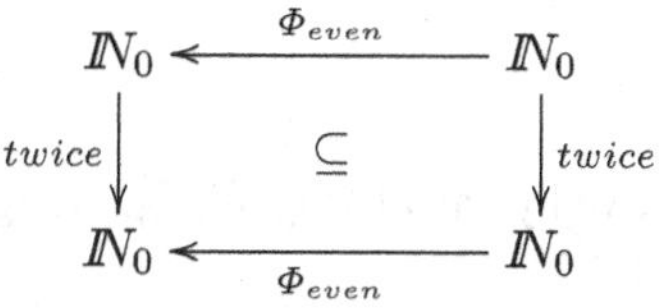

In retrospect, PF-statement (48) of proof obligation (44) is interesting from a number of viewpoints: notationally, it is of great economy; conceptually, it really purports the idea that ESC has to do with types, which are now regarded as predicates (encoded by coreflexives); last of not least, it is of great calculational value, as we shall soon see.

Let us generalize what we have obtained thus far:

Definition 1 (Predicative types of functions). *Let function* $B \xleftarrow{f} A$ *and predicates* $\mathbb{B} \xleftarrow{p} A$ *and* $\mathbb{B} \xleftarrow{q} B$ *be given. We say that* f *has* predicative type

$$\Phi_q \xleftarrow{f} \Phi_p \tag{49}$$

wherever

$$f \cdot \Phi_p \subseteq \Phi_q \cdot f \tag{50}$$

holds, cf. diagram

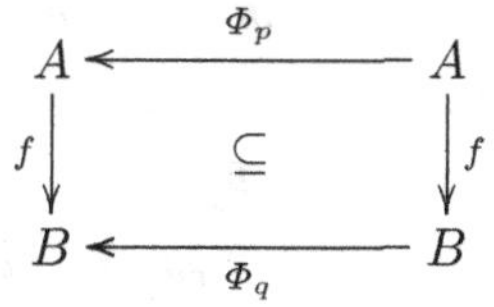

Condition (50) — which is equivalent to

$$f \cdot \Phi_p \subseteq \Phi_q \cdot \top \tag{51}$$

as we have seen above — is the PF-transform of ESC proof obligation $\langle \forall\ x\ :\ p\ x\ :\ q\ (f\ x) \rangle$ *stating that function* f *ensures property* q *on the output once property* p *is granted on the input.* □

Stating that a given function is of a particular predicative type is an assertion which needs to be checked. Predicative types obey to a number of interesting and useful properties which can be proved using the PF-calculus alone. Such properties, together with the relational calculus itself, make proof obligation discharge more structured and easier, as we shall soon see. Prior to this, we need to present a little more of the relational calculus itself.

9 More about the Relational Calculus

Coreflexives. Recall from section 3 that unary predicates PF-transform to fragments of id (coreflexives) as captured by the following universal property:

$$\Psi = \Phi_p \ \Leftrightarrow\ \langle \forall\ y, x\ ::\ y\, \Psi\, x \Leftrightarrow y = x\ \wedge\ p\, y \rangle \tag{52}$$

Via cancellation $\Psi := \Phi_p$, (52) yields

$$y\, \Phi_p\, x\ \Leftrightarrow\ y = x\ \wedge\ p\, y \tag{53}$$

A set S can also be PF-transformed into a coreflexive by calculating $\Phi_{(\in S)}$, cf. eg. the following graphic display of the transform of set $\{1, 2, 3, 4\}$:

$$\Phi_{(\in \{1,2,3,4\})} \quad =$$

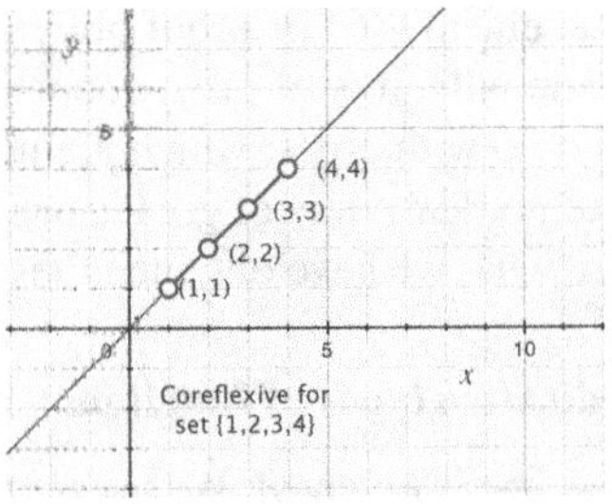

Thanks to the isomorphism between predicates and coreflexives implicit in (52), it is easy to show that predicate algebra can be expressed in terms of coreflexives alone [7]. In particular, given predicates p, q, we have

$$\Phi_{p\,\wedge\,q} = \Phi_p \cdot \Phi_q \tag{54}$$

$$\Phi_{p \vee q} = \Phi_p \cup \Phi_q \tag{55}$$

$$\Phi_{\neg p} = id - \Phi_p \tag{56}$$

$$\Phi_{false} = \bot \tag{57}$$

$$\Phi_{true} = id \tag{58}$$

where $false$ (resp. $true$) denote the everywhere FALSE (resp. everywhere TRUE) predicates and $R - S$ denotes relational difference (19).

Coreflexives are symmetric and transitive relations, that is,

$$\Phi^\circ = \Phi = \Phi \cdot \Phi \tag{59}$$

hold for Φ coreflexive. The fact that meet of coreflexives is composition

$$\Phi \cap \Psi = \Phi \cdot \Psi \tag{60}$$

is of great calculational advantage since it enables one to pipeline restrictions (or conditions) while taking advantage of the central role played by composition in the whole calculus.

Exercise 5. Given a function $B \xleftarrow{f} A$, show that $\mathsf{img}\, f$ is the coreflexive Φ_p of predicate $p\, b \triangleq \langle \exists\, a\ ::\ b = f\ a \rangle$. □

Domain and range. The coreflexive fragments of kernel and image are named *domain* (δ) and *range* (ρ)

$$\delta\, R \ \triangleq\ \mathsf{ker}\, R \cap id \tag{61}$$

$$\rho\, R \ \triangleq\ \mathsf{img}\, R \cap id \tag{62}$$

Therefore:

$$R \cdot \delta\, R \ =\ R \ =\ \rho\, R \cdot R \tag{63}$$

Clearly:

$$\delta\, R = \mathsf{ker}\, R \Leftrightarrow R \text{ is injective} \tag{64}$$

$$\rho\, R = \mathsf{img}\, R \Leftrightarrow R \text{ is simple} \tag{65}$$

$$\delta\, R = R = \rho\, R \Leftrightarrow R \text{ is coreflexive} \tag{66}$$

In particular, range and image of functions coincide.

From the definitions above we easily recover their pointwise equivalents. For instance, let us calculate $\rho\, twice$:

$$
\begin{array}{ll}
 & y(\rho\, twice)x \\
\Leftrightarrow & \quad \{\ (65)\ \} \\
 & y(twice \cdot twice^\circ)x \\
\Leftrightarrow & \quad \{\ \text{exercise 5 ; coreflexives}\ \} \\
 & y = x \ \wedge\ \langle \exists\, k\ ::\ y = twice\ k \rangle \\
\Leftrightarrow & \quad \{\ \text{definition of } twice\ \} \\
 & y = x \ \wedge\ \langle \exists\, k\ ::\ y = 2k \rangle \\
\Leftrightarrow & \quad \{\ (53)\ ;\ \text{definition of } even\ (43)\ \} \\
 & y\ \Phi_{even}\ x
\end{array}
$$

So, the range of $twice$ is the same relation as Φ_{even}. Taking advantage of this, we check predicative type assertion (48) of the previous section:

$$
\begin{array}{ll}
& \Phi_{even} \xleftarrow{twice} \Phi_{even} \\
\Leftrightarrow & \quad \{ \text{ (49,50) } \} \\
& twice \cdot \Phi_{even} \subseteq \Phi_{even} \cdot twice \\
\Leftrightarrow & \quad \{ \; \Phi_{even} = \rho\, twice \text{ (above) } \} \\
& twice \cdot \Phi_{even} \subseteq \rho\, twice \cdot twice \\
\Leftrightarrow & \quad \{ \text{ (63) } \} \\
& twice \cdot \Phi_{even} \subseteq twice \\
\Leftarrow & \quad \{ \text{ composition is monotonic } \} \\
& \Phi_{even} \subseteq id \\
\Leftrightarrow & \quad \{ \; \Phi_{even} \text{ is coreflexive } \} \\
& \text{TRUE}
\end{array}
$$

This first ESC/PF exercise gives an idea of the flavour of discharging proof obligations by calculation. The example is very simple and so the distance between this and the equivalent pointwise proof stemming directly from (44) is not much. Non-trivial examples to be given later in sections 13 and 18 will provide a better idea of the advantages of doing things in the pointfree style.

It should be noted that the closed formulæ given above (61,62) do not provide the best way to infer properties such as the above. It is much simpler to rely on universal properties which domain and range enjoy and which are (once again) Galois connections, as explained below.

Structuring the calculus. As anticipated in section 3, Galois connections provide a convenient way to structure the relational calculus in the sense that they offer (universal) properties which implicitly capture the meaning of the two relational combinators (termed *adjoints*) involved in each connection[11].

A paradigmatic example is that of capturing the meaning of functions: it can be shown that functions are *exactly* those relations h which obey the following Galois connection, for all other (suitably typed) relations R, S:

$$h \cdot R \subseteq S \Leftrightarrow R \subseteq h^\circ \cdot S \tag{67}$$

Taking converses, this is equivalent to [12]

$$R \cdot h^\circ \subseteq S \Leftrightarrow R \subseteq S \cdot h \tag{68}$$

Again we stress on the resemblance with school algebra: like number n in (20), function h in (67,68) can be shifted back and forth in relational expressions by "swapping sign" (which in the relational context means taking converses).

[11] This approach to the relational calculus was pioneered in the 1990s by the Mathematics of Program Construction (MPC) school, see eg. references [1,29,20,62,7].

[12] These Galois connections are often referred to as *shunting rules* [13].

The fact that *at most* and equality coincide in the case of functions

$$f \subseteq g \Leftrightarrow f = g \Leftrightarrow f \supseteq g \tag{69}$$

is among several other beneficial consequences of these rules (see eg. [13]).

Exercise 6. Use the shunting rules (67,68) to show that $\underline{c} \cdot R$ is always simple and $S \cdot \underline{c}^\circ$ is always injective, for all suitably typed R, S. □

Domain and range are characterized by Galois connections

$$\delta\, R \subseteq \Phi \Leftrightarrow R \subseteq \top \cdot \Phi \tag{70}$$

$$\rho\, R \subseteq \Phi \Leftrightarrow R \subseteq \Phi \cdot \top \tag{71}$$

where Φ ranges over coreflexives, from which a number of properties arise, namely:

$$\top \cdot \delta\, R = \top \cdot R \tag{72}$$

$$\rho\, R \cdot \top = R \cdot \top \tag{73}$$

$$\Phi \subseteq \Psi \Leftrightarrow \Phi \subseteq \top \cdot \Psi \tag{74}$$

$$\delta\, R \subseteq \delta\, S \Leftrightarrow R \subseteq \top \cdot S \tag{75}$$

$$\delta\,(R \cdot S) = \delta\,(\delta\, R \cdot S) \tag{76}$$

$$\rho\,(R \cdot S) = \rho\,(R \cdot \rho\, S) \tag{77}$$

In general, all such Galois connections instantiate the equivalence at the top of table 2. It should be mentioned that some rules in this table appear in the literature under different guises and usually not identified as GCs[13]. For a thorough presentation of the relational calculus in terms of GCs see [1,7]. There are *many* advantages in such an approach: further to the systematic tabulation of operators (of which table 2 is just a sample), GCs have a rich algebra of properties, namely:

- both adjoints f and g in a GC are monotonic;
- lower adjoint f commutes with join and upper-adjoint g commutes with meet;
- two cancellation laws hold, $R \subseteq g(f\ R)$ and $f(g\ S) \subseteq S$, respectively known as *left-cancellation* and *right-cancellation*.

In summary, all relational combinators involved in table 2 are monotonic. The ones in the f-column distribute over $\cup$, eg.

$$(R \cup S)^\circ = R^\circ \cup S^\circ \tag{78}$$

$$f \cdot (R \cup S) = f \cdot R \cup f \cdot S \tag{79}$$

and the ones in the g-column distribute over $\cap$, eg.:

$$(R \cap S)^\circ = R^\circ \cap S^\circ \tag{80}$$

$$(R \cap S) \cdot f = R \cdot f \cap S \cdot f \tag{81}$$

[13] For instance, *shunting* rule (67) is called *cancellation law* in [66].

Table 2. Tabulation of Galois connections in the relational calculus (sample). The general formula given on top is a logical equivalence universally quantified on S and R. It has a left part involving lower adjoint f and a right part involving upper adjoint g. These are expressed using sections of binary operators. So, each line in the table corresponds in fact to a *family* of adjoints indexed by the argument frozen in each section, eg. h in $(h\cdot)$, $(h^\circ\cdot)$ in the line marked *shunting rule*.

$$(f\ R) \subseteq S \Leftrightarrow R \subseteq (g\ S)$$

Description	f	g	**Comment**
converse	$(\_)^\circ$	$(\_)^\circ$	
shunting rule	$(h\cdot)$	$(h^\circ\cdot)$	h is a function
"converse" *shunting* rule	$(\cdot h^\circ)$	$(\cdot h)$	h is a function
difference	$(\_ - R)$	$(R \cup\ )$	
Left-division	$(R\cdot)$	$(R \setminus\ )$	read "R under ..."
Right-division	$(\cdot R)$	$(\ / R)$	read "... over R"
domain	δ	$(\top\cdot)$	left $\subseteq$ restricted to coreflexives
range	ρ	$(\cdot\top)$	left $\subseteq$ restricted to coreflexives

Simplicity. Simple relations (also known as partial functions) will be particularly relevant in the sequel because of their ubiquity in software modeling. In particular, they can be used to model data structures "embodying a functional dependency" such as eg. mappings from object identifiers to object attribute values [47,48].

In the same way simple relations generalize functions as shown in figure 1, *shunting* rules (67, 68) generalize to

$$S \cdot R \subseteq T \Leftrightarrow (\delta\, S) \cdot R \subseteq S^\circ \cdot T \tag{82}$$

$$R \cdot S^\circ \subseteq T \Leftrightarrow R \cdot \delta\, S \subseteq T \cdot S \tag{83}$$

for S simple. In the case of coreflexives (which are special cases of simple relations), rules (82,83) instantiate to

$$\Phi \cdot R \subseteq S \Leftrightarrow \Phi \cdot R \subseteq \Phi \cdot S \tag{84}$$

$$R \cdot \Phi \subseteq S \Leftrightarrow R \cdot \Phi \subseteq S \cdot \Phi \tag{85}$$

Harpoon arrows $B \xleftarrow{R} A$ or $A \xrightarrow{R} B$ in diagrams indicate that R is simple. Later on we will need to describe simple relations at pointwise level. The notation we shall adopt for this purpose is borrowed from VDM [32], where it is known as *mapping comprehension*. This notation exploits the applicative nature of a simple relation S by writing $b\ S\ a$ as

$$a \in dom\ S \wedge b = S\ a \tag{86}$$

where $\wedge$ should be understood non-strict on the right argument[14] and $dom\ S$ is the set-theoretic version of coreflexive $\delta\, S$, that is,

$$\delta\, S = \Phi_{(dom\ S)} \tag{87}$$

holds (cf. the isomorphism between sets and coreflexives). In this way, relation S itself can be written as $\{a \mapsto S\ a \mid a \in dom\ S\}$ and projection $f \cdot S \cdot g^{\circ}$ as

$$\{g\ a \mapsto f(S\ a) \mid a \in dom\ S\} \tag{88}$$

provided S satisfies functional dependency $g \rightarrow f$, to ensure simplicity (see exercise 8).

Exercise 7. Further to exercise 2 show that condition

$$M \cdot N^{\circ} \subseteq id \tag{89}$$

(which ensures that the union of two simple relations M and N is simple) converts to pointwise notation as follows,

$$\langle \forall\, a \ :\ a \in (dom\ M \cap dom\ N) :\ (M\ a) = (N\ a)\rangle$$

— a condition known as (map) *compatibility* in the VDM terminology [22]. □

Exercise 8. A relation S is said to satisfy functional dependency $g \rightarrow f$ wherever projection $f \cdot S \cdot g^{\circ}$ is simple, that is, iff

$$\mathsf{ker}\,(g \cdot S^{\circ}) \subseteq \mathsf{ker}\, f \tag{90}$$

holds [45].

1. Show that (90) trivially holds wherever g is injective and S is simple, for all (suitably typed) f.
2. Resort to (86), (90) and to the rules of both the PF-transform and the Eindhoven quantifier calculus (appendix A) to show that the healthiness condition (90) imposed on mapping comprehension (88) is equivalent to

$$\langle \forall\, a, b \ :\ a, b \in dom\ S \ \wedge\ (g\ a) = (g\ b) :\ f(S\ a) = f(S\ b)\rangle$$ □

10 Building Up the ESC/PF Calculus

What we have seen so far about the PF relational calculus is enough to start developing our own calculus of ESC predicative type assertions, stemming from definition 1. Let us see, for instance, what happens wherever the input predicate in (49) is a disjunction:

$$\begin{array}{ll} & \Phi_q \stackrel{f}{\longleftarrow} \Phi_{p_1} \cup \Phi_{p_2} \\ \Leftrightarrow & \quad \{\ (50)\ \} \\ & f \cdot (\Phi_{p_1} \cup \Phi_{p_2}) \subseteq \Phi_q \cdot f \end{array}$$

[14] VDM embodies a logic of partial functions (LPF) which takes this into account [32].

$\Leftrightarrow$ { distribution (79) }

$f \cdot \Phi_{p_1} \cup f \cdot \Phi_{p_2} \subseteq \Phi_q \cdot f$

$\Leftrightarrow$ { $\cup$-universal (22) }

$f \cdot \Phi_{p_1} \subseteq \Phi_q \cdot f \ \wedge \ f \cdot \Phi_{p_2} \subseteq \Phi_q \cdot f$

$\Leftrightarrow$ { (50) twice }

$\Phi_q \xleftarrow{\ f\ } \Phi_{p_1} \ \wedge \ \Phi_q \xleftarrow{\ f\ } \Phi_{p_2}$

Thus distributive law

$$\Phi_q \xleftarrow{\ f\ } \Phi_{p_1} \cup \Phi_{p_2} \ \Leftrightarrow \ \Phi_q \xleftarrow{\ f\ } \Phi_{p_1} \ \wedge \ \Phi_q \xleftarrow{\ f\ } \Phi_{p_2} \tag{91}$$

holds. The dual rule,

$$\Phi_{q_1} \cdot \Phi_{q_2} \xleftarrow{\ f\ } \Phi_p \ \Leftrightarrow \ \Phi_{q_1} \xleftarrow{\ f\ } \Phi_p \ \wedge \ \Phi_{q_2} \xleftarrow{\ f\ } \Phi_p \tag{92}$$

is calculated in the same way.

The fact that predicative arrows compose,

$$\Psi \xleftarrow{\ g \cdot h\ } \Phi \ \Leftarrow \ \Psi \xleftarrow{\ g\ } \Upsilon \ \wedge \ \Upsilon \xleftarrow{\ h\ } \Phi \tag{93}$$

follows straight from (49, 50), as does the obvious rule concerning identity

$$\Psi \xleftarrow{\ id\ } \Phi \ \Leftrightarrow \ \Phi \subseteq \Psi \tag{94}$$

whereby $\Phi \xleftarrow{\ id\ } \Phi$ always holds. Thus it makes sense to draw predicative diagrams such as, for instance,

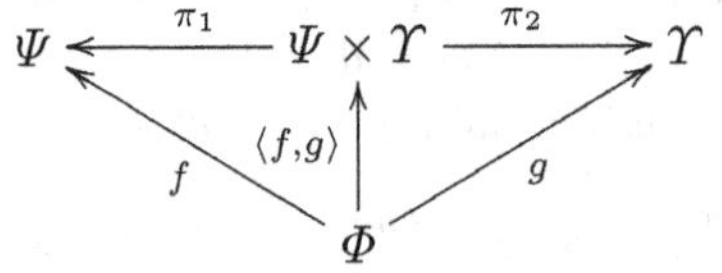

$$\begin{array}{ccc} \Psi & \xleftarrow{\ \pi_1\ } \Psi \times \Upsilon \xrightarrow{\ \pi_2\ } & \Upsilon \\ & \quad\scriptstyle{f} \ \ \uparrow \langle f,g \rangle \ \ \scriptstyle{g} & \\ & \Phi & \end{array} \tag{95}$$

where predicates (coreflexives) are promoted to objects (nodes in diagrams). In this case, the diagram explains the ESC behaviour of the combinator which pairs the results of two functions,

$$\langle f, g \rangle c \ \triangleq \ (f\,c, g\,c) \tag{96}$$

recall table 1. In the literature, this is often referred to as the *split* or *fork* combinator. The two projections π_1, π_2 are such that

$$\pi_1(a, b) = a \ \wedge \ \pi_2(a, b) = b \tag{97}$$

and $\Psi \times \Upsilon$ instantiates relational product $R \times S$ of table 1. The diagram expresses the two cancellation properties

$$\pi_1 \cdot \langle f, g \rangle = f \ \wedge \ \pi_2 \cdot \langle f, g \rangle = g \tag{98}$$

The question is: is diagram (95) properly typed?

We defer to section 11 the discussion about the arrows labelled with π_1, π_2 (which are instances of a more general result) and focus on arrow $\langle f, g\rangle$. We need to recall the universal property of relational *splits*

$$X \subseteq \langle R, S\rangle \;\Leftrightarrow\; \pi_1 \cdot X \subseteq R \wedge \pi_2 \cdot X \subseteq S \tag{99}$$

(another Galois connection, see exercise 9) and that $\times$-absorption holds [13]:

$$\langle R \cdot T, S \cdot U\rangle = (R \times S) \cdot \langle T, U\rangle \tag{100}$$

Then we reason:

$$\begin{array}{cl}
& \Psi \times \Upsilon \xleftarrow{\langle f,g\rangle} \Phi \\
\Leftrightarrow & \quad \{ \text{(49,50)} \} \\
& \langle f, g\rangle \cdot \Phi \subseteq (\Psi \times \Upsilon) \cdot \langle f, g\rangle \\
\Leftrightarrow & \quad \{ \text{absorption (100)} \} \\
& \langle f, g\rangle \cdot \Phi \subseteq \langle \Psi \cdot f, \Upsilon \cdot g\rangle \\
\Leftrightarrow & \quad \{ \text{universal property (99)} \} \\
& \pi_1 \cdot \langle f, g\rangle \cdot \Phi \subseteq \Psi \cdot f \;\wedge\; \pi_2 \cdot \langle f, g\rangle \cdot \Phi \subseteq \Upsilon \cdot g \\
\Leftrightarrow & \quad \{ \text{cancellations (98)} \} \\
& f \cdot \Phi \subseteq \Psi \cdot f \;\wedge\; g \cdot \Phi \subseteq \Upsilon \cdot g \\
\Leftrightarrow & \quad \{ \text{(49,50) twice} \} \\
& \Psi \xleftarrow{f} \Phi \;\wedge\; \Upsilon \xleftarrow{g} \Phi
\end{array}$$

In summary, we have calculated ESC/PF rule

$$\Psi \times \Upsilon \xleftarrow{\langle f,g\rangle} \Phi \;\Leftrightarrow\; \Psi \xleftarrow{f} \Phi \wedge \Upsilon \xleftarrow{g} \Phi \tag{101}$$

which justifies the existence of arrow $\langle f, g\rangle$ in diagram (95).

Exercise 9. Show that

$$\langle R, S\rangle = (\pi_1^\circ \cdot R) \cap (\pi_2^\circ \cdot S) \tag{102}$$

is the PF-transform of the clause given for this combinator in table 1. Furthermore infer (99) from (102) and universal property (21). □

Let us finally see how to handle conditional expressions of the form $if\ (c\ x)\ then\ (f\ x)$ $else\ (g\ x)$, which PF-transform into the following version of McCarthy's conditional combinator:

$$c \rightarrow f\ , g \;=\; f \cdot \Phi_c \cup g \cdot \Phi_{\neg c} \tag{103}$$

In this case, (51) offers a better standpoint for calculation than (50), as the reader may check in calculating the following rule for conditionals:

$$\Phi_q \xleftarrow{\;c\to f,g\;} \Phi_p \;\Leftrightarrow\; \Phi_q \xleftarrow{\;f\;} \Phi_p \cdot \Phi_c \;\wedge\; \Phi_q \xleftarrow{\;g\;} \Phi_p \cdot \Phi_{\neg c} \tag{104}$$

Further ESC/PF rules can calculated on the same basis, either elaborating on the predicate structure or on the combinator structure. However, all the cases above involve functions only and the semantics of computations are, in general, relations. So our strategy is to generalize definition 1 to relations and develop the calculus on such a generic basis. Before this, let us present a generic result which still has to do with functions and is of great interest to type checking.

11 ESC "for free"

In his well-known paper *Theorems for free!* [64], Philip Wadler writes:

> *From the type of a polymorphic function we can derive a theorem that it satisfies. (...) How useful are the theorems so generated? Only time and experience will tell.*

The generosity of this quotation stems from John Reynolds *abstraction theorem* on parametric polymorphism [54] of which several applications have been found in the meantime, namely in program transformation [59], abstract interpretation and safety analysis [3], relation calculus [49], program correctness [63], etc.[15]

In this section we identify a class of ESC/PF rules which are corollaries of this theorem and which, as such, do not need to be discharged. We follow the pointfree styled presentation of this theorem given in [3], which is remarkably elegant: let f be a polymorphic *function* $f : t$, whose type t can be written according to the following <<grammar>> of types:

$t := t' \leftarrow t''$

$t := \mathsf{F}(t_1, \ldots, t_n)$ for n-ary parametric type F

$t := v$ for v a type variable (= polymorphism <<dimension>>)

Let V be the set of type variables involved in type t, $\{R_v\}_{v \in V}$ be a V-indexed family of relations (f_v in case all such R_v are functions) and R_t be a relation defined inductively as follows:

$$R_{t:=t' \leftarrow t''} = R_{t'} \leftarrow R_{t''} \tag{105}$$

$$R_{t:=\mathsf{F}(t_1,\ldots,t_n)} = \mathsf{F}(R_{t_1}, \ldots, R_{t_n}) \tag{106}$$

$$R_{t:=v} = R_v \tag{107}$$

where $R_{t'} \leftarrow R_{t''}$ is defined by (37) and symbol F is overloaded in (106): it denotes a parametric type on the left hand side and the n-ary *relator* [35,8] which captures its semantics on the right hand side. (More details to follow.)

[15] For the automatic generation of free theorems (in Haskell syntax) see Janis Voigtlaender's home page: `http://linux.tcs.inf.tu-dresden.de/~voigt/ft`

The *free theorem of type* t then reads as follows: *given any function* $f : t$ *and* V *as above,* $f\ R_t\ f$ *holds for any relational instantiation of type variables in* V. Note that this theorem is a result about t and holds for *any* polymorphic function of type t *independently* of its actual definition[16].

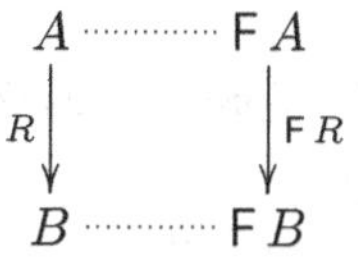

Before proceeding to the application of this theorem, we need to explain the meaning of F in (106). Technically, the parametricity of F is captured by regarding it as a *relator* [8], a concept which extends *functors* to relations: $\mathsf{F}\,R$ is a relation from $\mathsf{F}\,A$ to $\mathsf{F}\,B$ wherever R is a relation from A to B (see diagram aside). By definition, relators are monotonic

$$R \subseteq S \Rightarrow \mathsf{F}\,R \subseteq \mathsf{F}\,S \tag{108}$$

and commute with composition, converse and the identity:

$$\mathsf{F}\,(R \cdot S) = (\mathsf{F}\,R) \cdot (\mathsf{F}\,S) \tag{109}$$

$$\mathsf{F}\,(R^{\circ}) = (\mathsf{F}\,R)^{\circ} \tag{110}$$

$$\mathsf{F}\,id = id \tag{111}$$

The most simple relators are the *identity* relator Id, which is such that $\mathsf{Id}\ A = A$ and $\mathsf{Id}\ R = R$, and the *constant* relator K which, for a particular concrete data type K, is such that $\mathsf{K}\ A = K$ and $\mathsf{K}\ R = id_K$.

Relators can also be multi-parametric. Two well-known examples of binary relators are product and sum,

$$R \times S = \langle R \cdot \pi_1, S \cdot \pi_2 \rangle \tag{112}$$

$$R + S = [i_1 \cdot R\,, i_2 \cdot S] \tag{113}$$

where π_1, π_2 are the projections of a Cartesian product (97), i_1, i_2 are the injections of a disjoint union, and the *split/either* relational combinators are defined by (102) and

$$[R\,, S] = (R \cdot i_1^{\circ}) \cup (S \cdot i_2^{\circ}) \tag{114}$$

respectively. By putting product, sum, identity and constant relators together with fixpoint definitions one is able to specify a large class of parametric structures — referred to as *polynomial* — such as those implementable in Haskell, for instance.

Let us see how the free theorem of projections π_1 and π_2 justifies (for free) arrows $\Psi \xleftarrow{\pi_1} \Psi \times \Upsilon$ and $\Psi \times \Upsilon \xrightarrow{\pi_2} \Upsilon$ in diagram (95). The polymorphic type of π_1 being $t = a \leftarrow a \times b$, one has $R_t = R_a \leftarrow R_a \times R_b$. We reason:

$$\pi_1 (R_t) \pi_1$$

$\Leftrightarrow$ { abbreviating $R_a, R_b := R, S$ }

$$\pi_1 (R \leftarrow R \times S) \pi_1$$

$\Leftrightarrow$ { (37) }

[16] See [3] for comprehensive evidence on the power of this theorem when combined with Galois connections.

$$
\begin{array}{ll}
& \pi_1 \cdot (R \times S) \subseteq R \cdot \pi_1 \\
\Leftrightarrow & \{ \ (38) \ \} \\
& R \xleftarrow{\pi_1} (R \times S)
\end{array}
$$

Thus, $R \xleftarrow{\pi_1} R \times S$ holds for *all* (suitably typed) R, S, thus covering coreflexives Ψ and Υ as special cases. (The calculation of $R \times S \xrightarrow{\pi_2} S$ is identical.)

The free theorem of a polymorphic type conveys the idea that types too "are relations". Its wide scope is better appreciated once dealing with higher-order combinators. Let us see the case of functional composition $(\cdot)$, which is of type $t = (c \leftarrow a) \leftarrow (b \leftarrow a) \leftarrow (c \leftarrow b)$:

$$
\begin{array}{ll}
& (\cdot) R_t (\cdot) \\
\Leftrightarrow & \{ \ (109) \text{ to } (111) \ \} \\
& (\cdot)((R_c \leftarrow R_a) \leftarrow (R_b \leftarrow R_a) \leftarrow (R_c \leftarrow R_b))(\cdot) \\
\Leftrightarrow & \{ \ \text{introducing abbreviations such as in the previous calculation} \ \} \\
& (\cdot)((U \leftarrow R) \leftarrow (S \leftarrow R) \leftarrow (U \leftarrow S))(\cdot) \\
\Leftrightarrow & \{ \ (37) \ \} \\
& (\cdot) \cdot (U \leftarrow S) \subseteq ((U \leftarrow R) \leftarrow (S \leftarrow R)) \cdot (\cdot) \\
\Leftrightarrow & \{ \ (67) \ \} \\
& (U \leftarrow S) \subseteq (\cdot)^\circ \cdot ((U \leftarrow R) \leftarrow (S \leftarrow R)) \cdot (\cdot) \\
\Leftrightarrow & \{ \ (13) \text{ assuming } \forall\text{-quantification implicit} ; (27) \ \} \\
& f(U \leftarrow S)g \Rightarrow (f\cdot)((U \leftarrow R) \leftarrow (S \leftarrow R))(g\cdot) \\
\Leftrightarrow & \{ \ (37) \text{ twice} \ \} \\
& f \cdot S \subseteq U \cdot g \Rightarrow (f\cdot) \cdot (S \leftarrow R) \subseteq (U \leftarrow R) \cdot (g\cdot) \\
\Leftrightarrow & \{ \ (67) \text{ again} \ \} \\
& f \cdot S \subseteq U \cdot g \Rightarrow (S \leftarrow R) \subseteq (f\cdot)^\circ \cdot (U \leftarrow R) \cdot (g\cdot) \\
\Leftrightarrow & \{ \ (13) ; (27) \text{ again} \ \} \\
& f \cdot S \subseteq U \cdot g \Rightarrow h(S \leftarrow R)j \Rightarrow (f \cdot h)(U \leftarrow R)(g \cdot j) \\
\Leftrightarrow & \{ \ (37) \ \} \\
& f \cdot S \subseteq U \cdot g \ \wedge \ h \cdot R \subseteq S \cdot j \Rightarrow f \cdot h \cdot R \subseteq U \cdot g \cdot j
\end{array}
$$

Substituting $f, j, R, S, U := g, h, \Phi, \Upsilon, \Psi$ we obtain

$$
g \cdot \Upsilon \subseteq \Psi \cdot g \ \wedge \ h \cdot \Phi \subseteq \Upsilon \cdot h \ \Rightarrow \ g \cdot h \cdot \Phi \subseteq \Psi \cdot g \cdot h
$$

which is nothing but composition rule (93) already presented. So, (93) is an example of "ESC for free", as is the $\Rightarrow$ part of equivalence (101)[17].

Reference [12] elaborates on these corollaries of the free theorem of functional combinators in building a category Pred of "predicates as objects" proposed as a suitable universe for describing coalgebraic systems subject to invariants. Pred's objects are predicates, represented by coreflexives. An arrow $\Psi \xleftarrow{f} \Phi$ in Pred means a function which ensures property Ψ on its output whenever property Φ holds on its input. Arrows in Pred can therefore be seen as ESC proof-obligations concerning the functions involved.

Exercise 10. From the free theorem of $1 \xleftarrow{!} A$ and fact $\mathsf{ker}\,! = \top$ infer

$$f \cdot R \subseteq \top \cdot S \Leftrightarrow R \subseteq \top \cdot S \tag{115}$$

□

12 Calculating Pre-conditions for ESC

Wherever a function f does not ensure preservation of a given invariant inv, that is, $\Phi_{inv} \xleftarrow{f} \Phi_{inv}$ does not hold, there is always a pre-condition pre which enforces this at the cost of *partializing* f. In the limit, pre is the everywhere false predicate. Programmers often become aware of the need for such pre-conditions at runtime, in the testing phase. One can do better and find it much earlier, at specification (modeling) time, when trying to discharge the standard proof obligation

$$\langle \forall\, a \;:\; inv\ a :\ inv(f\ a) \rangle \tag{116}$$

which then extends to

$$\langle \forall\, a \;:\; inv\ a \wedge pre\ a :\ inv(f\ a) \rangle \tag{117}$$

Bound to *invent pre*, one will hope to guess the *weakest* such pre-condition. Otherwise, future use of f will be spuriously constrained. However, how can one be sure of having hit such weakest pre-condition?

As it will be explained below, predicate $inv(f\ a)$ in (117) is itself the weakest pre-condition for inv to hold upon execution of f. In our ESC/PF approach we will proceed as follows: we take the PF-transform of $inv(f\ a)$ — at data level — as starting point and attempt to rewrite it into the conjunction of predicate $inv\ a$ (or weaker) and possibly "something else" — the *calculated* pre-condition pre. So we strengthen (117) to equivalence

$$inv\ a \wedge pre\ a \Leftrightarrow inv(f\ a) \tag{118}$$

thus meaning that pre will be not only sufficient but also necessary for inv to be maintained by f. This method works provided all calculation steps are equivalences. Let us start by detailing this strategy.

---

[17] See eg. [49] for the derivation of the free theorem of the functional *split* combinator.

Weakest pre-conditions. Back to definition 1, let us transform (49) according to the PF-calculus studied so far:

$$\Phi_q \xleftarrow{f} \Phi_p$$

$$\Leftrightarrow \quad \{ (51) \}$$

$$f \cdot \Phi_p \subseteq \Phi_q \cdot \top$$

$$\Leftrightarrow \quad \{ (71) \}$$

$$\rho(f \cdot \Phi_p) \subseteq \Phi_q$$

On the other hand,

$$f \cdot \Phi_p \subseteq \Phi_q \cdot \top$$

$$\Leftrightarrow \quad \{ (67) \}$$

$$\Phi_p \subseteq f^\circ \cdot \Phi_q \cdot \top$$

Putting everything together, we obtain GC

$$\rho(f \cdot \Phi_p) \subseteq \Phi_q \;\Leftrightarrow\; \Phi_p \subseteq f^\circ \cdot \Phi_q \cdot \top \tag{119}$$

which is the expected composition of GCs (71) and (67). The left hand side of (119) tells that Φ_p is *sufficient* as a pre-condition for f to ensure Φ_q on the output. Its right hand side tells that $f^\circ \cdot \Phi_q \cdot \top$ is the largest (weakest) such condition[18]. In other words, $f^\circ \cdot \Phi_q \cdot \top$ is *necessary* for q to hold on f's output.

Weakest pre-conditions have been studied extensively in the literature, both in the pointwise and pointfree style [19,6]. As we shall soon see, they have a calculus of their own which is closely related to that of predicative types. This connection between the two calculi will be given in section 15, where it will be presented in its full generality, that is, concerning relations in general instead of functions.

Let us, for the moment, refrain from going into such foundational work and see two examples of ESC ensured by weakest pre-condition PF-calculation.

13 ESC/PF Calculus at Work — Case Study 1

Recalling the mobile phone case study of section 2, we want to ensure that $store$ maintains invariant $inv = noDuplicates \wedge leq10$, that is, to check $\Phi_{inv} \xleftarrow{store} \Phi_{inv}$. Thanks to ESC/PF rule (92), we know we can split this into $\Phi_{noDuplicates} \xleftarrow{store} \Phi_{inv} \;\wedge\; \Phi_{leq10} \xleftarrow{store} \Phi_{inv}$. We address the first of these arrows in this section.

Thanks to the pipelined structure of $store$ (7), we can split the problem in two. First we address $\Phi_{noDuplicates} \xleftarrow{(c:)} \Phi_{inv}$ and then we promote this result to $store$.

When compared to the definition of injective function (31), the pointwise definition of $noDuplicates$ (4) is suggestive of what needs to be done towards a calculational,

[18] Back to points, this is predicate $\langle \lambda\, x \;::\; q(f\ x) \rangle$.

PF-argument: a list has no duplicates if and only if, regarded as a (partial) function from indices to elements, it is injective. Thus we can represent a list l of elements in C by a *simple* relation in $I\!N \rightharpoonup C$ telling which elements take which positions in list, and define

$$noDuplicates\ L \ \triangleq\ L^\circ \cdot L \subseteq id \tag{120}$$

In this context, appending c at the front of list L becomes relational operator

$$c : L \ \triangleq\ \underline{c} \cdot \underline{1}^\circ \cup L \cdot succ^\circ \tag{121}$$

where $succ\ n \triangleq n+1$ is the successor function in $I\!N_0$. (Mind that L indices exclude 0.) Back to points and using mapping notation for simple relations (88), the body of (121) becomes the expected $\{1 \mapsto c\} \cup \{i+1 \mapsto (L\ i) \mid i \leftarrow dom\ L\}$.

13.1 ESC Calculations for $(c\ :)$

First of all, we need to show that $(c\ :)$ preserves simplicity:

$c : L$ is simple

$\Leftrightarrow$ { (121) followed by (33) }

$L \cdot succ^\circ$ is simple $\wedge$ $\underline{c} \cdot \underline{1}^\circ$ is simple $\wedge$ $L \cdot succ^\circ \cdot \underline{1} \cdot \underline{c}^\circ \subseteq id$

$\Leftrightarrow$ { exercise 6; $succ^\circ \cdot \underline{1} = \underline{0}$ }

$L \cdot succ^\circ$ is simple $\wedge$ $L \cdot \underline{0} \cdot \underline{c}^\circ \subseteq id$

$\Leftrightarrow$ { $succ$ is an injection, thus $succ^\circ \cdot succ = id$ }

L is simple $\wedge$ $L \cdot \underline{0} \cdot \underline{c}^\circ \subseteq id$

$\Leftrightarrow$ { 0 is not in the domain of L }

L is simple $\wedge$ $\bot \cdot \underline{c}^\circ \subseteq id$

$\Leftrightarrow$ { $\bot$ is at most anything }

L is simple

Since all steps in the calculation are equivalences, L being simple is the *weakest* pre-condition for $c : L$ being simple.

Next we calculate with $noDuplicates(c : L)$ aiming at splitting this into invariant $noDuplicates\ L$ plus "something else" — the calculated weakest pre-condition for $noDuplicates$ preservation:

$noDuplicates(c : L)$

$\Leftrightarrow$ { (121, 120) }

$\underline{c} \cdot \underline{1}^\circ \cup L \cdot succ^\circ$ is injective

$\Leftrightarrow$ { (32) }

$\underline{c} \cdot \underline{1}^\circ$ is injective $\wedge$ $L \cdot succ^\circ$ is injective $\wedge$ $(\underline{c} \cdot \underline{1}^\circ)^\circ \cdot L \cdot succ^\circ \subseteq id$

$$\Leftrightarrow \quad \{ \text{ exercise 6; definition of injective ; shunting (67,68) } \}$$

$$succ \cdot L^\circ \cdot L \cdot succ^\circ \subseteq id \wedge \underline{c}^\circ \cdot L \subseteq \underline{1}^\circ \cdot succ$$

$$\Leftrightarrow \quad \{ \text{ shunting again (67,68) } \}$$

$$L^\circ \cdot L \subseteq succ^\circ \cdot succ \wedge \underline{c}^\circ \cdot L \subseteq \underline{1}^\circ \cdot succ$$

$$\Leftrightarrow \quad \{ \ker succ = id \}$$

$$L^\circ \cdot L \subseteq id \wedge \underline{c}^\circ \cdot L \subseteq \underline{1}^\circ \cdot succ$$

$$\Leftrightarrow \quad \{ \text{ definition } \}$$

$$L \text{ is injective } \wedge \underline{c}^\circ \cdot L \subseteq \underline{1}^\circ \cdot succ \tag{122}$$

In summary, we have calculated:

$$c : L \text{ has no duplicates} \Leftrightarrow \underbrace{L \text{ is injective}}_{\text{no duplicates in } L} \wedge \underbrace{\underline{c}^\circ \cdot L \subseteq \underline{1}^\circ \cdot succ}_{wp} \tag{123}$$

We finish the exercise by calculating the pointwise-expansion of wp:

$$\underline{c}^\circ \cdot L \subseteq \underline{1}^\circ \cdot succ$$

$$\Leftrightarrow \quad \{ \text{ go pointwise: (27) twice } \}$$

$$\langle \forall\, n \;:\; c\, L\, n :\; 1 = 1 + n \rangle$$

$$\Leftrightarrow \quad \{ \text{ (86) } \}$$

$$\langle \forall\, n \;:\; n \in dom\ L \ \wedge\ c = L\, n :\; 1 = 1 + n \rangle$$

$$\Leftrightarrow \quad \{ \ 1 = 1 + n \text{ always false } (n \notin dom\ L)\ ; \forall\text{-trading (173) } \}$$

$$\langle \forall\, n \;:\; n \in dom\ L :\; c = L\, n \Rightarrow \text{FALSE} \rangle$$

$$\Leftrightarrow \quad \{ \text{ predicate calculus } \}$$

$$\langle \forall\, n \;:\; n \in dom\ L :\; c \neq L\, n \rangle$$

We obtain the expected pre-condition preventing c from being in the list already. In summary:

$$\Phi_{noDuplicates} \xleftarrow{(c:)} \Phi_{noDuplicates} \wedge wp\ c$$

holds, for $wp\ c\ L \triangleq \langle \forall\, n \;:\; n \in dom\ L :\; c \neq L\, n \rangle$.

13.2 ESC Calculation for $(c\ :) \cdot filter(c\ \neq)$

Next we address arrow $\Phi_{noDuplicates} \xleftarrow{store} \Phi_{inv}$. Note that, looking at (7), it is sufficient to show that $(c\ :) \cdot filter(c\ \neq)$ preserves $noDuplicates$, since $take\ n\ L$ is at most L, for all n, and *smaller than injective is injective* (exercise 1). Also note that, defined over PF-transformed lists, $filter$ becomes

$$filter\ p\ L \;\triangleq\; \Phi_p \cdot L \tag{124}$$

Thus

$$filter(c \neq)L = (\neg\rho\,\underline{c}) \cdot L \tag{125}$$

where the negated range operator $(\neg\rho)$ is defined by $\neg\rho\,R \triangleq id - \rho\,R$ and satisfies property

$$\Phi \subseteq \neg\rho\,R \Leftrightarrow \Phi \cdot R \subseteq \bot \tag{126}$$

That filtering preserves simplicity follows immediately from exercise 1 (*smaller than simple is simple*). Concerning the injectivity of $c : (filter(c \neq)L)$, we reason:

$$
\begin{array}{ll}
& c : (filter(c \neq)L) \text{ is injective} \\
\Leftrightarrow & \quad \{ \ (123)\,;(125) \ \} \\
& (\neg\rho\,\underline{c}) \cdot L \text{ is injective } \wedge\ \underline{c}^{\circ} \cdot (\neg\rho\,\underline{c}) \cdot L \subseteq \underline{1}^{\circ} \cdot succ \\
\Leftrightarrow & \quad \{ \ \text{converses} \ \} \\
& (\neg\rho\,\underline{c}) \cdot L \text{ is injective } \wedge\ L^{\circ} \cdot (\neg\rho\,\underline{c}) \cdot \underline{c} \subseteq succ^{\circ} \cdot \underline{1} \\
\Leftrightarrow & \quad \{ \ (\neg\rho\,\underline{c}) \cdot \underline{c} = \bot \text{ by left-cancellation of (126)} \ \} \\
& (\neg\rho\,\underline{c}) \cdot L \text{ is injective } \wedge\ L^{\circ} \cdot \bot \subseteq succ^{\circ} \cdot \underline{1} \\
\Leftrightarrow & \quad \{ \ \bot \text{ is below anything} \ \} \\
& (\neg\rho\,\underline{c}) \cdot L \text{ is injective}
\end{array}
$$

In this case, the calculated (weakest) pre-condition is even weaker than the invariant to maintain, since L injective implies $(\neg\rho\,\underline{c}) \cdot L$ injective. (*Smaller than injective is injective*, recall exercise 1 once again.) In summary, we have checked:

$$\Phi_{noDuplicates} \xleftarrow{(c:)\cdot filter(c\neq)} \Phi_{noDuplicates}$$

In retrospect, note that not having PF-transformed lists into simple relations would lead to defining $noDuplicates$ inductively on lists, in turn leading to an inductive proof. The PF-transform has, in a sense, "converted induction into deduction" (calculation).

Exercise 11. Show that (126) stems from Galois connection [1]

$$\Phi \subseteq \neg\delta\,R \Leftrightarrow R \subseteq \bot/\Phi \tag{127}$$

(among others) where $\neg\delta\,R = id - \delta\,R$. □

14 From Functional to Relational ESC

Computer programs have, in general, a relational semantics, as they can be partial (eg. non-terminating) and non-deterministic. What is the impact of moving from function $A \xrightarrow{f} B$ to relation $A \xrightarrow{R} B$ in definition 1? We reason:

$$R \cdot \Phi_p \subseteq \Phi_q \cdot R$$

$$
\begin{array}{ll}
\Leftrightarrow & \{\ (47, 21)\ \} \\
& R \cdot \Phi_p \subseteq \Phi_q \cdot \top \\
\Leftrightarrow & \{\ (23)\ \} \\
& \Phi_p \subseteq R \setminus (\Phi_q \cdot \top) \\
\Leftrightarrow & \{\ (13)\ ;\ (53)\ \} \\
& \langle \forall\, a\ :\ p\,a :\ a(R \setminus (\Phi_q \cdot \top))a \rangle \\
\Leftrightarrow & \{\ \text{table 1}\ \} \\
& \langle \forall\, a\ :\ p\,a :\ \langle \forall\, b\ :\ bRa :\ b(\Phi_q \cdot \top)a \rangle\rangle \\
\Leftrightarrow & \{\ (53)\ ;\ \text{table 1}\ \} \\
& \langle \forall\, a\ :\ p\,a :\ \langle \forall\, b\ :\ bRa :\ q\,b \rangle\rangle
\end{array}
$$

This means that, for all inputs to R satisfying p, all outputs (if any) will satisfy q[19]. So p is sufficient for ensuring q on the output. What is the weakest such p? It is easy to repeat the reasoning which lead to (119), this time for relation R instead of function f, and for GC (23) instead of (67):

$$
\rho\,(R \cdot \Phi_p) \subseteq \Phi_q \Leftrightarrow \Phi_p \subseteq \underbrace{R \setminus (\Phi_q \cdot \top)}_{R \,\blacklozenge\, \Phi_q} \tag{128}
$$

Notation $R \blacklozenge \Phi$ for the weakest (liberal) pre-conditions is taken from [6]. Adjective *liberal* stresses the fact that the condition encompasses all input values for which R is undefined. Thus the definition which follows:

Definition 2 (Relational predicative types). *Let* $B \xleftarrow{R} A$ *be a relation and* $\mathbb{B} \xleftarrow{p} A$ *and* $\mathbb{B} \xleftarrow{q} B$ *be predicates. We shall say that* R *has* predicative type

$$
\Phi_q \xleftarrow{R} \Phi_p \tag{129}
$$

wherever

$$
R \cdot \Phi_p \subseteq \Phi_q \cdot R \tag{130}
$$

holds. The following are equivalent ways of stating (130):

$$
\begin{array}{rcl}
\Phi_q \xleftarrow{R} \Phi_p & \Leftrightarrow & R \cdot \Phi_p \subseteq \Phi_q \cdot \top \qquad (131) \\
& \Leftrightarrow & \Phi_p \subseteq R \,\blacklozenge\, \Phi_q \qquad (132)
\end{array}
$$

□

Relationship with Hoare Logic. Suppose $R = [\![P]\!]$ is the semantics of a given program P running over state space S, that is, $S \xrightarrow{R=[\![P]\!]} S$. Writing $s \overset{P}{\mapsto} s'$ for $s' R s$, meaning that

[19] This will be related to the concept of *satisfiability* [32] in the sequel.

program P *may* reach state s' once executing over starting state s, fact $\Phi_q \xleftarrow{[\![P]\!]} \Phi_p$ PF-transforms to

$$\langle \forall\, s \,:\, p\, s :\, \langle \forall\, s' \,:\, s \overset{P}{\mapsto} s' :\, q\, s' \rangle \rangle \tag{133}$$

which is nothing but the meaning of Hoare triple

$$\{p\}P\{q\} \tag{134}$$

Hoare triples are thus special cases of predicative types, as suggested in the introduction by writing (2). In summary, "declaration"

$$\Psi \xleftarrow{R} \Phi \tag{135}$$

can be regarded as the type assertion that, if fed with values (or starting on states) "of type Φ" computation R yields results (or moves to states) "of type Ψ" (if it terminates). So ESC proof obligations and Hoare triples are one and the same device: a way to type computations, be them specified as (always terminating, deterministic) functions or encoded into (possibly non-terminating, non-deterministic) programs. This means that all relational ESC/PF calculation rules to follow apply to Hoare triples.

Satisfiability. Definition 2 is related to another notion of predicative typing known as *satisfiability* [32]: given R, p and q as in definition 2, R is said to be *satisfiable* with respect to (p, q) iff

$$\langle \forall\, a \,:\, p\, a :\, \langle \exists\, b \,:\, q\, b :\, bRa \rangle \rangle$$

holds, that is

$$\Phi_p \subseteq R^\circ \cdot \Phi_q \cdot R \tag{136}$$

in PF-notation. (As expected, shifting R from the left to the right hand side of (130) turns universal into existential quantification.) Usually, p and q are the invariants associated to (respectively) the input and output types of operations whose semantics are captured by pre/post-condition pairs "à la VDM", that is, post-conditions relating outputs to inputs, of pattern

$$R : (b : B) \leftarrow (a : A)$$
$$\textbf{pre} \ \ldots a \ldots$$
$$\textbf{post} \ \ldots b \ldots a \ldots$$

In this case, the satisfiability condition becomes, using a VDM-like syntax

$$\langle \forall\, a \,:\, a \in A :\, \text{pre-}R\, a \Rightarrow \langle \exists\, b \,:\, b \in B :\, \text{post-}R(b, a) \rangle \rangle \tag{137}$$

Clearly, (137) has to do with a particular semantic interpretation of R's non-determinism: *vagueness*. For instance, post-condition $b = 2a \vee b = a + 1$ for $A, B := Even$ (43) specifies an operation which is satisfiable but fails to maintain inv-$Even$.

The relationship between invariant preservation (130) and satisfiability (136) depends on the kind of relation R involved. For R simple, satisfiability is stronger than invariant preservation. For R entire, the former is weaker than the latter (see exercise 12 below). Therefore, both notions coincide in the case of functions.

Exercise 12. Show that

- for R entire, (130) entails (136) and, for R simple, (136) entails (130). Hint: resort to the shunting rules of simple relations.
- (136) can be written alternatively as

$$\Phi_p \subseteq \delta\,(\Phi_q \cdot R) \tag{138}$$

and therefore as

$$\Phi_p \subseteq \top \cdot \Phi_q \cdot R \tag{139}$$

Hint: resort to the properties of δ and of coreflexive relations in general (section 9).

□

15 Relational ESC/PF Calculus

We are now in position to list rules of the relational ESC/PF calculus stemming from definition 2. Some of these rules actually extend those already given in section 10. In general, they help in breaking complexity of ESC/PF obligations. Note that most rules are *equivalences*, not just implications, as they tend to be written in eg. Hoare logic. So they contribute to ensuring ESC/PF predicative types *by construction*.

Relational ESC/PF rules. We begin by presenting and justifying the rule which extends relators to predicative types:

- **Relators**: rule

$$\mathsf{F}\,\Psi \xleftarrow{\mathsf{F}\,R} \mathsf{F}\,\Phi \;\Leftarrow\; \Psi \xleftarrow{R} \Phi \tag{140}$$

holds for every relator F.

This is easy to justify:

$$
\begin{array}{cl}
 & \mathsf{F}\,\Psi \xleftarrow{\mathsf{F}\,R} \mathsf{F}\,\Phi \\
\Leftrightarrow & \{\ (130)\ \} \\
 & \mathsf{F}\,R \cdot \mathsf{F}\,\Phi \subseteq \mathsf{F}\,\Psi \cdot \mathsf{F}\,R \\
\Leftrightarrow & \{\ (109)\ \} \\
 & \mathsf{F}(R \cdot \Phi) \subseteq \mathsf{F}(\Psi \cdot R) \\
\Leftarrow & \{\ (108)\ \} \\
 & R \cdot \Phi \subseteq \Psi \cdot R \\
\Leftrightarrow & \{\ (130)\ \} \\
 & \Psi \xleftarrow{R} \Phi
\end{array}
$$

Further to (92,94,104) and (140), the following rules hold:

- **Trivia**:

$$id \xleftarrow{R} \Phi \;\Leftrightarrow\; \text{TRUE} \;\Leftrightarrow\; \Phi \xleftarrow{R} \bot \tag{141}$$

- **Trading**:

$$\Upsilon \xleftarrow{R} \Phi \cdot \Psi \;\Leftrightarrow\; \Upsilon \xleftarrow{R \cdot \Phi} \Psi \tag{142}$$

  As we shall see soon, (142) is useful for trading coreflexives between the input type of a given ESC arrow and the relation typed by the arrow.
- **Composition (Fusion)**:

$$\Psi \xleftarrow{R \cdot S} \Phi \;\Leftarrow\; \Psi \xleftarrow{R} \Upsilon \wedge \Upsilon \xleftarrow{S} \Phi \tag{143}$$

  This rule extends (93) to relations.
- **Split by conjunction**:

$$\Psi_1 \cdot \Psi_2 \xleftarrow{R} \Phi \;\Leftrightarrow\; \Psi_1 \xleftarrow{R} \Phi \wedge \Psi_2 \xleftarrow{R} \Phi \tag{144}$$

  This equivalence generalizes (92).
- **Weakening/strengthening**:

$$\Psi \xleftarrow{R} \Phi \;\Leftarrow\; \Psi \supseteq \Theta \wedge \Theta \xleftarrow{R} \Upsilon \wedge \Upsilon \supseteq \Phi \tag{145}$$

- **Separation**:

$$\Upsilon \cdot \Theta \xleftarrow{R} \Phi \cdot \Psi \;\Leftarrow\; \Upsilon \xleftarrow{R} \Phi \wedge \Theta \xleftarrow{R} \Psi \tag{146}$$

  This rule follows from (144,145).
- **Splitting**:

$$\Psi \times \Upsilon \xleftarrow{\langle R,S \rangle} \Phi \;\Leftrightarrow\; \Psi \xleftarrow{R} \Phi \cdot \delta\, S \wedge \Upsilon \xleftarrow{S} \Phi \cdot \delta\, R \tag{147}$$

  This generalizes (101) from functions to arbitrary relations.
- **Product**:

$$\Phi' \times \Psi' \xleftarrow{R \times S} \Phi \times \Psi \;\Leftrightarrow\; \Phi' \xleftarrow{R} \Phi \wedge \Psi' \xleftarrow{S} \Psi \tag{148}$$

  Note that rule (140) already ensures part $\Leftarrow$ of equivalence (148).
- **Conditional**: equivalence

$$\Psi \xleftarrow{\quad c \rightarrow R,S \quad} \Phi \;\Leftrightarrow\; \Psi \xleftarrow{R} \Phi \cdot \Phi_c \wedge \Psi \xleftarrow{S} \Phi \cdot \Phi_{\neg c} \tag{149}$$

  where

$$c \rightarrow R\,,S \;\triangleq\; R \cdot \Phi_c \cup S \cdot \Phi_{\neg c} \tag{150}$$

  generalizes (103) to relations[20].

[20] For a wider generalization of conditionals to relations see eg. [1].

The interested reader is welcome to provide PF-calculations for all rules listed above.

Exercise 13. The Hoare logic rule corresponding to (143) is

$$\frac{\{p\}P_1\{q\}\ ,\ \{q\}P_2\{s\}}{\{p\}P_1;P_2\{s\}}$$

for $\Phi = \Phi_p$, $\Psi = \Phi_s$, $\Upsilon = \Phi_q$, $S = [\![P_1]\!]$, $R = [\![P_2]\!]$ and $[\![P;Q]\!] = [\![Q]\!] \cdot [\![P]\!]$. Check which other Hoare logic rules correspond to which ESC/PF rules, bearing in mind that some of latter may split into two of the former because they are equivalences, not implications. $\square$

Formal correspondence with WLP calculus. Recall from (128) that the weakest (liberal) pre-condition operator $(R \mathbin{\dot{\backslash}})$ is the upper adjoint of a GC which combines two adjoints already seen — range (71) and left division (23). The pointwise version $wlp\ R\ q$ of $R \mathbin{\dot{\backslash}} \Phi_q$ is

$$wlp\, R\, q \triangleq \langle \bigvee\ p\ :\ \langle \forall\, b, a\ :\ b\, R\, a\ \wedge\ p\, a :\ q\, b \rangle\ :\ p \rangle$$

Also recall (132), which tells that checking $\Phi_q \xleftarrow{R} \Phi_p$ is the same as first calculating $R \mathbin{\dot{\backslash}} \Phi_q$ and then showing that this is weaker than Φ_p. This leads to the constructive method for ESC which has already been adopted in the case study of section 13.

Besides this practical application, (132) is central to the close relationship between the ESC/PF calculus and the WLP-calculus. In fact, the two approaches are related by indirect equality (15). Let us take as example a rule of the latter calculus

$$R \mathbin{\dot{\backslash}} (\Upsilon \cdot \Psi) = (R \mathbin{\dot{\backslash}} \Upsilon) \cdot (R \mathbin{\dot{\backslash}} \Psi)$$

which holds since $(R \mathbin{\dot{\backslash}})$ is an upper-adjoint and therefore distributes over meet, ie. composition in the case of coreflexives [9]. We reason:

$$
\begin{array}{cl}
& R \mathbin{\dot{\backslash}} (\Upsilon \cdot \Psi) = (R \mathbin{\dot{\backslash}} \Upsilon) \cdot (R \mathbin{\dot{\backslash}} \Psi) \\
\Leftrightarrow & \quad \{ \text{ indirect equality (15) } \} \\
& \langle \forall\, \Phi\ ::\ \Phi \subseteq R \mathbin{\dot{\backslash}} (\Upsilon \cdot \Psi)\ \Leftrightarrow\ \Phi \subseteq (R \mathbin{\dot{\backslash}} \Upsilon) \cdot (R \mathbin{\dot{\backslash}} \Psi) \rangle \\
\Leftrightarrow & \quad \{ \text{ (60) ; (21) } \} \\
& \langle \forall\, \Phi\ ::\ \Phi \subseteq R \mathbin{\dot{\backslash}} (\Upsilon \cdot \Psi)\ \Leftrightarrow\ \Phi \subseteq R \mathbin{\dot{\backslash}} \Upsilon\ \wedge\ \Phi \subseteq R \mathbin{\dot{\backslash}} \Psi \rangle \\
\Leftrightarrow & \quad \{ \text{ (132) three times, omitting universal quantification } \} \\
& \Upsilon \cdot \Psi \xleftarrow{R} \Phi\ \ \Leftrightarrow\ \ \Upsilon \xleftarrow{R} \Phi\ \wedge\ \Psi \xleftarrow{R} \Phi
\end{array}
$$

We thus obtain (144), the equivalent ESC/PF-rule. A more interesting example is the transformation of WLP-rule

$$(S \cdot R) \mathbin{\dot{\backslash}} \Phi = R \mathbin{\dot{\backslash}} (S \mathbin{\dot{\backslash}} \Phi)$$

into ESC/PF format:

$$
\begin{array}{ll}
 & R \mathbin{\blacktriangleleft} (S \mathbin{\blacktriangleleft} \phi) = (S \cdot R) \mathbin{\blacktriangleleft} \phi \\
\Leftrightarrow & \qquad \{ \text{ indirect equality (15) } \} \\
 & \psi \subseteq R \mathbin{\blacktriangleleft} (S \mathbin{\blacktriangleleft} \phi) \Leftrightarrow \psi \subseteq (S \cdot R) \mathbin{\blacktriangleleft} \phi \\
\Leftrightarrow & \qquad \{ \text{ (132) twice } \} \\
 & (S \mathbin{\blacktriangleleft} \phi) \xleftarrow{R} \psi \;\Leftrightarrow\; \phi \xleftarrow{(S \cdot R)} \psi
\end{array}
$$

The outcome is a ESC/PF rule which, still involving the $\blacktriangleleft$ operator, is an advantageous replacement for (143), since it is an equivalence.

16 Case Study 2 — Verified File System

Our second group of experiments with the ESC/PF calculus has to do with a real-life project. In the context of the Verified Software Initiative [28], we want to validate a formal model of a file system as part of a broader exercise on providing a verified file system (VFS) on flash memory — a challenge put forward by Rajeev Joshi and Gerard Holzmann of NASA JPL [34].

An explanation of the overall approach to the problem, involving not only formal modeling but also model checking in Alloy and theorem proving in HOL [26] can be found in [21]. Below we shall be concerned only with showing the role of the PF-transform in statically checking the model by pen-and-paper calculation.

As explained in [21], the problem has two levels — the POSIX level and the NAND flash level. The work so far has focussed on the top level, taking as working document Intel's *Flash File System Core Reference Guide* [16]. This is a layered collection of APIs, of which we are considering FS (file system), the top one. Figure 2 gives an idea of what is to be modeled for each file system operation, in this case the one which enables file/directory deletion.

Data model. By inspecting reference guide [16] we have arrived at a formal, relational model of the file system structure which, stripped of details irrelevant for the operation of figure 2, can be depicted in the relational diagram which follows:

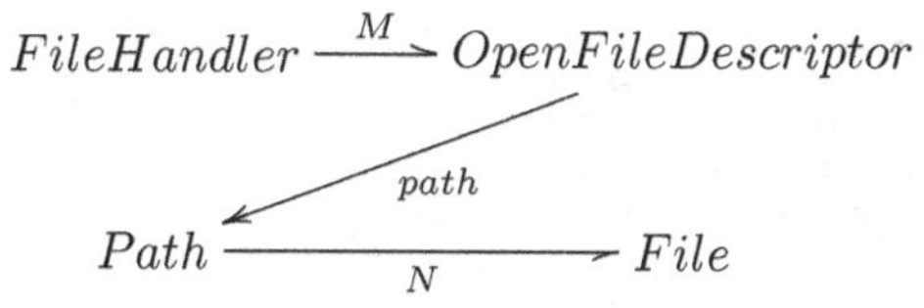

(151)

This tells that there are two simple relations in the model, one (N in the diagram) relating paths to file contents and another (M in the diagram) giving details of each opened file identified by a file handler. These two data structures are linked by function $path$ which selects paths from the information recorded in $OpenFileDescriptor$s and is central to the main invariant of the model — the referential integrity condition which ensures that non-existing files cannot be opened:

$$
\begin{array}{l}
System = \{table : OpenFileDescriptorTable, fs : FStore\} \\
\textbf{inv}\ \ sys \triangleq \langle \forall\, d\ :\ d \in rng\ (table\ sys) :\ path\, d \in dom\ (fs\ sys)\rangle
\end{array} \qquad (152)
$$

In this "linguistic version" of diagram (151) the choice of long identifiers is justified by practical reasons, due to the overall complexity of the whole model. While datatypes

$$
\begin{array}{l}
OpenFileDescriptorTable = FileHandler \rightharpoonup OpenFileDescriptor \\
OpenFileDescriptor = \{path : Path, ...\}
\end{array}
$$

are subject to no invariant (in this simplified version), file stores should be such that father directories always exist and are indeed directories:

$$
\begin{array}{l}
FStore = Path \rightharpoonup File \\
\textbf{inv}\ \ store \triangleq \langle \forall\, p\ :\ p \in dom\ store :\ dirName(p) \in dom\ store\ \wedge \\
\qquad\qquad fileType(attributes(store(dirName\, p))) = Directory\rangle
\end{array} \qquad (153)
$$

The function $dirName : Path \rightarrow Path$ tells the father path of a given path. There exists a topmost path *Root* in the path hierarchy which, according to the requirements [16], is such that $dirName\ Root = Root$. Files have attributes and $fileType$ is one such attribute. For space economy, we omit all other details of the model's data types.

File System API Reference intel®

4.6 FS_DeleteFileDir

Deletes a single file/directory from the media

Syntax

```
FFS_Status    FS_DeleteFileDir (
        mOS_char      *full_path,
        UINT8         static_info_type );
```

Parameters

Parameter	Description
*full_path	(IN) This is the full path of the filename for the file or directory to be deleted.
static_info_type	(IN) This tells whether this function is called to delete a file or a directory.

Error Codes/Return Values

FFS_StatusSuccess	Success
FFS_StatusNotInitialized	Failure
FFS_StatusInvalidPath	Failure
FFS_StatusInvalidTarget	Failure
FFS_StatusFileStillOpen	Failure

Fig. 2. Example of API specification in [16]. (Permission to reproduce this excerpt is kindly granted by Intel Corporation).

Modeling the operations. Let us focus on the API operation which enables file deletion (figure 2) modeled after the requirements in [16] as follows:

$$
\begin{array}{l}
FS\_DeleteFileDir : Path \to System \to (System \times FFS\_Status) \\
FS\_DeleteFileDir\ p\ sys \triangleq \\
\quad if\ p \neq Root \wedge p \in dom\ (fs\ sys) \wedge \text{pre-}FS\_DeleteFileDir\_System\ p\ sys \\
\quad then\ (FS\_DeleteFileDir\_System\ p\ sys, FFS\_StatusSuccess) \\
\quad else\ (sys, FS\_DeleteFileDir\_Exception\ p\ sys)
\end{array}
$$

This is a function that either deletes the $FStore$ entry whose path p is given or raises an exception, leaving the state unchanged and returning the appropriate error code (of type FFS_Status). Function $FS\_DeleteFileDir\_Exception$ returning error codes does not interfere with ESC and is therefore omitted. By contrast, the core of the success trace is the (partial) function which updates the system once the specified entry can indeed be deleted:

$$
\begin{array}{l}
FS\_DeleteFileDir\_System : Path \to System \to System \\
FS\_DeleteFileDir\_System\ p\ (h, t) \triangleq \\
\qquad (h, FS\_DeleteFileDir\_FStore\ \{p\}\ t) \\
\textbf{pre}\ \langle \forall\ d\ :\ d \in rng\ h :\ path\ d \neq p \rangle\ \wedge\ \text{pre-}FS\_DeleteFileDir\_FStore\ \{p\}\ t
\end{array}
$$

This, in turn, calls a function whose scope is the $FStore$ component of $System$. This is where things actually happen:

$$
\begin{array}{l}
FS\_DeleteFileDir\_FStore : \mathcal{P}Path \to FStore \to FStore \\
FS\_DeleteFileDir\_FStore\ s\ store \triangleq\ store \setminus s \\
\textbf{pre}\ \langle \forall\ p\ :\ p \in dom\ store\ \wedge\ dirName\ p \in s :\ p \in s \rangle
\end{array}
\tag{154}
$$

This function actually deletes sets of entries (and not individual ones) using the *domain restricted by* operator $M \setminus S$ typical of model-oriented specification languages such as VDM or Z, whose meaning is *select the largest sub-relation of M whose keys are not in S*. Formally, the PF-transform of this operator is

$$
[\![M \setminus S]\!] = M \cdot \Phi_{(\notin S)} \tag{155}
$$

Note that $FS\_DeleteFileDir\_System$ and $FS\_DeleteFileDir\_FStore$ are subject to pre-conditions *invented* by the software analyst who wrote the model. Such pre-conditions are the main target of our reasoning below. Several questions arise: how *"good"* are these? are they *sufficient* for the invariants to be maintained? are they too *strong*? which are concerned with ESC alone and which are restrictions posed by the API specifier derived from POSIX recommendations or constraints?

Before answering these questions, we should say that real problems such as this have the merit of showing *where the complexity actually is*, and part of it has to do with the (often intricate) structure of datatypes involving nested invariants. This calls for an effective way of calculating which invariants hold at which levels of a given data model in terms of the associated coreflexives, as shown next.

17 Invariant Structural Synthesis

Let us denote by F_p the fact that data type constructor F is constrained by invariant p. Of course, F itself can be defined in terms of other type constructors constrained by their own invariants. We write $\in_{\mathsf{F}_p}$ to denote the coreflexive which captures *all* constraints involved in declaring type F_p. This is defined by induction on the structure of type constructors (relators)[21]:

$$\in_{\mathsf{F}_p} = (\in_{\mathsf{F}}) \cdot \Phi_p \tag{156}$$

$$\in_{\mathsf{K}} = id \tag{157}$$

$$\in_{\mathsf{Id}} = id \tag{158}$$

$$\in_{\mathsf{F}\times\mathsf{G}} = \in_{\mathsf{F}} \times \in_{\mathsf{G}} \tag{159}$$

$$\in_{\mathsf{F}+\mathsf{G}} = \in_{\mathsf{F}} + \in_{\mathsf{G}} \tag{160}$$

$$\in_{\mathsf{F}\cdot\mathsf{G}} = \mathsf{F}(\in_{\mathsf{G}}) \tag{161}$$

For instance, $Even = (I\!N_0)_{even}$, recall (43). Thus $\in_{Even} = \Phi_{even}$ by direct application of (156) and (157). In the calculation of $\in_{System}$ which follows we abbreviate its invariant declared in (152) by predicate ri (for "referential integrity") and $FStore$'s invariant (153) by pc (for "paths closed"):

$$
\begin{array}{ll}
& \in_{System} \\
= & \{ \text{ definition of } System \text{ (152) } \} \\
& \in_{(OpenFileDescriptorTable \times FStore)_{ri}} \\
= & \{ \text{ (156) and datatype definitions } \} \\
& (\in_{FileHandler \rightharpoonup OpenFileDescriptor} \times \in_{(Path \rightharpoonup File)_{pc}}) \cdot \Phi_{ri} \\
= & \{ \text{ (157) and (156) } \} \\
& (id \times \in_{Path \rightharpoonup File} \cdot \Phi_{pc}) \cdot \Phi_{ri} \\
= & \{ \text{ (157) } \} \\
& (id \times \Phi_{pc}) \cdot \Phi_{ri}
\end{array}
\tag{162}
$$

18 ESC/PF Calculus at Work — Case Study 2

Now that we know the pointfree structure $(id \times \Phi_{pc}) \cdot \Phi_{ri}$ of the overall invariant which we have to ESC for, let us investigate the structure of the operation we want to check — $FS\_DeleteFileDir$. Our main goal is to discharge proof obligation

$$\in_{System \times FFS\_Status} \xleftarrow{FS\_DeleteFileDir\ p} \in_{System} \tag{163}$$

[21] The choice of symbol "$\in$" instead of "$\in$", which would be more natural regarding its use in eg. (42), is due to the fact that notation $\in_{\mathsf{F}}$ is already taken by *structural membership* [29], a related but different concept.

We start by using the PF-transform to "find structure" in the specification text. By freezing parameter p (which is not active in the specification of the operation) and PF-transforming $FS\_DeleteFileDir\ p$ we obtain a PF-expression which has the "shape" of a McCarthy conditional (150)

$$c \rightarrow \langle f, \underline{k} \rangle\ ,\ \langle id, g \rangle \tag{164}$$

where

- c abbreviates section $(c\ \ p)$ of the condition of the main if-then-else, that is $c\ p\ sys \triangleq p \neq Root \wedge p \in dom\ (fs\ sys) \wedge$ pre-$FS\_DeleteFileDir\_System\ p\ sys$
- f abbreviates $FS\_DeleteFileDir\_System\ p$
- k abbreviates $FFS\_StatusSuccess$, the success output code
- g abbreviates $FS\_DeleteFileDir\_Exception\ p$.

Facing complexity. What's the advantage of PF-pattern (164)? Below we show how to apply the ESC/PF calculus of section 15 to (164) in a "divide and conquer" manner, thus breaking the complexity of the target proof obligation (163):

$$\in_{System \times FFS\_Status} \xleftarrow{FS\_DeleteFileDir\ p} \in_{System}$$

$\Leftrightarrow \quad \{$ (164), (159) and $\in_{FFSstatus} = id$ (157) $\}$

$$\in_{System} \times id \xleftarrow{c \rightarrow \langle f, \underline{k} \rangle, \langle id, g \rangle} \in_{System}$$

$\Leftrightarrow \quad \{$ conditional (149) $\}$

$$\in_{System} \times id \xleftarrow{\langle f, \underline{k} \rangle} \in_{System} \cdot \Phi_c \ \wedge\ \in_{System} \times id \xleftarrow{\langle id, g \rangle} \in_{System} \cdot \Phi_{\neg c}$$

$\Leftrightarrow \quad \{$ splitting (101) $\}$

$$\in_{System} \xleftarrow{f} \in_{System} \cdot \Phi_c \ \wedge\ id \xleftarrow{\underline{k}} \in_{System} \cdot \Phi_c$$
$$\wedge$$
$$\in_{System} \xleftarrow{id} \in_{System} \cdot \Phi_{\neg c} \ \wedge\ id \xleftarrow{g} \in_{System} \cdot \Phi_{\neg c}$$

$\Leftrightarrow \quad \{$ (141), (94) $\}$

$$\in_{System} \xleftarrow{f} \in_{System} \cdot \Phi_c$$

$\Leftrightarrow \quad \{$ trading (142) and unfolding $\in_{System}$ (162) $\}$

$$(id \times \Phi_{pc}) \cdot \Phi_{ri} \xleftarrow{f \cdot \Phi_c} (id \times \Phi_{pc}) \cdot \Phi_{ri}$$

$\Leftarrow \quad \{$ separating (146) $\}$

$$\Phi_{ri} \xleftarrow{f \cdot \Phi_c} \Phi_{ri} \ \wedge\ id \times \Phi_{pc} \xleftarrow{f \cdot \Phi_c} id \times \Phi_{pc}$$

Clearly, the focus has moved from the main function to $FS\_DeleteFileDir\_System\, p$ (abbreviated to f above) with respect to two (now *separate*) proofs: one concerning path referential integrity (ri) and the other concerning path closure (pc).

It can be further observed that condition c splits in two independent parts, that is, $\Phi_c = \Phi_{c_1} \times \Phi_{c_2}$ where[22]

$$c_1\, p\, h \triangleq \langle \forall\, d : d \in rng\, h : path\, d \neq p \rangle$$
$$c_2\, p\, t \triangleq p \neq Root \wedge p \in dom\, t \wedge \text{pre-}FS\_DeleteFileDir\_FStore\, \{p\}\, t$$

Moreover,

$$\begin{aligned} f &= FS\_DeleteFileDir\_System\, p \\ &= id \times FS\_DeleteFileDir\_FStore\, \{p\} \qquad (165) \\ &= id \times f_2 \qquad (166) \end{aligned}$$

introducing abbreviation f_2 to save space. So we can calculate further:

$$\Phi_{ri} \xleftarrow{f \cdot \Phi_c} \Phi_{ri} \;\wedge\; id \times \Phi_{pc} \xleftarrow{f \cdot \Phi_c} id \times \Phi_{pc}$$

$\Leftrightarrow$ $\{ \ \Phi_c = \Phi_{c_1} \times \Phi_{c_2}$; $f = id \times f_2$; $\times$-relator (109) $\}$

$$\Phi_{ri} \xleftarrow{f \cdot \Phi_c} \Phi_{ri} \;\wedge\; id \times \Phi_{pc} \xleftarrow{\Phi_{c_1} \times f_2 \cdot \Phi_{c_2}} id \times \Phi_{pc}$$

$\Leftrightarrow$ $\{$ (148) ; (141) $\}$

$$\Phi_{ri} \xleftarrow{f \cdot \Phi_c} \Phi_{ri} \;\wedge\; \Phi_{pc} \xleftarrow{f_2 \cdot \Phi_{c_2}} \Phi_{pc}$$

$\Leftrightarrow$ $\{$ trading (142) $\}$

$$\Phi_{ri} \xleftarrow{f} \Phi_{ri} \cdot \Phi_c \;\wedge\; \Phi_{pc} \xleftarrow{f_2} \Phi_{pc} \cdot \Phi_{c_2} \qquad (167)$$

Going "in-the-small". So much for ESC/PF calculation *in-the-large*. Going *in-the-small* means spelling out invariants, functions and pre-conditions and reason as in the previous case study.

Let us pick the first proof obligation in (167), $\Phi_{ri} \xleftarrow{f} \Phi_{ri} \cdot \Phi_c$. Following (132) as earlier on, we go pointwise and try to rewrite weakest pre-condition $ri(f(M, N))$ — where M handles open file descriptors and N file contents, recall diagram (151) — into $ri(M, N)$ and a pre-condition, which will be the weakest for maintaining ri provided all steps in the calculation are equivalences. Then we compare the outcome with what the designer wrote (Φ_c).

Taking advantage of the fact that both data structures M and N are relations, we choose to start by PF-transforming ri

$$ri(M, N) \triangleq \rho\,(path \cdot M) \subseteq \delta\, N$$

[22] Note the somewhat arbitrary decision of adding condition $p \neq Root$ to c_2. We shall have more to say about this. Also note the notation convention of abbreviating sections $(c_1\, p)$ and $(c_2\, p)$ by c_1 and c_2 in coreflexives' subscripts.

according to diagram (151) and thus investing on PF-notation again. This expression for ri, which clearly spells out the referential integrity constraint relating paths in opened file descriptors and paths in the file store N, further transforms to

$$ri(M, N) \triangleq path \cdot M \subseteq N^\circ \cdot \top \tag{168}$$

cf. diagram

$$\begin{array}{ccc} OpenFileDescriptor & \xleftarrow{M} & FileHandler \\ {\scriptstyle path}\Big\downarrow & \subseteq & \Big\downarrow{\scriptstyle \top} \\ Path & \xleftarrow[N^\circ]{\qquad\qquad} & File \end{array}$$

On the other hand, (165, 166) and (155) lead to

$$\begin{aligned} ri(f(M, N)) &= ri(FS\_DeleteFileDir\_System\ p\ (M, N)) \\ &= ri(M, N \cdot \Phi_{(\notin\{p\})}) \end{aligned}$$

In the calculation below we generalize $\{p\}$ to any set S of paths:

$$\begin{array}{cl} & ri(M, N \cdot \Phi_{(\notin S)}) \\ \Leftrightarrow & \quad \{\ (168)\ \} \\ & path \cdot M \subseteq (N \cdot \Phi_{(\notin S)})^\circ \cdot \top \\ \Leftrightarrow & \quad \{\ \text{converses } (26{,}59)\ \} \\ & path \cdot M \subseteq \Phi_{(\notin S)} \cdot N^\circ \cdot \top \\ \Leftrightarrow & \quad \{\ (47)\ \} \\ & path \cdot M \subseteq N^\circ \cdot \top \cap \Phi_{(\notin S)} \cdot \top \\ \Leftrightarrow & \quad \{\ \cap\text{-universal } (21)\ \} \\ & path \cdot M \subseteq N^\circ \cdot \top\ \wedge\ path \cdot M \subseteq \Phi_{(\notin S)} \cdot \top \\ \Leftrightarrow & \quad \{\ (168)\ ;\ \text{shunting } (67)\ \} \\ & ri(M, N)\ \wedge\ \underbrace{M \subseteq path^\circ \cdot \Phi_{(\notin S)} \cdot \top}_{wp} \end{array}$$

The obtained weakest pre-condition wp converts back to the pointwise $\langle \forall\ b\ :\ b \in rng\ M\ :\ path\ b \notin S \rangle$ which instantiates to $\langle \forall\ b\ :\ b \in rng\ M\ :\ path\ b \neq p \rangle$ for $S := \{p\}$. This is in fact a conjunct of pre-$FS\_DeleteFileDir\_System$, itself a conjunct of $c\ p$, the condition of $FS\_DeleteFileDir$'s if-then-else. So we are done as far invariant ri is concerned.

Before moving to invariant *pc*, note two levels of reasoning in ESC/PF calculations: the *in-the-large* level using the ESC/PF arrow calculus and the *in-the-small* level, where PF-notation describes data and properties of data, typically invariants.

Checking for paths-closed invariant preservation. Our last ESC/PF exercise has to do with the remaining proof obligation

$$\Phi_{pc} \xleftarrow{FS\_DeleteFileDir\_FStore\ \{p\}} \Phi_{pc} \cdot \Phi_{c_2} \tag{169}$$

where $FS\_DeleteFileDir\_FStore\ \{p\}$ PF-transforms to

$$(FS\_DeleteFileDir\_FStore\ S)\ N = N \cdot \Phi_{(\notin S)} \tag{170}$$

generalizing $\{p\}$ to an arbitrary set of paths S, as we have seen. The PF-transform of invariant *pc*,

$$pc\ N \triangleq \underline{Directory} \cdot N \subseteq fileType \cdot attributes \cdot N \cdot dirName \tag{171}$$

is explained by the rectangle added below to diagram (151):

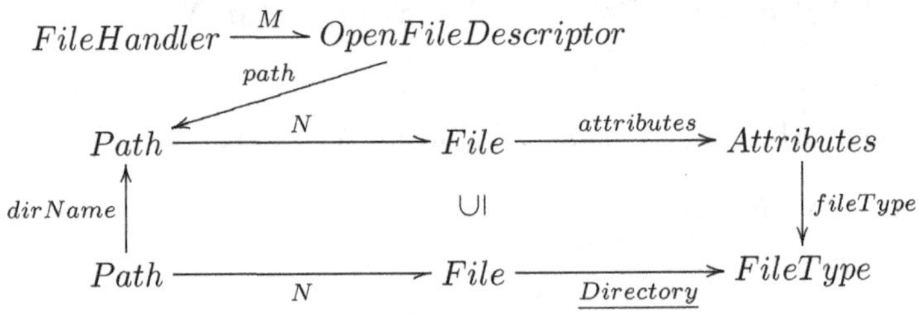

Again, our strategy will be to ignore Φ_{c_2} in (169) for a moment and calculate the weakest pre-condition for $FS\_DeleteFileDir\_FStore\ S$ to preserve *pc*; then we compare Φ_{c_2} with the pre-condition thus obtained. For improved readability, we introduce abbreviations $ft := fileType \cdot attributes$ and $d := \underline{Directory}$:

$$
\begin{array}{ll}
& pc(FS\_DeleteFileDir\_FStore\ S\ N) \\
\Leftrightarrow & \quad \{\ (170) \text{ and } (171)\ \} \\
& d \cdot (N \cdot \Phi_{(\notin S)}) \subseteq ft \cdot (N \cdot \Phi_{(\notin S)}) \cdot dirName \\
\Leftrightarrow & \quad \{\ \text{shunting } (69)\ \} \\
& d \cdot N \cdot \Phi_{(\notin S)} \cdot dirName^{\circ} \subseteq ft \cdot N \cdot \Phi_{(\notin S)} \\
\Leftrightarrow & \quad \{\ (46)\ \} \\
& d \cdot N \cdot \Phi_{(\notin S)} \cdot dirName^{\circ} \subseteq ft \cdot N \cap \top \cdot \Phi_{(\notin S)} \\
\Leftrightarrow & \quad \{\ \cap\text{-universal ; shunting}\ \} \\
& d \cdot N \cdot \Phi_{(\notin S)} \subseteq ft \cdot N \cdot dirName \ \wedge\ d \cdot N \cdot \Phi_{(\notin S)} \subseteq \top \cdot \Phi_{(\notin S)} \cdot dirName \\
\Leftrightarrow & \quad \{\ \top \text{ absorbs } d\ (115)\ \} \\
& \underbrace{d \cdot N \cdot \Phi_{(\notin S)} \subseteq ft \cdot N \cdot dirName}_{\text{weaker than } pc(N)} \ \wedge\ \underbrace{N \cdot \Phi_{(\notin S)} \subseteq \top \cdot \Phi_{(\notin S)} \cdot dirName}_{wp}
\end{array}
$$

This ends the PF-calculation of this ESC proof obligation. It remains to compare c_2 with wp just above which, back to points, re-writes to:

$$\langle \forall\, q \;:\; q \in dom\, N \;\wedge\; q \notin S :\; dirName\, q \notin S \rangle$$

$$\Leftrightarrow \qquad \{ \text{ predicate logic } \}$$

$$\langle \forall\, q \;:\; q \in dom\, N \;\wedge\; (dirName\, q) \in S :\; q \in S \rangle$$

This is pre-condition (154) which, in words, means: *if parent directory of existing path q is marked for deletion than so must be q.* Condition c_2 involves this pre-condition, for $S := \{p\}$,

$$\langle \forall\, q \;:\; q \in dom\, N \;\wedge\; (dirName\, q) = p :\; q = p \rangle$$

but adds further constraints. So c_2 is stronger than the calculated weakest pre-condition and, thanks to (132), we are done. In particular, c_2 doesn't allow for $Root$ deletion. Condition wp enables so (since $dirName\ Root = Root$) provided no other files exist in the file system.

The interest of these observations, which we have reached by calculation, lies in the fact that the POSIX standard itself [58] is ambiguous in this matter. Whether the minimal $FStore$ is the empty relation or whether it must be the root directory's singleton is a bit of a philosophical question. In the POSIX System Interface [58] one reads, concerning the `rmdir()` system call:

> *The rmdir() function shall remove a directory whose name is given by path. The directory shall be removed only if it is an empty directory. If the directory is the root directory or the current working directory of any process, it is unspecified whether the function succeeds, or whether it shall fail and set errno to [EBUSY].*

Another aspect of the starting specification is clause $p \in dom\ (fs\ sys)$. From the calculations above we infer that no harm arises from trying to delete a non-existing file, as nothing happens to the system. So, the corresponding error code should be interpreted more as a warning than as an exception.

19 Alloy Friendship

The "everything is a relation" lemma of Alloy and the PF-flavour of its notation turn the Alloy Analyzer into a very helpful tool supporting the PF-transform on practical grounds. This tool has been developed by the Software Design Group at MIT for analyzing models written in a simple structural modeling language based on first-order logic. Being a model checker, it does not discharge proofs as such but is very useful in finding (via counter-examples) design flaws, as reported in [21] concerning the VFS project.

Space constraints prevent us from giving the Alloy model in detail. We focus on invariant pc which PF-transforms to (171). Note the similarity between (171) and the corresponding code in Alloy syntax,

```
pred pcInvariant[t: FStore]{
  RelCalc/Simple[t.map, Path]
  (t.map).(File->Directory)
          in dirName.(t.map).attributes.fileType
}
```

where predicate `Simple` is available from library `RelCalc` (it checks for relation simplicity), composition is written in reverse order and `map` has to do with the declaration of *FStore* as an Alloy signature [30]:

```
sig FStore {
  map: Path -> File,
}
```

Note how `File->Directory` elegantly represents the constant function $\underline{Directory}$ in (171). The alternative, pointwise version of *pc* is written in Alloy as follows:

```
pred pcInvariantPW[t: FStore]{
   RelCalc/Simple[t.map, Path]
   all p: Path |
        p in RelCalc/dom[t.map] =>
             p.dirName in RelCalc/dom[t.map] &&
                  t.map[p.dirName].attributes.fileType =
                                                 Directory
}
```

Checking (not proving!) the equivalence of these two alternative predicates can be expressed in Alloy by running assertion

```
assert equivPWPF {
  all t: FStore | pcInvariant[t] <=> pcInvariantPW[t]
}
```

See [21] for more about the role of Alloy in the VFS case study.

Exercise 14. Alloy will find counter-examples to the assertion above once the simplicity requirement `RelCalc/Simple[t.map, Path]` is dropped from both predicates. Resort to the PF-calculus and show why the calculations which lead to (171) are not valid for arbitrary N. □

20 Conclusions

In full-fledged formal software development one is obliged to provide mathematical proofs that desirable properties of software systems hold. An important class of such properties has to do with (extended) type checking and includes those which ensure that datatype invariants are not violated by some trace of the system at runtime. A way to prevent this consists of abstractly modeling the intended system using a formal language, formulating such proof obligations and proving them. Because this is not done at run-time, this class of proof belongs to the *static* world of software quality checking and is known under the ESC (*extended static checking*) acronym.

ESC proofs can either be performed as paper-and-pencil exercises or, in case of sizeable models, be supported by theorem provers and model checkers. Real-life case studies show that *all* such approaches to adding quality to a formal model are useful in their own way and have a proper place in software engineering using formal methods.

The main novelty of the approach put forward in the current paper resides in the chosen method of proof construction: first-order formulæ in proof obligations are subject to the PF-transform before they are reasoned about. This "Laplace flavoured" transformation eliminates quantifiers and bound variables and reduces complex formulas to algebraic relational expressions which are more agile to calculate with. Suitable relational encoding of recursive structures often makes it possible to perform non-inductive proofs over such structures.

The overall approach is structured in two layers: one is a formal set of rules (the ESC/PF calculus) which enable one to break complex proof obligations into smaller ones, by exploiting both the structure of the predicates involved (expressed as coreflexive relations) and the PF structure of the software operations being checked. This is referred to as the *in-the-large* ESC/PF level, which uses arrow notation clearly reminding the user that one is doing (extended) type checking.

One moves into the *in-the-small* level wherever discharging elementary proofs, that is, ESC-arrows which cannot be further decomposed by *in-the-large* calculation. In spite of the reasoning going pointwise at this level, the PF-calculus turns up again wherever the particular data structures are encoded as relations and invariants as PF-formulæ involving such relations. As already stressed in [48], this is a novel ingredient in PF-calculation, since most work on the pointfree relation calculus has so far been focused on reasoning about programs (ie. algorithms) [13]. Advantages of our proposal to *uniformly* PF-transform both programs and data are already apparent at practical level, see eg. the work reported in [41]. The approach contrasts with the VDM tradition where universal quantifications over finite lists and finite mappings are carried out by induction on such structures [32]. It should be noted, however, that not *every* proof obligation leads to such calculations. The encoding of lists into simple relations, for instance, does not take *finiteness* aspects (eg. counting elements, etc) into account.

Last but not least, this paper helps in better characterizing the notion of *type* of an arbitrary piece of code, since Hoare logic is shown to be under the umbrella of ESC/PF, as is the weakest pre-condition calculus.

21 Future Work

This paper finds its roots in the excellent background for computer science research developed by the MPC (Mathematics of Program Construction) group [1,29,13,7]. Surely there is still much to explore. For instance, Voermans's PhD thesis [62] investigates the use of PERs (partial equivalence relations) to model datatypes subject to axioms, as in the classic abstract data type (ADT) tradition. Coreflexives are minimal PERs, so the view of *coreflexives as types* implicit in the current paper can surely be extended to that of *PERs as types*. How much is gained in this generalization needs to be balanced against what is likely to be lost.

The idea that the proposed ESC/PF calculus bridges Hoare logic and type theory needs to be better exploited, in particular concerning the work by Kozen [36] on subsuming propositional Hoare logic under Kleene algebra with tests (of which the relational calculus is a well known instance [7]) and the work emerging on *Hoare type theory* (HTT) [40], which should be carefully studied. Still on the type theory track, the alternative use of dependent types to model types subject to invariants and the way in which ESC proofs are carried out by systems such as Agda [14] should be compared to the current paper's approach.

The arrow notation adopted in the ESC/PF calculus not only is adequate to express proof obligation discharge as a type-system kind of problem, but also triggers synergies with similar notation used in other branches of computing. Pick functional dependence (FD) theory [38], for instance, where one writes $f \stackrel{R}{\rightarrow} g$ to mean that in database relation R (set of tuples), attribute g is functionally dependent on attribute f:

$$\langle \forall\, t, t' \;:\; t, t' \in R :\; f\, t = f\, t' \Rightarrow g\, t = g\, t' \rangle$$

Compare, for instance, (145) with the *decomposition* axiom of FDs

$$h \stackrel{R}{\rightarrow} k \Leftarrow h \geq f \;\wedge\; f \stackrel{R}{\rightarrow} g \;\wedge\; g \geq k$$

where $\leq$ compares (sets of) attributes. In the PF-approach to FD-theory developed in [45,47][23], R in $f \stackrel{R}{\rightarrow} g$ is modeled by a coreflexive relation and attributes f, g by functions. (So functions and coreflexives swap places when compared with ESC arrows.) Checking how much structure is shared among these two (so far apart) theories is something the PF-transform has potential for.

As far as tool support is concerned, reference [41] already presents visible progress in the automation of the relational calculus applied to ESC-like situations. Calculations are performed using a Haskell term rewriting system written in the strategic programming style. Another related line of research is the design of the *Galculator* [56], a prototype of a proof assistant of a special brand: it is solely based on the algebra of Galois connections. When combined with the PF-transform and tactics such as indirect equality (15), it offers a powerful, generic device to tackle the complexity of proofs in program verification. Moreover, we think the ESC/PF calculus could be of help in designing a *generic* proof obligation generator which could be instantiated to particular tool-sets such as, for instance, the one developed by Vermolen [61] for VDM.

The ESC/PF calculus can be further developed taking into account other aspects of model-based reasoning such as, for instance, refinement [32,66]. The reader is left with an exercise which provides a foretaste of ESC rules entailed by operation refinement.

Exercise 15. The refinement ordering on pre/post-specification pairs viewed as binary relations can be defined by

$$S \vdash R \;\;\triangleq\;\; \delta\, S \subseteq (R \setminus S) \cap \delta\, R \qquad (172)$$

meaning that S (the specification) is smaller domain-wise and vaguer range-wise than R (the implementation) [50]. That is, implementations can only be more defined and more deterministic than specifications.

[23] Also recall exercise 8 from section 9 of the current paper.

From $\Psi \xleftarrow{S} \Phi$ and $S \vdash R$ infer $\Psi \xleftarrow{R} \Phi \cdot \delta S$. □

Acknowledgments

Part of this research was carried out in the context of the PURE Project *(Program Understanding and Re-engineering: Calculi and Applications)* funded by FCT contract POSI/ICHS/44304/2002.

The author wishes to thank the organizers of the PURECAFE meetings for the opportunity to present his first ideas about ESC/PF at one of the seminars, back to 2004 [43]. He also thanks Simão Sousa for pointing him to HTT.

The work of Claudia Necco and Joost Visser on putting the ESC/PF into practice is also gratefully acknowledged. Thanks are also due to Miguel Ferreira and Samuel Silva for their interest in the VFS project at Minho.

References

1. Aarts, C., Backhouse, R.C., Hoogendijk, P., Voermans, E., van der Woude, J.: A relational theory of datatypes (December 1992), www.cs.nott.ac.uk/~rcb
2. Alves, T.L., Silva, P.F., Visser, J., Oliveira, J.N.: Strategic term rewriting and its application to a VDM-SL to SQL conversion. In: Fitzgerald, J.S., Hayes, I.J., Tarlecki, A. (eds.) FM 2005. LNCS, vol. 3582, pp. 399–414. Springer, Heidelberg (2005)
3. Backhouse, K., Backhouse, R.C.: Safety of abstract interpretations for free, via logical relations and Galois connections. SCP 15(1-2), 153–196 (2004)
4. Backhouse, R., Michaelis, D.: Exercises in quantifier manipulation. In: Uustalu, T. (ed.) MPC 2006. LNCS, vol. 4014, pp. 70–81. Springer, Heidelberg (2006)
5. Backhouse, R.C.: On a relation on functions. In: Dijkstra, W. (ed.) Beauty is our business: a birthday salute to Edsger, New York, NY, USA, pp. 7–18. Springer, Heidelberg (1990)
6. Backhouse, R.C.: Fixed point calculus. In: Summer School and Workshop on Algebraic and Coalgebraic Methods in the Mathematics of Program Construction, Lincoln College, Oxford, UK, April 10-14 (2000)
7. Backhouse, R.C.: Mathematics of Program Construction. Univ. of Nottingham. Draft of book in preparation, 608 pages (2004)
8. Backhouse, R.C., de Bruin, P., Hoogendijk, P., Malcolm, G., Voermans, T.S., van der Woude, J.: Polynomial relators. In: AMAST 1991, pp. 303–362. Springer, Heidelberg (1992)
9. Backhouse, R.C., Woude, J.: Demonic operators and monotype factors. Mathematical Structures in Computer Science 3(4), 417–433 (1993)
10. Backus, J.: Can programming be liberated from the von Neumann style? a functional style and its algebra of programs. CACM 21(8), 613–639 (1978)
11. Barbosa, L.S., Oliveira, J.N.: Transposing partial components — an exercise on coalgebraic refinement. Theoretical Computer Science 365(1), 2–22 (2006)
12. Barbosa, L.S., Oliveira, J.N., Silva, A.M.: Calculating invariants as coreflexive bisimulations. In: Meseguer, J., Roşu, G. (eds.) AMAST 2008. LNCS, vol. 5140, pp. 83–99. Springer, Heidelberg (2008)
13. Bird, R., de Moor, O.: Algebra of Programming. Series in Computer Science. Prentice-Hall International, Englewood Cliffs (1997) C.A.R. Hoare (series editor)
14. Bove, A., Dybjer, P.: Dependent types at work. Lecture Notes for the LerNet Summer School, Piriapolis, Uruguay, 47 p. (Feburary 2008)

15. Claessen, K., Hughes, J.: Quickcheck: a lightweight tool for random testing of Haskell programs. In: ICFP, pp. 268–279 (2000)
16. Intel Corporation. Intel Flash File System Core Reference Guide. Doc. Ref. 304436-001 (October 2004)
17. CSK. The Integrity Checking: Using Proof Obligations (2007)
18. Cunha, A., Oliveira, J.N., Visser, J.: Type-safe two-level data transformation. In: Misra, J., Nipkow, T., Sekerinski, E. (eds.) FM 2006. LNCS, vol. 4085, pp. 284–299. Springer, Heidelberg (2006)
19. Dijkstra, E.W., Scholten, C.S.: Predicate calculus and program semantics. Springer, New York (1990)
20. Doornbos, H., Backhouse, R., van der Woude, J.: A calculational approach to mathematical induction. Theoretical Computer Science 179(1-2), 103–135 (1997)
21. Ferreira, M.A., Silva, S.S., Oliveira, J.N.: Verifying Intel FLASH file system core specification. In: Modelling and Analysis in VDM: Proceedings of the Fourth Overture/VDM++ Workshop at FM 2008, Turku, Finland, May 26, 2008. University of Newcastle, Computer Science. Technical Report CS-TR-1099 (2008)
22. Fitzgerald, J., Larsen, P.G.: Modelling Systems: Practical Tools and Techniques for Software Development, 1st edn. Cambridge University Press, Cambridge (1998)
23. Fitzgerald, J., Larsen, P.G., Mukherjee, P., Plat, N., Verhoef, M.: Validated Designs for Object–oriented Systems. Springer, New York (2005)
24. Flanagan, C., Leino, K.R.M., Lillibridge, M., Nelson, G., Saxe, J.B., Stata, R.: Extended static checking for Java. In: PLDI, pp. 234–245 (2002)
25. Freyd, P.J., Ščedrov, A.: Categories, Allegories. Mathematical Library, vol. 39. North-Holland, Amsterdam (1990)
26. Gordon, M.J.C., Melham, T.F.: Introduction to HOL: A Theorem Proving Environment for Higher Order Logic. Cambridge University Press, Cambridge (1993)
27. Hoare, C.A.R.: An axiomatic basis for computer programming. CACM 12(10), 576–580 (1969)
28. Hoare, C.A.R., Misra, J.: Verified software: theories, tools, experiments — vision of a Grand Challenge project. In: Proceedings of IFIP working conference on Verified Software: theories, tools, experiments (2005)
29. Hoogendijk, P.: A Generic Theory of Data Types. PhD thesis, University of Eindhoven, The Netherlands (1997)
30. Jackson, D.: Software abstractions: logic, language, and analysis. MIT Press, Cambridge (2006)
31. Jacobs, B.: Introduction to Coalgebra. Towards Mathematics of States and Observations. Draft Copy. Institute for Computing and Information Sciences, Radboud University Nijmegen, P.O. Box 9010, 6500 GL Nijmegen, The Netherlands
32. Jones, C.B.: Systematic Software Development Using VDM, 1st edn. Series in Computer Science. Prentice-Hall Int., Englewood Cliffs (1986) (1990)
33. Peyton Jones, S.L.: Haskell 98 Language and Libraries. Cambridge University Press, Cambridge (2003); also published as a Special Issue of the Journal of Functional Programming 13(1) (Janurary 2003)
34. Joshi, R., Holzmann, G.J.: A mini challenge: build a verifiable filesystem. Formal Asp. Comput. 19(2), 269–272 (2007)
35. Kawahara, Y.: Notes on the universality of relational functors. Mem. Fac. Sci. Kyushu Univ (Series A, Mathematics) 27(2), 275–289 (1973)
36. Kozen, D.: On Hoare logic and Kleene algebra with tests. Trans. Computational Logic 1(1), 60–76 (2000)
37. Kreyszig, E.: Advanced Engineering Mathematics, 6th edn. J. Wiley & Sons, Chichester (1988)

38. Maier, D.: The Theory of Relational Databases. Computer Science Press (1983)
39. Meyer, B.: Applying "design by contract". IEEE Computer 25(10), 40–51 (1992)
40. Nanevski, A., Morrisett, G., Birkedal, L.: Polymorphism and separation in Hoare type theory. In: ICFP 2006, pp. 62–73. ACM, New York (2006)
41. Necco, C., Oliveira, J.N., Visser, J.: ESC/PF: Static checking of relational models by calculation (2008) (submitted)
42. Oliveira, J.N.: Bagatelle in C arranged for VDM SoLo. JUCS 7(8), 754–781 (2001)
43. Oliveira, J.N.: Constrained datatypes, invariants and business rules: a relational approach. PUReCafé talk, DI-UM, 2004.5.20, PURE PROJECT (POSI/CHS/44304/2002) (2004)
44. Oliveira, J.N.: Calculate databases with 'simplicity'. Presentation at the IFIP WG 2.1 #59 Meeting, Nottingham, UK (September 2004) (slides available from the author's website)
45. Oliveira, J.N.: Data dependency theory made generic — by calculation. Presentation at the IFIP WG 2.1 #62 Meeting, Namur, Belgium (December 2006)
46. Oliveira, J.N.: Reinvigorating pen-and-paper proofs in VDM: the pointfree approach. In: Presented at the Third OVERTURE Workshop, Newcastle, UK, November 27-28 (2006)
47. Oliveira, J.N.: Pointfree foundations for (generic) lossless decomposition (2008) (submitted)
48. Oliveira, J.N.: Transforming Data by Calculation. In: Lämmel, R., Visser, J., Saraiva, J. (eds.) GTTSE 2007. LNCS, vol. 5235, pp. 134–195. Springer, Heidelberg (2008)
49. Oliveira, J.N., Rodrigues, C.J.: Transposing relations: from Maybe functions to hash tables. In: Kozen, D. (ed.) MPC 2004. LNCS, vol. 3125, pp. 334–356. Springer, Heidelberg (2004)
50. Oliveira, J.N., Rodrigues, C.J.: Pointfree factorization of operation refinement. In: Misra, J., Nipkow, T., Sekerinski, E. (eds.) FM 2006. LNCS, vol. 4085, pp. 236–251. Springer, Heidelberg (2006)
51. Ore, O.: Galois connexions. Trans. Amer. Math. Soc. 55, 493–513 (1944)
52. Pierce, B.C.: Types and programming languages. MIT Press, Cambridge (2002)
53. Pratt, V.: Origins of the calculus of binary relations. In: Proc. of the 7th Annual IEEE Symp. on Logic in Computer Science, Santa Cruz, CA, pp. 248–254. IEEE Comp. Soc., Los Alamitos (1992)
54. Reynolds, J.C.: Types, abstraction and parametric polymorphism. Information Processing 83, 513–523 (1983)
55. Russo, L.: The Forgotten Revolution: How Science Was Born in 300BC and Why It Had to Be Reborn. Springer, Heidelberg (2003)
56. Silva, P.F., Oliveira, J.N.: 'Galculator': functional prototype of a Galois-connection based proof assistant. In: PPDP 2008: Proceedings of the 10th international ACM SIGPLAN conference on Principles and practice of declarative programming, pp. 44–55. ACM, New York (2008)
57. Spivey, J.M.: The Z Notation — A Reference Manual. Series in Computer Science. Prentice-Hall International, Englewood Cliffs (1989) C.A.R. Hoare (series editor)
58. Open Group Technical Standard. Standard for information technology - Portable operating system interface (POSIX). System interfaces. IEEE Std 1003.1, 2004 edn. The Open Group Technical Standard. Base Specifications, Issue 6. Includes IEEE Std 1003.1-2001, IEEE Std 1003.1-2001/Cor 1-2002 and IEEE Std 1003.1-2001/Cor 2-2004. System Interfaces (2004)
59. Takano, A., Meijer, E.: Shortcut to deforestation in calculational form. In: Proc. FPCA 1995 (1995)
60. Tarski, A., Givant, S.: A Formalization of Set Theory without Variables. American Mathematical Society, vol. 41. AMS Colloquium Publications, Providence (1987)
61. Vermolen, S.D.: Automatically discharging VDM proof obligations using HOL. Master's thesis, Radboud University Nijmegen, Computing Science Department (June-August 2007)
62. Voermans, T.S.: Inductive Datatypes with Laws and Subtyping — A Relational Model. PhD thesis, University of Eindhoven, The Netherlands (1999)

63. Voigtländer, J.: Proving correctness via free theorems: The case of the destroy/build-rule. In: Glück, R., de Moor, O. (eds.) Symposium on Partial Evaluation and Semantics-Based Program Manipulation, San Francisco, California, Proceedings, pp. 13–20. ACM Press, New York (2008)
64. Wadler, P.L.: Theorems for free! In: 4th International Symposium on Functional Programming Languages and Computer Architecture, London, pp. 347–359. ACM, New York (1989)
65. Wang, S., Barbosa, L.S., Oliveira, J.N.: A Relational Model for Confined Separation Logic. In: TASE 2008, pp. 263–270. IEEE Computer Society, Los Alamitos (2008)
66. Woodcock, J., Davies, J.: Using Z: Specification, Refinement, and Proof. Prentice-Hall, Inc., Upper Saddle River (1996)

A Background — Eindhoven Quantifier Calculus

When writing $\forall, \exists$-quantified expressions is useful to know a number of rules which help in reasoning about them. Throughout this paper we adopt the Eindhoven quantifier notation and calculus [7,4] whereby

$$\langle \forall\, x\ :\ R:\ T \rangle$$
$$\langle \exists\, x\ :\ R:\ T \rangle$$

mean, respectively

- *"for all x in range R it is the case that T"*
- *"there exists x in range R such that T"*.

Some useful rules about $\forall, \exists$ follow, taken from [7][24]:

- Trading:

$$\langle \forall\, i\ :\ R \wedge S:\ T \rangle = \langle \forall\, i\ :\ R:\ S \Rightarrow T \rangle \tag{173}$$
$$\langle \exists\, i\ :\ R \wedge S:\ T \rangle = \langle \exists\, i\ :\ R:\ S \wedge T \rangle \tag{174}$$

- One-point:

$$\langle \forall\, k\ :\ k = e:\ T \rangle = T[k := e] \tag{175}$$
$$v\langle \exists\, k\ :\ k = e:\ T \rangle = T[k := e] \tag{176}$$

- de Morgan:

$$\neg\langle \forall\, i\ :\ R:\ T \rangle = \langle \exists\, i\ :\ R:\ \neg T \rangle \tag{177}$$
$$\neg\langle \exists\, i\ :\ R:\ T \rangle = \langle \forall\, i\ :\ R:\ \neg T \rangle \tag{178}$$

Nesting:

$$\langle \forall\, a,b\ :\ R \wedge S:\ T \rangle = \langle \forall\, a\ :\ R:\ \langle \forall\, b\ :\ S:\ T \rangle\rangle \tag{179}$$
$$\langle \exists\, a,b\ :\ R \wedge S:\ T \rangle = \langle \exists\, a\ :\ R:\ \langle \exists\, b\ :\ S:\ T \rangle\rangle \tag{180}$$

[24] As forewarned in [7], the application of a rule is invalid if *(a)* it results in the capture of free variables or release of bound variables; *(b)* a variable ends up occurring more than once in a list of dummies.

- Empty range:

$$\langle \forall\, k \ : \ \text{FALSE} : \ T \rangle = \text{TRUE} \tag{181}$$

$$\langle \exists\, k \ : \ \text{FALSE} : \ T \rangle = \text{FALSE} \tag{182}$$

- Splitting:

$$\langle \forall\, j \ : \ R : \ \langle \forall\, k \ : \ S : \ T \rangle\rangle = \langle \forall\, k \ : \ \langle \exists\, j \ : \ R : \ S \rangle : \ T \rangle \tag{183}$$

$$\langle \exists\, j \ : \ R : \ \langle \exists\, k \ : \ S : \ T \rangle\rangle = \langle \exists\, k \ : \ \langle \exists\, j \ : \ R : \ S \rangle : \ T \rangle \tag{184}$$

Combinator Parsing: A Short Tutorial

S. Doaitse Swierstra

Center for Software Technology, Utrecht University, The Netherlands
doaitse@swierstra.net

Abstract. There are numerous ways to implement a parser for a given syntax; using parser combinators is a powerful approach to parsing which derives much of its power and expressiveness from the type system and semantics of the host programming language. This tutorial begins with the construction of a small library of parsing combinators. This library introduces the basics of combinator parsing and, more generally, demonstrates how domain specific embedded languages are able to leverage the facilities of the host language. After having constructed our small combinator library, we investigate some shortcomings of the naïve implementation introduced in the first part, and incrementally develop an implementation without these problems. Finally we discuss some further extensions of the presented library and compare our approach with similar libraries.

1 Introduction

Parser combinators [2,4,8,15] occupy a unique place in the field of parsing; they make its possible to write expressions which look like grammars, but actually describe parsers for these grammars. Most mature parsing frameworks entail voluminous preprocessing, which read in the syntax at hand, analyse it, and produce target code for the input grammar. By contrast, a relatively small parser combinator library can achieve comparable parsing power by harnessing the facilities of the language. In this tutorial we develop a mature parser combinator library, which rivals the power and expressivity of other frameworks in only a few hundred lines of code. Furthermore it is easily extended if desired to do so. These advantages follow from the fact that we have chosen to embed context-free grammar notation into a general purpose programming language, by taking the *Embedded Domain Specific Language* (EDSL) approach.

For many areas special purpose programming languages have been defined. The implementation of such a language can proceed along several different lines. On the one hand one can construct a completely new compiler, thus having complete freedom in the choice of syntax, scope rules, type system, commenting conventions, and code generation techniques. On the other hand one can try to build on top of work already done by extending an existing host language. Again, here one can pursue several routes; one may extend an existing compiler, or one can build a library implementing the new concepts. In the latter case one automatically inherits –but is also limited to– the syntax, type system and

A. Bove et al. (Eds.): LerNet ALFA Summer School 2008, LNCS 5520, pp. 252–300, 2009.

code generation techniques from the existing language and compilers for that language. The success of this technique thus depends critically on the properties of the host language.

With the advent of modern functional languages like Haskell [11] this approach has become a really feasible one. By applying the approach to build a combinator parsing library we show how Haskell's type system (with the associated class system) makes this language an ideal platform for describing EDSLs . Besides being a kind of user manual for the constructed library this tutorial also serves as an example of how to use Haskell concepts in developing such a library. Lazy evaluation plays a very important role in the semantics of the constructed parsers; thus, for those interested in a better understanding of lazy evaluation, the tutorial also provides many examples. A major concern with respect to combinator parsing is the ability or need to properly define and use parser combinators so that functional values (trees, unconsumed tokens, continuations, etc.) are correctly and efficiently manipulated.

In Sect. 2 we develop, starting from a set of basic combinators, a parser combinator library, the expressive power of which extends well above what is commonly found in *EBNF*-like formalisms. In Sect. 3 we present a case study, describing a sequence of ever more capable pocket calculators. Each subsequent version gives us a chance to introduce some further combinators with an example of their use.

Sect. 4 starts with a discussion of the shortcomings of the naïve implementation which was introduced in Sect.2, and we present solutions for all the identified problems, while constructing an alternative, albeit much more complicated library. One of the remarkable points here is that the basic interface which was introduced in Sect. 2 does not have to change, and that –thanks to the facilities provided by the Haskell class system– all our derived combinators can be used without having to be modified.

In Section 5 we investigate how we can use the progress information, which we introduced to keep track of the progress of parsing process, introduced in Sect. 4 to control the parsing process and how to deal with ambiguous grammars. In Sect. 6 we show how to use the Haskell type and class system to combine parsers which use different scanner and symbol type intertwined. In Sect. 7 we extend our combinators with error reporting properties and the possibility to continue with the parsing process in case of erroneous input. In Sect. 8 we introduce a class and a set of instances which enables us to make our expressions denoting parsers resemble the corresponding grammars even more. In Sect. 9 we touch upon some important extensions to our system which are too large to deal with in more detail, in Sect. 10 we provide a short comparison with other similar libraries and conclude.

2 A Basic Combinator Parser Library

In this section we describe how to embed grammatical descriptions into the programming language Haskellin such a way that the expressions we write closely resemble context- free grammars, but actually are descriptions of parsers for such languages. This technique has a long history, which can be traced back to the use of recursive descent parsers [2], which became popular because of their ease of use, their nice integration with semantic processing, and the absence of the need to (write and) use an off-line parser generator. We assume that the reader has a basic understanding in the concept of a context-free grammar, and probably also has seen the use of parser generators, such as YACC or ANTLR.

Just like most normal programming languages, embedded domain specific languages are composed of two things:

1. a collection of primitive constructs
2. ways to compose and name constructs

and when embedding grammars things are no different. The basic grammatical concepts are *terminal* and *non-terminal* symbols, or *terminals* and *non-terminals* for short. They can be combined by *sequential composition* (multiple constructs occurring one after another) or by *alternative composition* (a choice from multiple alternatives).

Note that one may argue that non-terminals are actually not primitive, but result from the introduction of a naming scheme; we will see that in the case of parser combinators, non-terminals are not introduced as a separate concept, but just are Haskell names referring to values which represent parsers.

2.1 The Types

Since grammatical expressions will turn out to be normal Haskell expressions, we start by discussing the types involved; and not just the types of the basic constructs, but also the types of the composition mechanisms. For most embedded languages the decisions taken here heavily influence the shape of the library to be defined, its extendability and eventually its success.

Basically, a parser takes a list of symbols and produces a tree. Introducing type variables to abstract from the symbol type s and the tree type t, a first approximation of our *Parser* type is:

$$\textbf{type}\ \mathit{Parser}\ s\ t = [s] \to t$$

Parsers do not need to consume the entire input list. Thus, apart from the tree, they also need to return the part of the input string that was not consumed:

$$\textbf{type}\ \mathit{Parser}\ s\ t = [s] \to (t, [s])$$

The symbol list $[s]$ can be thought of as a *state* that is transformed by the function while building the tree result.

Parsers can be ambiguous: there may be multiple ways to parse a string. Instead of a single result, we therefore have a list of possible results, each consisting of a parser tree and unconsumed input:

$$\textbf{type}\ \mathit{Parser}\ s\ t = [s] \to [(t, [s])]$$

This idea was dubbed by Wadler [17] as the "list of successes" method, and it underlies many backtracking applications. An added benefit is that a parser can return the empty list to indicate failure (no successes). If there is exactly one solution, the parser returns a singleton list.

Wrapping the type with a constructor P in a **newtype** definition we get the actual *Parser* type that we will use in the following sections:

$$\mathbf{newtype}\ \mathit{Parser}\ s\ t = P\ ([s] \to [(t, [s])])$$
$$\mathit{unP}\ (P\ p) = p$$

2.2 Basic Combinators: *pSym*, *pReturn* and *pFail*

As an example of the use of the *Parser* type we start by writing a function which recognises the letter `'a'`: keeping the "list of successes" type in mind we realise that either the input starts with an `'a'` character, in which case we have precisely one way to succeed, i.e. by removing this letter from the input, and returning this character as the witness of success paired with the unused part of the input. If the input does not start with an `'a'` (or is empty) we fail, and return the empty list, as an indication that there is no way to proceed from here:

```
pLettera :: Parser Char Char
pLettera = P (λinp → case inp of
                       (s : ss) | s ≡ 'a' → [('a', ss)]
                       otherwise →          []
             )
```

Of course, we want to abstract from this as soon as possible; we want to be able to recognise other characters than `'a'`, and we want to recognise symbols of other types than *Char*. We introduce our first basic parser constructing function *pSym*:

```
pSym ::    Eq s ⇒ s → Parser s s
pSym a = P (λinp → case inp of
                     (s : ss) | x ≡ a → [(s, ss)]
                     otherwise        → []
           )
```

Since we want to inspect elements from the input with terminal symbols of type s, we have added the *Eq s* constraint, which gives us access to equality ($\equiv$) for values of type s. Note that the function *pSym* by itself is strictly speaking not a parser, but a function which returns a parser. Since the argument is a run-time value it thus becomes possible to construct parsers at run-time.

One might wonder why we have incorporated the value of s in the result, and not the value a? The answer lies in the use of *Eq s* in the type of *Parser*; one should keep in mind that when $\equiv$ returns *True* this does not imply that the compared values are guaranteed to be bit-wise equal. Indeed, it is very common for a scanner –which pre-processes a list of characters into a list of tokens to be recognised– to merge different tokens into a single class with an extra attribute indicating which original token was found. Consider e.g. the following *Token* type:

```
data Token = Identifier      -- terminal symbol used in parser
           | Ident String    -- token constructed by scanner
           | Number Int
           | If_Symbol
           | Then_Symbol
```

Here, the first alternative corresponds to the terminal symbol as we find it in our grammar: we want to see an identifier and from the grammar point of view we do not care which one. The second alternative is the token which is returned by the scanner, and which contains extra information about which identifier was actually scanned; this is the value we want to use in further semantic processing, so this is the value we return as witness from the parser. That these symbols are the same, as far as parsing is concerned, is expressed by the following line in the definition of the function ≡:

```
instance Eq Token where
  (Ident _) ≡ Identifier = True
  ...
```

If we now define:

```
pIdent = pSym Identifier
```

we have added a special kind of terminal symbol.

The second basic combinator we introduce in this subsection is *pReturn*, which corresponds to the ϵ-production. The function always succeeds and as a witness returns its parameter; as we will see the function will come in handy when building composite witnesses out of more basic ones. The name was chosen to resemble the monadic *return* function, which injects values into the monadic computation:

```
pReturn :: a → Parser s a
pReturn a = P (λinp → [(a, inp)])
```

We could have chosen to let this function always return a specific value (e.g. ()), but as it will turn out the given definition provides a handy way to inject values into the result of the overall parsing process.

The final basic parser we introduce is the one which always fails:

```
pFail = P (const [])
```

One might wonder why one would need such a parser, but that will become clear in the next section, when we introduce *pChoice*.

2.3 Combining Parsers: <*>, <|>, <$> and *pChoice*

A grammar production usually consists of a sequence of terminal and non-terminal symbols, and a first choice might be to use values of type [*Parser s a*] to represent such productions. Since we usually will associate different types to different parsers, this does not work out. Hence we start out by restricting ourselves to productions of length 2 and introduce a special operator <*> which combines two parsers into a new one. What type should we choose for this operator? An obvious choice might be the type:

$$Parser\ s\ a \rightarrow Parser\ s\ b \rightarrow Parser\ s\ (a, b)$$

in which the witness type of the sequential composition is a pair of the witnesses for the elements of the composition. This approach was taken in early libraries [4]. A problem with this choice is that when combining the resulting parser with further parsers, we end up with a deeply nested binary Cartesian product. Instead of starting out with simple types for parsers, and ending up with complicated types for the composed parsers, we have taken the opposite route: we start out with a complicated type and end with a simple type. This interface was pioneered by Röjemo [12], made popular through the library described by Swierstra and Duponcheel [15], and has been incorporated into the Haskell libraries by McBride and Paterson [10]. Now it is know as the *applicative interface.* It is based on the idea that if we have a value of a complicated type $b \rightarrow a$, and a value of type b, *we can compose them into a simpler type by applying the first value to the second one.* Using this insight we can now give the type of <*>, together with its definition:

$$\begin{array}{ll}
(<\!\!*\!\!>) & ::\ Parser\ s\ (b \rightarrow a) \rightarrow Parser\ s\ b \rightarrow Parser\ s\ a \\
P\ p_1 <\!\!*\!\!> P\ p_2 & = P\ (\lambda inp \rightarrow [(v_1\ v_2, ss_2) \mid (v_1, ss_1) \leftarrow p_1\ inp \\
 & \qquad\qquad\qquad\qquad\qquad\quad ,\ (v_2, ss_2) \leftarrow p_2\ ss_1 \\
 & \qquad\qquad\qquad\quad] \\
 & \qquad)
\end{array}$$

The resulting function returns all possible values $v_1\ v_2$ with remaining state ss_2, where v_1 is a witness value returned by parser p_1 with remaining state ss_1. The state ss_1 is used as the starting state for the parser p_2, which in its turn returns the witnesses v_2 and the corresponding final states ss_2. Note how the types of the parsers were chosen in such a way that the value of type $v_1\ v_2$ matches the witness type of the composed parser.

As a very simple example, we give a parser which recognises the letter 'a' twice, and if it succeeds returns the string "aa":

$$\begin{array}{ll}
pString_aa = & (pReturn\ (:) <\!\!*\!\!> pLettera) \\
 & <\!\!*\!\!> \\
 & (pReturn\ (\lambda x \rightarrow [x]) <\!\!*\!\!> pLettera)
\end{array}$$

Let us take a look at the types. The type of (:) is $a \rightarrow [a] \rightarrow [a]$, and hence the type of *pReturn* (:) is $Parser\ s\ (a \rightarrow [a] \rightarrow [a])$. Since the type of *pLettera* is *Parser Char Char*, the type of *pReturn* (:) <*> *pLettera* is $Parser\ Char\ ([Char] \rightarrow [Char])$. Similarly the type of the right hand side operand is $Parser\ Char\ [Char]$, and hence the type of the complete expression is $Parser\ Char\ [Char]$. Having chosen <*> to be left associative, the first pair of parentheses may be left out. Thus, many of our parsers will start out by producing some function, followed by a sequence of parsers each providing an argument to this function.

Besides sequential composition we also need *choice*. Since we are using lists to return all possible ways to succeed, we can directly define the operator $<|>$ by returning the concatenation of all possible ways in which either of its arguments can succeed:

$$(<|>) \quad :: Parser\ s\ a \rightarrow Parser\ s\ a \rightarrow Parser\ s\ a$$
$$P\ p_1 <|> P\ p_2 = P\ (\lambda inp \rightarrow p_1\ inp +\!\!+\ p_2\ inp)$$

Now we have seen the definition of $<|>$, note that *pFail* is both a left and a right unit for this operator:

$$pFail <|> p \equiv p \equiv p <|> pFail$$

which will play a role in expressions like

$$pChoice\ ps = foldr\ (<|>)\ pFail\ ps$$

One of the things left open thus far is what precedence level these newly introduced operators should have. It turns out that the following minimises the number of parentheses:

infixl 5 $<*>$
infixr 3 $<|>$

As an example to see how this all fits together, we write a function which recognises all correctly nested parentheses – such as `"()(()())"`– and returns the maximal nesting depth occurring in the sequence. The language is described by the grammar $S \rightarrow$ `'('` S `')'` $S \mid \epsilon$, and its transcription into parser combinators reads:

$$parens :: Parser\ Char\ Int$$
$$parens = pReturn\ (\lambda\_\ b\ \_\ d \rightarrow (1 + b)\ \text{`}max\text{`}\ d)$$
$$<*> pSym\ \text{'('} <*> parens <*> pSym\ \text{')'} <*> parens$$
$$<|> pReturn\ 0$$

Since the pattern *pReturn* ... $<*>$ will occur quite often, we introduce a third combinator, to be defined in terms of the combinators we have seen already. The combinator $<\$>$ takes a function of type $b \rightarrow a$, and a parser of type *Parser s b*, and builds a value of type *Parser s a*, by applying the function to the witness returned by the parser. Its definition is:

infix 7 $<\$>$
$$(<\$>) :: (b \rightarrow a) \rightarrow (Parser\ s\ b) \rightarrow Parser\ s\ a$$
$$f <\$> p = pReturn\ f <*> p$$

Using this new combinator we can rewrite the above example into:

$$parens = (\lambda\_\ b\ \_\ d \rightarrow (1 + b)\ \text{`}max\text{`}\ d)$$
$$<\$> pSym\ \text{'('} <*> parens <*> pSym\ \text{')'} <*> parens$$
$$<|> pReturn\ 0$$

Notice that left argument of the $<\$>$ occurrence has type $a \rightarrow (Int \rightarrow (b \rightarrow (Int \rightarrow Int)))$, which is a function taking the four results returned by the parsers to the right of the `<$>` and constructs the result sought; this all works because we have defined `<*>` to associate to the left.

Although we said we would restrict ourselves to productions of length 2, in fact we can just write productions containing an arbitrary number of elements. Each extra occurrence of the `<*>` operator introduces an anonymous non-terminal, which is used only once.

Before going into the development of our library, there is one nasty point to be dealt with. For the grammar above, we could have just as well chosen $S \rightarrow S$ `'('` S `')'` $\mid \epsilon$, but unfortunately the direct transcription into a parser would not work. Why not? Because the resulting parser is left recursive: the parser *parens* will start by calling itself, and this will lead to a non-terminating parsing process. Despite the elegance of the parsers introduced thus far, this is a serious shortcoming of the approach taken. Often, one has to change the grammar considerably to get rid of the left-recursion. Also, one might write left-recursive grammars without being aware of it, and it will take time to debug the constructed parser. Since we do not have an off-line grammar analysis, extra care has to be taken by the programmer since the system just does not work as expected, without giving a proper warning; it may just fail to produce a result at all, or it may terminate prematurely with a stack-overflow.

2.4 Special Versions of Basic Combinators: `<*`, `*>`, `<$` and *opt*

As we see in the *parens* program the values witnessing the recognition of the parentheses themselves are not used in the computation of the result. As this situation is very common we introduce specialised versions of `<$>` and `<*>`: in the new operators `<$`, `<*` and `*>`, the missing bracket indicates which witness value is not to be included in the result:

```
infixl 3 `opt`
infixl 5 <*, *>
infixl 7 <$

f <$ p  = const <$> pReturn f <*> p
p <* q  = const <$> p         <*> q
p *> q  = id    <$  p         <*> q
```

We use this opportunity to introduce two further useful functions, *opt* and *pParens* and reformulate the *parens* function:

```
pParens :: Parser s a → Parser s a
pParens p = id <$ pSym '(' <*> p <* pSym ')'

opt :: Parser s a → a → Parser s a
p `opt` v  = p <|> pReturn v

parens     = (max.(1+)) <$> pParens parens <*> parens `opt` 0
```

As a final combinator, which we will use in the next section, we introduce a combinator which creates the parser for a specific keyword given as its parameter:

$$pSyms\ [\,] = pReturn\ [\,]$$
$$pSyms\ (x : xs) = (:) \mathbin{<\$>} pSym\ x \mathbin{<*>} pSyms\ xs$$

3 Case Study: Pocket Calculators

In this section, we develop –starting from the basic combinators introduced in the previous section– a series of pocket calculators, each being an extension of its predecessor. In doing so we gradually build up a small collection of useful combinators, which extend the basic library.

To be able to run all the different versions we provide a small driver function $run :: (Show\ t) \Rightarrow Parser\ Char\ t \rightarrow String \rightarrow IO\ ()$ in appendix A. The first argument of the function *run* is the actual pocket calculator to be used, whereas the second argument is a string prompting the user with the kind of expressions that can be handled. Furthermore we perform a little bit of preprocessing by removing all spaces occurring in the input.

3.1 Recognising a Digit

Our first calculator is extremely simple; it requires a digit as input and returns this digit. As a generalisation of the combinator *pSym* we introduce the combinator *pSatisfy*: it checks whether the current input token satisfies a specific predicate instead of comparing it with the expected symbol:

$$\begin{array}{l} pDigit = pSatisfy\ (\lambda x \rightarrow \texttt{'0'} \leqslant x \wedge x \leqslant \texttt{'9'}) \\ pSatisfy :: (s \rightarrow Bool) \rightarrow Parser\ s\ s \\ pSatisfy\ p = P\ (\lambda inp \rightarrow \textbf{case}\ inp\ \textbf{of} \\ \qquad\qquad\qquad\qquad (x : xs) \mid p\ x \rightarrow [(x, xs)] \\ \qquad\qquad\qquad\qquad otherwise \quad \rightarrow [\,] \\ \qquad\qquad\quad) \\ pSym\ a = pSatisfy\ (\equiv a) \end{array}$$

A demo run now reads:

```
*Calcs> run pDigit "5"
Give an expression like: 5 or (q) to quit
3
Result is: '3'
Give an expression like: 5 or (q) to quit
a
Incorrect input
Give an expression like: 5 or (q) to quit
q
*Calcs>
```

In the next version we slightly change the type of the parser such that it returns an *Int* instead of a *Char*, using the combinator <\$>:

$$\begin{array}{l} pDigitAsInt :: Parser\ Char\ Int \\ pDigitAsInt = (\lambda c \rightarrow fromEnum\ c - fromEnum\ \texttt{'0'}) <\$> pDigit \end{array}$$

3.2 Integers: *pMany* and *pMany1*

Since single digits are very boring, let's change our parser into one which recognises a natural number, i.e. a (non-empty) sequence of digits. For this purpose we introduce two new combinators, both converting a parser for an element to a parser for a sequence of such elements. The first one also accepts the empty sequence, whereas the second one requires at least one element to be present:

$$\begin{array}{l} pMany, pMany1 :: Parser\ s\ a \rightarrow Parser\ s\ [a] \\ pMany\ p\ \ = (:) <\$> p <\ast> pMany\ p\ `opt`\ [\,] \\ pMany1\ p = (:) <\$> p <\ast> pMany\ p \end{array}$$

The second combinator forms the basis for our natural number recognition process, in which we store the recognised digits in a list, before converting this list into the *Int* value:

$$\begin{array}{l} pNatural :: Parser\ Char\ Int \\ pNatural = foldl\ (\lambda a\ b \rightarrow a * 10 + b)\ 0 <\$> pMany1\ pDigitAsInt \end{array}$$

From here it is only a small step to recognising signed numbers. A $-$ sign in front of the digits is mapped onto the function *negate*, and if it is absent we use the function *id*:

$$\begin{array}{l} pInteger :: Parser\ Char\ Int \\ pInteger = (negate <\$\ (pSyms\ \texttt{"-"})\ `opt`\ id) <\ast> pNatural \end{array}$$

3.3 More Sequencing: *pChainL*

In our next version, we will show how to parse expressions with infix operators of various precedence levels and various association directions. We start by parsing an expression containing a single + operator, e.g. "2+55". Note again that the result of recognising the + token is discarded, and the operator (+) is only applied to the two recognised integers:

$$pPlus = (+) <\$> pInteger <\ast\ pSyms\ \texttt{"+"} <\ast> pInteger$$

We extend this parser to a parser which handles any number of operands separated by +-tokens. It demonstrates how we can make the result of a parser to differ completely from its "natural" abstract syntax tree.

$$\begin{array}{l} pPlus' = applyAll <\$> pInteger <\ast> pMany\ ((+) <\$\ pSyms\ \texttt{"+"} <\ast> pInteger) \\ \quad applyAll :: a \rightarrow [a \rightarrow a] \rightarrow a \\ \quad applyAll\ x\ (f : fs) \ = \ applyAll\ (f\ x)\ fs \\ \quad applyAll\ x\ [\,] \qquad\ = \ x \end{array}$$

Unfortunately, this approach is a bit too simple, since we are relying on the commutativity of + for this approach to work, as each integer recognized in the call to *pMany* becomes the first argument of the (+) operator. If we want to do the same for expressions with − operators, we have to make sure that we *flip* the operator associated with the recognised operator token, in order to make the value which is recognised as second operand to become the right hand side operand:

```
pMinus' = applyAll <$> pInteger <*> pMany (flip (-) <$ pSyms "-"
                                                    <*> pInteger
                                          )
flip f x y = f y x
```

From here it is only a small step to the recognition of expressions which contain both + and − operators:

```
pPlusMinus = applyAll <$> pInteger
                      <*> pMany (  ( flip (-) <$ pSyms "-"
                                   <|>
                                     flip (+) <$ pSyms "+"
                                   ) <*> pInteger
                                )
```

Since we will use this pattern often we abstract from it and introduce a parser combinator *pChainL*, which takes two arguments:

1. the parser for the separator, which returns a value of type $a \to a \to a$
2. the parser for the operands, which returns a value of type a

Using this operator, we redefine the function *pPlusMinus*:

```
pChainL :: Parser s (a -> a -> a) -> Parser s a -> Parser s a
pChainL op p = applyAll <$> p <*> pMany (flip <$> op <*> p)
pPlusMinus' = ((-) <$ pSyms "-" <|> (+) <$ pSyms "+")
              `pChainL`
              pInteger
```

3.4 Left Factoring: *pChainR*, <**> and <??>

As a natural companion to *pChainL*, we would expect a *pChainR* combinator, which treats the recognised operators right-associatively. Before giving its code, we first introduce two other operators, which play an important role in fighting common sources of inefficiency. When we have the parser *p*:

```
p =     f <$> q <*> r
    <|> g <$> q <*> s
```

then we see that our backtracking implementation may first recognise the *q* from the first alternative, subsequently can fail when trying to recognise *r*, and will then continue with recognising *q* again before trying to recognise an *s*. Parser generators recognise such situations and perform a grammar transformation (or equivalent action) in order to share the recognition of q between the two alternatives. Unfortunately, we do not have an explicit representation of the underlying grammar at hand which we can inspect and transform [16], and without further help from the programmer there is no way we can identify such a common *left-factor*. Hence, we have to do the left-factoring by hand. Since this situation is quite common, we introduce two operators which assist us in this process. The first one is a modification of <*>, which we have named <**>; it differs from <*> in that it applies the result of its right-hand side operand to the result of its left-hand side operand:

$$(\text{<**>}) :: Parser\ s\ b \rightarrow Parser\ s\ (b \rightarrow a) \rightarrow Parser\ s\ a$$
$$p \text{ <**> } q = (\lambda a\ f \rightarrow f\ a) \text{ <\$> } p \text{ <*> } q$$

With help of this new operator we can now transcribe the above example, introducing calls to *flip* because the functions f and g now get their second arguments first, into:

$$p = q \text{ <**> } (flip\ f \text{ <\$> } r \text{ <|> } flip\ g \text{ <\$> } s)$$

In some cases, the element s is missing from the second alternative, and for such situations we have the combinator <??>:

$$(\text{<??>}) :: Parser\ s\ a \rightarrow Parser\ s\ (a \rightarrow a) \rightarrow Parser\ s\ a$$
$$p \text{ <??> } q = p \text{ <**> } (q \text{ `opt` } id)$$

Let us now return to the code for *pChainR*. Our first attempt reads:

$$\begin{aligned} pChainR\ op\ p = &\ id \quad \text{<\$> } p \\ \text{<|>} &\ flip\ (\$) \text{ <\$> } p \text{ <*> } (flip \text{ <\$> } op \text{ <*> } pChainR\ op\ p) \end{aligned}$$

which can, using the refactoring method, be expressed more elegantly by:

$$pChainR\ op\ p = r\ \textbf{where}\ r = p \text{ <??> } (flip \text{ <\$> } op \text{ <*> } r)$$

3.5 Two Precedence Levels

Looking back at the definition of *pPlusMinus*, we see still a recurring pattern, i.e. the recognition of an operator symbol and associating it with its semantics. This is the next thing we are going to abstract from. We start out by defining a function that associates an operator terminal symbol with its semantics:

$$pOp\ (sem, symbol) = sem \text{ <\$ } pSyms\ symbol$$

Our next library combinator *pChoice* takes a list of parsers and combines them into a single parser:

$$pChoice = foldr\ (\text{<|>})\ pFail$$

Using these two combinators, we now can define the collective additive operator recognition by:

```
anyOp  = pChoice . map pOp
addops = anyOp [((+), "+"), ((-), "-")]
```

Since multiplication has precedence over addition, we can now define a new non-terminal *pTimes*, which can only recognise operands containing multiplicative operators:

```
pPlusMinusTimes = pChainL addops pTimes
pTimes          = pChainL mulops pInteger
mulops          = anyOp [((*), "*")]
```

3.6 Any Number of Precedence Levels: *pPack*

Of course, we do not want to restrict ourselves to just two priority levels. On the other hand, we are not looking forward to explicitly introduce a new non-terminal for each precedence level, so we take a look at the code, and try to see a pattern. We start out by substituting the expression for *pTimes* into the definition of *pPlusMinusTimes*:

```
pPlusMinusTimes = pChainL addops (pChainL mulops pInteger)
```

in which we recognise a *foldr*:

```
pPlusMinusTimes = foldr pChainL pInteger [addops, mulops]
```

Now it has become straightforward to add new operators: just add the new operator, with its semantics, to the corresponding level of precedence. If its precedence lies between two already existing precedences, then just add a new list between these two levels. To complete the parsing of expressions we add the recognition of parentheses:

```
pPack       :: Eq s => [s] -> Parser s a -> [s] -> Parser s a
pPack o p c = pSyms o *> p <* pSyms c

pExpr   = foldr pChainL pFactor [addops, mulops]
pFactor = pInteger <|> pPack "(" pExpr ")"
```

As a final extension we add recognition of conditional expressions. In order to do so we will need to recognise keywords like **if**, **then**, and **else**. This invites us to add the companion to the *pChoice* combinator:

```
pSeq :: [Parser s a] -> Parser s [a]
pSeq (p : pp) = (:) <$> p <*> pSeq pp
pSeq []       = pReturn []
```

Extending our parser with conditional expressions is now straightforward:

```
pExpr       = foldr pChainL pFactor [addops, mulops] <|> pIfThenElse
pIfThenElse = choose <$  pSyms "if"
                     <*> pBoolExpr
                     <*  pSyms "then"
                     <*> pExpr
                     <*  pSyms "else"
```

```
                    <*>    pExpr
choose c t e = if c then t else e
pBoolExpr  = foldr pChainR pRelExpr [orops, andops]
pRelExpr   =        True <$ pSyms "True"
               <|> False <$ pSyms "False"
               <|> pExpr <**> pRelOp <*> pExpr
andops = anyOp [((∧), "&&")]
orops  = anyOp [((∨), "||")]
pRelOp = anyOp [((≤), "<="), ((≥), ">="),
                ((≡), "=="), ((≢), "/="),
                ((<), "<"), ((>) , ">")]
```

3.7 Monadic Interface: *Monad* and *pTimes*

The parsers described thus far have the expressive power of context-free grammars. We have introduced extra combinators to capture frequently occurring grammatical patterns such as in the EBNF extensions. Because parsers are normal Haskell values, which are computed at run-time, we can however go beyond the conventional context-free grammar expressiveness by using the result of one parser to construct the next one. An example of this can be found in the recognition of XML-based input. We assume the input be a tree-like structure with tagged nodes, and we want to map our input onto the data type *XML*. To handle situations like this we make our parser type an instance of the class *Monad*:

```
instance Monad (Parser s) where
return = pReturn
P pa >>= a2pb = P (λinput → [b_input'' | (a, input') ← pa input
                                         , b_input''  ← unP (a2pb a) input']
                  )
data XML = Tag String [XML] | Leaf String
pXML =       do t ← pOpenTag
                Tag t <$> pMany pXML <* pCloseTag t
       <|> Leaf <$> pLeaf
pTagged p   = pPack "<" p ">"
pOpenTag    = pTagged pIdent
pCloseTag t = pTagged (pSym '/' *> pSyms t)
pLeaf       = ...
pIdent      = pMany1 (pSatisfy (λc → 'a' ≤ c ∧ c ≤ 'z'))
```

A second example of the use of monads is in the recognition of the language $\{a^n b^n c^n | n >= 0\}$, which is well known not to be context-free. Here, we use the number of `'a'`'s recognised to build parsers that recognise exactly that number of `'b'`'s and `'c'`'s. For the result, we return the original input, which has now been checked to be an element of the language:

$$
\begin{aligned}
pABC = \mathbf{do}\ & as \leftarrow pMany\ (pSym\ \texttt{'a'}) \\
& \mathbf{let}\ n = length\ as \\
& bs \leftarrow p\_n\_Times\ n\ (pSym\ \texttt{'b'}) \\
& cs \leftarrow p\_n\_Times\ n\ (pSym\ \texttt{'c'}) \\
& return\ (as +\!\!+\ bs +\!\!+\ cs)
\end{aligned}
$$

$$
\begin{aligned}
&p\_n\_Times :: Int \rightarrow Parser\ s\ a \rightarrow Parser\ s\ [a] \\
&p\_n\_Times\ 0\ p = pReturn\ [\,] \\
&p\_n\_Times\ n\ p = (:)\ \texttt{<\$>}\ p\ \texttt{<*>}\ p\_n\_Times\ (n-1)\ p
\end{aligned}
$$

3.8 Conclusions

We have now come to the end of our introductory section, in which we have introduced the idea of a combinator language and have constructed a small library of basic and non-basic combinators. It should be clear by now that there is no end to the number of new combinators that can be defined, each capturing a pattern recurring in some input to be recognised. We finish this section by summing up the advantages of using an EDSL.

full abstraction. Most special purpose programming languages have –unlike our host language Haskell– poorly defined abstraction mechanisms, often not going far beyond a simple macro-processing system. Although –with a substantial effort– amazing things can be achieved in this way as we can see from the use of TEX, we do not think this is the right way to go; programs become harder to get correct, and often long detours –which have little to do with the actual problem at hand– have to be taken in order to get things into acceptable shape. Because our embedded language inherits from Haskell –by virtue of being an embedded language– all the abstraction mechanisms and the advanced type system, it takes a head start with respect to all the individual implementation efforts.

type checking. Many special purpose programming languages, and especially the so-called scripting languages, only have a weak concept of a type system; simply because the type system was not considered to be important when the design took off and compilers should remain small. Many scripting languages are completely dynamically typed, and some see this even as an advantage since the type system does not get into their way when implementing new abstractions. We feel that this perceived shortcoming is due to the very basic type systems found in most general purpose programming languages. Haskell however has a very powerful type system, which is not easy to surpass, unless one is prepared to enter completely new grounds, as with dependently typed languages such as Agda (see paper in this volume by Bove and Dybjer). One of the huge benefits of working with a strongly typed language is furthermore that the types of the library functions already give a very good insight in the role of the parameters and what a function is computing.

clean semantics. One of the ways in which the meaning of a language construct is traditionally defined is by its denotational semantics, i.e. by mapping the language construct onto a mathematical object, usually being a function. This fits very well with the embedding of domain specific languages in Haskell, since functions are the primary class of values in Haskell. As a result, implementing a DSL in Haskell almost boils down to giving its denotational semantics in the conventional way and getting a compiler for free.

lazy evaluation. One of the formalisms of choice in implementing the context sensitive aspects of a language is by using attribute grammars. Fortunately, the equivalent of attribute grammars can be implemented straightforwardly in a lazily evaluated functional language; inherited attributes become parameters and synthesized attributes become part of the result of the functions giving the semantics of a construct [14,13].

Of course there are also downsides to the embedding approach. Although the programmer is thinking he writes a program in the embedded language, he is still programming in the host language. As a result of this, error messages from the type system, which can already be quite challenging in Haskell, are phrased in terms of the host language constructs too, and without further measures the underlying implementation shines through. In the case of our parser combinators, this has as a consequence that the user is not addressed in terms of terminals, non-terminals, keywords, and productions, but in terms of the types implementing these constructs.

There are several ways in which this problem can be alleviated. In the first place, we can try to hide the internal structure as much as possible by using a lot of **newtype** constructors, and thus defining the parser type by:

$$\mathbf{newtype}\ \mathit{Parser'}\ s\ a = \mathit{Parser'}\ ([s] \rightarrow [(a,[s])])$$

A second approach is to extend the type checker of Haskell such that the generated error messages can be tailored by the programmer. Now, the library designer not only designs his library, but also the domain specific error messages that come with the library. In the Helium compiler [5], which handles a subset of Haskell, this approach has been implemented with good results. As an example, one might want to compare the two error messages given for the incorrect program in Fig. 1. In Fig. 2 we see the error message generated by a version of Hugs, which does not even point near the location of the error, and in which the internal representation of the parsers shines through. In Fig. 3, taken from [6], we see that Helium, by using a specialised version of the type rules which are provided by the programmer of the library, manages to address the application programmer in terms of the embedded language; it uses the word *parser* and explains that the types do not match, i.e. that a component is missing in one of the alternatives. A final option in the Helium compiler is the possibility to program the search for possible corrections, e.g. by listing functions which are likely to be confused by the programmer (such as $<\!\!*\!\!>$ and $<\!\!*$ in programming parsers, or $:$ and $+\!\!+$ by beginning Haskell programmers). As we can see in Fig. 4 we can now pinpoint the location of the mistake even better and suggest corrective actions.

```
data Expr     = Lambda Patterns Expr     -- can contain more alternatives
type Patterns = [Pattern]
type Pattern  = String

pExpr :: Parser Token Expr
pExpr
  =  pAndPrioExpr
 <|> Lambda <$  pSyms "\\"
            <*> many  pVarid
            <*  pSyms "->"
            <*  pExpr          -- <* should be <*>
```

Fig. 1. Type incorrect program

```
ERROR "Example.hs":7 - Type error in application
*** Expression     : pAndPrioExpr <|> Lambda <$ pSyms "\\"
                       <*> many pVarid <* pSyms "->" <* pExpr
*** Term           : pAndPrioExpr
*** Type           : Parser Token Expr
*** Does not match : [Token] -> [(Expr -> Expr,[Token])]
```

Fig. 2. Hugs, version November 2002

```
Compiling Example.hs
(7,6): The result types of the parsers in the operands of <|> don't match
  left parser    : pAndPrioExpr
    result type : Expr
  right parser   : Lambda <$ pSyms "\\" <*> many pVarid <* pSyms "->"
                                                         <* pExpr
    result type : Expr -> Expr
```

Fig. 3. Helium, version 1.1 (type rules extension)

```
Compiling Example.hs
(11,13): Type error in the operator <*
  probable fix: use <*> instead
```

Fig. 4. Helium, version 1.1 (type rules extension and sibling functions)

4 Improved Implementations

Since the simple implementation which was used in section 2 has quite a number of shortcomings we develop in this section a couple of alternative implementations of the basic interface. Before doing so we investigate the problems to be solved, and then deal with them one by one.

4.1 Shortcomings

Error reporting. One of the first things someone notices when starting to use the library is that when erroneous input is given to the parser the result is [], indicating that it is not possible to get a correct parse. This might be acceptable in situations where the input was generated by another program and is expected to be correct, but for a library to be used by many in many different situations this is unacceptable. At least one should be informed about the position in the input where the parser got stuck, and what symbols were expected.

Online Results. A further issue to be investigated is at what moment the result of the parser will become available for further processing. When reading a long list of records –such as a BiBTeX file–, one is likely to want to process the records one by one and to emit the result of processing it as soon as it has been recognised, instead of first recognising the complete list, storing that list in memory, and finally –after we know that the input does not contain errors– process all the elements.

When we inspect the code for the sequential composition closely however, and investigate when the first element of the resulting list will be produced, we see that this is only the case after the right-hand side parser of <*> returns its first result. For the root symbol this implies that we get only to see the result after we have found our first complete parse. So, taking the observation of the previous subsection into account, at the end of the first complete parse we have stored the complete input and the complete result in memory. For long inputs this may become prohibitively costly, especially since garbage collection will take a lot of time without actually collecting a lot of garbage.

To illustrate the difference consider the parser:

$\mathit{parse}\ (\mathit{pMany}\ (\mathit{pSym}\ \texttt{'a'}))\ (\mathit{listToStr}\ (\texttt{'a'} : \bot)$

The parsers we have seen thus far will produce $\bot$ here. An online parser will return `'a'` $: \bot$ instead, since the initial `'a'` could be succesfully recognised irrespective of what is behind it in the input.

Error Correction. Although this is nowadays less common, it would be nice if the parser could apply (mostly small) error repairing steps, such as inserting a missing closing parenthesis or **end** symbol. Also spurious tokens in the input stream might be deleted. Of course the user should be properly informed about the steps which were taken in order to be able to proceed parsing.

Space Consumption. The backtracking implementation may lead to unexpected space consumption. After the parser p in a sequential composition p <*> q has found its first complete parse, parsing by q commences. Since this may fail further alternatives for p may have to be tried, even when it is obvious from the grammar that these will all fail. In order to be able to continue with the backtracking process (i.e. go back to a previous choice point) the implementation keeps a reference in the input which was passed to the composite parser. Unfortunately this is also the case for the root symbol, and thus the complete input is kept in memory at least until the first complete parse has been found, and its witness has been selected as the one to use for further processing

This problem is well known from many systems based on backtracking implementations. In Prolog we have the *cut* clause to explicitly indicate points beyond which no backtracking should take place, and also some parser combinator libraries [9] have similar mechanisms.

Conclusions. Although the problems at first seem rather unrelated they are not. If we want to have an online result this implies that we want to start processing a result without knowing whether a complete parse can be found. If we add error correction we actually change our parsers from parsers which may fail to parsers which will always succeed (i.e. return a result), but probably with an error message. In solving the problems mentioned we will start with the space consumption problem, and next we change the implementation to produce online results. As we will see special measures have to be taken to make the described parsers instances of the class *Monad*.

We will provide the full code in this tutorial. Unfortunately when we add error reporting and error correction our way of presenting code in an incremental way leads to code duplication. So we will deal with the last two issues separately in Sect. 7.

4.2 Parsing Classes

Since we will be giving many different implementations and our aim is to construct a library which is generally usable, we start out by defining some classes.

Applicative. Since the basic interface is useable beyond the basic parser combinators from Sect. 3 we introduce a class for it: *Applicative*.[1]

```
class Applicative p where
  (<*>)   :: p (b → a) → p b → p a
  (<|>)   :: p a       → p a → p a
  (<$>)   :: (b → a)   → p b → p a
  pReturn :: a               → p a
  pFail   ::                   p a
  f <$> p = pReturn f <*> p
instance Applicative p ⇒ Functor p where
  fmap = (<$>)
```

The class *Describes*. Although for parsing the input is just a sequence of terminal symbols, in practice the situation is somewhat different. We assume our grammars are defined in terms of terminal *symbols*, whereas we can split our input state into the next *token* and a a new *state*. A token may contain extra position information or more detailed information which is not relevant for the parsing process. We have seen an example already of the latter; when parsing we may want to see an identifier, but it is completely irrelevant which identifier

[1] We do not use the class *Applicative* from the module *Control.Applicative*, since it provides standard implementations for some operations for which we want to give optimized implementations, as the possibility arises.

is actually recognised. Hence we want check whether the current token matches with an expected symbol. Of course these values do not have to be of the same type. We capture the relation between input *tokens* and terminal *symbols* by the class *Describes*:

```
class symbol `Describes` token where
  eqSymTok :: symbol → token → Bool
```

Recognising a single symbol: *Symbol*. The function *pSym* takes as parameter a terminal *symbol*, but returns a parser which has as its witness an input *token*. Because we again will have many different implementations we make *pSym* a member of a class too.

```
class Symbol p symbol token where
  pSym :: symbol → p token
```

Generalising the Input: *Provides*. In the previous section we have taken the input to be a list of tokens. In reality this may also be a too simple approach. We may e.g. want to maintain position information, or extra state which can be manipulated by special combinators. From the parsing point of view the thing that matters is that the input state can provide a *token* on demand if possible:

```
class Provides state symbol token | state symbol → token where
  splitState :: symbol → state → Maybe (token, state)
```

We have decided to pass the expected *symbol* to the function *splitState*. Since we will also be able to switch *state* type we have decided to add a functional dependecy *state symbol* → *token*, stating that the *state* together with the expected *symbol* type determines how a token is to be produced. We can thus switch from one scanning stategy to another by passing a symbol of a different type to pSym!

Calling a parser: *Parser*. We will often have to check whether we have read the complete input, and thus we introduce a class containing the function *eof* (end-of-file) which tells us whether more tokens have to be recognised:

```
class Eof state where
  eof :: state → Bool
```

Because our parsers will all have different interfaces we introduce a function *parse* which knows how to call a specific parser and how to retrieve the result:

```
class Parser p where
    parse :: p state a → state → a
```

The instances of this class will serve as a typical example of how to use a parser of type *p* from within a Haskell program. For specific implementations of *p*, and in specific circumstances one may want to vary on the given standard implementations.

4.3 From Depth-First to Breadth-First

In this section we will define four instances of the *Parser* class:

1. the type R ('recognisers') in subsection 4.4
2. the type P_h ('history parsers') in subsection 4.5,
3. the type P_f ('future parsers') in subsection 4.6, and
4. the type P_m ('monad parsers') in subsection 4.7.

All four types will be polymorphic, having two type parameters: the type of the state, and the type of the witness of the correct parse. This is a digression from the parser type in Sect. 2, which was polymorphic in the *symbol* type and the witness type.

All four types will be functions, which operate on a state rather than a list of symbols. The state type must be an instance of *Provides* together with a symbol and a token type, and the symbol and the token must be an instance of *Describes*.

A further digression from section 2 is that the parsers in this section are not ambiguous. Instead of a list of successes, they return a single result.

As a final digression, the result type of the parsers is not a pair of a witness and a final state, but a witness only wrapped in a *Steps* datatype. The *Steps* datatype will be introduced below. It is an encoding of whether there is failure or success, and in the case of success, how much input was consumed.

As we explained before, the list-of-successes method basically is a depth-first search technique. If we manage to change this depth-first approach into a breath-first approach, then there is no need to hang onto the complete input until we are finished parsing. If we manage to run all alternative parsers in parallel we can discard the current input token once it has been inspected by all active parsers, since it will never be inspected again.

Haskell's lazy evaluation provides a nice way to drive all the active alternatives in a step by step fashion. The main ingredient for this process is the data type *Steps*, which plays a crucial role in all our implementations, and describes the type of values constructed by all parsers to come. It can be seen as a lazily constructed trace representing the progress of the parsing process.

```
data Steps a where
  Step :: Steps a → Steps a
  Fail ::           Steps a
  Done :: a       → Steps a
```

Instead of returning just a witness from the parsing process we will return a nested application of *Step*'s, which has eventually a *Fail* constructor indicating a failed branch in our breadth-first search, or a *Done* constructor which indicates that parsing completed successfully and presents the witness of that parse. For each successfully recognised symbol we get a *Step* constructor in the resulting *Steps* sequence; thus the number of *Step* constructors in the result of a parser tells us up to which point in the input we have successfully proceeded, and more specifically if the sequence ends in a *Fail* the number of *Step*-constructors tell us where this alternative failed to proceed.

The function driving our breadth-first behaviour is the function *best*, which compares two *Steps* sequences and returns the "best" one:

$$\begin{aligned}
&best :: Steps\ a \rightarrow Steps\ a \rightarrow Steps\ a\\
&Fail\quad \text{`}best\text{`}\ r \quad = r\\
&l\quad \text{`}best\text{`}\ Fail \quad = l\\
&(Step\ l)\ \text{`}best\text{`}\ (Step\ r) = Step\ (l\ \text{`}best\text{`}\ r)\\
&_\quad \text{`}best\text{`}\ _ \quad = error\ \texttt{"incorrect parser"}
\end{aligned}$$

The last alternative covers all the situations, where either one parser completes and another is still active (*Step*'*best*' *Done*,*Done*'*best*' *Step*), or where two active parsers complete at the same time (*Done* / *Done*) as a result of an ambiguity in the grammar. For the time being we assume that such situations will not occur.

The alternative which takes care of the conversion from depth-first to breadth-first is the one in which both arguments of the *best* function start with a *Step* constructor. In this case we discover that both alternatives can make progress, so the combined parser can make progress by immediately returning a *Step* constructor; we do however not decide nor reveal yet which alternative eventually will be chosen. The expression *l* '*best*' *r* in the right hand side is lazily evaluated, and only unrolled further when needed, i.e. when further pattern matching takes place on this value, and that is when all *Step* constructors corresponding to the current input position have been merged into a single *Step*. The sequence associated with this *Step* constructor is internally an expression, consisting of further calls to the function *best*. Later we will introduce more elaborate versions of this type *Steps*, but the idea will remain the same, and they will all exhibit the breadth-first behaviour.

In order to retrieve a value from a *Steps* value we write a function *eval* which retrieves the value remembered by the *Done* at the end of the sequence, provided it exists:*

$$\begin{aligned}
&eval :: Steps\ a \rightarrow a\\
&eval\ (Step\ l) \ \ = eval\ l\\
&eval\ (Done\ v) = v\\
&eval\ Fail \quad\ \ = error\ \texttt{"should not happen"}
\end{aligned}$$

4.4 Recognisers

After the preparatory work introducing the *Steps* data type, we introduce our first 'parser' type, which we will dubb *recogniser* since it will not present a witness; we concentrate on the recognition process only. The type of *R* is polymorphic in two type parameters: *st* for the state, and *a* for the witness of the correct parse. Basically a recogniser is a function taking a state and returning *Steps*. This *Steps* value starts with the steps produced by the recogniser itself, but ends with the steps produced by a continuation which is passed as the first argument to the recogniser:

$$\begin{aligned}
&\textbf{newtype}\ R\ st\ a = R\ (\forall\ r.(st \rightarrow Steps\ r) \rightarrow st \rightarrow Steps\ r)\\
&unR\ (R\ p) = p
\end{aligned}$$

Note that the type *a* is not used in the right hand side of the definition. To make sure that the recognisers and the parsers have the same kind we have included this type parameter here too; besides making it possible to to make use of all the calsses we introduce for parsers it also introduces extra check on the wellformedness of recognisers. Furthermore we can now, by provinding a top level type specification use the same expression to just recognise something or to parse with building a result.

We can now make *R* an instance of *Applicative*, that is implement the five classic parser combinators for it. Note that the parameter *f* of the operator <$> is irnored, since it does not play a role in the reognition process, and the same holds for the parameter *a* of *pReturn*.

```
instance Applicative (R st) where
          R p <*> R q = R (λk st → p (q k) st)
          R p <|> R q = R (λk st → p k st `best` q k st)
          f <$>   R p = R p
          pReturn a   = R (λk st → k st)
          pFail       = R (λk st → Fail)
```

We have abstained from giving point-free definitions, but one can easily see that sequential composition is essentially function composition, and that *pReturn* is the identity function wrapped in a constructor.

Next we provide the implementation of *pSym*, which resembles the definition in the basic library. Note that when a symbol is succesfully recognised this is reflected by prefixing the result of the call to the continuation with a *Step*:

```
instance (symbol `Describe` s token, Provides state symbol token)
   ⇒ Symbol (R state) symbol token where
   pSym a = R (λk h st → case splitState a st of
                            Just (t, ss) → if a `eqSymTok` t
                                            then Step (k ss)
                                            else Fail
                            Nothing      → Fail)
```

4.5 History Based Parsers

After the preparatory work introducing the *Steps* data type and the recognisers, we now introduce our first parser type, which we will call *history* parsers. The type P_h takes the same type parameters as the recogniser: *st* for the state, and *a* for the witness of the correct parse. The actual parsing function takes, besides the continuation and the state an extra parameter in its second position..

The second parameter is the 'history': a stack containing all the values recognised as the left hand side of a <*> combinator which have thus far not been paired with the result of the corresponding right hand side parser. The first parameter is again the 'continuation', a function which is responsible, being passed the history extended with the newly recognised witness, to produce the final result from the rest of the input.

In the type P_h, we have local type variables for the type of the history h, and the type of the witness of the final result r:

$$\textbf{newtype}\ P_h\ st\ a = P_h\ (\forall\ r\ h\ .\ ((h, a) \rightarrow st \rightarrow Steps\ r) \rightarrow h \rightarrow st \rightarrow Steps\ r)$$

$$unP_h\ (P_h\ p) = p$$

We can now make P_h an instance of *Applicative*, that is, implement the five classic parser combinators for it.

In the definition of *pReturn*, we encode that the history parameter is indeed a stack, growing to the right and implemented as nested pairs. The new witness is pushed on the history stack, and passed on to the continuation k.

In the definition of f<\$>, the continuation is modified to sneak in the application of the function f.

In the definition of alternative composition <|>, we call both parsers and exploit the fact that they both return *Steps*, of which we can take the *best*. Of course, *best* only lazily unwraps both *Steps* up to the point where one of them fails.

In the definition of sequential composition <*>, the continuation-passing style is again exploited: we call p, passing it q as continuation, which in turn takes a modification of the original continuation k. The modification is that two values are popped from the history stack: the witness b from parser q, and the witness $b2a$ from parser p; and a new value $b2a\ b$ is pushed onto the history stack which is passed to the orginal continuation k:

$$
\begin{array}{l}
\textbf{instance}\ Applicative\ (P_h\ state)\ \textbf{where} \\
\quad P_h\ p <\!\!*\!\!> P_h\ q = P_h\ (\lambda k \rightarrow p\ (q\ apply_h) \\
\qquad\qquad\qquad\qquad \textbf{where}\ apply_h = \lambda((h, b2a), b) \rightarrow k\ (h, b2a\ b)) \\
\quad P_h\ p <\!|\!> P_h\ q = P_h\ (\lambda k\ h\ st \rightarrow p\ k\ h\ st\ \text{`}best\text{`}\ q\ k\ h\ st) \\
\quad f\quad <\!\$\!> P_h\ p = P_h\ (\lambda k \quad\quad \rightarrow p\ \$\ \lambda(h, a) \rightarrow k\ (h, f\ a)) \\
\quad pFail \qquad\quad\ = P_h\ (\lambda k\ \_\ \_ \rightarrow Fail \quad) \\
\quad pReturn\ a \quad\ = P_h\ (\lambda k\ h \quad \rightarrow k\ (h, a) \quad)
\end{array}
$$

Note that we have given a new definition for <\$>, which is slightly more efficient than the default one; instead of pushing the function f on the stack with a *pReturn* and popping it off later, we just apply it directly to recognised result of the parser p. In Fig. 5 we have given a pictorial representation of the flow of data associated with this parser type. The top arrows, flowing right, correspond to the accumulated history, and the arrows directly below them to the state which is passed on. The bottom arrows, flowing left, correspond to the final result which is returned through all the continuation calls.

In a slightly different formulation the stack may be respresented implicitly using extra continuation functions. From now on we will use a somewhat simpler type for $P - h$ and thus we also provide a new instance definition for the class *Applicative*. It is however useful to keep te pictorial representation of the earlier type in mind.:

$$P_h\ st\ a = P_h\ (\forall\ r.(a \rightarrow st \rightarrow Steps\ r) \rightarrow st \rightarrow Steps\ r$$

$$\textbf{instance}\ Applicative\ (P_h\ state)\ \textbf{where}$$

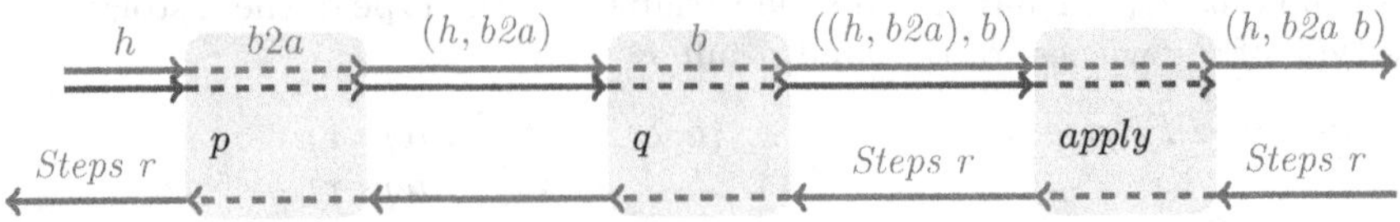

Fig. 5. Sequential composition of history parsers

$$
\begin{aligned}
&(P_h\ p) \mathbin{<\!\!*\!\!>} (P_h\ q) &&= P_h\ (\lambda k \rightarrow p\ (\lambda f \rightarrow q\ (\lambda a \rightarrow k\ (f\ a))))\\
&(P_h\ p) \mathbin{<\!|\!>} (P_h\ q) &&= P_h\ (\lambda k\ inp \rightarrow p\ k\ inp\ \text{`}best\text{`}\ q\ k\ inp)\\
&f \mathbin{<\!\$\!>} (P_h\ p) &&= P_h\ (\lambda k \rightarrow p\ (\lambda a \rightarrow k\ (f\ a)))\\
&pFail &&= P_h\ (\lambda k \rightarrow const\ noAlts)\\
&pReturn\ a &&= P_h\ (\lambda k \rightarrow k\ a)
\end{aligned}
$$

The definition of *pSym* is straightforward; the recognised token is passed on to the continuation:

```
instance (symbol`Describes' token, Provides state symbol token)
  => Symbol (P_h state) symbol token where
  pSym a = P_h (λk st → case splitState a st of
                          Just (t, ss) → if a `eqSymTok` t
                                         then Step (k t ss)
                                         else Fail
                          Nothing      → Fail)
```

Finally we make P_h an instance of *Parser* by providing a function *parse* that checks whether all input was consumed; if so we initialise the return sequence with a *Done*with the final conctructed witness.

```
instance Eof state => Parser (P_h state) where
  parse (P_h p)
    = eval.p (λr rest → if eof rest then Done r else Fail)
```

Since we will later be adding error recovery to the parsers constructed in this chapter, which will turn every illegal input into a legal one, we will assume in this section that there exists *always precisely one way of parsing the input.* If there is more than one way then we have to deal with ambiguities, which we will also show how to deal with in section 5.

4.6 Producing Results Online

The next problem we are attacking is producting the result online. The history parser accumulates its result in an extra argument, only to be inserted at the end of the parsing process with the *Done* constructor. In this section we introduce the counterpart of the history parser, the *future* parser, which is named this way because the "stack" we are maintaining contains elements which still have to come into existence. The type of future parsers is:

$$\textbf{newtype}\ P_f\ st\ a = P_f\ (\forall\ r.(st \to Steps\ r) \to st \to Steps\ (a, r))$$
$$unP_f\ (P_f\ p) = p$$

We see that the history parameter has disappeared and that the parameter of the *Steps* type now changes; instead of just passing the result constructed by the call to the continuation unmodified to the caller, the constructed witness a is pushed onto the stack of results constructed by the continuation; this stack is made an integral part of the data type *Steps* by not only representing progress information but also constructed values in this sequence.

In our programs we will make the stack grow from the right to the left; this maintains the suggestion introduced by the history parsers that the values to the right correspond to input parts which are located further towards the end of the input stream (assuming we read the stream from left to right). One way of pushing such a value on the stack would be to traverse the whole future sequence until we reach the *Done* constructor and then adding the value there, but that makes no sense since then the result again will not be available online. Instead we extend our *Steps* data type with an extra constructor. We remove the *Done* constructor, since it can be simulated with the new *Apply* constructor. The *Apply* constructor makes it possible to store function values in the progress sequence:

$$\begin{aligned}&\textbf{data}\ Steps\ a\ \textbf{where}\\ &\quad Step :: \quad Steps\ a \to Steps\ a\\ &\quad Fail :: \quad Steps\ a\\ &\quad Apply :: (b \to a) \to Steps\ b \to Steps\ a\end{aligned}$$

$$\begin{aligned}&eval :: Steps\ a \to a\\ &eval\ (Step\ \ \ l) \ = eval\ l\\ &eval\ (Fail\ \ \ ls) = error\ \texttt{"no result"}\\ &eval\ (Apply\ f\ l\ ) = f\ (eval\ l)\end{aligned}$$

As we have seen in the case of the history parsers there are two operations we perform on the stack: pushing a value, and popping two values, applying the one to the other and pushing the result back. For this we define two auxiliary functions:

$$\begin{aligned}&push\ \ :: v \to Steps\ r \to Steps\ (v, r)\\ &push\ v = Apply\ (\lambda s \to (v, s))\\ &apply_f :: Steps\ (b \to a, (b, r)) \to Steps\ (a, r)\\ &apply_f = Apply\ (\lambda(b2a,\ \tilde{}(b, r)) \to (b2a\ b, r))\end{aligned}$$

One should not confuse the *Apply* constructor with the $apply_f$ function. Keep in mind that the *Apply* constructor is a very generally applicable construct changing the value (and possibly the type) represented by the sequence by prefixing the sequence with a function value, whereas the $apply_f$ function takes care of combining the values of two sequentially composed parsers by applying the result of the first one to the result of the second one. An important rôle is played by the ~-symbol. Normally, Haskell evaluates arguments to functions far enough to check that it indeed matches the pattern. The tilde prevents this by making Haskell assume that the pattern always matches. Evaluation of the argument is thus slightly more lazy, which is critically needed here: the function *b2a* can already return that part of the result for which evaluation of its argument is not needed!

The code for the the function *best* now is a bit more involved, since there are extra cases to be taken care of: a *Steps* sequence may start with an *Apply* step. So before calling the actual function *best* we make sure that the head of the stream is one of the constructors that indicates progress, i.e. a *Step* or *Fail* constructor. This is taken care of by the function *norm* which pushes *Apply* steps forward into the progress stream until a progress step is encountered:

$$\begin{array}{l}
norm :: Steps\ a \rightarrow Steps\ a \\
norm\ (Apply\ f\ (Step\ l\ \ \ )) = Step\ (Apply\ f\ l) \\
norm\ (Apply\ f\ Fail\ \ \ \ \ \ \ \ \ ) = Fail \\
norm\ (Apply\ f\ (Apply\ g\ l)) = norm\ (Apply\ (f . g)\ l) \\
norm\ steps\ = steps
\end{array}$$

Our new version of *best* now reads:

$$\begin{array}{l}
l\ `best`\ r = norm\ l\ `best'`\ norm\ r \\
\quad \mathbf{where}\ \begin{array}{lll}
Fail & `best'`\ r & = r \\
l & `best'`\ Fail & = l \\
(Step\ l) & `best'`\ (Step\ r) & = Step\ (l\ `best`\ r) \\
_ & `best'`\ _ & = Fail
\end{array}
\end{array}$$

We as well make P_f an instance of *Applicative*:

$$\begin{array}{l}
\mathbf{instance}\ Applicative\ (P_f\ st)\ \mathbf{where} \\
\quad \begin{array}{ll}
P_f\ p \mathbin{<\!\!*\!\!>} P_f\ q & = P_f\ (\lambda k\ st \rightarrow apply_f\ (p\ (q\ k)\ st)) \\
P_f\ p \mathbin{<|>} P_f\ q & = P_f\ (\lambda k\ st \rightarrow p\ k\ st\ `best`\ q\ k\ st\ ) \\
pReturn\ a & = P_f\ (\lambda k\ st \rightarrow push\ a\ (k\ st)\ \ \ \ \ \ \ ) \\
pFail & = P_f\ (\lambda_\ _\ \rightarrow Fail\ )
\end{array}
\end{array}$$

Just as we did for the history parsers we again provide a pictorial representation of the data flow in case of a sequential composition $<\!\!*\!\!>$ in Fig. 6:

Also the definitions of *pSym* and *parse* pose no problems. The only question is what to take as the initial value of the *Steps* sequence. We just take $\bot$, since the types guarantee that it will never be evaluated. Notice that if the parser constructs the value *b*, then the result of the call to the parser in the function

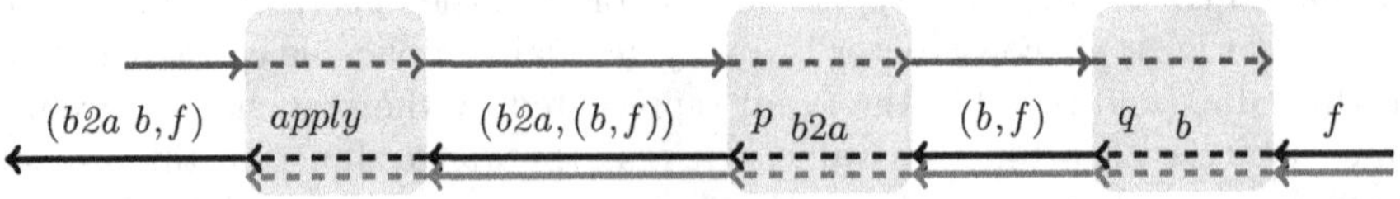

Fig. 6. Sequential composition of future parsers

parse will be $(b, \bot)$ of which we select the first component after converting the returned sequence to the value represented by it.

```
instance (symbol `Describes` token, state `Provides` token)
            ⇒ Symbol (P_f state) symbol token where
  pSym a = P_f (λk st → case splitState a st of
                          Just (t, ss) → if a `eqSymTok` t
                                          then Step (push t (k ss))
                                          else Fail
                          Nothing      → Fail
               )
instance Eof state ⇒ Parser (P_f state)
where
  parse (P_f p) = fst.eval.p (λinp → if eof inp then ⊥ else error "end")
```

4.7 The Monadic Interface

As with the parsers from the introduction we want to make our new parsers instances of the class *Monad* too, so we can again write functions like *pABC* (see page 265). Making history parsers an instance of the class *Monad* is straightforward:

```
instance Applicative (P_h state) ⇒ Monad (P_h state) where
  P_h p >>= a2q = P_h (λk → p (λa → unP_h (a2q a) k))
  return = pReturn
```

At first sight this does not seem to be a problem to proceed similarly for future parsers. Following the pattern of sequential composition, we call p with the continuation $unP_h\ (a2q\ a)\ k$; the only change is that instead of applying the result of p to the result of q we use the result of p to build the continuation in $a2q\ a$. And indeed the following code type-checks perfectly:

```
instance Applicative (P_f state) ⇒ Monad (P_f state) where
  P_f p >>= pv2q = P_f (λk st →
                        let steps = p (q k) st
                            q     = unP_f (pv2q pv)
                            pv    = fst (eval steps)
                        in Apply snd steps
                       )
  return = pReturn
```

Unfortunately execution of the above code may lead to a black hole, i.e. a non-terminating computation, as we will explain with the help of Fig. 7. Problems occur when inside p we have a call to the function *best* which starts to compare two result sequences. Now suppose that in order to make a choice the parser p does not provide enough information. In that case the continuation q is called once for each branch of the choice process, in order to provide further steps of which we hope they will lead us to a decision. If we are lucky the value of pv is not needed by $q\ pv$ in order to provide the extra needed progress information.

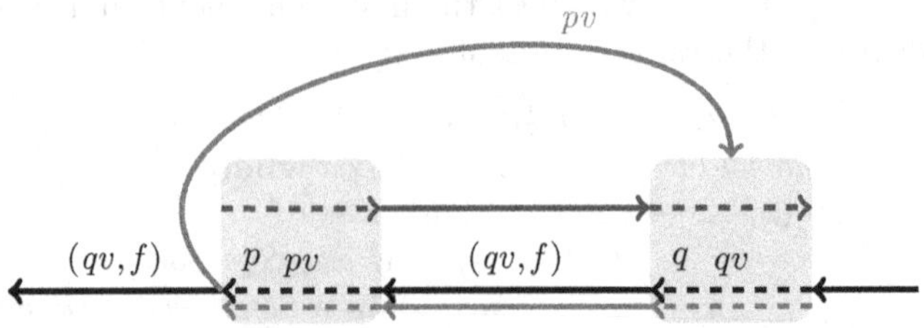

Fig. 7. Erroneous implementation of monadic future parsers

But if we are unlucky the value is needed; however the *Apply* steps contributing to *pv* will have been propagated into the sequence returned by *q*. Now we have constructed a loop in our computation: *pv* depends on the outcome of *best*, *best* depends on the outcome of *q pv*, and *q pv* depends on the value of *pv*.

The problem is caused by the fact that each branch taken in *p* has its own call to the continuation *q*, and that each branch *may lead to a different value for pv*, but we get only one in our hands: the one which belongs to the successful alternative. So we are stuck.

Fortunately we remember just in time that we have introduced a different kind of parser, the history based ones, which have the property that they pass the value produced along the path taken inside them to the continuation. Each path splitting somewhere in *p* can thus call the continuation with the value which will be produced if this alternative wins eventually. That is why their implementation of *Monad*'s operations is perfectly fine. This brings us to the following insight: the reason we moved on from history based parsers to future based parsers was that we wanted to have an online result. But the result of the left-hand side of a monadic bind is not used at all in the construction of the result. Instead it is removed from the result stack in order to be used as a parameter to the right hand side operand of the monadic bind. So the solution to our problem lies in *using a history based parser as the left hand side of a monadic bind*, and a future based parser at the right hand side. Of course we have to make sure that they share the *Steps* data type used for storing the result. In Fig. 8 we have given a pictorial representation of the associated data flow.

Unfortunately this does not work out as expected, since the type of the ≫= operator is *Monad m* ⇒ *m b* → (*b* → *m a*) → *m a*, and hence requires the left and right hand side operands to be based upon the same functor *m*. A solution is to introduce a class *GenMod*, which takes two functor parameters instead of one:

```
infixr 1 >>>=
class GenMonad m_1 m_2 where
  (>>>=) :: m_1 b → (b → m_2 a) → m_2 a
```

Now we can create two instances of *GenMonad*. In both cases the left hand side operand is the history parser, and the right hand side operand is either a history or a future based parser:

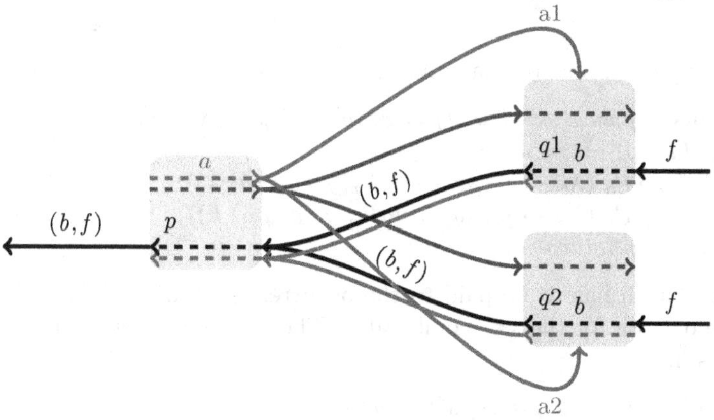

Fig. 8. Combining future based and history based parsers

```
instance Monad (P_h state)
  ⇒      GenMonad (P_h state) (P_h state) where
  (>>>=) = (>>=)  -- the monadic bind defined before
instance GenMonad (P_h state) (P_f state) where
  (P_h p) >>>= pv2q = P_f (λk → p (λpv → unP_h (pv2q pv) k))
```

Unfortunately we are now no longer able to use the **do** notation because that is designed for *Monad* expressions rather than for *GenMonad* expressions which was introduced for monadic expressions, and thus we still cannot replace the implementation in the basic library by the more advanced one we are developing. Fortunately there is a trick which makes this still possible: *we pair the two implementations, and select the one which we need*:

```
data P_m state a = P_m (P_h state a) (P_f state a)
unP_m_h (P_m (P_h h) _      ) = h
unP_m_f (P_m _      (P_f f)) = f
```

Our first step is to make this new type again instance of *Applicative*:

```
instance  ( Applicative (P_h st), Applicative (P_f st))
            ⇒ Applicative (P_m st) where
(P_m hp fp)   <*> ~(P_m hq fq) = P_m (hp <*> hq) (fp <*> fq)
(P_m hp fp)   <|> (P_m hq fq)  = P_m (hp <|> hq) (fp <|> fq)
pReturn a                      = P_m (pReturn a) (pReturn a)
pFail                          = P_m pFail        pFail
instance    (symbol `Describes` token, state `Provides` token)
  ⇒         Symbol (P_m state) symbol token where
  pSym a = P_m (pSym a) (pSym a)
instance Eof state ⇒ Parser (P_m state) where
  parse (P_m _ (P_f fp))
```

$= fst.eval.fp\ (\lambda rest \rightarrow \textbf{if}\ eof\ rest\ \ \textbf{then}\ \bot$
$\qquad\qquad\qquad\qquad\qquad\qquad\qquad \textbf{else}\ error\ \texttt{"parse"})$

This new type can now be made into a monad by:

$$
\begin{array}{l}
\textbf{instance}\ Applicative\ (P_m\ st) \Rightarrow Monad\ (P_m\ st)\ \textbf{where} \\
\quad (P_m\ (P_h\ p)\ \_) \gg= a2q = \\
\qquad P_m\ (P_h\ (\lambda k \rightarrow p\ (\lambda a \rightarrow unP_{m\_h}\ (a2q\ a)\ k))) \\
\qquad\quad (P_f\ (\lambda k \rightarrow p\ (\lambda a \rightarrow unP_{m\_f}\ (a2q\ a)\ k))) \\
\quad return = pReturn
\end{array}
$$

Special attention has to be paid to the occurrence of the ~ symbol in the left hand side pattern for the <*> combinator. The need for it comes from recursive definitions like:

$pMany\ p = (:)\ \texttt{<\$>}\ p\ \texttt{<*>}\ pMany\ p\ `opt`\ [\,]$

If we match the second operand of the <*> occurrence strictly this will force the evaluation of the call *pMany p*, thus leading to an infinite recursion!

5 Exploiting Progress Information

Before continuing discussing the mentioned shortcomings such as the absence of error reporting and error correction which will make the data types describing the result more complicated, we take some time to show how the introduced *Steps* data type has many unconventional applications, which go beyond the expressive power of context-free grammars. Because both our history and future parsers now operate on the same *Steps* data type we will focus on extensions to that data type only.

5.1 Greedy Parsing

For many programming languages the context-free grammars which are provided in the standards are actually ambiguous. A common case is the dangling **else**. If we have a production like:

stat ::= `"if"` *expr* `"then"` *stat* [`"else"` *stat*]

then a text of the form `if ... then ... if ... then ... else ...` has two parses: one in which the **else** part is associated with the first **if** and one in which it is associated with the second. Such ambiguities are often handled by accompanying text in the standard stating that the second alternative is the interpretation to be chosen. A straightforward way of implementing this, and this is how it is done in quite a few parser generators, is to apply a greedy parsing strategy: if we have to choose between two alternatives and the first one can make progress than take that one. If the greedy strategy fails we fall back to the normal strategy.

In our approach we can easily achieve this effect by introducing a biased choice operator $\ll\mid>$, which for all purposes acts like <|>, but chooses its left alternative if it starts with the successful recognition of a token:

```
class Greedy p where
  (<<|>) :: p a -> p a -> p a
best_gr :: Steps a -> Steps a -> Steps a
l@(Step _ _) `best_gr` _ = l
l            `best_gr` r = l `best` r
instance Best_gr (Ph st) where
  Ph p <<|> Ph q = Ph (\k st -> p k st `best_gr` q k st)
```

The instance declarations for the other parser types are similar.

This common solution usually solves the problem adequately. It may however be the case that we only want to take a specific alternative if we can be sure that some initial part can completely be recognised. As a preparation for the discussion on error correction we show how to handle this. We extend the data type *Steps* with one further alternative:

```
data Steps a = ...
             | Success (Steps a)
```

and introduce yet another operator $<\!\!<\!\!<|>$ which performs its work in cooperation with a function *try*. In this case we only provide the implementation for the P_f case:

```
class Try p where
  (<<<|>) :: p a -> p a -> p a
  try ::     p a -> p a
instance Try (Pf state) where
  Pf p <<<|> Pf q = Pf (\k st -> let l = p k st
                                 in maybe (l `best` q k st) id (hasSuccess id l)
                       )
       where hasSuccess f (Step l   ) = hasSuccess (f.Step)    l
             hasSuccess f (Apply g l) = hasSuccess (f.Apply g) l
             hasSuccess f (Success l) = Just (f l)
             hasSuccess f (Fail     ) = Nothing
  try (Pf p) = Pf (p.(Success.))
```

The function *try* does little more than inserting a *Success* marker in the result sequence, once its argument parser has completed successfully. The function *hasSuccess* tries to find such a marker. If found then the marker is removed and success (*Just*) reported, otherwise failure (*Nothing*) is returned. In the latter case our good old friend *best* takes its turn to compare both sequences in parallel as before. One might be inclined to think that in case of failure of the first alternative we should just take the second, but that is a bit too optimistic; the right hand side alternative might fail even earlier.

Unfortunately this simple approach has its drawback: what happens if the programmer forgets to mark an initial part of the left hand side alternative with *try*? In that case the function will never find a *Success* constructor, and our parsing process fails. We can solve this problem by introducing yet another parser type which guarantees that *try* has been used and thus that such a *Success* constructor may occur. We will not pursue this alternative here any further, since it will make our code even more involved.

5.2 Ambiguous Grammars

One of the big shortcomings of the combinator based approach to parsing, which is aggravated by the absence of global grammar analysis, is that we do not get a warning beforehand if our underlying grammar is ambiguous. It is only when we try to choose between two result sequences in the function *best* and discover that both end successfully, that we find out that our grammar allows more than one parse. Worse however is that parse times also may grow exponentially. For each successful parse for a given non-terminal the remaining part of the input is completely parsed. If we were only able to memoise the calls to the continuations, i.e. we can see that the same function is called more than once with the same argument, we could get rid of the superfluous work. Unfortunately continuations are anonymous functions which are not easily compared. If the programmer is however prepared to do some extra work by indicating that a specific non-terminal may lead to more than a single parse, we can provide a solution.

The first question to be answered is what to choose for the result of an ambiguous parser. We decide to return a list of all produced witnesses, and introduce a function *amb* which is used to label ambiguous non-terminals; the type of the parser that is returned by *amb* reflects that more than one result can be expected.

```
class Ambiguous p where
  amb :: p a → p [a]
```

For its implementation we take inspiration from the *parse* functions we have seen thus far. For history parsers we discovered that a grammar was ambiguous by simultaneously encountering a *Done* marker in the left and right operand of a call to *best*. So we model our *amb* implementation in the same way, and introduce a new marker End_h which becomes yet an extra alternative in our result type:

```
data Steps a where
      ...
      | End_h :: ([a], [a] → Steps r) → Steps (a, r) → Steps (a, r)
      ...
```

To recognise the end of a potentially ambiguous parse we insert an End_h mark in the result sequence, which indicates that at this position a parse for the ambiguous non-terminal was completed and we should continue with the call to the continuation. Since we want to evaluate the call to the common continuation only once we bind the current continuation k and the current state in the value of type $[a] \to Steps\ r$; the argument of this function will be the list of all witnesses recognised at the point corresponding to the occurrence of the End_h constructor in the sequence:

$$
\begin{array}{l}
\textbf{instance } \mathit{Ambiguous}\ (P_h\ \mathit{state})\ \textbf{where} \\
\quad \mathit{amb}\ (P_h\ p) = \\
\quad\quad P_h\ (\lambda k \rightarrow \mathit{removeEnd}_h.p\ (\lambda a\ st' \rightarrow \mathit{End}_h\ ([a], \lambda as \rightarrow k\ as\ st')\ \mathit{noAlts})) \\
\mathit{noAlts} = \mathit{Fail}
\end{array}
$$

We thus postpone the call to the continuation itself. The second parameter of the End_h constructor represents the other parsing alternatives that branch within the ambiguous parser, but have not yet completed and thus contain and End_h marker further down the sequence.

All parses which reach their End_h constructor at the same point are collected in a common End_h constructor. We only provide the interesting alternatives in the new function *best*:

$$
\begin{array}{llll}
\mathit{End}_h\ (as, k\_\ st)\ l & \text{`}\mathit{best}'\text{`}\ \mathit{End}_h\ (bs, \_)\ r & = & \mathit{End}_h\ (as +\!\!+\ bs, k\_st) \\
 & & & \quad (l\ \text{`}\mathit{best}\text{`}\ r) \\
\mathit{End}_h\ as\ l & \text{`}\mathit{best}'\text{`}\ r & = & \mathit{End}_h\ as\ (l\ \text{`}\mathit{best}\text{`}\ r) \\
l & \text{`}\mathit{best}'\text{`}\ \mathit{End}_h\ bs\ r & = & \mathit{End}_h\ bs\ (l\ \text{`}\mathit{best}\text{`}\ r)
\end{array}
$$

If an ambiguous parser succeeds at least once it will return a sequence of *Step*'s which has the length of input consumed, followed by an End_h constructor which holds all the results and continuations of the parses that completed successfully at this point, and a sequence representing the best result for all other parses which were successful up-to this point. Note that all the continuations which are stored are the same by construction.

The expression $kas\ st'$ binds the ingredients of the continuation; it can immediately be called once we have constructed the complete list containing the witnesses of all successful parses. The tricky work is done by the function *removeEnd*, which hunts down the result sequence in order to locate the End_h constructors, and to resume the *best* computation which was temporarily postponed until we had collected all successful parses with their common continuations.

$$
\begin{array}{ll}
\mathit{removeEnd}_h :: \mathit{Steps}\ (a, r) \rightarrow \mathit{Steps}\ r & \\
\mathit{removeEnd}_h\ (\mathit{Fail} &) = \mathit{Fail} \\
\mathit{removeEnd}_h\ (\mathit{Step}\ l &) = \mathit{Step}\ (\mathit{removeEnd}_h\ l) \\
\mathit{removeEnd}_h\ (\mathit{Apply}\ f\ l &) = \mathit{error}\ \texttt{"not in history parsers"} \\
\mathit{removeEnd}_h\ (\mathit{End}_h\ (as, k\_st)\ r &) = k\_st\ as\ \text{`}\mathit{best}\text{`}\ \mathit{removeEnd}_h\ r
\end{array}
$$

In the last alternative the function $removeEnd_h$ has forced the evaluation of all alternatives which are active up to this point. The result of the completed parsers here have been collected in the value *as*, which can now be passed to the function, thus resuming the parsing process at this point. Other parsers for the ambiguous non-terminal which have not completed yet are all represented by the second component. So the function $removeEnd_h$ still has to force further evaluation of these sequences, and remove the End_h constructor. The parsers terminating at this point of course still have to compete wih the still active parsers to finally reach a decision.

Without making this explicit we have gradually moved from a situation were the calls to the function *best* immediately construct a single sequence, to a situation where we have markers in the sequence which may be used to stop and start evaluation.

The situation for the online parsers is a bit different, since we want to keep as much of the online behaviour as possible. As an example we look at the following set of definitions, where the parser r is marked as an ambiguous parser:

$$p \mathrel{<\!\!+\!\!+\!\!>} q = (+\!\!+) \mathrel{<\$>} p \mathrel{<*>} q$$
$$a = (:[\,]) \mathrel{<\$>} pSym \text{ 'a'}$$
$$a2 = a \mathrel{<\!\!+\!\!+\!\!>} a$$
$$a3 = a \mathrel{<\!\!+\!\!+\!\!>} a \mathrel{<\!\!+\!\!+\!\!>} a$$
$$r = amb\ (a \mathrel{<\!\!+\!\!+\!\!>} (a2 \mathrel{<\!\!+\!\!+\!\!>} a3 \mathrel{<|>} a3 \mathrel{<\!\!+\!\!+\!\!>} a2)$$

In section 7 we will introduce error repair, which will guarantee that each parser always constructs a result sequence when forced to do so. This has as a consequence that if we access the value computed by an ambiguous parser we can be sure that this value has a length of at least 1, and thus we should be able to match, in the case of the parser r above, the resulting value successfully against the pattern $((a:\_):\_)$ as soon as parsing has seen the first `'a'` in the input. As before we add yet another marker type to the type *Steps*:

$$\textbf{data}\ Steps\ a\ \textbf{where}$$
$$\ldots$$
$$End_f :: [Steps\ a] \rightarrow Steps\ a \rightarrow Steps\ a$$
$$\ldots$$

We now give the code for the P_f case:

$$\begin{array}{l}
\textbf{instance}\ Ambiguous\ (P_f\ state)\ \textbf{where} \\
\quad amb\ (P_f\ p) = P_f\ (\lambda k\ inp \rightarrow combineValues.removeEnd_f\ \$ \\
\qquad\qquad\qquad\qquad p\ (\lambda st \rightarrow End_f\ [k\ st]\ noAlts)\ inp) \\
removeEnd_f :: Steps\ r \rightarrow Steps\ [r] \\
removeEnd_f\ (Fail) \qquad\qquad\quad = Fail \\
removeEnd_f\ (Step\ l) \qquad\qquad = Step\ (removeEnd_f\ l) \\
removeEnd_f\ (Apply\ f\ l) \qquad\ = Apply\ (map'\ f)\ (removeEnd_f\ l) \\
removeEnd_f\ (End_f\ (s:ss)\ r) = Apply\ (:(map\ eval\ ss))\ s \\
\qquad\qquad\qquad\qquad\qquad\qquad `best` \\
\qquad\qquad\qquad\qquad\qquad removeEnd_f\ r \\
combineValues :: Steps\ [(a,r)] \rightarrow Steps\ ([a],r) \\
combineValues\ lar = Apply\ (\lambda lar' \rightarrow (map\ fst\ lar', snd\ (head\ lar')))\ lar \\
map'\ f\ \tilde{}(x:xs) \quad = f\ x : map\ f\ xs
\end{array}$$

The hard work is again done in the last alternative of $removeEnd_f$, where we apply the function *eval* to all the sequences. Fortunately this *eval* is again lazily evaluated, so not much work is done yet. The case of *Apply* is also interesting, since it covers the case of the first a in the example; the $map'\ f$ adds this value to all successful parses. We cannot use the normal *map* since this function is strict in the list constructor of its second argument, and we may already want to expose the call to f (e.g. to produce the value `'a'`:) without proceeding with the match. The function *map'* exploits the fact that its list argument is guaranteed to be non-empty, as a result of the error correction to be introduced.

Finally we use the function *combineValues* to collect the values recognised by the ambiguous parser, and combine the result of this with the sequence produced by the continuation. It looks all very expensive, but lazy evaluation makes that a lot of work is actually not performed; especially the continuation will be evaluated only once, since the function *fst* does not force evaluation of the second component of its argument tuple.

5.3 Micro-steps

Besides the greedy parsing strategy which just looks at the next symbol in order to decide which alternative to choose, we sometimes want to give precedence to one parse over the other. An example of this is when we use the combinators to construct a scanner. The string `"name"` should be recognised as an identifier, whereas the string `"if"` should be recognised as a keyword, and this alternative thus has precedence over the interpretation as an identifier. We can easily get the desired effect by introducing an extra kind of step, which looses from *Step* but wins from *Fail*. The occurrence of such a step can be seen as an indication that a small penalty has to be paid for taking this alternative, but that we are happy to pay this price if no other alternatives are available. We extend the type *Steps* with a step *Micro* and add the alternatives:

```
(Micro l)   `best'` r@(Step _) = r
l@(Step _) `best'` (Micro _)  = l
(Micro l)   `best'` (Micro r)  = Micro (l `best'` r)
...
```

The only thing still to be done is to add a combinator which inserts this small step into a progress sequence:

```
class Micro p where
  micro :: p a → p a
instance Micro (P_f state) where
  micro (P_f p) = P_f (p.(Micro.))
```

The other instances follow a similar pattern. Of course there are endless variations possible here. One might add a small integer cost to the micro step, in order to describe even finer grained disambiguation strategies.

6 Embedding Parsers

With the introduction of the function *splitState* we have moved the responsibility for the scanning process, which converts the input into a stream of tokens, to the *state* type. Usually one is satisfied to have just a single way of scanning the input, but sometimes one may want to use a parser for one language as sub-parser in the parser for another language. An example of this is when one has a Haskell parser and wants to recognise a *String* value. Of course one could offload the recognition of string values to the tokeniser, but wouldn't it be nice if we could just call the parser for strings as a sub-parser, which uses single characters as its token type? A second example arises when one extend a language like Java with a sub-language like AspectJ, which again has Java as a sub-language. Normally this creates all kind of problems with the scanning process, but if we are able to switch from scanner type, many problems disappear.

In order to enable such an embedding we introduce the following class:

$$\begin{array}{l}\textbf{class}\ \mathit{Switch}\ p\ \textbf{where}\\ \quad \mathit{pSwitch} :: (\mathit{st1} \rightarrow (\mathit{st2}, \mathit{st2} \rightarrow \mathit{st1})) \rightarrow p\ \mathit{st2}\ a \rightarrow p\ \mathit{st1}\ a\end{array}$$

It provides a new parser combinator *pSwitch* that can temporarily parse with a different state type *st2* by providing it with a splitting function which splits the original state of type *st1* into a state of type *st2* and a function which will convert the final value of type *st2* back into a value of type *st1*:

$$\begin{array}{l}\textbf{instance}\ \mathit{Switch}\ P_h\ \textbf{where}\\ \quad \mathit{pSwitch}\ \mathit{split}\ (P_h\ p) = P_h\ (\lambda k\ \mathit{st1} \rightarrow \textbf{let}\ (\mathit{st2}, b) = \mathit{split}\ \mathit{st1}\\ \qquad\qquad\qquad\qquad\qquad\qquad\quad \textbf{in}\ p\ (\lambda \mathit{st2}' \rightarrow k\ (b\ \mathit{st2}'))\ \mathit{st2})\\ \textbf{instance}\ \mathit{Switch}\ P_f\ \textbf{where}\\ \quad \mathit{pSwitch}\ \mathit{split}\ (P_f\ p) = P_f\ (\lambda k\ \mathit{st1} \rightarrow \textbf{let}\ (\mathit{st2}, b) = \mathit{split}\ \mathit{st1}\\ \qquad\qquad\qquad\qquad\qquad\qquad\quad \textbf{in}\ p\ (\lambda \mathit{st2}' \rightarrow k\ (b\ \mathit{st2}'))\ \mathit{st2})\\ \textbf{instance}\ \mathit{Switch}\ P_m\ \textbf{where}\\ \quad \mathit{pSwitch}\ \mathit{split}\ (P_m\ (p, q)) = P_m\ (\mathit{pSwitch}\ \mathit{split}\ p, \mathit{pSwitch}\ \mathit{split}\ q)\end{array}$$

Using the function *pSwitch* we can map the state to a different state and back; by providing different instances we can thus use different versions of *splitState*.

A subtle point to be addressed concerns the breadth-first strategy; if we have two alternatives working on the same piece of input, but are using different scanning strategies, the two alternatives may get out of sync by accepting a different number of tokens for the same piece of input. Although this may not be critical for the breadth-first process, it may spoil our recognition process for ambiguous parsers, which depend on the fact that when *End* markers meet the corresponding input positions are the same. We thus adapt the function *splitState* such that it not only returns the next token, but also an *Int* value indicating how much input was consumed. We also adapt the *Step* alternative to record the progress made:

$$\begin{array}{l}\textbf{type}\ \mathit{Progress} = \mathit{Int}\\ \textbf{data}\ \mathit{Steps}\ a\ \textbf{where}\\ \qquad \ldots\\ \qquad \mathit{Step} :: \mathit{Progress} \rightarrow \mathit{Steps}\ a\end{array}$$

Of course also the function *best′* needs to be adapted too. We again only show the relevant changes:

$$\begin{array}{l}\mathit{Step}\ n\ l\ \text{`}\mathit{best}'\text{`}\ \ \mathit{Step}\ m\ r\\ \qquad \mid n \equiv m = \mathit{Step}\ n\ (l\ \text{`}\mathit{best}'\text{`}\ r)\end{array}$$

$$| \; n < m = Step\ n\ (l \text{ `}best\text{'} \ Step\ (m - n)\ r)$$
$$| \; n > m = Step\ m\ (Step\ (n - m)\ l \text{ `}best\text{'} \ r)$$

The changes to all other functions, such as *eval*, are straightforward.

7 Error Reporting and Correcting

In this section we will address two issues: the reporting of errors and the automatic repair of errors, such that parsing can continue.

7.1 Error Reporting

An important feature of proper error reporting is an indication of the longest valid prefix of the input, and which symbols were expected at that point. We have seen already that the number of *Step* constructors provides the former. So we will focus on the latter. For this we change the *Fail* alternative of the *Steps* data type, in order to record symbols that were expected at the point of failure:

data *Steps a* **where**
  ...
  $Fail :: [String] \rightarrow Steps\ a$
  ...

In the functions *pSym* we replace the occurrences of *Fail* with the expression *Fail* [*show a*], where *a* is the symbol we were looking for, i.e. the argument of *pSym*. The reason that we have chosen to represent the information as a collection of *String*'s makes it possible to combine *Fail* steps from parsers with different symbol types, which arises if we embed one parser into another.

In the function *best* we have to change the lines accordingly; the most interesting line is one where two failing alternatives are merged, which in the new situation becomes:

$$Fail\ ls \text{ `}best\text{'}\ Fail\ rs = Fail\ (ls +\!\!+ rs)$$

An important question to be answered is how to deal with erroneous situations. The simplest approach is to have the function *eval* emit an *error* message, reporting the number of accepted tokens and the list of expected symbols. One might be tempted to change the function *eval* to return an *Either a* [*String*], returning either the evaluated result or the list of expected symbols. Keep in mind however that this would completely defeat all the work we did in order to get online results. If one is happy to use the history parsers this is however a perfect solution.

7.2 Error Repair

The situation becomes more interesting if we want to perform some form of error repair. We distinguish two actions we can perform on the input [18], *inserting* an expected symbol and *deleting* the current token. Ideally one would like to try all possible combinations of such actions, and continue parsing to see which combination leads to the least number of error messages. Unfortunately this soon becomes infeasible. If we encounter e.g. the expression `"2 4"` then it can be repaired by inserting a binary operator between both integers, and from the parser's point of view these are all equivalent, leading us to the situation we encountered in the case of the ambiguous non-terminals: a non-terminal may not be ambiguous, but its corrections may turn it into one which behaves like an ambiguous one. The approach we will take is to generate a collection of possible repairs, each with an associated cost, and then select the best one out of these, using a limited look-ahead.

To get an impression of the kind of repairs we will be implementing consider the following program:

```
test p inp = parse ((,) <$> p <*> pEnd) (listToStr inp)
```

The function *test* calls its parameter parser followed by a call to *pEnd* which returns the list of constructed errors and deleted possibly unconsumed input. The constructor (,) pairs the error messages with the result of the parser and the function *listToStr* convert a list of characters into an appropriate input stream type.

We define the following small parsers to be tested, including an ambiguous parser and a monadic parser to show the effects of the error correction:

```
a        = (λa → [a]) <$> pSym 'a'
b        = (λa → [a]) <$> pSym 'b'
p <++> q = (++) <$> p <*> q
a2       =     a <++> a
a3       =     a <++> a2
pMany p = (λa b → b + 1) <$> p <*> pMany p <<|> pReturn 0
pCount 0 p = pReturn []
pCount n p = p <++> pCount (n − 1) p
```

Now we have three calls to the function *test*, all with erroneous inputs:

```
main = do print (test a2                                "bbab"      )
          print (test (do {l ← pMany a; pCount l b}) "aaacabbb")
          print (test (amb   (  (++) <$> a2 <*> a3
                            <|> (++) <$> a3 <*> a2)) "aaabaa")
```

Running the program will generate the following outputs, in which each result tuple contains the constructed witness and a list of error messages, each reporting the correcting action, the position in the input where it was performed, and the set of expected symbols:

```
("aa",          [ Deleted  'b' 0 ["'a'"],
                  Deleted  'b' 1 ["'a'"],
                  Deleted  'b' 3 ["'a'"],
                  Inserted 'a' 4 ["'a'"]])
["bbbb"],       [ Deleted  'c' 3 ["'a'","'b'"],
```

```
                          Inserted 'b' 8 ["'b'"]])
 (["aaaaa"],            [ Deleted  'b' 3 ["'a'","'a'"]])
```

Before showing the new parser code we have to answer the question how we are going to communicate the repair steps. To allow for maximal flexibility we have decided to let the *state* keep track of the accumulated error messages, which can be retrieved (and reset) by the special parser *pErrors*. We also add an extra parser *pEnd* which is to be called as the last parser, and which deletes superfluous tokens at the end of the input:

class *p* ‘*AsksFor*‘ *errors* **where**
  pErrors :: *p errors*
  pEnd :: *p errors*
class *Eof state* **where**
  eof :: *state* → *Bool*
  deleteAtEnd :: *state* → *Maybe* (*Cost*, *state*)

In order to cater for the most common case we introduce a new class *Stores*, which represents the retreival of errors, and extend the class *Provides* with two more functions which report the corrective actions tken to the *state*:

class *state* ‘*Stores*‘ *errors* **where**
  getErrors :: *state* → (*errors*, *state*)
class *Provides state symbol token* **where**
where
splitState :: *symbol* → *state* → *Maybe* (*token*, *state*)
insertSym :: *symbol* → *state* → *Strings* → *Maybe* (*Cost*, *token*, *state*)
deleteTok :: *token* → *state* → *state* → *Strings* → *Maybe* (*Cost*, *state*)

The function *getErrors* returns the accumulated error messages and resets the maintained set. The function *insertSym* takes as argument the symbol to be inserted, the current state and a set of strings describing what was expected at this location. If the state decides that the symbol is acceptable for insertion, it returns the costs associated with the insertion, a token which should be used as the witness for the successful insertion action, and a new state. The function *deleteTok* takes as argument the token to be deleted, the old state which was passed to *splitState* –which may e.g. contain the position at which the token to be deleted is located–, and the new state that was returned from *splitState*. It returns the cost of the deletion, and the new state with the associated error message included.

In Fig. 9 we give a reference implementation which lifts, using *listToStr*, a list of tokens to a state which has the required interface and provides a stream of tokens. One fine point remains to be discussed, which is the commutativity of insert and delete actions. Inserting a symbol and then deleting the current token has the same effect as first deleting the token and then inserting a symbol. This is why the function *deleteTok* returns a *Maybe*; if it is called on a state into which just a symbol has been inserted it should return *Nothing*. The data type *Error* represents the error messages which are stored in the state, and *pos* maintains

```
instance Eq a ⇒ Describes a a where
  eqSymTok = (≡)
data Error t s pos = Inserted s pos Strings
                   | Deleted t pos Strings
                   | DeletedAtEnd t
          deriving Show
data Str t = Str    {input    :: [t]
                    , msgs     :: [Error t t Int]
                    , pos      :: !Int
                    , deleteOk :: !Bool}
listToStr ls = Str ls [] 0 True
instance Provides (Str a) a where
  splitState _ (Str    []       _ _      _ ) = Nothing
  splitState _ (Str    (t : ts) msgs pos ok) = Just (t, Str ts msgs (pos + 1) True, 1)
instance Eof (Str a) where
  eof (Str i          _ _ _)             = null i
  deleteAtEnd      (Str (i : ii) msgs pos ok)
                   = Just (5, Str ii (msgs ++ [DeletedAtEnd i]) pos ok)
  deleteAtEnd      _
                   = Nothing
instance Corrects (Str a) a a where
  insertSym s (Str i    msgs pos      ok) exp
          = Just (5, s, Str i (msgs ++ [Inserted s pos exp]) pos False)
  deleteTok i (Str  ii   _          pos True)
              (Str   _   msgs pos' True)  exp
          = (Just (5, Str ii (msgs ++ [Deleted i pos' exp]) pos True))
  deleteTok _ _ _                   _
          = Nothing
instance Stores (Str a) [Error a a Int] where
  getErrors (Str    inp msgs pos ok      ) = (msgs, Str inp [] pos ok)
```

Fig. 9. A reference implementation of *state*

the current input position. Note also that the function *splitState* returns the extra integer, which represents how far the input state was "advanced"; here the value is always 1.

Given the defined interfaces we can now define the proper instances for the parser classes we have introduced. Since the code is quite similar we only give the version for P_f. The occurrence of the *Fail* constructor is a bit more involved than expected, and will be explained soon. The function *pErrors* uses *getErrors* to retrieve the error messages, which are inserted into the result sequence using a *push*. The function *pEnd* uses the recursive function *del* to remove any remaining tokens from the input, and to produce error messages for these deletions. Having reached the end of the input it retrieves all pending error messages and hands them over to the result:

$$
\begin{array}{l}
\textbf{instance}\ (\mathit{Eof\ state}, \mathit{Stores\ state\ errors}) \Rightarrow \mathit{AsksFor}\ (P_f\ \mathit{state})\ \mathit{errors}\ \textbf{where} \\
\quad \mathit{pErrors} = P_f\ (\lambda k\ \mathit{inp} \to \textbf{let}\ (\mathit{errs}, \mathit{inp}') = \mathit{getErrors\ inp} \\
\qquad\qquad\qquad\qquad\qquad \textbf{in}\ \mathit{push\ errs}\ (k\ \mathit{inp}')) \\
\quad \mathit{pEnd} = P_f\ (\lambda k\ \mathit{inp} \to \\
\qquad \textbf{let}\ \mathit{del\ inp} = \quad \textbf{case}\ \mathit{deleteAtEnd\ inp}\ \textbf{of} \\
\qquad\qquad\qquad\qquad \mathit{Nothing} \to \textbf{let}\ (\mathit{errors}, \mathit{state}) = \mathit{getErrors\ inp} \\
\qquad\qquad\qquad\qquad\qquad\qquad \textbf{in}\ \mathit{push\ errors}\ (k\ \mathit{state}) \\
\qquad\qquad\qquad\qquad \mathit{Just}\,(i, \mathit{inp}') \to \mathit{Fail}\ [\,]\ [\mathit{const}\ (\mathit{Just}\ (i, \mathit{del\ inp}'))] \\
\qquad \textbf{in}\ \mathit{del\ inp} \\
\qquad)
\end{array}
$$

Of course, if we want to base any decision about how to proceed with parsing on what errors have been produced thus far, the P_h version of *pErrors* should be used. If we just want to decide whether to proceed or not, the fact that results are produced online can be used too. If we find a non-empty error message embedded in the resulting value, we may decide not to inspect the rest of the returned value at all; and since we do not inpect it, parsing will not produce it either.

7.3 Repair Strategies

As we have seen we have associated a cost with each repair step. In order to decide how to proceed we change the type *Step* once more. Since this will be the final version we present its complete definition here:

$$
\begin{array}{llll}
\multicolumn{4}{l}{\textbf{data}\ \mathit{Steps}\ a\ \textbf{where}} \\
\mathit{Step} & :: & \mathit{Progress} \to \mathit{Steps}\ a & \to \mathit{Steps}\ a \\
\mathit{Fail} & :: & [\mathit{String}] \to [[\mathit{String}] \to \mathit{Maybe}\ (\mathit{Int}, \mathit{Steps}\ a)] & \to \mathit{Steps}\ a \\
\mathit{Apply} & :: & \forall\, b.(b \to a) \to \mathit{Steps}\ b & \to \mathit{Steps}\ a \\
\mathit{End}_h & :: & [(a, [a] \to \mathit{Steps}\ r)] \to \mathit{Steps}\ (a, r) & \to \mathit{Steps}\ (a, r) \\
\mathit{End}_f & :: & [\mathit{Steps}\ a] \to \mathit{Steps}\ a & \to \mathit{Steps}\ a
\end{array}
$$

In the first component of the *fail* alternative the *String*'s describing the expected symbols are collected. The interesting part is the second component of the *Fail* alternative, which is a list of functions, each taking the list of expected symbols, and possibly returning a repair step containing an *Int* cost for this step and the result sequence corresponding to this path. The interesting alternative of *best'*, where all this information is collected, is:

$$\mathit{Fail}\ \mathit{sl}\ \mathit{fl}\ \text{`}\mathit{best}'\text{`}\ \mathit{Fail}\ \mathit{sr}\ \mathit{fr} = \mathit{Fail}\ (\mathit{sl} +\!\!+\ \mathit{sr})\ (\mathit{fl} +\!\!+\ \mathit{fr})$$

In figure Fig. 10 we give the final definition of *pSym* for the P_f case.

The local functions *del* and *ins* take care of the deletion of the current token and the insertion of the expected symbol, and are returned where appropriate if recognition of the expected symbol a fails.

In the *best'* alternative just given we see that the function stops working and just collects information about how to proceed. Now it becomes the task of the function *eval* to start the suspended parsing process:

$$\mathit{eval}\ (\mathit{Fail}\ \mathit{ss}\ \mathit{fs}) = \mathit{eval}\ (\mathit{getCheapest}\ 3\ [c \mid f \leftarrow \mathit{fs}, \textbf{let}\ \mathit{Just}\ c = f\ \mathit{ss}])$$

```
instance (Show symbol, Describes symbol token, Corrects state symbol token)
         ⇒ Symbol (P_f state) symbol token where
  pSym a = P_f (
    let p = λk inp →
      let ins ex =         case insertSym a inp ex of
                           Just (c_i, v, st_i) →   Just (c_i, push v (k st_i))
                           Nothing               → Nothing
          del s ss ex
                         = case deleteTok s ss inp ex of
                           Just (c_d, st_d) → Just (c_d, p k st_d)
                           Nothing →          Nothing
      in case splitState a inp of
         Just (s, ss, pr) → if a `eqSymTok` s
                            then    Step pr (push s (k ss))
                            else    Fail [show a] [ins, del s ss]
         Nothing →                  Fail [show a] [ins]
    in p)
```

Fig. 10. The definition of *pSym* for the P_f case

Once *eval* is called we know that all expected symbols and all information how to proceed has been merged into a single *Fail* constructor. So we can construct all possible ways how to proceed by applying the elements from *ls* to the set of expected symbols *ss*, and selecting those cases where actually something can be repaired. The returned progress sequences themselves of course can contain further *Fail* constructors, and thus each alternative actually represents a tree of ways of how to proceed; the branches of such a tree are either *Step*'s with which we associate cost 0, or further repair steps each with its own costs. For each tree we compute the cheapest path up-to n steps away from the root using the function *traverse*, and use the result to select the progress sequence containing the path with the lowest accumulated cost. The first parameter of *traverse* is the number of tree levels still to be inspected, the second argument the tree, the third parameter the accumulated costs from the root up-to the current node, and the last parameter the best value found for a tree thus far, which is used to prune the search process.

```
getCheapest :: Int → [(Int, Steps a)] → Steps a
getCheapest _ [] = error "no correcting alternative found"
getCheapest n l = snd $ foldr (λ(w, ll) btf@(c, l)
                              → if w < c
                                then let new = (traverse n ll w c)
                                     in if new < c then (new, ll) else btf
                                else btf
                              ) (maxBound, error "getCheapest") l

traverse :: Int → Steps a → Int → Int → Int
traverse 0 _           = λv c → v
traverse n (Step ps l) = traverse (n − 1) l
```

$$
\begin{array}{l}
\mathit{traverse}\ n\ (\mathit{Apply}\ \_\ l) \quad = \quad \mathit{traverse}\ n\ l \\
\mathit{traverse}\ n\ (\mathit{Fail}\ m\ \mathit{m2ls}) = \\
\quad \lambda v\ c \to \mathit{foldr}\ (\lambda(w, l)\ c' \to \quad \mathbf{if}\ v + w < c' \\
\qquad\qquad\qquad\qquad\qquad\qquad\qquad \mathbf{then}\ \mathit{traverse}\ (n-1)\ l\ (v+w)\ c' \\
\qquad\qquad\qquad\qquad\qquad\qquad\qquad \mathbf{else}\ c' \\
\qquad\qquad\qquad)\ c\ (\mathit{catMaybes}\ \$\ \mathit{map}\ (\$m)\ \mathit{m2ls}) \\
\mathit{traverse}\ n\ (\mathit{End}_h\ ((a, \mathit{lf}) : \_)\ r) = \mathit{traverse}\ n\ (\mathit{lf}\ [a]\ \text{`}\mathit{best}\text{`}\ \mathit{removeEnd}_h\ r) \\
\mathit{traverse}\ n\ (\mathit{End}_f\ (l : \_) \qquad r) = \mathit{traverse}\ n\ (l\ \text{`}\mathit{best}\text{`}\ r)
\end{array}
$$

8 An Idiomatic Interface

McBride and Paterson [10] investigate the *Applicative* interface we have been using throughout this tutorial. Since this extension of the pattern of sequential composition is so common they propose an intriguing use of functional dependencies to enable a very elegant way of writing applicative expressions. Here we shortly re-introduce the idea, and give a specialised version for the type *Parser* we introduced for the basic library.

Looking at the examples of parsers written with the applicative interface we see that if we want to inject a function into the result then we will always do this with a *pReturn*, and if we recognise a keyword then we always throw away the result. Hence the question arises whether we can use the types of the components of the right hand side of a parser to decide how to incorporate it into the result. The overall aim of this exercise is that we will be able to replace an expression like:

```
choose <$ pSyms "if" <*> pExpr <* pSyms "then" <*> pExpr
                               <* pSyms "else" <*> pExpr
```

by the much shorter expression:

```
start choose "if" pExpr "then" pExpr "else" pExpr stop
```

or by nicely formatting the start and stop tokens as a pair of brackets by:

```
[: choose "if" pExpr "then" pExpr "else" pExpr :]
```

The core idea of the trick lies in the function *idiomatic* which takes two arguments: an accumulating argument in which it constructs a parser, and the next element from the expression. Based on the type of this next element we decide what to do with it: if it is a parser too then we combine it with the parser constructed thus far by using sequential composition, and if it is a *String* then we build a keyword parser out of it which we combine in such a way with the thus far constructed parser that the witness is thrown away. We implement the choice based on the type by defining a collection of suitable instances for the class *Idiomatic*:

```
class Idiomatic f g | g -> f where
  idiomatic :: Parser Char f -> g
```

We start by discussing the standard case:

```
instance Idiomatic f r ⇒ Idiomatic (a → f) (Parser Char a → r) where
  idiomatic isf is = idiomatic (isf <*> is)
```

which is to be read as follows: if the next element in the sequence is a parser returning a witness of type a, and the parser we have constructed thus far expects a value of that type a to build a parser of type f, and we know how to combine the rest of g with this parser of type f, then we combine the accumulated parser recognising a value of type $a \to f$ and the argument parser recognising an a, and call the function *idiomatic* available from the context to consume further elements from the expression.

If we encounter the *stop* marker, we return the accumulated parser. For this marker we introduce a special type *Stop*, and declare an instance which recognises this *Stop* and returns the accumulated parser.

```
data Stop = Stop
stop = Stop
instance Idiomatic x (Stop → Parser Char x) where
  idiomatic ix Stop = ix
```

Now let us assume that the next element in the input is a function instead of a parser. In this case the *Parser Char a* in the previous instance declaration is replaced by a function of some type $a \to b$, and we expect our thus far constructed parser to accept such a value. Hence we get:

```
instance Idiomatic f g ⇒ Idiomatic ((a → b) → f) ((a → b) → g) where
  idiomatic isf a2b = idiomatic (isf <*> pReturn a2b)
```

Once we have this instance it is now easy to define the function *start*. Since we can prefix every parser with a *id*<$> fragment, we can define *start* as the initialisation of the accumulated parser by the parser which always succeeds with an *id*:

```
start :: ∀ a g.(Idiomatic (a → a) g) ⇒ g
start = idiomatic (pReturn id)
```

Finally we can provide extra instances at will, as long as we do not give more than one for a specific type. Otherwise we would get an overloading ambiguity. As an example we define two further cases, one for recognising a keyword and once for recognising a single character:

```
instance Idiomatic f g ⇒ Idiomatic f (String → g) where
  idiomatic isf str = idiomatic (isf <* pKey str)
instance Idiomatic f g ⇒ Idiomatic f (Char   → g) where
  idiomatic isf c   = idiomatic (isf <* pSym c)
```

9 Further Extensions

In the previous sections we have developed a library which provides a lot of basic functionality. Unfortunately space restrictions prevent us from describing many more extensions to the library in detail, so we will sketch them here. Most of them are efficiency improvements, but we will also show an example of how to use the library to dynamically generate large grammars, thus providing solutions to problems which are infeasible when done by traditional means, such as parser generators.

9.1 Recognisers

In the basic library we had operators which discarded part of the recognised result since it was not needed for constructing the final witness; typical examples of this are e.g. recognised keywords, separating symbols such as commas and semicolons, and bracketing symbols. The only reason for their presence in the input is to make the program readable and unambiguously parseable.

Of course it is not such a great idea to first perform a lot of work in constructing the result, only having to even more work to get rid of it again. Fortunately we have already introduced the *recognisers* which can be combined with the other types of parsers P_h, P_f and P_m. We introduce yet another class:

```
class Applicative p ⇒ ExtApplicative p st where
  (<*) :: p a      → R st b → p a
  (*>) :: R st b → p a      → p a
  (<$) :: a        → R st b → p a
```

The instances of this class again follow the common pattern. We only give the implementation for P_h:

```
instance ExtApplicative (P_h st) st where
  P_h p <* R r = P_h (p.(r.) )
  R r *> P_h p = P_h (r.p    )
  f <$ R r     = P_h (r.($f))
```

9.2 Parsing Permutation Phrases

A nice example of the power of parser combinators is when we want to recognise a sequence of elements of different type, in which the order in which they appear in the input does not matter; examples of such a situation are in the recognition of a BibTeX entry or the attribute declarations allowed at a specific node in an XML-tree. In [1] we show how to proceed in such a case, so here we only sketch the idea which heavily depends on lazy evaluation.

We start out by building a data structure which represents all possible permutations of the parsers for the individual elements to be recognised. This structure is a tree, in which each path from the root to a leaf represents one of the possible permutations. From this tree we generate a parser, which initially is prepared to accept any of the elements; after having recognised the first element it continues to recognise a permutation of the remaining elements, as described by the appropriate subtree. Since the tree describing all the permutations and the parser corresponding to it are constructed lazily, only the parsers corresponding to a permutation actually occurring in the input will be generated. All the chosen alternative has to do in the end is to put the elements in some canonical order.

9.3 Look-ahead Computations

Conventional parser generators analyse the grammar, and based on the results of this analysis try to build efficient recognisers. In an earlier paper [15] we have shown how the computation of *first sets*, as known from the theory about $LL(1)$ grammar analysis, can be performed for grammars described by combinator parsers. We plan to add such an analysis to our parsers too, thus speeding up the parsing process considerably in cases where we have to deal with a larger number of alternatives.

A subtle point here is the question how to deal with monadic parsers. As we described in [15] the static analysis does not go well with monadic computations, since in that case we dynamically build new parses based on the input produced thus far: the whole idea of a static analysis is that it is static. This observation has lead John Hughes to propose *arrows* for dealing with such situations [7]. It is only recently that we realised that, although our arguments still hold in general, they do not apply to the case of the $LL(1)$ analysis. If we want to compute the symbols which can be recognised as the first symbol by a parser of the form $p \gg= q$ then we are only interested in the starting symbols of the right hand side if the left hand side can recognise the empty string; the good news is that in that case we statically know what value will be returned as a witness, and can pass this value on to q, and analyse the result of this call statically too. Unfortunately we will have to take special precautions in case the left hand side operator contains a call to *pErrors* in one of the empty derivations, since then it is no longer true that the witness of this alternative can be determined statically.

10 Conclusions

We have come to end of a fairly long tutorial, which we hope to extend in the future with sections describing the yet missing abstract interpretations. We hope nevertheless that the reader has gained a good insight in the possibilities of using Haskell as a tool for embedding domain specific languages. There are a few final remarks we should like to make.

In the first place we claim that the library we have developed can be used outside the context of parsing. Basically we have set up a very general infrastructure for describing search algorithms, in which a a tree is generated representing possible solutions. Our combinators can be used for building such trees and searching such trees for possible solutions in a breadth-first way.

In the second place the library we have described is by far not the only one existing. Many different (Haskell) libraries are floating around, some more mature than others, some more dangerous to use than others, some resulting in faster parsers, etc. One of the most used libraries is *Parsec*, originally constructed by Daan Leijen, which gained its popularity by packaged with the distribution of the GHC compiler. The library distinguishes itself from our approach in that the underlying technique is the more conventional back-tracking technique, as described in the first part of our tutorial. In order to alleviate some of the mentioned disadvantages of that approach, the programmer has the possibility to commit the search process at specific points, thus cutting away branches from the search tree. Although this technique can be very effective it is also more dangerous: unintentionally branches which should remain alive may be pruned away. The programmer really has to be aware of how his grammar is parsed in order to know where to safely put the annotations. But if he knows what he is doing, fast parsers can be constructed. Another simplifying aspect is that *Parsec* just stops if it cannot make further progress; a single error message is produced, describing what was expected at the farthest point reached.

A relatively new library was constructed by Malcolm Wallace [19], which contains many of the aspects we are dealing with: building results online, and combing a monadic interface with an applicative one. It does however not perform error correction.

Another library which implements a breadth-first strategy are Koen Claessen's parallel parsers [3], which are currently being used in the implementation of the GHC *read* functions. They are based on a rewriting process, and as a result do not lend themselves well to an optimising implementation.

Concluding we may say that parser combinators are providing an ever lasting source of inspiration for research into Haskell programming patterns which has given us a lot of insight in how to implement Embedded Domain Specific Languages in Haskell.

Acknowledgements. I thank current and past members of the Software Technology group at Utrecht University for commenting on earlier versions of this paper, and for trying out the library described here. I want to thank Alesya Sheremet for working out some details of the monadic implementation, and the anonymous referee for his/her comments, and Magnus Carlsson for many suggestions for improving the code.

References

1. Baars, A.I., Löh, A., Swierstra, S.D.: Parsing permutation phrases. J. Funct. Program. 14(6), 635–646 (2004)
2. Burge, W.H.: Recursive Programming Techniques. Addison-Wesley, Reading (1975)
3. Claessen, K.: Parallel parsing processes. Journal of Functional Programming 14(6), 741–757 (2004)
4. Fokker, J.: Functional parsers. In: Jeuring, J.T., Meijer, H.J.M. (eds.) AFP 1995. LNCS, vol. 925, pp. 1–23. Springer, Heidelberg (1995)
5. Heeren, B.: Top Quality Type Error Messages. PhD thesis, Utrecht University (2005)
6. Heeren, B., Hage, J., Swierstra, S.D.: Scripting the type inference process. In: Eighth ACM Sigplan International Conference on Functional Programming, pp. 3–13. ACM Press, New York (2003)
7. Hughes, J.: Generalising monads to arrows. Science of Computer Programming 37(1-3), 67–111 (2000)
8. Hutton, G., Meijer, E.: Monadic parsing in Haskell. J. Funct. Program. 8(4), 437–444 (1998)

9. Leijen, D.: Parsec, a fast combinator parser. Technical Report UU-CS-2001-26, Institute of Information and Computing Sciences, Utrecht University (2001)
10. Mcbride, C., Paterson, R.A.: Applicative programming with effects. Journal of Functional Programming 18(1), 1–13 (2008)
11. Peyton Jones, S.: Haskell 98 Language and Libraries. Cambridge University Press, Cambridge (2003), `http://www.haskell.org/report`
12. Röjemo, N.: Garbage collection and memory efficiency in lazy functional languages. PhD thesis, Chalmers University of Technology (1995)
13. Swierstra, S.D., Baars, A., Löh, A., Middelkoop, A.: uuag - Utrecht university attribute grammar system
14. Swierstra, S.D., Azero Alocer, P.R., Saraiava, J.: Designing and implementing combinator languages. In: Swierstra, S.D., Henriques, P., Oliveira, J. (eds.) AFP 1998. LNCS, vol. 1608, pp. 150–206. Springer, Heidelberg (1999)
15. Swierstra, S.D., Duponcheel, L.: Deterministic, error-correcting combinator parsers. In: Launchbury, J., Meijer, E., Sheard, T. (eds.) AFP 1996. LNCS, vol. 1129, pp. 184–207. Springer, Heidelberg (1996)
16. Viera, M., Swierstra, S.D., Lempsink, E.: Haskell, do you read me?: constructing and composing efficient top-down parsers at runtime. In: Haskell 2008: Proceedings of the first ACM SIGPLAN symposium on Haskell, pp. 63–74. ACM, New York (2008)
17. Wadler, P.: How to replace failure with a list of successes. In: Jouannaud, J.-P. (ed.) FPCA 1985. LNCS, vol. 201, pp. 113–128. Springer, Heidelberg (1985)
18. Wagner, R.A., Fischer, M.J.: The string-to-string correction problem. J. ACM 21(1), 168–173 (1974)
19. Wallace, M.: Partial parsing: Combining choice with commitment. In: Chitil, O., Horváth, Z., Zsók, V. (eds.) IFL 2007. LNCS, vol. 5083, pp. 93–110. Springer, Heidelberg (2008)

A Driver Function for Pocket Calculators

The driver function for the pocket calculators:

```
run :: (Show t) => Parser Char t -> String -> IO ()
run p c =
    do putStrLn ("Give an expression like: "
                 ++ c ++ " or (q) to quit")
       inp <- getLine
       case inp of
           "q" -> return ()
           _   -> do putStrLn (case unP p (filter (/= ' ') inp) of
                                  ((v, "") : _) -> "Result is: " ++ show v
                                  _             -> "Incorrect input")
       run p c
```

Author Index